The Papacy:
Its History, Dogmas, Genius, and Prospects

Rev. J. A. Wylie, LL.D.

Table of Contents

Book I: History of the Papacy.

Chapter I: Origin of the Papacy.

The Papacy, next to Christianity, is the great FACT of the modern world. Of the two, the former, unhappily, has proved in some respects the more powerful spring in human affairs, and has acted the more public part on the stage of the world. Fully to trace the rise and development of this stupendous system, were to write a history of Western Europe. The decay of empires, — the extinction of religious systems, — the dissolution and renewal of society, — the rise of new States, — the change of manners, customs, and laws, — the policy of courts, — the wars of kings, — the decay and revival of letters, of philosophy and of arts, — all connect themselves with the history of the Papacy, to whose growth they ministered, and whose destiny they helped to unfold. On so wide a field of investigation neither our time nor our limits permit us to enter. Let it suffice that we indicate, in general terms, the main causes that contributed to the rise of this tremendous Power, and the successive stages that marked the course of its portentous development.

The first rise of the Papacy is undoubtedly to be sought for in the corruption of human nature. Christianity, though pure in itself, was committed to the keeping of imperfect beings. The age, too, was imperfect, and abounded with causes tending to corrupt whatever was simple, and materialize whatever was spiritual. Society was pervaded on all sides with sensuous and material influences. These absolutely unfitted the age for relishing, and especially for retaining, truth in its abstract form, and for perceiving the beauty and grandeur of a purely spiritual economy. The symbolic worship of the Jew, heaven-appointed, had taught him to associate religious truth with visible rites, and to attribute considerably more importance to the observance of the outward ceremony than to the cultivation of the inward habit, or the performance of the mental act. Greece, too, with all its generous sensibilities, its strong emotions, and its quick perception and keen relish of the beautiful, was a singularly gross and materialized land. Its voluptuous poetry and sensuous mythology had unfitted the intellect of its people for appreciating the true grandeur of a simple and spiritual system. Italy, again, was the land of gods and of arms. The former was a type of human passions; and the latter, though lightened by occasional gleams of heroic virtue and patriotism, exerted, on the whole, a degrading and brutalizing effect upon the character and genius of the people, withdrawing them from efforts of pure mind, and from the contemplation of the abstract and the spiritual. It was in this complex corruption, — the degeneracy of the individual and the degeneracy of society, owing to the unspiritualizing influences then powerfully at work in the Jewish, the Grecian, and the Roman worlds, — that the main danger of Christianity consisted; and in this element it encountered an antagonist a thousand times more formidable than the sword of Rome. Amid these impure matters did the Papacy germinate, though not till a subsequent age did it appear above ground. The corruption took a different form, according to the prevailing systems and the predominating tastes of the various countries. The Jew brought with him into the Church the ideas of the synagogue, and attempted to graft the institutions of Moses upon the doctrines of Christ; the Greek, unable all at once to unlearn the lessons and cast off the yoke of the Academy, attempted to form an alliance between the simplicity of the gospel and his own subtle and highly imaginative philosophy; while the Roman, loath to think that the heaven of his gods should be swept away as the creation of an unbridled fancy, recoiled from the change, as we would from the dissolution of the material heavens; and, though he embraced Christianity, he still clung to the forms and shadows of a polytheism in the truth and reality of which he could no longer believe. Thus the Jew, the Greek, the Roman, were alike in that they corrupted the simplicity of the gospel; but they differed in that each corrupted it after his own fashion. Minds there were of a more vigorous cast originally, or more largely endowed with the Spirit's grace, who were able to take a more tenacious grasp of truth, and to appreciate more highly her spirituality and simplicity; but as regards the majority of converts, especially towards the end of the first century and the beginning of the second, it is undeniable that they felt, in all their magnitude, the difficulties now enumerated.

The new ideas had a painful conflict to maintain with the old. The world had taken a mighty step in advance. It had accomplished a transition from the symbolic to the spiritual, — from the fables, allegories, and myths, which a false philosophy and a sensuous poetry had invented to amuse its infancy, to the clear, definite, and spiritual ideas which Christianity had provided for the exercise of its manhood. But it seemed as if the transition was too great. There was a felt inability in the human mind, as yet, to look with open face upon TRUTH; and men were fain to interpose the veil of symbol between themselves and the glory of that Majestic Form. It was seen that the world could not pass by a single step from infancy to manhood, — that the Creator had imposed certain laws upon the growth of the species, as on that of the individual, — upon the development of the social, as on that of the personal mind; and that these laws could not be violated. It was seen, in short, that so vast a reformation could not be made; it must grow. So much had been foreshadowed, we apprehend, by those parables of the Saviour which were intended as illustrative of the nature of the gospel kingdom and the manner of its progress: "The kingdom of heaven cometh not with observation;" "It is like a grain of mustard-seed, the least of all seeds; but when it is grown, it is the greatest among herbs, and becometh a tree;" "It is like unto leaven, which a woman took, and hid in three measures of meal, till the whole was leavened." Not in a single day was the master idea of Christianity to displace the old systems, and inaugurate itself in their room. It was to progress in obedience to the law which regulates the growth of all great changes. First, the seed had to be deposited in the bosom of society; next, a process of germination had to ensue; the early and the latter rains of the Pagan and the Papal persecutions had to water it; and it was not till after ages of silent growth, during which society was to be penetrated and leavened by the quickening spirit of the gospel, that Christianity would begin her universal and triumphant reign.

But as yet the time was not come for a pure spiritual Christianity to attain dominion upon the earth. The infantile state of society forbade it. As, in the early ages, men had not been able to retain, even when communicated to them, the knowledge of one self-existent, independent, and eternal Being, so now they were unable to retain, even when made known to them, the pure spiritual worship of that Being. From this it might have been inferred, though prophecy had been silent on the point, that the world had yet a cycle of progress to pass through ere it should reach its manhood; that an era was before it, during which it would be misled by grievous errors, and endure, in consequence, grievous sufferings, before it could attain the faculty of broad, independent, clear, spiritual conception, and become able to think without the help of allegory, and to worship without the aid of symbol. This reconciles us to the fact of the great apostasy, so stumbling at first view. Contemplated in this light, it is seen to be a necessary step in the world's progress towards its high destinies, and a necessary preparation for the full unfolding of God's plans towards the human family.

The recovery of the world from the depth into which the Fall has plunged it, is both a slow and a laborious process. The instrumentality which God has ordained for its elevation is knowledge. Great truths are discovered, one after one; they are opinion first, — they become the basis of action next; and thus society is lifted up, by slow degrees, to the platform where the Creator has ordained it shall ultimately stand. A great principle, once discovered, can never be lost; and thus the progress of the world is steadily onward. Truth may not be immediately operative. To recur to the Saviour's figure, it may be the seed sown in the earth. It may be confined to a single bosom, or to a single book, or to a single school; but it is part of the constitution of things; it is agreeable to the nature of God, and in harmony with his government; and so it cannot perish. Proofs begin to gather around it; events fall out which throw light upon it: the martyr dies for it; society suffers by neglecting to shape its course in conformity with it; other minds begin to embrace it; and after reaching a certain stage, its adherents increase in geometrical progression: at last the whole of society is leavened; and thus the world is lifted a stage higher, never again to be let down. The stage, we say, once fully secured, is never altogether lost; for the truth, in fighting its way, has left behind it so many monuments of its power, in the shape of the errors and sufferings, as well as of the emancipation, of mankind, that it becomes a great landmark in the progress of our race. It attains in the social mind all the clearness and certainty of an axiom. The history of the world, when read aright, is not so much a record of the follies and wickedness of mankind, as it is a series of moral demonstrations, — a slow process of experimental and convincing proof, — in reference to great principles, and that on a scale so large, that the whole world may see it, and understand it, and come to act upon it. Society can be saved not otherwise than as the individual is saved: it must be convinced of sin; its mind must be enlightened; its will renewed; it must be brought to embrace and act upon truth; and when in this way it has been sanctified, society shall enter upon its rest.

This we take to be the true theory of the world's progress. There is first an objective revelation of truth; there is second a subjective revelation of it. The objective revelation is the work of God alone; the subjective revelation, that is, the reception of it by society, is the work of God and man combined. The first may be done in a day or an hour; the second is the slow operation of an age. Thus human progression takes the form of a series of grand epochs, in which the world is suddenly thrown forward in its course, and then again suddenly stands still, or appears to retrograde. The first is known, in ordinary speech, as reformation or revolution; the second is termed re-action. There is, however, in point of fact, no retrogression: what we mistake for retrogression is only society settling down, after the sun-light burst of newly-revealed truth is over, to study, to believe, and to apply the principles which have just come into its possession. This is a work of time, often of many ages; and not unfrequently does it go on amid the confusion and conflict occasioned by the opposition offered to the new ideas by the old errors. Among the epochs of the past, — the grand objective revelations, — we may instance, as the more influential ones, the primeval Revelation, the Mosaic Economy, the Christian Era, and the Reformation. Each of these advanced the world a stage, from which it never altogether fell back into its former condition: society always made good its advance. Nevertheless, each of these epochs was followed by a re-action, which was just society struggling to lay hold upon the principles made known to it, thoroughly to incorporate them with its own structure, and so to make ready for a new and higher step. The world progresses much as the tide rises on the beach. Society in progress presents as sublime and fearful a spectacle as the ocean in a storm. As the mountain billow, crested with foam, swells huge and dark against the horizon, and comes rolling along in thunder, it threatens not only to flood the beach, but to submerge the land; but its mighty force is arrested and dissolved on its sandy barrier: the waters retire within the ocean's bed, as if they had received a counter-stroke from the earth. One would think that the ocean had spent its power in that one effort; but it is not so. The resistless energies of the great deep recruit themselves in an instant: another mountain wave is seen advancing; another cataract of foaming waters is poured along the beach; and now the level of the tide stands higher than before. Thus, by a series of alternate flows and ebbs does the ocean fill its shores. This natural phenomenon is but the emblem of the manner in which society advances. After some great epoch, the new ideas seem to lose ground, — the waters are diminished; but gradually the limit between the new ideas and the old prejudices comes to be adjusted, and then it is found that the advantage is on the side of truth, and that the general level of society stands perceptibly higher. Meanwhile, preparation is being made for a new conquest. The regenerative instrumentalities with which the Creator has endowed the world, by the truths which He has communicated, are silently at work at the bottom of society. Another mighty wave appears upon its agitated surface; and, rolling onwards in irresistible power against the dry land of superstition, it adds a new domain to the empire of Truth.

But while it is true that the world has been steadily progressive, and that each successive epoch has placed society on a higher platform than that which went before it, it is at the same time a fact, that the development of superstition has kept equal pace with the development of truth. From the very beginning the two have been the counterparts of each other, and so will it be, doubtless, while they exist together upon the earth. In the early ages idolatry was unsophisticated in its creed and simple in its forms, just as the truths then known were few and simple. Under the Jewish economy, when truth became embodied in a system of doctrines with an appointed ritual, then, too, idolatry provided its system of metaphysical subtleties to ensnare the mind, and its splendid ceremonial to dazzle the senses. Under the Christian dispensation, when truth has attained its amplest development, in form at least, if not as yet in degree, idolatry is also more fully developed than in any preceding era. Papal idolatry is a more subtle, complicated, malignant, and perfected system than Pagan idolatry was. This equal development is inevitable in the nature of the case. The discovery of any one truth necessitates the invention of the opposite error. In proportion as truth multiplies its points of assault, error must necessarily multiply its points of defence. The extension of the one line infers the extension of the other also. Nevertheless there is an essential difference betwixt the two developments. Every new truth is the addition of another impregnable position to the one side; whereas every new error is but the addition of another untenable point to the other, which only weakens the defence. Truth is immortal, because agreeable to the laws by which the universe is governed; and therefore, the more it is extended, the more numerous are the points on which it can lean for support upon God's government; the more that error is extended, the more numerous the points in which it comes into collision and conflict with that government. Thus the one develops into strength, the other into weakness. And thus, too, the full development of the one is the harbinger of its triumph, — the full development of the other is the precursor of its downfall.

Idolatry at the first was one, and necessarily so, for it drew its existence from the same springs which were seated in the depth of the early ages.

But, though one originally, in process of time it took different forms, and was known by different names, in the several countries. The Magian philosophy had long prevailed in the East; in the West had arisen the polytheism of Rome; while in Greece, forming the link between Asia and Europe, and combining the contemplative and subtle character of the Eastern idolatries with the grossness and latitudinarianism of those of the West, there flourished a highly imaginative but sensuous mythology. As these idolatries were one in their essence, so they were one in their tendency; and the tendency of all was, to draw away the heart from God, to hem in the vision of man by objects of sense, and to create a strong disrelish for the contemplation of a spiritual Being, and a strong incapacity for the apprehension and retention of spiritual and abstract truth. These idolatries had long since passed their prime; but the powerful bent they had given to the human mind still existed. It was only by a slow process of counteraction that that evil bias could be overcome. So long had these superstitions brooded over the earth, and so largely had they impregnated the soil with their evil principles, that their eradication could not be looked for but by a long and painful conflict on the part of Christianity. It was to be expected, that after the first flush of the gospel's triumph there would come a recoil; that the ancient idolatries, recovering from their panic, would rally their forces, and appear again, not in any of their old forms, — for neither does superstition nor the gospel ever revive under exactly its old organization, — but under a new form adapted to the state of the world, and the character of the new antagonist now to be confronted; and that Satan would make a last, and, of course, unexampled struggle, before surrendering to Christ the empire of the world. It was to be expected also, in the coming conflict, that all these idolatries would combine into one phalanx. It was extremely probable that the animosities and rivalships which had hitherto kept them apart would cease; that the schools and sects into which they had been divided would coalesce; that, recognising in Christianity an antagonist that was alike the foe of them all, the common danger would make them feel their common brotherhood; and thus, that all these false systems would come to be united into one comprehensive and enormous system, containing within itself all the principles of hostility, and all the elements of strength, formerly scattered throughout them all; and that in this combined and united form would they do battle with the Truth.

It was not long till symptoms began to appear of such a move on the part of Satan, — of such a resuscitation of the ancient Paganisms. The shadow began to go back on the dial of Time. The spiritual began to lose ground before the symbolic and the mythological. The various idolatries which had formerly covered the wide space which the gospel now occupied, — subjugated, but not utterly exterminated, — began to pay court to Christianity. They professed, as the handmaids, to do homage to the Mistress; but their design in this insidious friendship was not to aid her in her glorious mission, but to borrow her help, and so reign in her room. Well they knew that they had been overtaken by that decrepitude which, sooner or later, overtakes all that is sprung of earth; but they thought to draw fresh vitality from the living side of Christianity, and so rid themselves of the burden of their anility. The Magian religion wooed her in the East; Paganism paid court to her in the West: Judaism, too, esteeming, doubtless, that it had a better right than either, put in its claim to be recognized. Each brought her something of its own, which, it pretended, was necessary to the perfection of Christianity. Judaism brought her dead symbols; the Magian and Greek philosophies brought her refined and subtle, but dead speculations and doctrines; and the Paganism of Rome brought her dead divinities. On all hands was she tempted to part with the substance, and to embrace again the shadow. Thus did the old idolatries muster under the banner of Christianity. They rallied in her support, — so they professed; but, in reality, to unite their arms for her overthrow.

Two things might have been expected to happen. First, that the rising corruption would reach its maturest proportion in that country where external influences most favoured its development; and second, that when developed, it would exhibit the master traits and leading peculiarities of each of the ancient paganisms. Both these anticipations were exactly realised. It was not in Chaldea, nor in Egypt, the seats of the Magian philosophy, nor was it in Greece, that Popery arose, for these countries now retained little besides the traditions of their former power. It was in the soil of the Seven Hills, amid the trophies of unnumbered victories, the symbols of universal empire, and the gorgeous rites of a polluting polytheism, that Romanism, *velut arbor oevo*, grew up. By a law similar to that which guides the seed to the spot best fitted for its germination, did the modern Paganism strike its roots in the soil which the ancient Paganism had most largely impregnated with its influences and tendencies. The surrounding heresies were speedily overshadowed and dwarfed. The Gnostic, and other errors, declined in the proportion in which Romanism waxed in stature, its mighty trunk drawing to itself all those corrupt influences which would otherwise have afforded nourishment to them. In process of time they disappeared, though rather through a process of absorption than of extinction. The result presents us with a sort of Pantheism, — the only sort of Pantheism that is real, — in which the expiring idolatries returned into the bosom of their parent divinity, and had their existence prolonged in its existence. The Papacy is a new Babel, in which the old redoubtable idolatries are the builders. It is a spiritual Pantheon, in which the local and vagrant superstitions find again a centre and a home. It is a grand mausoleum, in which the corpses of the defunct Paganisms, like the mummied monks of Kreutzberg, are laid out in ghastly pomp, while their disembodied spirits still live in the Papacy, and govern the world from their grave. Analyse Popery, and you will find all these ancient systems existing in it. The Magian philosophy flourishes anew under the monastic system; for in the conventual life of Rome we find the contemplative moods and the ascetic habits which so largely prevailed in Egypt and over all the East; and here, too, we find the fundamental principle of that philosophy, namely, that the flesh is the seat of evil, and, consequently, that it becomes a duty to weaken and mortify the body. In Popery we find the predominating traits of the Grecian philosophy, more especially in the subtle casuistry of the Popish schools, combined with a sensuous ritual, the celebration of which is often accompanied, as in Greece of old, with gross licentiousness. And last of all, there is palpably present in Popery the polytheism of ancient Rome, in the gods and goddesses which, under the title of saints, fill up the calendar and crowd the temples of the Romish Church. Here, then, all the old idolatries live over again. There is nothing new about them but the organization, which is more perfect and complete than ever. To add one other illustration to those already given, the Papacy is a gigantic realization of our Lord's parable. The Roman empire, on the introduction of Christianity, was swept and garnished; the unclean spirit which inhabited it had been driven out of it; but the demon had never wandered far from the region of the Seven Hills; and finding no rest, he returned, bringing with him seven other spirits more wicked than himself, which took possession of their old abode, and made its last state worse than its first. The name of Popery, truly, is Legion! "There are many Antichrists," said the apostle John; for in his days the various systems of error had not been combined into one. But the Roman apostacy acquired ultimately the dominion, and, marshalling the other heresies beneath its banner, gave its own name to the motley host, and became known as the Antichrist of prophecy and of history.

Popery, then, we hold to be an after-growth of Paganism, whose deadly wound, dealt by the spiritual sword of Christianity, was healed. Its oracles had been silenced, its shrines demolished, and its gods consigned to oblivion; but the deep corruption of the human race, not yet cured by the promised effusion of the Spirit upon all flesh, revived it anew, and, under a Christian mask, reared other temples in its honour, built it another Pantheon, and replenished it with other gods, which, in fact, were but the ancient divinities under new names. All idolatries, in whatever age or country they have existed, are to be viewed but as successive developments of the one grand apostacy. That apostacy was commenced in Eden, and consummated at Rome. It had its rise in the plucking of the forbidden fruit; and it attained its acme in the supremacy of the Bishop of Rome, — Christ's Vicar on earth. The hope that he would "be as God," led man to commit the first sin; and that sin was perfected when the Pope "exalted himself above all that is called God, or that is worshipped; so that he, as God, sitteth in the temple of God, showing himself that he is God." Popery is but the natural development of this great original transgression. It is just the early idolatries ripened and perfected. It is manifestly an enormous expansion of the same intensely malignant and fearfully destructive principle which these idolatries contained. The ancient Chaldean worshipping the sun, — the Greek deifying the powers of nature, — and the Roman exalting the race of primeval men into gods, are but varied manifestations of the same evil principle, namely, the utter alienation of the heart from God, — its proneness to hide itself amid the darkness of its own corrupt imaginations, and to become a god unto itself. That principle received the most fearful development which appears possible on earth, in the Mystery of Iniquity which came to be seated on the Seven Hills; for therein man deified himself, became God, nay, arrogated powers which lifted him high above God. Popery is the last, the most matured, the most subtle, the most skilfully contriven, and the most essentially diabolical form of idolatry which the world ever saw, or which, there is reason to believe, it ever will see. It is the *ne plus ultra* of man's wickedness, and the *chef d'oeuvre* of Satan's cunning and malignity. It is the greatest calamity, next to the Fall, which ever befell the human family. Farther away from God the world could not exist at all. The cement that holds society together, already greatly weakened, would be altogether destroyed, and the social fabric would instantly fall in ruins.

Having thus indicated the origin of Romanism, we shall attempt in the three following chapters to trace its rise and progress.

Chapter II: Rise and Progress of Ecclesiastical Supremacy.

The first pastors of the Roman Church aspired to no rank above their brethren. The labours in which they occupied themselves were the same as those of the ordinary ministers of the gospel. As pastors, they watched with affectionate fidelity over their flock; and, when occasion offered, they added to the duties of the pastorate the labours of the evangelist. All of them were eminent for their piety; and some of them to the graces of the Christian added the accomplishments of the scholar. Clemens of Rome may be cited as an instance. He was the most distinguished Christian writer, after the apostles, of the first century. Even after the gospel had found entrance within the walls of Rome, Paganism maintained its ground amongst the villages of the Campagna. Accordingly, it became the first care of the pastors of the metropolis to plant the faith and found churches in the neighbouring towns. They were led to embark in this undertaking, not from the worldly and ambitious views which began, in course of time, to actuate their successors, but from that pure zeal for the diffusion of Christianity for which these early ages were distinguished. It was natural that churches founded in these circumstances should cherish a peculiar veneration for the men to whose pious labours they owed their existence; and it was equally natural that they should apply to them for advice in all cases of difficulty. That advice was at first purely paternal, and implied neither superiority on the part of the person who gave it, nor dependence on the part of those to whom it was given. But in process of time, when the Episcopate at Rome came to be held by men of worldly spirit, — lovers of the pre-eminence, — the homage, at first voluntarily rendered by equals to their equal, — was exacted as a right; and the advice, at first simply fraternal, took the form of a command, and was delivered in a tone of authority. These beginnings of assumption were small; but they were beginnings, and power is cumulative. It is the law of its nature to grow, at a continually accelerating rate, which, though slow at the outset, becomes fearfully rapid towards the end. And thus the pastors of Rome, at first by imperceptible degrees, and at last by enormous strides, reached their fatal pre-eminence.

Such was the state of matters in the first century, during which the authority of the presbyter or bishop — for these two titles were employed in primitive times to distinguish the same office and the same order of men — did not extend beyond the limits of the congregation to which they ministered. But in the second century another element began to operate. In that age it became customary to regulate the consideration and rank which the bishops of the Christian Church enjoyed, by that of the city in which they resided. It is easy to see the influence and dignity which would thence accrue to the bishops of Rome, and the prospects of grandeur and power which would thus open to the aspiring prelates who now occupied that see. Rome was the mistress of the world. During ages of conquest her dominion had been gradually extending, till at last it had become universal and supreme; and now she exercised a mysterious and potent charm over the nations. Her laws were received, and her sway submitted to, throughout the whole civilized earth. The first Rome was herein the type of the second Rome; and if the spectacle which she exhibited of a centralized and universal despotism did not suggest to the aspiring prelates of the capital the first ideas of a spiritual empire alike centralized and universal, there is no question that it contributed most material aid towards the attainment of such an object, — an object which, we know, they had early proposed, and which they had begun with great vigor, steadiness, and craft, to prosecute. It acted as a secret but powerful stimulant upon the minds of the Roman bishops themselves, and it operated with all the force of a spell upon the imaginations of those over whom they now began to arrogate power. Herein we discover one of the grand springs of the Papacy. As the free states that formerly existed in the world had rendered up their wealth, their independence, and their deities, to form one colossal empire, why, asked the bishops of Rome, should not the various churches throughout the world surrender their individuality and their powers of self-government to the metropolitan see, in order to form one mighty Catholic Church? Why should not Christian Rome be the fountain of law and of faith to the world, as Pagan Rome had been? Why should not the symbol of unity presented to the world in the secular empire be realized in the real unity of a Christian empire? If the occupant of the temporal throne had been a king of kings, why should not the occupant of the spiritual chair be a bishop of bishops? That the bishops of Rome reasoned in this way is a historical fact. The Council of Chalcedon established the superiority of the Roman see on this very ground. "The fathers," say they, "justly conferred the dignity on the throne of the presbyter of Rome, because that was the imperial city." The mission of the gospel is to unite all nations into one family. Satan presented the world with a mighty counterfeit of this union, when he united all nations under the despotism of Rome, that thus, by counterfeiting, he might defeat the reality.

The rise of Provincial Ecclesiastical Councils wrought in the same way. The Greeks, copying the model of their Amphictyonic Council, were the first to adopt the plan of assembling the deputies of the churches of a whole province to deliberate on affairs of consequence. The plan in a short time was received throughout the whole empire. The Greeks called such assemblies *Synods*; the Latins termed them *Councils*, and styled their laws or resolutions *Canons*. In order to temper the deliberations and to execute the resolutions of the assembly, it was requisite that one should be chosen as president; and the dignity was usually conferred on the presbyter of greatest weight for his piety and wisdom. That the tranquillity of the Church might not be disturbed by annual elections, the person raised by the suffrages of his brethren to the presidential chair was continued in it for life. He was regarded only as the first among equals; but the title of Bishop began now to acquire a new significance, and to raise itself above the humble appellation of Presbyter. The election to the office of perpetual president fell not unfrequently upon the bishop of the metropolitan city; and thus the equality that reigned among the pastors of the primitive Church came to be still farther disturbed.

The fourth century found the primitive simplicity of the Church, as regards the form of her government, but little encroached upon. If we except the perpetual president of the Provincial Synod, a rank of equal honour and a title of equal dignity were enjoyed by all the pastors or bishops of the Church. But this century brought great changes along with it, and paved the way for still greater changes in the centuries that followed it. Under Constantine the empire was divided into four prefectures, these four prefectures into dioceses, and the dioceses into provinces. In making this arrangement, the State acted within its own province; but it stepped out of it altogether when it began, as it now did, to fashion the Church upon the model of the Empire. The ecclesiastical and civil arrangements were made, as nearly as possible, to correspond. Pious emperors believed that, in assimilating the two, they were doing both the State and the Church a service, — and the imperial wishes were powerfully seconded and formally sanctioned by ambitious prelates and intriguing councils. The new arrangements, impressed by a human policy upon the Church, became every day more marked, as did likewise the gradation of rank amongst the pastors. Bishop rose above bishop, not according to the eminence of his virtue or the fame of his learning, but according to the rank of the city in which his charge lay. The chief city of a province gave the title of METROPOLITAN, and likewise of Primate, to its bishop. The metropolis of a diocese conferred on its pastor the dignity of EXARCH. Over the exarchs were placed four presidents or patriarchs, corresponding to the four praetorian prefects created by Constantine. But it is probable that the title of Patriarch, which is of Jewish origin, was at first common to all bishops, and gradually came to be employed as a term of dignity and eminence. The first distinct recognition of the order occurs in the Council of Constantinople, A.D. 381. At that time we find but three of these great dignitaries in existence, — the Bishops of Rome, Antioch, and Alexandria; but a fourth was now added. The Council, taking into consideration that Constantinople was the residence of the Emperor, decreed "that the Bishop of Constantinople should have the prerogative, next after the Bishop of Rome, because his city was called New Rome." In the following century the Council of Chalcedon declared the bishops of the two cities on a level as regarded their spiritual rank. But the practice of old Rome was more powerful than the decree of the fathers. Despite the rising grandeur of her formidable rival, the city on the Tiber continued to be the one city of the earth, and her pastor to hold the foremost place among the patriarchs of the Christian world. In no long time wars broke out between these four spiritual potentates. The primates of Alexandria and Antioch threw themselves for protection upon the patriarch of the west; and the concessions they made as the price of the succour which was extended to them tended still more to enhance the importance of the Roman see.

This gradation of rank necessarily led to a gradation of jurisdiction and power. First came the Bishop, who exercised authority in his parish, and to whom the individual members of his flock were accountable. Next came the Metropolitan, who administered the ecclesiastical affairs of the province, exercised superintendence over all its bishops, convened them in synods, and, assisted by them, heard and determined all questions touching religion which arose within the limits of his jurisdiction. He possessed, moreover, the privilege of having his consent asked to the ordination of bishops within his province. Next came the Exarchs or Patriarchs, who exercised authority over the metropolitans of the diocese, and held diocesan synods, in which all matters pertaining to the welfare of the Church in the diocese were deliberated upon and adjudicated. There needed but one step more to complete this gradation of rank and authority, — a primacy among the exarchs. In due time an arch-Patriarch arose. As might have been foreseen, the seat of the prince of the patriarchs was Rome. A gradation which aimed at making the civil and ecclesiastical arrangements exactly to correspond, and which fixed the chief seats of the two authorities at the same places, made it inevitable that the primate of all Christendom should appear nowhere but at the metropolis of the Roman world. It was now seen what a tower of strength was Rome. Her prestige alone had lifted her bishop from the humble rank of presbyter to the pre-eminent dignity of arch-patriarch; and in this she gave the world a pledge of the future dominion and grandeur of her popes.

A gradation of rank and titles, however suitable to the genius and conducive to the ends of a temporal monarchy, consorts but ill with the character and objects of a spiritual kingdom: in fact, it forms a positive and powerful obstruction to the development of the one and the attainment of the other. It is only as a spiritual agent that the Church can be serviceable to society: she can make the task of government easy only by eradicating the passions of the human heart. A sound policy would have dictated the necessity of preserving intact the spiritual element, seeing the Church is powerful in proportion as she is spiritual. With a most infatuated persistency, the very opposite policy was pursued. Religion was robbed of her rights as a co-ordinate power. She was bound round with the trappings of state; the spiritual was enchained, the carnal had free scope given it, and then the Church was asked to do her office as a spiritual institute! A defunct organization, she was required to impart life!

The condition under which alone it appears possible for both Church and State to preserve their independence and vigour, is not *incorporation*, but *co-ordination*. God created society as he created man at the beginning, not ONE, but TWAIN. There is a secular body and there is a spiritual body upon the earth. We must accept the fact, and deal with it in such a way as will allow of the great ends being gained which God intended to serve by ordaining this order of things. If we attempt to incorporate the two, — the common error hitherto, — we contradict the design of God, by making one what he created twain. All former attempts at amalgamation have ended in the dominancy of the one principle, the subserviency of the other, and the corruption and injury of both. If, on the other hand, we aim at effecting a total disseverance, we not less really violate the constitution of society, and arrive at the same issue as before: we virtually banish the one principle, and install the other in undivided and absolute supremacy. Co-ordination is the only solution of which the problem admits; and it is the true solution, just because it is an acceptance of the fact as God has ordained it. It declares that society is neither matter solely nor spirit solely, but both; that, therefore, there is the secular jurisdiction and the spiritual jurisdiction; that these two have distinct characters, distinct objects, and distinct spheres; and that each in its own sphere is independent, and can claim from the other a recognition of its independence. Had the constitution of society been understood, and the principle of co-ordination recognised, the Papacy could not have arisen. But, unhappily, the State drew the Church into conformity first, which ended inevitably in incorporation; and this, again, in the dominancy of the spiritual over the secular element, as will always be the case in the long run, the spiritual being the stronger. The crime met a righteous punishment; for the State, which had begun by enslaving the Church, was itself enslaved in the end by that very arrogance and ambition which it had taught the Church to cherish. But we pursue our melancholy story of the decline of Christianity and the rise of the Papacy.

Rome had the art to turn all things to her advantage. There was nothing that fell out that did not minister to her growth, and help onward the accomplishment of her vast designs; — the rivalship of sects, the jealousies of churchmen, the intrigues of courts, the growth of ignorance and superstition find the triumph of barbarian arms. It seemed as if the natural operation of events was suspended in her case, and that what to other systems wrought nought but evil, to her brought only good. The great shocks by which powerful empires were broken in pieces, and the face of the world changed, left the Church unscathed. While other systems and confederations were falling into ruin, she continued steadily to advance. From the mighty wreck of the empire she uprose in all the vigour of youth. She had shared in its grandeur, but she did not share in its fall. She saw the barbaric flood from the north overwhelm southern Europe; but from her lofty seat on the Seven Hills she looked securely down on the deluge that rolled beneath her. She saw the crescent, hitherto triumphant, cease to be victorious the moment it approached the confines of her special and sacred territory. The same arms that had overthrown other countries only contributed to her grandeur. The Saracens brought to an end the patriarchate of Alexandria and of Antioch; thus leaving the see of Rome, more especially after the breach with Constantinople, undisputed mistress of the west. What could be concluded from so many events, whose issues to the Papacy were so opposite from their bearing on all besides, but that, while other states were left to their fate, Rome was defended by an invisible arm? Instinct she must be with a divine life, otherwise how could she survive so many disasters? No wonder that the blinded nations mistook her for a god, and prostrated themselves in adoration. We cannot write the history of the period; but we may be permitted to point out the general bearing of the occurrences which we have classified as above, upon the development of the Papacy.

The disputes which arose in the churches of the east favored the pretensions of the Roman Church, and helped to pave her way to universal domination. Desirous to silence an opponent by citing the opinion of the western Church, the eastern clergy not unfrequently submitted questions at issue among themselves to the judgment of the Roman bishop. Every such application was registered by Rome as a proof of superior authority on her part, and of submission on the part of the east. The germinating superstition of the times, — owing principally to the prevalence of the Platonic philosophy, from the subtle disquisitions and specious reasonings of which Christianity suffered far more than she did from the persecuting edicts of emperors and pro-consuls, — likewise aided the advance of the Papacy. This superstition, which was in truth, as we have already explained, nothing but the revived Paganism of a former age, continued to increase from an early part of the third century and onward. The simplicity of the Christian faith began to be corrupted by novel and heathenish opinions, and the worship of the Church to be burdened by ridiculous and idolatrous ceremonies. When the Church exchanged the catacombs for the magnificent edifices which the wealth, the policy, and sometimes the piety of princes erected, she exchanged also the simplicity of life and purity of faith, of which so many affecting memorials remain to our day, for the accommodating spirit of the schools, and the easy manners of the court. Already, in the fourth century, we find images introduced into churches, the bones of martyrs hawked about as relics, the tombs of saints become the resort of pilgrims, and monks and hermits swarming in the various countries. We find the pagan festivals, slightly disguised, adopted into the Christian worship; the homage offered anciently to the gods transferred to the martyrs; the Lord's Supper dispensed sometimes at funerals; the not improbable origin of masses; and the churches filled with the blaze of lamps and tapers, the smoke of incense, the perfume of flowers, and the goodly show of gorgeous robes, crosiers, mitres, and gold and silver vases; reminding one of the not unsimilar spectacles which might be witnessed in the pagan temples. "The religion of Constantine," remarks Gibbon, "achieved in less than a century the final conquest of the Roman empire; but the victors themselves were insensibly subdued by the arts of their vanquished rivals." And as it had fared with the worship of the Church, so had it fared with her government. First, the people were excluded from all share in the administration of affairs; next, the rights and privileges of the presbyters were invaded; while the bishops, who had usurped the powers of both people and presbyters, contended with one another respecting the limits of their respective jurisdictions, and imitated, in their manner of living, the state and magnificence of princes. At last the Church elected her chief bishop in the midst of tumults and fearful slaughter. "Hence it came to pass," says Mosheim, that at the conclusion of this century there remained no more than a mere shadow of the ancient government of the Church." Notwithstanding that the Church contained every man of the age who was distinguished for erudition and eloquence, we look in vain for any really serious attempt to check this career of spiritual infatuation. There was one moment peculiarly critical, inasmuch as it offered signal opportunities of retrieving the errors of the past, and preventing the more tremendous errors of the future. Galled by the yoke of ceremonies, the Christian people began to evince a desire to return to the simplicity of early times. There needed only a powerful voice to call that feeling into action. Many eyes were already turned to one whose commanding eloquence and venerable piety made him the most conspicuous person of his times. The destiny of ages hung on the decision of Augustine. Had he declared for reform, the history of the Papacy might have been cut short; the ambition of a Hildebrand and a Clement, the bigotry and despotism of a Philip and a Ferdinand, the fanaticism and cruelties of a Dominic, and the carnage of a St. Bartholomew, might never have existed. But the Bishop of Hippo, alas! hesitated, — gave his voice in favour of the growing superstition. All was lost. The history of the Church becomes from that hour little better than the history of superstition, hypocrisy, knavery, and blood. Poisonous plants thrive best amid corruption; and thus the young Papacy drew nutriment from the follies and superstitions of the age.

The time was now come when the empire should fall. Hosts of barbarians from the deserts of the north were already assembled on its frontier. The distracted State, threatened with destruction, leant for aid upon the arm of the Church, whose infancy it had first attempted to crush, and next condescended to shelter. Thus the decline of the imperial accelerated the rise of the spiritual power. In the year 378 came the law of Gratian and Valentinian II., empowering the metropolitans to judge the inferior clergy, and empowering the Bishop of Rome (Pope Damasus), either in Person or by deputy, to judge the metropolitans. An appeal might be carried from the tribunal of the metropolitan to the Roman bishop, but from the judgment of the pontiff there was no appeal; his sentence was final. This law was addressed to the praetorian prefects of Gaul and Italy, and thus it included the whole western empire, for the latter prefect exercised jurisdiction over western Illyricum and Africa, as well as over Italy. Thus did the Roman bishop acquire legal jurisdiction over all the western clergy. When the bishops applied to the Pope in doubtful cases, his letters conveying the desired advice were styled *Decretal Epistles*; and to these decretals the Roman canonists came afterwards to attach as much importance as to the Holy Scriptures. In order to the due publication and enforcement of these decrees, bishops were appointed to represent the Pope in the various countries; and it became customary to ordain no bishops without the sanction of these papal vicars. The jurisdiction thus conferred on the Roman bishop over the west was submitted to with reluctance: it received only a partial submission from the churches of Africa, and was successfully resisted for some considerable time by those of Britain and Ireland.

The edict of Gratian and Valentinian II., which was coincident, as respects the date of its promulgation and the powers which it conferred, with the decree of a synod of Italian bishops, forms a marked epoch in the growth of the ecclesiastical supremacy. Up till this time the jurisdiction of the Bishop of Rome had been exercised within the somewhat narrow limits of the civil prefect. His direct power extended only over the vicarage of Rome or the ten suburban provinces. However, within this territory his authority was of a more absolute kind than that which the exarchs of the east exercised within their dioceses. The latter functionaries could ordain only their metropolitans, whereas the Roman prelate possessed the right to ordain every bishop within the limits of his jurisdiction. Thus, if his authority was less extensive than that of the oriental patriarch, it was already of a more solid kind. But now it underwent a sudden and vast enlargement. By the edict of the Emperor, and the sanction of the Italian bishops, the Roman prelate took his place at the head of the western clergy. A post so distinguished, though conferring as yet, on the whole, but a nominal authority, must have offered vast facilities for acquiring real and substantial power. When was it that the occupants of Peter's chair lacked either the capacity to comprehend or the tact to improve the advantages of their position? Ambition and genius have ever alike seemed intuitive to them. Lifted thus to the supremacy of the west by royal favour and clerical subserviency, — twin elevatory powers at all stages of the rise of this terrible despotism, — the pontiff began to arrogate all the prerogatives which ecclesiastical law confers upon patriarchs, and to exercise them in an arbitrary and irresponsible manner. He obtruded his interference in the ordination of all bishops, even those of humblest rank; thus passing by, and virtually ignoring, the rights of metropolitans. He encouraged appeals to his see, in the well-founded hope of drawing into his own hands the management of all affairs. He convoked synods, but rather to display the magnificence and power of Peter's see, than to benefit by the counsel of his brethren in difficult cases. Usurping the legislative as well as the judicial functions of the Church, he dictated to his secretary whatever he believed, or pretended to believe, to be right and fitting in matters pertaining to the Church; and the decretal, to which all submitted, was equally authoritative with the canons of councils, and finally with the commandments of Holy Scripture. Thus did the occupant of the fisherman's chair craftily weave the intricate web of his tyrannical and blasphemous power over all the churches and clergy of the west.

Another well-marked stage in the rise of the ecclesiastical supremacy is A.D. 445. In that year came the memorable edict of Valentinian III. and Theodosius II., in which the Roman pontiff was styled the "Director of all Christendom," and the bishops and universal clergy were commanded to obey him as their ruler. It is believed that the decree was issued on the application of Pope Leo. Amongst other advantages enjoyed by the pontiff was that of ready access to the Court, and thus he sometimes became the prompter of the imperial policy. The suggestions noted down by his secretary, submitted to the Emperor, and approved of by him, were ushered into the world with the customary forms and the full authority of an imperial edict. "Henceforth," that is, from the publication of the decree we have just noted, "the power of the Roman bishops," says Ranke, "advanced beneath the protection of the Emperor himself." At about the distance of a century from the decree of Theodosius came the celebrated letter of

Justinian to the Pope, in which the Emperor still farther enlarged the prerogatives which previous edicts had conferred upon the Bishop of Rome.

These imperial recognitions of a rank which the councils of the Church had previously conferred, tended greatly, as may easily be conceived, to consolidate and advance the arrogant assumptions of the Roman bishop. They gave solidity to his power, by investing him with a positive and legal jurisdiction. The code of Justinian, which had been published a few years before this time, was now the law of western Europe. Its influence, too, was favourable to the growth of the ecclesiastical supremacy. Contemporarily with the publication of Justinian's code, was the rise of the Benedictine order. In the course of a century the Benedictines had spread themselves over the west, preaching everywhere the doctrine of implicit submission to the see of Rome. Last of all came the edict of the Emperor Phocas, in A.D. 606, constituting Boniface III. Universal Bishop. This was the last in a series of edicts which had for their object to make the Bishop of Rome "Lord over God's heritage." In so infamous a cause no one was so worthy to perform the crowning act as the tyrannical and brutal Phocas. It was the hand of a murderer which placed upon the brow of Boniface the mitre of a universal episcopate.

The ecclesiastical supremacy had now a *legal* existence, but it must become *real* also. So vast a power, extending over so many interests, and over such a multitude of persons, and covering so large a portion of the globe, no imperial fiat could create; it must grow. Planted by councils, buttressed by edicts, with a congenial element of vitality and increase in the thickening superstition of the times, it henceforward made rapid progress. It throve so well, in fact, and shot up into such portentous height, that before all was over, the authority that had evoked it would fain have bidden it away, but could not; like the necromancer who forgets his spell, and is unable to lay the spirit he has raised. The suckling in the cradle to which the State offered its breasts could never surely grow into the hydra that was to strangle the empire! Power, when once it has begun to grow, enlarges its volume like the rolling river, and accelerates its speed like the falling avalanche. On a sudden all things become favourable to it. At every turn, it finds, ready-made to its hand, helps to speed it onward. Its faults, be they ever so great, never lack apologists; and its excellencies, however small they be, always find willing and eloquent panegyrists. Its wealth converts enemies into friends; the timid grow courageous in its cause; and the indifferent and lukewarm find a hundred reasons for being active and zealous in its service. The cause of Rome was the rising cause, and therefore it enjoyed all these advantages, and many more besides. With a dexterity and skill which have never elsewhere been equalled, the Vatican could manufacture, out of materials the most heterogeneous and unpromising, props and defences of its ill-gotten supremacy. The incautious admission of an opponent, the exaggerated and high-flown language of a eulogist, were alike accepted by Rome as formal and measured acknowledgments of her right. The hyperbolical and sycophantish terms in which a prelate sued for protection, or a heretic implored forgiveness, were registered as documentary proofs of the prerogatives and powers of the Roman see. The sectary was encouraged or put down, just as it suited the policy of the pontiffs; and the shield of the vanquished heretic Rome hung up as a trophy of her prowess. Monarchs were incited to quarrel with one another: Rome stood by till the conflict was ended; and then, siding with the stronger party, she divided the spoils with the victor. The clergy even, who might naturally have been supposed to be averse to the rise of such a domination, were conciliated by being taught to find their own dignity in that of the Roman see, and to share with the pontiff dominion over the laity. By these, and an hundred other arts, which triumphantly vindicate to the Roman pontiffs an unquestionable supremacy in knavery and hypocrisy, it came to pass, that in process of time, the one Bishop of Rome had absorbed all the bishops of the west. There was but one huge episcopate, with its head upon the Seven Hills; while its hundred limbs, like these of the giant Briareus of classic mythology, were stretched out over Europe, forming a monster of so anomalous and nondescript a character, that nowhere shall we find a figure adequately to depict it, save among the inspired hieroglyphics of the Apocalypse, where it is portrayed under the symbol of a beast, of lamb-like mien but dragon-ferocity.

At last the empire of the west was dissolved. The seat which had been occupied so long by the master of the world was now empty. This had been noted beforehand in prophecy as the instant sign of the coming of Antichrist, that is, of his full revelation; for, as we have already seen, the Mystery of Iniquity was operative in the apostles' days. "He who now letteth will let," said Paul, alluding to the imperial power, which, so long as it existed, was an effectual obstruction to the papal supremacy, — "he who now letteth will let, till he be taken out of the way; and then shall that

Wicked be revealed." The overthrow of the empire contributed most materially towards the elevation of the Bishop of Rome; for, *first*, it took the Caesars out of the way. "A secret hand," says De Maistre, "chased the emperors from the Eternal City, to give it to the head of the Eternal Church." *Second*, It compelled the bishops of Rome, now deprived of the imperial influence which had hitherto helped them so mightily in their struggles for pre-eminence, to fall back on another element, and that an element which constitutes the very essence of the Papacy, and on which is founded the whole complex fabric of the spiritual and temporal domination of the popes. The rank of Rome, as the seat of government and the metropolis of the world, had lifted her bishop to a proud preeminence above his peers. But Rome was the head of empire no longer: the prestige of her name, which in all ages has struck the imagination so powerfully, and through the imagination captivated the judgment, she still retained; for by no change could she become bereft of her immortal memories: but the subject nations no longer called her Mother and Ruler. With Rome would have fallen her bishop, had he not, as if by anticipation of the crisis, reserved till this hour the masterstroke of his policy. He now boldly cast himself upon an element of much greater strength than that of which the political convulsions of the times had deprived him, namely, that the Bishop of Rome is the successor of Peter, the prince of the Apostles, and, in virtue of being so, is Christ's Vicar on earth. In making this claim, the Roman pontiffs vaulted at once over the throne of kings to the seat of gods: Rome became once more the mistress of the world, and her popes the rulers of the earth.

The principle had been tacitly adopted by many of the clergy, and more especially by the bishops of Rome, before this time; but now it was formally and openly advanced, as the basis of a claim of authority over all churches and bishops, and ultimately of dominion over sovereigns. Of this we adduce the following testimonies. In the middle of the fifth century, we find the fundamental dogma of the Papacy, that the Church is founded on Peter, and that the popes are his representatives, proclaimed by the papal legate in the midst of the Council of Chalcedon, and virtually sanctioned by the silence of the fathers who were sitting in judgment on the case of Dioscorus. "For these causes," said the legate, "Leo, archbishop of Old Rome, doth by us and by the Synod, with the authority of St. Peter, who is the rock and foundation of the Church, and the ground of faith, depose him (Dioscorus) from his episcopal dignity." We find the fathers of the same council hailing with acclamation the voice of Leo as the voice of Peter. A shout followed the reading of the Pope's letter: — "Peter speaks in Leo." As a farther proof that the Popes had now shifted their dignity from an *imperial* to a *pontifical* foundation, we may instance the case of Hilary, the successor of Leo, who accepted from the Terragonese bishop, as a title to which he had unquestionable right, the appellation "Vicar of Peter, to whom, since the resurrection of Christ, belonged the keys of the kingdom." In a spirit of equal arrogance, we find Pope Gelasius, bishop of Rome from A.D. 492 to 496, asserting that it became kings to learn their duty from bishops, but especially from the *"Vicar of the blessed Peter."* We find the same Pope asserting, in a Roman council, A.D. 495, that to the see of Rome belonged the primacy, in virtue of Christ's own delegation; and that from the authority of the keys there was excepted none living, but only (mark how modest Rome then was!) the dead. The council in which these lofty claims were put forth concluded its session with a shout of acclamation to Gelasius, "In thee we behold Christ's Vicar."

In the violent contention which raged between Symmachus and Laurentius, both of whom had been elected to the pontificate on the same day, we are furnished with another proof that at the beginning of the sixth century not only was this lofty prerogative claimed by the popes, but that it was generally acquiesced in by the clergy. We find the council convoked by Theodoric demurring to investigate the charges alleged against Pope Symmachus, on the grounds set forth by his apologist Ennodius, which were, "that the Pope, as God's Vicar, was the judge of all, and could himself be judged by no one." "In this apology," remarks Mosheim, "the reader will perceive that the foundations of that enormous power which the popes of Rome afterwards acquired were now laid." Thus did the pontiffs, providing timeously against the changes and revolutions of the future, place the fabric of the primacy upon foundations that should be immoveable for all time. The primacy had been promulgated by synodical decrees, ratified by imperial edicts; but the pontiffs perceived that what synods and emperors had given, synods and emperors might take away. The enactments of both, therefore, were discarded, and the *Divine right* was put in their room, as the only basis of power which neither lapse of years nor change of circumstances could overthrow. Rome was henceforward indestructible.

"Dum domus Aeneae capitoli immobile saxum
Accolet, imperiumque Romanus pater habebit."

Thus was accomplished in the destinies of the Papacy a change of so vast a character, that the imagination can with difficulty realize it. Quickened with a new life, Rome returned from her grave to exercise universal dominion a second time. The element of power which was lost when the empire fell was at best of an extraneous kind: it was influence reflected from without upon Rome, — foreign in its character and earthly in its source. But the element on which she now cast herself was of a nature analogous to the Papacy, and so, incorporating with it, that element became its life. It made Rome self-existent and invincible, — invincible to every principle save one, and that principle was to remain in abeyance for a full thousand years. The day of Luther was yet afar off. It was this element that gave to Rome the superhuman power she wielded over the world. It was this which enabled her to plant or to pluck up its kingdoms, to bind monarchs to her chariot-wheel, to throw reason and intellect into chains, and to restore once more the dominion of the pagan night. In so subtle a device we can discover a deeper policy and a more consummate craft than that of man. It was Rome's invisible director that counselled so bold a step. This step was as successful as bold. It opened a new career to the ambition of Rome, and revealed to her, though yet at a great distance, and with many an intervening change and struggle, that seat of godlike power to which she was ultimately to attain, and towards which she now began, with slow and painful steps, to climb. Most marvellous and astonishing it truly was, that at a time when Rome was placed in most imminent jeopardy, and society itself was perishing around her, she should lay the foundations of her power, and by her prompt interposition save herself and the world from the dissolution to which both appeared to be tending. Her adherents in all ages have seen in this nothing less than a proof, alike incontrovertible and marvellous, of her Divinity. The Cardinal Baronius speaks the sentiments of all Roman Catholics when he breaks out in the following impassioned strain, in reference to a supposed grant of the kingdom of Hungary, by Stephen, to the Roman see: — "It fell out, by a wonderful providence of God, that at the very time when the Romish Church might appear ready to fall and perish, even then distant kings approach the apostolic see, which they acknowledge and venerate as the only temple of the universe, — the sanctuary of piety, the pillar of truth, the immoveable rock. Behold kings, not from the east, as of old they came to the cradle of Christ, but from the north: led by faith, they humbly approach the cottage of the fisher, the

Church of Rome herself offering not only gifts out of their treasures, but bringing even kingdoms to her, and asking kingdoms from her."

Thus have we traced the history of the Papacy, from its rise in primitive times, to its formal though but partial development in the sixth century. Aided by the various influences we have enumerated, — the prestige and rank of Rome, — the institution of the order, first of metropolitan, and next of patriarch, — the edicts of emperors, — the reference of disputed questions by other Churches to the Bishop of Rome, — and, most of all, the pretence that the occupant of the Roman see was the successor of Peter and the Vicar of Christ, — together with that crafty, astute, and persevering policy which enabled the Roman bishops to make the most of apparent concessions to them of preeminence and authority, — the pastors of Rome were now supreme over the great body of the clergy of the west; and thus the ecclesiastical supremacy was attained. They were now in a fair way, too, of becoming the superiors of kings, for there was no usurpation of prerogative, no exercise of dominion, temporal or spiritual, which the claim now put forth by the Roman bishop to be Christ's Vicar would not cover. We are now to follow the several steps by which the Papacy gradually rose to the height of power in which we find it shortly before the breaking out of the Reformation.

Chapter III: Rise and Progress of the Temporal Sovereignty.

Over the abyss in which the Roman empire of the west had been engulphed there now floated the portentous form of the Papacy. If the idolatrous nations, in their victorious march from the Upper Danube to southern Europe, had not brought the gods of their ancestors along with them, they were not on that account the less pagan. Their conversion to Christianity was merely nominal. Ignorant of its doctrines, destitute of its spirit, and captivated by its splendid ceremonial, they were scarcely conscious of any change, when they transferred to the saints of the Roman Church the worship they had been accustomed to pay to their Scandinavian deities. The process by which these nations, from being pagan, became Christian, may be adequately likened to the contrivance by which the statue of Jupiter at Rome was converted from the representative of the prince of pagan deities to the representative of the prince of Christian apostles, namely, by the substitution of the two keys for the thunderbolt. After the same manner the newly arrived nations were taught to wear the outward badges of the Christian faith, but at heart they were as much pagan as before. Most of the new tribes became professors of the Arian faith. In this heresy were involved the barbarians which occupied Italy, Africa, Spain, and Gaul; and the Popes were obliged to exercise the utmost circumspection and management, in order to surmount the perils and profit by the advantages presented by the new order of things. The convulsions, combinations, and heresies of the times, formed a maze so intricate and dangerous, that no power less wary and sagacious than the papal could have threaded its way with safety through it. The bark of Peter was now navigating a sea full of rocks and maelstroms, and had to shape its course,

"Harder beset,
And more endangered, than when Argo passed
Through Bosphorus, betwixt the justling rocks,
Or when Ulysses on the larboard shunn'd
Charybdis, and by the other Whirlpool steer'd."
PARADISE LOST.

In A.D. 496, an event took place destined to exercise a momentous influence on the fate of the Papacy and of Europe. In that year Clovis, king of the Franks, in fulfilment of a vow made on the field of Tolbiac, where he was victorious over the Allemanni, was baptized at Rheims. "On the memorable day," observes Gibbon, "when Clovis descended from the baptismal font, he alone in the Christian world deserved the name and prerogatives of a catholic king." Rome hailed the auspicious event as a token of a long series of similar triumphs; and she rewarded the devotion of Clovis by bestowing upon him the title,-which he has transmitted downward through 1400 years to his successors the kings of France,-*of Eldest Son of the Church*. During the course of the sixth century, others of the barbarian kings, the Burgundians of southern Gaul and Savoy, the Bavarians, the Visigoths of Spain, the Suevi of Portugal, and the Anglo-Saxons of Britain,-presented themselves before the apostolic throne as its spiritual vassals. Thus, the dominion which their swords had taken away, their superstition restored to Rome. The various nations who were now masters of the western empire found in the Papacy, and nowhere else, to use Muller's words, "a point of union." The sagacious measures of pope Gregory the Great contributed at this juncture material assistance to the rising Papacy. The barbarian kings being now submissive to the Roman faith, Gregory exerted himself, with a large measure of success, to establish it as a law throughout their kingdoms, that the metropolitan should receive the sanction of the pontiff. For this end it now became the practice to send from Rome a pallium to the metropolitan, in token of investiture; and without the pall he could not lawfully enter on the exercise of his functions. The zeal of Boniface, the apostle of Germany a century later, completed what Pope Gregory had commenced. This man, a Briton by birth, travelled throughout Germany and Gaul, preaching profound submission to Peter and his representative the Roman bishop; and he succeeded in inducing the German and Frank bishops to take the vow he himself had taken of implicit obedience to the Roman see. Henceforward, without the pallium no metropolitan entered upon the duties of his office. How much this tended to consolidate the spiritual supremacy, and to pave the way for the temporal usurpations of the popes, it is not difficult to perceive.

In the seventh century, we find a prevalent disposition among the princes of the west to submit themselves implicitly, in all matters that pertained to religion, to the Roman see. In their pagan state they had been accustomed to undertake no affair of consequence without the advice and consent of their priests, by whom they were held in the most degrading vassalage; and after their conversion they transferred this implicit obedience to the Roman clergy, who most willingly accepted the implied superiority and power, and used every means to improve and extend their influence. "It was the sturdy shoulders of these children of the idolatrous north," remarks Dr. D'Aubigné, "that succeeded in placing on the supreme throne of Christendom a pastor of the banks of the Tiber." The people venerated the clergy, and the clergy were bound to implicit obedience to the pontiff. By this time, too, the *unity of the Church*, not in the Scriptural, but Romish sense,-not as consisting in one baptism, one faith, one hope; but as consisting in one outward body governed by a visible head, the Roman pontiff,-had established itself in the minds of men. The term POPE or FATHER, originally a divine, and next an imperial title, formerly given to all bishops, now came to be restricted to the Bishop of Rome, according to the saying afterwards employed by Gregory VII., that there was but one pope in the world. The overthrow of the Ostrogoths and Vandals about this time, by the arms of Belisarius, contributed also to the expansion of the Papacy. The former had established themselves in Italy, and the latter in Sardinia and Corsica; and their near presence enabled them to overawe the popedom; but their extirpation by the victorious general of Justinian rid the Pope of these formidable neighbours, and tended to the authority as well as the security of the Roman see.

But it was in the eighth century that the most considerable addition was made to the temporal power of the popes. A singular combination of dangers at that period threatened the very existence of the Papacy. The iconoclast disputes, then raging with extreme violence, had engendered a deep and lasting variance between the Roman see and the emperors of the east. The Arian kings of Lombardy, intent on the conquest of all Italy, were brandishing their swords before the very gates of Rome; while in the west, the Saracens, who had overrun Africa and conquered Spain, were arrived at the passes of the Pyrenees, and threatened to enter Italy and plant the crescent on the Seven Hills. Pressed on all sides, the Pope turned his eyes to France. He wrote to the mayor of the palace, and so framed the terms of his letter, that Peter, with all the saints, supplicated the Gallic soldier to hasten to the rescue of *his* chosen city, and of that church where his bones reposed. The succour was not more earnestly craved than it was cordially and promptly granted. The bold Pepin had just seated himself on the throne of the pusillanimous Childeric, and needed the papal confirmation of his usurped dignity. Bargaining for this, he girded on the sword, crossed the

Alps, defeated the Lombards, and, wresting from them the cities they had taken from the Greek emperor, he laid the keys of the conquered towns upon the altar of St. Peter. This was in the year 755; and by this act was laid the foundation of the temporal power of the popes.

The gifts thus bestowed by Pepin were confirmed by his yet more distinguished son Charlemagne. The Lombards had again become troublesome to the Pope; in fact, they were besieging him in his city of Rome. The pontiff again supplicated the aid of France; and Charlemagne, in answer to his prayer, entered Italy at the head of his army. Defeating the Lombards, he visited the Pope in his capital; and so profound was his deference for the see of Rome, that he kissed the steps of St. Peter as he ascended, and, at the interview that followed, ratified and enlarged the donations of his father Pepin to the Church. A second time Charlemagne appeared in the Eternal City. The factions that now reigned in Rome threatened to put an end, by their violence, to the authority of the pontiff; and the third time did France interpose to save the Papacy from apparent destruction. Charlemagne, says Machiavelli, decreed, "that his Holiness, being God's Vicar, could not be subject to the judgment of man." Charlemagne was now master of nearly all the Romano-Germanic nations of the west; and, as a recompense for these repeated succours, the Pope (Leo III.), on Christmas eve, A.D. 800, placed upon the head of the French king the crown of the western empire. In this act the pontiff displayed his power not less than his gratitude. As one who had crowns and kingdoms at his disposal, we behold him selecting the son of Pepin, and placing upon his brow the imperial diadem.. In this light at least have the partisans of Rome regarded the act. They have "generally maintained," says Mosheim, "that Leo. III., by a *divine right*, vested in him as Bishop of Rome, transported the western empire from the Greeks to the Franks." "Whereas formerly," says Machiavelli, in his History of Florence, "the popes were confirmed by the emperors, the emperor now, in his election, was to be beholden to the pope; by which means the power and dignity of the empire declined, and the Church began to advance, and by these steps to usurp upon the authority of temporal princes." One thing at least is clear, that great advantages accrued to both parties from this proceeding. It added new lustre to the dignity of Charlemagne, and gave the title to him who already possessed the power; while, on the other hand, it greatly enlarged the temporal possessions of the Church, and secured a powerful friend and protector to the Pope in the person of the Emperor. Thus the perils which had threatened to destroy the Papacy tended ultimately to consolidate it; and thus did Rome, skilled to profit alike by the weakness and the strength of monarchs, steadily pursue that profound scheme of policy, the object of which was to chain kings, priests, and people, to the pontifical chair. Henceforward the Pope takes his place among the monarchs of the earth. First the Vandals and Ostrogoths, and now the Lombards, had fallen before him. Their territories were given to the Church, and formed the patrimony of St. Peter; and the haughty pastor by whom these powers had been supplanted, unaware that prophecy had pointed very significantly to the fact, and marked it as a noted stage in the rise of Antichrist, now appeared in the glories of the triple crown.

While the Papacy was laboriously building up its external defences, conciliating princes, contracting alliances with powerful monarchs, and intriguing to acquire in its own right temporal sovereignty, let us mark the growth of that superstition in which lay the life and strength of the Popedom. These two,-the inward principle and the outward development,-we find ever advancing *pari passu*. By the time the barbarians arrived in southern Europe, Christianity had been grossly corrupted. It lacked, as a consequence, the power to dispel the ignorance or to purify the morals of those whom the convulsions of the times brought into contact with it. As they issued from their native forests, so were they received within the pale of the Church,-uninstructed, unreformed, unchristianized. The only change the Christianity of the age exacted had respect to the names of those divinities in whose honour the invading nations continued to celebrate the same rites, slightly modified, which they had been accustomed to pay to their Druidical and Scandinavian idols. It follows that the term Christendom is simply a geographical expression. The nations that inhabit western Europe have not till this hour been evangelized, if we except the partial enlightenment of the Reformation. The barbarism of the times had extinguished the light of philosophy and of letters. No polite study, no elegant art, no useful science, helped to tame the fierceness, refine the manners, or expand the intellect, of these nations. The clergy, wallowing in wealth, and abandoning themselves to dissolute pleasures, were grossly and shamefully ignorant, and unable to compose the homilies which they recited in the presence of the people. The genius of Charlemagne saw and bewailed these evils; but neither his power nor his munificence,-and both were largely employed,-could avail to reform these gross abuses. The singular infelicity of the times rendered all his attempts at reformation abortive. If we except a few individuals, belonging chiefly to Ireland and Britain, where the enlightened and beneficent patronage of Alfred the Great maintained a better order of things, no illustrious names illumined the darkness of that barbarous night. Till partially restored by the Saracens in the tenth century, learning and science were unknown in the west. The state of matters as regards religion was even more deplorable. We have already seen the height to which superstition had risen in the fourth century. We will search in vain, amid the ignorance, the follies, the vices, of the eighth and ninth centuries, for the early purity of the gospel, the simple grandeur of its worship, or the attractive virtues of its first confessors. A general dissolution of manners characterized the age: the corruption had infected all classes, not excepting even the clergy, who, instead of being examples of virtue, were notorious for their impieties and vices. In the same proportion in which they declined in piety and learning, did they increase in riches and influence. A notion now began to be propagated, that crimes might be expiated by donations to the Church at the moment of death. This proved a fertile source of wealth to the clergy. Rich legacies and ample donations of lands and houses flowed in upon the churches and monasteries, the gifts of men who hoped by these generous deeds, performed at the expense of their heirs, to obliterate the sins of a lifetime, and purchase salvation for their souls. By and by, bequests on a yet larger scale began to be made. It was at this time customary for princes to distribute munificent gifts among their followers, partly as the reward of past services, and partly with a view to secure their support in future. The great credit which the clergy enjoyed with the people made it a matter of the last importance to secure their influence. Whole provinces, with their cities, castles, and fortresses, were not unfrequently bestowed upon them; and over the domains so bestowed they were permitted to exercise sovereign jurisdiction. Raised thus to the rank of temporal princes, they vied with dukes and sovereigns in the splendour of their court and the number of their retinue. They raised armies, imposed taxes, waged bloody wars, and by their ceaseless intrigues and boundless ambition plunged Europe into interminable broils and conflicts. Those men who were bound by their sacred calling to preach to the world the vanity of human grandeur, furnished in their own persons the most scandalous examples of worldly pride and ambition. To fulfil their sublime mission as ministers of Christ,- to instruct the ignorant, reclaim the wandering, succour the distressed, and console the dying,-formed no part of their care. These duties were forsaken for the more tempting paths of pleasure and wealth, the intrigues of courts, and the tumults of camps. A crafty priesthood, moreover, made it an inviolable rule, that property gifted to the Church should be regarded as the property of God, and be held for ever inalienable. Henceforward to touch it was sacrilege; and whoever adventured on so bold an act was destined to experience the full measure of the Church's vengeance. The natural law which limits the growth of bodies corporate was set aside by this kind of spiritual entail; and the wealth of the Church, and, by consequence, her power, grew to be enormous.

The evils of the time were LEGION; but all flowed from one colossal error: the cardinal truth of Christianity, that *salvation is of grace*, was completely obscured. By the most plausible pretexts and the most subtle devices was man led away from God, and taught to centre all his hopes in himself. Faith was overthrown, and works were put in its room. The sacrifice of Christ was neglected, and man became his own saviour. We trace the operation of this grand error in the superstitious and burdensome rites in which all holiness now began to be placed. Sanctification was no longer sought in a pure heart and a mind enlightened by divine truth, but in certain external rites, which were seldom either important or dignified. To nourish the passions and mortify the body was now the grand secret of holiness. Pilgrimages were undertaken, and their merits were regulated by the length and the perils of the way, and the renown of the shrine visited. Penances were imposed, fasts were enjoined; and in proportion to the severity of the suffering and the rigour of the abstinence, was the efficacy of the act to atone for sin, and recommend to the favour of God. A mind debased by ignorance, and not unfrequently by vice, and a body emaciated by flagellations and fastings, was a sure sign of eminent sanctity. Piety no longer consisted in love to God and obedience to his will, but in the observance of the most frivolous ceremonies, to which there attached an extraordinary value and a mysterious influence. To endow a convent or erect a cathedral was among the most illustrious deeds which one could perform. To possess a finger or a toe of a saint was a rare privilege; and the owner of so inestimable a treasure derived therefrom unspeakably more benefit than could possibly accrue from the possession of any moral or spiritual excellence, however exalted. Relics so precious were sought for with a perseverance and a zeal that set all difficulties at defiance; and what was so eagerly sought was in most cases happily found. The caves of Egypt, the sands of Libya, and the deserts of Syria, were ransacked. The bones of dead men, and, if history may be credited, of the lower animals, were exhumed, were hawked over Christendom, and purchased at a high rate. They were worn as amulets, or enshrined in cabinets of silver and gold; and, being placed in cathedrals, were exhibited at stated times to the devout. To abandon society, with the obligations it imposes and the duties it exacts, and to consume life in the midst of filth, indolence, and vice, was accounted an effort of uncommon holiness. To shirk the plough and the loom, and mount the wallet of the beggar,-to abscond from the ranks of honest industry, and fleece the labouring classes in predatory bands or as single sorners,-was to be heroically self-denied and virtuous. Such holy men were rather unpleasantly common; for the west, as formerly the east, now began to swarm with monks and hermits. Such of the pagan sophists as lived to witness the rise of this superstition, no less amazed than indignant, pointed the keen shafts of their powerful satire against that filthy race, which had renounced the beautiful mythology of Greece and the martial gods of Rome, to fall prostrate before the bones and mouldering relics of the dead.

So wretched did man's condition become, so soon as he turned away from God, and sought salvation in himself. In the same hour in which he forsook the light he lost his liberty. When he surrendered his faith he parted with his peace. From that moment his life became barren of all good, because he strove to produce by an effort of his will, what God had ordained to spring only from love. Hope, too, forsook the breast, in which she found no solid footing, and a "doubtsome faith," the result partly of scepticism and partly of indifference, took her place. The overmastering force of evil desires began now to be felt; and man found his own strength but a feeble substitute for the grace of God. Having taken upon himself the burden of his own salvation, he laboured, in a round of mortifying and painful acts, to accomplish a task utterly beyond his power. His success was far indeed from being in proportion to his efforts. But in this lay one of the deep artifices of Popery. That system employed the defilement of guilt, the slavery of fear, the thrall of sensuality, to complete its conquest over man. Having put out his eyes, Popery led man away to grind in her prison-house. The perfection of error is the perfection of slavery; and man surrendered himself without a struggle to the dominion of this tyrant. It was not till Truth came at the Reformation, that his prison-doors were opened, and that the bondman was loosed and led forth.

But the master corruption of the age was image-worship. Blinded by error, and grown carnal in their imaginations, men saw not the true glory of the sanctuary, and sought to beautify it with the fictitious splendour of statues and pictures. The promise, "Lo, I am with you," was forgotten; and when the worshipper ceased to realize the presence of a spiritual Being, the hearer of his prayer, he strove to stimulate his flagging devotion by corporeal representations. The churches, already polluted with relics, began now to be disgraced with images. Pictures of the saints and the martyrs covered the walls, while the vestibules and niches were occupied with statues of Christ and the apostles. These were first introduced under pretext of doing honour to those whom they represented; but the feeling, by a natural and unavoidable process, rapidly degenerated into worship. This was a master-stroke of the enemy. In no other way could he so effectually have withdrawn the contemplation of man from the region of the spiritual, and defaced, and ultimately destroyed in his mind, all true conceptions of the invisible Jehovah. It trained man, even in his devotions, to think only of what he saw; and from thinking only of what he sees, the step is an easy one to believe only in what he sees. It brought man from the heavens, and chained him to the earth. The rise of image-worship was the return of the ancient idolatry. The body ecclesiastic had ceased to be Christian, and had become pagan. The Church, planted by the labours of the apostles, and watered by the blood of martyrs, had disappeared; and an idolatrous and polytheistic institute had been substituted in its room. There was not less cause than formerly for the lament, "I planted thee a noble vine; how then art thou become the degenerate plant of a strange vine?"

We enter at greater length on the subject of image-worship, because it forms an important branch of the idolatry of Rome, and because it is intimately connected with the rise of the temporal sovereignty. It was in the east that this superstition first arose, but it was in the west that it found its most zealous patrons and champions; and none discovered greater ardour in this evil cause than the popes of Rome. Its rise was as early as its progress was gradual. "The first notice," says Gibbon, "of the use of pictures is in the censure of the Council of Illiberis, three hundred years after the Christian era." "The first introduction of a symbolic worship," continues the historian, "was in the veneration of the cross and of relics. . . . . . But a memorial more interesting than the skull or the sandals of a departed worthy, is a faithful copy of his person and features, delineated by the arts of painting or sculpture. . . . . By a slow though inevitable progression, the honours of the original were transferred to the copy; the devout Christian prayed before the image of a saint, and the pagan rites of genuflexion, luminaries, and incense, again stole into the Catholic Church. . . . . The use, and even the worship, of images was firmly established before the end of the sixth century." From this time the idolatry rapidly increased. Writing of the seventh century, we find Gibbon stating that "the throne of the Almighty was darkened by a cloud of martyrs, and saints, and angels." In this Gibbon is confirmed by the testimony of Mosheim, who states that "in this age, (*i. e.* the seventh century), they who were called Christians worshipped the wooden cross, the images of saints, and bones of men, they know not whom."

A century later, the famous dispute between the eastern emperors and the western popes had broken out. The Christians of the east, alarmed by the magnitude of the abuse, and stung by the reproaches of the Jews, and the railleries-all the more severe that they were merited-of the Mussulmans, who now reigned at Damascus, strove to effect a partial reformation. Their wishes were powerfully seconded by the Emperor Leo, III., who proscribed by edict the worship of images, and ordered the churches to be cleansed. These proceedings roused the ire of the reigning pontiff, Gregory II. The eloquence of the monks was evoked, and the thunders of excommunication were hurled against the imperial iconoclast; and Leo was pronounced an apostate, because he worshipped as the apostles and primitive Christians had worshipped, and because he sought to lead back his people to the same scriptural model. When it was found that the spiritual artillery had failed to take effect, earthly weapons were employed. Italy was excited to revolt, and a contest was commenced, which was continued for a hundred and twenty years. The Italians were absolved by the pontiff from their allegiance to the Emperor, and the revenue of Italy ceased to be sent to Constantinople. To chastise these rebellious proceedings, Leo despatched his fleet to the coast of Italy; but the Italians, inspired by fanaticism and rebellion, made a desperate resistance, and after a vast loss of life, and the ravage of several of the fairest provinces of the empire, the expedition was forced to return without having accomplished its object. The quarrel was taken up by successive emperors on the one side and successive popes on the other, and prosecuted with unabated violence and various success. Councils were convoked to give judgment in the matter. The Council of Constantinople, A.D. 754, summoned by Constantine Copronymus, condemned the worship, and also the use, of images. The Council of Nice, in Bithynia, A.D. 786, known as the second Nicene Council, convoked by the fair but flagitious Irene, the widow and murderess of Leo IV., reversed the sentence of the Council of Constantinople, and restored the worship of images. Leo V. condemned these idols to a second exile, but they were recalled by the Empress Theodora, A.D. 842, never more to be expelled from the east, till they and their worshippers were extirpated together in the fourteenth century by the sword of the Turks. Rome and Italy yielded in this matter the most profound submission to the Popes, who showed themselves throughout the zealous and truculent defenders of image-worship. The churches of France, Germany, England, and Spain, held a middle course. They condemned the adoration of images, but they adopted the perilous course of tolerating them in their churches as "the memorials of faith and history." Of these sentiments was Charlemagne, who endeavoured, but in vain, to stem the torrent of superstition. The unanimous decree of the Council which he assembled at Frankfort, A.D. 794, could not counteract the influence arising from the example and authority of the pontiff. Charlemagne found that the power which had enabled him to become master of all the western nations, was not sufficient to enable him to cope successfully with the rising superstition of the age. The cause of image-worship continued silently to progress, and it speedily attained in the west, as it had already done in the east, a universal triumph.

Though the quarrel, as regards the main point in dispute, had the same issue, both in the east and in the west, it led nevertheless to a final separation between the two churches. It directly contributed, as we have already said, to lay the foundation of the Pope's temporal sovereignty. In the heat of the conflict, the Italian provinces were torn from the emperor, and their government was virtually assumed by the pontiffs. "In that schism," says Gibbon, "the Romans had tasted of freedom, and the popes of sovereignty." "Rome raised her throne," to use D'Aubigné's words, "between two revolts." On the one side Italy threw off the yoke of the eastern emperors; on the other, France discarded her ancient dynasty, and both revolts were zealously encouraged and formally sanctioned by the popes. It is difficult to say which of the two,-the Greek schism or the Gallic usurpation,-contributed most to elevate the Papacy to temporal sovereignty.

Such is the real origin of the Pope's power. According to his own claim, it is of heaven; but history refuses to let the claim pass current, and points unequivocally to a different quarter as the source of his prerogative. Of the two branches of his power,-the sacerdotal and the regal,-it is hard to determine which is the most disreputable and infamous in its beginnings. His mitre he had from the murderer Phocas; his crown from the usurper Pepin. A spotless and noble lineage forsooth! The pontifical trunk has one stem rooted rankly in blood, and the other foully grafted on rebellion. As a priest, the Pope is qualified to minister in the ensanguined temples of Moloch; as a sovereign, his title is indisputable to act the satrap under the arch-rebel and "anarch old." No one can glance a moment at the contour of his character, as seen in history, without feeling that the hideous likeness on which he gazes is that of the Antichrist. Every line of his visage, every passage of his history, is full of antagonism, is the very counterpart of that of the Saviour. "All these things will I give thee," said the tempter to Christ in the wilderness, "if thou wilt fall down and worship me." "Get thee hence, Satan," was the reply. The fiend returned after three hundred years, and, leading the pontiff to the summit of the Roman hill, showed him "all the kingdoms of the world and the glory of them." "All these," said he, "will I give thee, if thou wilt fall down and worship me." No second denial awaited the tempter: instantly the knee was bent, and the pontiff raised his head crowned with the tiara. Twice has Christianity been crowned in bitter derision and mockery of her character. Once with a crown of thorns by the blasphemers of Caiaphas' hall; and now again with the tiara, in the person of the pontiff. Never did she demean herself with such divine dignity as when the thorns girt her brow; but, ah! the burning shame of the tiara.

It is further worthy of notice, that at the same time, and to a great degree by the same acts, did the bishops of Rome establish the worship of images, and consolidate their own jurisdiction as temporal sovereigns. These two form analogous stages in the career of the Papacy. They manifest an equal decline and advance,-a decline in the spiritual, and an advance in the secular element. By the first, Rome perfected the corruption of her worship; by the second, she perfected the corruption of her government. There was a meetness, therefore, in the two being attained at the same period. These two constitute the leading branches of the Romish apostacy,-idolatry and tyranny. These are the two arms of the apostacy,-SUPERSTITION and the SWORD: both arms were now grown; and thus Rome was equipped for her terrible mission. Her inglorious task was to bow down the world in ignominious thraldom, and her two-edged sword made it equally easy to enslave the mind and to tyrannize over the body. Her idolatry was to display itself in yet grosser forms, and her political power was to be vastly enlarged by new accessions of dominion and influence; but the world had now a fair specimen of the leading principles and organization of the Roman Catholic Church. Rome was to be a temple of idols, not a sanctuary of truth; a hierarchy, not a brotherhood. Were we called upon to fix on a period when Rome completed her transition from Christianity to Paganism, we would fix on this era. Henceforward she did not deserve to be regarded in any sense as a Church. She was not simply a corrupt Church; she was a pagan institute. The symbols of the Apocalypse had now found their verification in the corruptions of Europe: the temple had been measured; the outer court and the city had been given over to the Gentiles; and the Church was restricted to the select company which ministered at the altar within.

Into this sad condition had the Roman Church now come. She had begun in the spirit and been made perfect in the flesh. The spiritual she had renounced, as containing neither truth, nor beauty, nor power. An impassable gulph now divided her from the form not less than from the spirit of the early Church. She stood before the world as the legitimate successor of those systems of error and idolatry which in former ages had burdened the earth and affronted heaven. Her members kneeled before idols, and her head wore an earthly crown. She "had left heaven and its spheres of light, to mingle in the vulgar interests of citizens and princes." An hundred and twenty years (the period of the iconoclast disputes) had God striven with the men of the western Church, as he strove with the antediluvians in the days of Noah, when the ark was a-building; but his waiting had been in vain; and henceforward Rome was to pursue her career without let or hinderance. The spirit had ceased to strive with her. The Gothic scourge, sent to turn her from those dumb idols, had failed to induce repentance or reformation. Righteously, therefore, was she given over to the dominion of grosser delusions, to the commission of more aggravated crimes, and to the infliction, at last, of an unspeakably tremendous doom.

Chapter IV: Rise and Progress of the Temporal Supremacy.

We left the Papacy, at the opening of the ninth century, reposing beneath the shadow of the Carlovingian monarchy. One grand stage in its progress had been accomplished. The battle for the temporal sovereignty had been fought and won. A crowned priest now sat upon the Seven Hills. From this time another and far mightier object began to occupy the ambition and exercise the genius of Rome. To occupy a seat overshadowed by the loftier throne of the emperors would not satisfy the vast ambition of the pontiffs, and accordingly there was now commenced the struggle for the temporal supremacy.

There was an obvious incompatibility between the lofty spiritual powers claimed by the pontiffs, and their subordination to secular authority; nevertheless, at this time, and for some ages afterwards, the popes *were* subject to the emperors. Charlemagne was lord paramount of Rome, and the territories of the Church were a fief of the Emperor. The son of Pepin wore the imperial diadem, and, in the words of Ranke, "performed unequivocal acts of sovereign authority in the dominions conferred on St. Peter." Nevertheless, he had received the empire in a way which left it undecided whether he owed it more to his own merit or to the pontiff's favour, and whether he held it solely in virtue of his own right, and not also, in good degree, as the gift of Leo. The Pope was nominally subject to the Emperor, but in many vital points the *first* was *last*; and he who now wrote himself "a servant of servants," was fulfilling in a bad sense what our Lord intended in a good, — "Whosoever will be the greatest among you, let him be the servant of all." The popes had not yet advanced a direct and formal claim to dispose of crowns and kingdoms, but the germ of such a claim was contained, first, in the acts which they now performed. They had already taken it upon them to sanction the transference of the crown of France from the Merovingian to the Carlovingian family. And on what principle had they done so? Why did the Pope, rather than any other prince, profess to give validity to Pepin's right to the throne of France? Why, seeing, as a temporal ruler, he was the least powerful and independent sovereign in Europe, did he, of all men, interpose his prerogative in the matter? The principle on which he proceeded was plainly this, — that in virtue of his spiritual character he was superior to earthly dignities, and had been vested in the power of controlling and disposing of such dignities. The same principle is yet more clearly involved in the bestowal of the imperial dignity on Charlemagne. That the popes themselves held this principle to be implied in these proceedings, though as yet they kept the claim in the background, is plain from the fact that, at an after period, and in more favourable circumstances, they founded on these acts in proof of the dependence of the emperors, and their own right to confer the empire. It was the usual manner of the Papacy to perform acts which, as they appeared to contain no principles hostile to the rights of society or the prerogatives of princes, were permitted to pass unchallenged at the time; but the Popes took care afterwards to improve them, by founding upon them the most extravagant and ambitious claims. In nothing have the plausibility and artifice of the system and its patrons been more plainly shown.

But, *second*, the principle on which the whole system of the popes was founded, virtually implied their supremacy over kings as well as over priests. They claimed to be the successors of Peter and the vicars of Christ. But Christ is Lord of the world as well as Head of the Church. He is a King of kings; and the popes aimed at exhibiting on earth an exact model or representation of Christ's government in heaven; and accordingly they strove to reduce monarchs to the rank of their vassals, and assume into their own hands the management of all the affairs of earth. If their claim was a just one, — if they were indeed the vicars of Christ and the vicegerents of God, as they affirmed, — there were plainly no bounds to their authority, either in temporal or spiritual matters. The symbol which to pontifical rhetoric has alone seemed worthy to shadow forth the more than mortal magnificence of the popes is the sun, which, they tell us, the Creator has set in the heavens as the representative of the pontifical authority; while the moon, shining with borrowed splendour, has formed the humble symbolization of the secular power. According to their theory, there was strictly but one ruler on earth, — the Pope. In him all authority was centred. From him all rule and jurisdiction emanated. From him kings received their crowns, and priests their mitres. To him all were accountable, while he was accountable to no one save God alone. The pontiffs, we say, judged it premature to startle the world as yet by an undisguised and open avowal of this claim: they accounted it sufficient, meanwhile, to embody its fundamental principles in the decrees of councils and in the pontifical acts, and allow them to lie dormant there, in the hope that a better age would arrive, when it would be possible to avow in plain terms, and enforce by direct acts, a claim which they had put forth only inferentially as yet. But to make good this claim was the grand object of Rome from the beginning; and this object she steadily pursued through a variety of fortune and a succession of centuries. The vastness of the object was equalled by the ability and perseverance with which it was prosecuted. The policy of Rome was profound, subtle, patient, unscrupulous, and audacious. And as she has had no rival as respects the greatness of the prize and the qualities with which she has contended for it, so neither has she had a rival in the dazzling success with which at last her contest was crowned.

With Charlemagne expired the military genius and political sagacity which had founded the empire. His power now passed into hands too feeble to save the state from convulsions or the empire from dissolution. Quarrels and disputes arose among the inheritors of his dominions. The popes were called in, and asked to employ their paternal authority and ghostly wisdom in the settlement of these differences. With a well-feigned coyness, but real delight at having found so plausible a pretext for advancing their own pretensions, they undertook the task, and executed it to such good purpose, that while they took care of the interests of their clients, they very considerably promoted their own. Hitherto the pontiff bad been raised to his dignity by the suffrages of the bishops, accompanied by the acclamation of the Roman people and the ratification of the emperor. For till the imperial consent had been signified, the newly-elected pontiff could not be legally consecrated. But this badge of subordination, if not of servitude, the popes resolved no longer to wear. Was it to be endured that the vicegerent of God should reign only by the sufferance of the French emperor? Must that authority which came direct from the great apostle be countersigned by a mere dignitary of earth? These ambitious projects the popes had found it prudent to repress hitherto; but now the sword of Charlemagne was in the dust, and they could deal as they listed with the puppets who had stood up in his room. A course of policy was adopted, consisting of alternate cajolery and browbeating, in which the emperors had decidedly the worst of it. Their privilege of giving a valid and legal right to the tiara was wrested from them; and the popes manoeuvred so successfully as to keep the imperial prerogative in abeyance till the times of Otho the Great. Inimitable adroitness did the

Papacy display in turning to account the troubles of the times. Like a knowing trader at a commercial crisis with plenty of ready cash in hand, the popes did such an amount of business in Peter's name, that they vastly increased the credit and revenues of his see. So wisely did they lay out their available stock of influence, that their house now became, and for some time afterwards continued to be, the first establishment in Europe. Of the many bidders for a share in the trade of the great Fisherman, none were admitted into the concern but such as brought with them, in some shape or other, good solid capital; and thus the business went on every day improving. Monarchs were aided, but on all such occasions the popes took care that the chair of Peter should receive in return sevenfold what it gave.

The posterity of Charlemagne at this time contested with one another, in a sanguinary war, their rights to the throne of their illustrious father. By large presents, and yet larger promises, Charles the Bald was fortunate enough to engage the reigning pontiff, John VIII., in his interests. From that moment the contest was no longer doubtful. Charles was proclaimed Emperor by the Pope in A.D. 876. A service so important deserved to be suitably acknowledged. The monarch's gratitude for his throne was embodied in an act, by which he surrendered for himself and his successors all right of interfering in the election to the pontifical chair. Henceforward, till the middle of the tenth century, the imperial sanction was dispensed with, and the pontiffs mounted the chair of Peter without acknowledging in the matter either king or kaisir. In this the pontificate had achieved a great victory over the empire. Nor was this the only advantage which the pontiffs gained in that struggle with the imperial power into which they had been temptingly drawn by the unsettled character of the times. In the case of Charles the Bald the Pope had nominated the Emperor. The same act was repeated in the case of his successors, Carloman and Charles the Gross. It was continued in the contests for the empire which followed the reigns of these princes. The candidate who was rich enough to offer the largest bribe, or powerful enough to appear with an army at the gates of Rome, was invariably crowned emperor in the Vatican. Thus, as the State dissolved, the Church waxed in strength. What the one lost the other drew to herself. The popes did not trouble the world with any formal statement of their principles on the head of the supremacy; they were content to embody them in acts. They were wise enough to know, that the speediest way of getting the world to acknowledge theoretic truth is to familiarize it with its practical applications, — to ask its approval of it, not as a theory, but as a fact. Thus the popes, by a bold course of dexterous management, and of audacious but successful aggression, laboured to weave the doctrine of the supremacy into the general policy of Europe. But for the rise, in the tenth century, of a new power superior to the Franks, Rome would now have reached the summit of her wishes.

No weapon was too base for the use of Rome. Her hand grasped with equal avidity the forged document and the hired dagger. Both were sanctified in her service. In the beginning of the ninth century came the decretals of Isidore. These professed to be a collection of the decrees and rescripts of the early councils and popes, the object of their infamous author, who is unknown, being to show that the see of Rome possessed from the very beginning all the prerogatives with which the intrigues of eight centuries had invested it. Their style was so barbarous, and their anachronisms and solecisms were so flagrant, that in no age but the most ignorant could they have escaped detection for a single hour. Rome, nevertheless, infallibly decreed the truth of what is now universally acknowledged to be false. These decretals supported her pretensions, and that with her decided the question of their authenticity or spuriousness. There are few who have earned so well the honours of canonization as this unknown forger. For ages the decretals possessed the authority of precedents, and furnished Rome with appropriate weapons in her contests with bishops and kings.

The French power was declining; that of the Germans had not yet risen. The pontifical influence was, on the whole, the predominating element in Europe; and the popes, having now no superior, and freed from all restraint, began to use the ample license which the times afforded them, for purposes so infamous, that they transcend description, and well-nigh belief. With the tenth century commence the dark annals of the Papacy. The popes, although wholly devoted to selfish and ambitious pursuits, had found it prudent hitherto to maintain the semblance of piety; but now even that pretence was laid aside. Thanks to Rome, the world was now prepared to see the mask thrown off. Europe had reached a pitch of ignorance and superstition, and the Papacy a height of insolence and truculence, which enabled the popes to defy with impunity the fear of man and the power of God. Not only were the forms of religion contemned; the ordinary decencies of manhood were flagrantly outraged. We dare not pollute our page with such things as the pontiffs of this age practised in the face of Rome and the world. The palaces of the worst emperors, the groves of pagan worship, saw nothing so foul as the orgies of the Vatican. Men sat in the chair of Peter, whose consciences were loaded with perjuries and adulteries, and whose hands were stained with murders; and claimed, as the vicars of Christ, a right to govern the Church and the world. The intrigues, the fraud, the violence, that now raged at Rome, may be conceived of from the fact, that from the death of Benedict IV., A.D. 903, to the elevation of John XII., A.D. 956, — an interval of only fifty-three years, — not fewer than thirteen popes held successively the pontificate. The attempt were vain to pursue these fleeting pontifical phantoms. Their brief but flagitious career was ended most commonly by the lingering horrors of the dungeon, or the quick despatch of the poignard. It is enough to mention the names of a John the Twelfth, a Boniface the Seventh, a John the Twenty-third, a Sixtus the Fourth, an Alexander the Sixth (Borgia), a Julius the Second. These names stand associated with crimes of enormous magnitude. This list by no means exhausts the goodly band of pontifical villains. Simony, the good-will of a prostitute, or the dagger of an assassin, opened their way to the pontifical throne; and the use they made of their power formed a worthy sequel to the infamous means by which they had obtained it. In the chair of Peter, the pontiffs of this and succeeding eras revelled in impiety, perjury, lewdness, sacrilege, sorcery, robbery, and blood; thus converting the palace of the apostle into an unfathomable sink of abomination and filth. "A mass of moral impurity," says Edgar, "might be collected from the Roman hierarchy, sufficient to crowd the pages of folios, and glut all the demons of pollution and malevolence." The age, too, was scandalized by frequent and flagrant schisms. These divided the nations of Christendom, engendered sanguinary wars, and unhinged society itself. For half a century rival pontifical thrones stood at Rome and Avignon; and Europe was doomed daily to listen to the dreadful vollies of spiritual thunder which the rival infallibilities, Urban and Clement, ever and anon launched at one another, and which, in almost one continuous and stunning roar, reverberated between the Tiber and the Rhone. There is no need to darken the horrors of the time by the fable (if fable it be) of a female pope, who is said about this time to have filled St. Peter's chair. The traditionary Pope Joan is found, perhaps, in the sister-prostitutes, the well-known Marozia and Theodora, who now governed Rome. Their influence, founded on their wealth, their beauty, and their intrigues, enabled them to place on the pontifical throne whom they would; and not unfrequently they promoted, without a blush, their paramours to the holy chair. Such were the dark transactions of the period, and such the scones that signalized the advent of the Papacy to temporal power. The revels of Ahasuerus and Haman were concluded with the bloody decree which delivered over a whole nation to the sword. The yet guiltier revels of the Papacy were, in like manner, followed in due time by ages of proscription and slaughter.

In tracing the rise of the temporal supremacy, we are now brought to the middle of the tenth century. Otho the Great appears upon the stage. With a vigorous hand did these German conquerors grasp the imperial diadem which the degenerate descendants of Charlemagne were no longer either worthy to wear or able to defend. Otho found the Papacy running a career of crime, and in some danger of perishing in its own corruption. He interposed his sword, and averted its otherwise inevitable fate. It did not suit the designs of the German emperors that the Papacy should suffer a premature extinction. It might be turned, they were not slow to perceive, to great account in the way of consolidating and extending their own imperial dignity, and therefore they strove to reform, not destroy, Rome. They rescued the chair of Peter from its worst foes, its occupants. They deposed several popes notorious for their vices, and exalted others of purer morals to the pontifical dignity. Thus the Papacy had found a new master; for Otho and his descendants were as much the liege lords of the popedom as the monarchs of the Carlovingian line had been. The popes were now obliged to surrender the powers they had usurped during the time that the imperial sceptre was in the feeble hands of the last of the posterity of Charlemagne. In particular, the rights of which Charles the Bald had been stripped were now given back. The emperors again nominated the pope. When a vacancy occurred in the chair of St. Peter, envoys from Rome announced the fact at the court of the emperor, and waited the signification of his will respecting a successor. This substantial right of interfering when a new pope was to be elected, which the emperors possessed, was very inadequately balanced by the empty and nominal power enjoyed by the popes, of placing the imperial crown on the emperor's head. "The prince elected in the German Diet," says Gibbon, "acquired from that instant the subject kingdoms of Italy and Rome; but he might not legally assume the titles of Emperor and Augustus, till he had received the crown from the hands of the Roman pontiff," — a sanction that could be withheld with difficulty so long as the emperor was master of Rome and her popes. But the intimate union now existing between the empire and the pontificate was productive of reciprocal advantages, and tended greatly to consolidate and extend the power of both. The rise of the French monarchy had been owing in no small degree to the favourable dispositions which the kings of France discovered towards the Church. The western Goths and Burgundians were sunk in Arianism; the Franks, from the beginning, had been truly Catholic; and the popes did all they could to foster the growth of a power which, from similarity of creed, as well as from motives of policy, was so likely to become their surest ally. The miraculous succours vouchsafed to the arms of the French resolve themselves, without doubt, into the material aids given by the popes and their agents to a people in whose success they felt a deep interest. Hence the legend, according to which St. Martin, in the form of a hind, discovered to Clovis the ford over the Vienne; and hence also that other fable which asserts that St. Hillary preceded the Frank armies in a column of fire. The St. Martin and the St. Hillary of these legends were doubtless some bishop, or other ecclesiastic, who rendered important services to the Frank monarch and his army, on the ground that, with the triumph of their arms was identified the progress of the Church.

The same influence was vigorously exerted, from the same motive, in behalf of the German power. Monks and priests preceded the imperial arms, especially in the east and north of Germany; and the annexation of these countries to the empire is to be attributed fully as much to the zeal of the ecclesiastics as to the valour of the soldiers. Nor did the German chiefs show that they were either unable to appreciate or unwilling to reward these important services. They lavished unbounded wealth upon the clergy, their policy being to bind thereby this important class to their interests. No one was more distinguished for his munificence in this respect than Henry II. This monarch created numerous rich benefices; but the rigour with which he insisted upon his right to nominate to the livings he had endowed betrayed the motives that prompted this great liberality. Abbots and bishops were exalted to the rank of barons and dukes, and invested with jurisdiction over extensive territories. "The bishoprics of Germany," says Gibbon, "were made equal in extent and privilege, superior in wealth and population, to the most ample states of the military order." "Baronial, and even ducal rights," says Ranke, "were held in Germany by the bishops and abbots of the empire, not within their own possessions only, but even beyond them. Ecclesiastical estates were no longer described as situated in certain counties, but these counties were described as situated in the bishopricks. In upper Italy, nearly all the cities were governed by the viscounts of their bishops." Military service was exacted of these ecclesiastical barons, in return for the possessions which they held; and not unfrequently did bishops appear at the head of their armed vassals, with lance in hand and harness on their backs. They were, moreover, addicted to the chase, of which the Germans in all ages have been passionately fond, and for which their vast forests have afforded ample scope. "Rude as the Germans of the middle ages were," observes Dunham, "to see a successor of St. Peter hallooing after his dogs certainly struck them as incongruous. Yet the bishops, in virtue of their fiefs, were compelled to send their vassals to the field; and no doubt they considered as somewhat inconsistent, a system which commanded them to kill men, but not beasts."

The acquisition of wealth formed an important element in the growth of the Papacy. The Roman law did not permit lands to be held on mortmain; nevertheless the emperors winked at the possession by the Church of immoveable possessions, whose revenues furnished stipends to her pastors and alms to her poor. No sooner did Constantine embrace Christianity, than an imperial edict invested the Church with a legal right to what she had possessed hitherto by tolerance only. Neither under the empire, nor under any of the ten kingdoms into which the empire was ultimately divided, did the Church ever obtain a territorial establishment; but the ample liberality, first of the Christian emperors, and next of the barbarian kings, did more than supply the want of a general provision. For ages, wealth had been flowing in upon the Church in a torrent; and now, from being the poorest she had become the wealthiest corporation in Europe. A race of princes had succeeded to the fishermen of Galilee; and the opulent nobles and citizens of the empire represented that society whose first bonds had been cemented in the catacombs under the city. Under the Carlovingian family, and the Saxon line of emperors, "many churches possessed seven or eight thousand mansi," says Hallam. "One with but two thousand passed for only indifferently rich. This vast opulence represented the accumulations and hoardings of many ages, and had been acquired by innumerable, and sometimes not very honourable, means. When a wealthy man entered a monastery, his estate was thrown into the common treasury of the brotherhood. When the son of a rich man took the cowl, he recommended himself to the Church by a donation of land. To die without leaving a portion of one's worldly goods to the priesthood came to be rare, and was regarded as a fraud upon the Church. The monks sometimes supplemented the incomes of their houses by intromitting with the funds of charities placed under their control. The wealthy sinner, when about to depart, expressed his penitence in a well-filled bag of gold, or in a certain number of broad acres; and the ravening baron was compelled to disgorge, with abundant interest, on the bed of death, the spoliations of church-property of which he had been guilty during his lifetime. The fiefs of the nobility, who had beggared themselves by profligacy, or in the epidemic folly of the crusades, were not unfrequently brought into the market; and, being offered at a cheap rate, the Church, which had abundance of ready money at her command, became the purchaser, and so augmented her possessions. It is but fair to state also, that the clergy helped, in that age, to add to the wealth and beauty of the country, by the cultivation of tracts of waste lands which were frequently gifted to them. The Church found additional sources of revenue in the exemption from taxes; though not from military service, which her lands enjoyed, and in the institution of tithes, which, in imitation of the Jewish law, was originated about the sixth century, formed the main topic of the sermons of the eighth, and finally obtained a civil sanction in the ninth, under Charlemagne. But, not content with these varied facilities of getting rapidly and enormously rich, the monks betook themselves to forging charters, — an exploit which their knowledge of writing enabled them to achieve, and which the ignorance of the age rendered of very difficult detection. "They did nearly enjoy," says Hallam, "one half of England, and, I believe, a greater proportion in some countries of Europe." This wealth was far beyond the measure of their own enjoyment, and they had no families to whom they might bequeath it. Such rapacity, then, does seem as unnatural as it was enormous. But, in truth, the Church had fallen as entirely under the dominion of an unreasonable and uncontrollable passion as the miser; she was, in fact, a corporate miser. This vast wealth, it may easily be apprehended, inflamed her insolence and advanced her power. The power of the Church became greater every day, — not its power as a Church, but as a confederation, — and might well excite alarm as to the future. Here was a body of men placed under one head, bound together by a community of interest and feeling, superior in intelligence, and therefore in influence, to the rest of the empire, enormously rich, and exercising civil jurisdiction over extensive tracts and vast populations. It was impossible to contemplate without misgivings, so numerous and compact a phalanx. It must have struck every one, that upon the moderation and fidelity of its members must depend the repose of the empire and the world in time to come. The emperors, secure, as they imagined themselves, in the possession of the supremacy, saw without alarm the rise of this formidable body. They looked upon it as one of the main props of their power, and felicitated themselves not a little in having been so fortunate as to entrench their prerogative behind so firm a bulwark. The appointment to all ecclesiastical benefices was in the emperor's hands; and in augmenting the wealth and grandeur of the clergy, they doubted not that they were consolidating their own authority. It required no prophet to divine, that so long as the imperial sceptre continued to be grasped by a strong hand and guided by a firm mind, which it had been since it came into the possession of the German race, no danger would arise; but that the moment this ceased to be the case, the pontificate, already almost on a level with the empire, would obtain the mastery. Rome had been often baulked in her grand enterprise; but now her accommodating, patient, and persevering policy was about to receive its reward. The hour was near when her grandest hopes and her loftiest pretensions were to be realized, — when the throne of God's vicegerent was to display itself in its fullest proportions, and be seen towering in proud supremacy above all the other thrones of earth.

The emergency that might have been foreseen had arisen. We behold on the throne of the empire a child, Henry IV. and in the chair of St. Peter, the astute Hildebrand. We find the empire torn by insurrections and tumults, whilst the Papacy is guided by the clear and bold genius of Gregory VII. Savoy had the honour to give birth to this man. He was the son of a carpenter, and comprehended from the first the true destiny of the Papacy, and the height to which its essential principles, vigorously maintained and fearlessly carried out, would exalt the popedom. To emancipate the pontificate from the authority of the empire, and to establish a visible theocracy with the vicar of Christ at its head, became the one grand object of his life. He brought to the execution of his task a profound genius, a firm will, a fearless courage, and a pliant policy, — a quality in which the popes have seldom been deficient. From the moment that he chid Leo IX. for accepting the tiara from the hands of the secular power, his spirit had governed Rome. At length, in A.D. 1073, he ascended the pontifical throne in person. "No sooner was this man made Pope," says Du Pin, "but he formed a design of becoming lord, spiritual and temporal, over the whole earth; the supreme judge and determiner of all affairs, both ecclesiastical and civil; the distributer of all manner of graces, of what kind soever; the disposer not only of archbishopricks, bishopricks, and other ecclesiastical benefices, but also of kingdoms, states, and the revenues of particular persons. To bring about this resolution, he made use of the ecclesiastical authority and the spiritual sword." The times were favourable in no ordinary degree. The empire of Germany was enfeebled by the disaffection of the barons; France was ruled by an infant sovereign, without capacity or inclination for affairs of state; England had just been conquered by the Normans; Spain was distracted by the Moors; and Italy was parcelled out amongst a multitude of petty princes. Everywhere faction was rife throughout Europe, and a strong government existed nowhere. The time invited him, and straightway Gregory set about his high attempt. His first care was to assemble a Council, in which he pronounced the marriage of priests unlawful. He next sent his legates throughout the various countries of Europe, to compel bishops and all ecclesiastics to put away their wives. Having thus dissevered the ties which connected the clergy with the world, and given them but one object for which to live, namely, the exaltation of the hierarchy, Gregory rekindled, with all the ardour and vehemence characteristic of the man, the war between the throne and the mitre. The object at which Gregory VII. aimed was twofold: — 1. To render the election to the pontifical chair independent of the emperors; and, 2. To resume the empire as a fief of the Church, and to establish his dominion over the kings and kingdoms of the earth. His first step towards the accomplishment of these vast designs was, as we have shown, to enact clerical celibacy. His second was to forbid all ecclesiastics to receive investiture at the hands of the secular power. In this decree he laid the foundation of the complete emancipation of the Church from the State; but half a century of wars and bloodshed was required to conduct the first enterprise, that of the investitures, to a successful issue; while a hundred and fifty years more of similar convulsions had to be gone through before the second, that of universal domination, was attained.

Let us here pause to review the rise of the war of investitures which now broke out, and which "during two centuries distracted the Christian world, and deluged a great portion of Italy with blood." In the primitive age the pastors of the Roman Church were elected by the people. When we come down to those times, still early, when the office of bishop began to take precedence of that of presbyter, we find the election to the episcopate effected by the joint suffrages of the clergy and people of the city or diocese. After the fourth century, when a regular gradation of offices or hierarchy was set up, the bishop chosen by the clergy and people had to be approved of by his metropolitan, as the metropolitan by his primate. It does not appear that the emperors interfered at all in these elections, farther than to signify their acceptance or rejection of the persons chosen to the very highest sees, — the patriarchates of Rome and Constantinople. In this their example was followed by the Gothic and Lombard kings of Italy. The people retained their influence in the election of their pastors and bishops down till a comparatively late period. We find popular election in existence in the end of the fourth century. A canon of the third Council of Carthage, in A.D. 397, decrees that no clergyman shall be ordained who has not been examined by the bishop and approved of by the suffrages of the people. Even at the middle of the sixth century popular election had not disappeared from the Church. We find the third Council of Orleans, held in A.D. 538, regulating by canon the election and ordination of metropolitans and bishops. As regarded the metropolitan, the Council enacted that he should be chosen by the bishops of the province, with the consent of the clergy and people of the city, "it being fitting," say the fathers, "that he who is to preside over all should be chosen by all." And, as respected bishops, it was decreed that they should be ordained by the metropolitan, and chosen by the clergy and people. "The people fully preserved their elective rights at Milan," observes Hallam, "in the eleventh century; and traces of their concurrence may be found in France and Germany in the next age." From the people the right passed to the sovereigns, who found a plausible pretext for granting investitures of bishops, in the vast temporalities attached to their sees. These possessions, which had originated mostly in royal gifts, were viewed somewhat in the light of fiefs, for which it was but reasonable that the tenant should do homage to the lord paramount. Hence the ceremony introduced by Charlemagne of putting the ring and crosier into the hands of the newly consecrated bishop. The bishops of Rome, like their brethren, were at first chosen by popular election. In process of time, the consent of the emperor was used to ratify the choice of the people. This prerogative came into the possession of Charlemagne along with the imperial crown, and was exercised by his posterity, — if we except the last of his descendants, during whose feeble reigns the prerogative which the imperial hands had let fall was caught up by the Roman populace. This right came next into the possession of the Saxon emperors, and was exercised by some of the race of Otho in a more absolute manner than it had ever been by either Greek or Carlovingian monarch. Henry III., impatient to put down the scandal of three rival popes, assembled a council at Sutri, which deposed all three, placed Henry's friend, the Bishop of Bamberg (Clement II.), in Peter's chair, and added this substantial boon, that henceforward the imperial throne should possess the entire nomination of the popes, without the intervention of clergy or laity. But what the magnanimity of Henry III. had gained came to be lost by the tender age and irresolute spirit of his son Henry IV. Nicolas II., in 1059, wrested the prerogative from the emperors, to place it, not in the people, but in a new body, which presents us with the origin of the conclave of cardinals. According to the pontifical decree, the seven cardinal bishops holding sees in the neighbourhood of Rome were henceforward to choose the pope. A vague recognition of some undefinable right possessed by the emperors and the people in the election was made in the decree, but it amounted in reality to little more than a permission to both to be present on the occasion, and to signify their acquiescence in what they had no power to prevent. The real author of this, and of similar measures, was Hildebrand, who was content meanwhile to wield, in the humble rank of a Roman archdeacon, the destinies of the Papacy, and to hide in the monk's garb that dauntless and comprehensive genius which in a few years was to govern Europe. Hildebrand in no long time took the quarrel into his own hands.

He ascended the pontifical throne, as we have already stated, in 1073, under the style of Gregory VII. He comprehended the Emperor's position with regard to the princes of Germany better than the Emperor himself did, and shaped his measures accordingly. He began by promulgating the decree against lay investitures, to which we have already adverted. He saw the advantage of having the barons on his side. He knew that they were impatient and envious of the power of Henry, who was at once weak and tyrannical; and he found it no difficult matter to gain them over to the papal interests, — first, by the decree of the Pope, which declared Germany an electoral monarchy; and, second, by the influence which the barons were still permitted to retain in the election of bishops. For although Gregory had deprived the Emperor of the right of investiture, and in doing so had broken the bond that held together the civil and spiritual institutions, as Ranke remarks, and declared a revolution, he did not claim the direct nomination of the bishops, but referred the choice to the chapters, over which the higher German nobility exercised very considerable influence. Thus the Pope had the aristocratic interests on his side in the conflict. Henry, reckless as impotent, proceeded to give mortal offence to his great antagonist. Hastily assembling a number of bishops and other vassals at Worms, he procured a sentence deposing Gregory from the popedom. He mistook the man and the times. Gregory, receiving the tidings with derision, assembled a council in the Lateran palace, and solemnly excommunicated Henry, annulled his right to the kingdoms of Germany and Italy, and absolved his subjects from their allegiance. Henry's recklessness was succeeded by panic. He felt that the spell of the pontifical curse was upon him; that his nobles, and bishops, and subjects, were fleeing from him or conspiring against him; and in prostration of spirit he resolved to beg in person the clemency of the Pope. He crossed the Alps in the depth of winter, and, arriving at the gates of the castle of Canossa, where the Pope was residing at the time, shut up with his firm adherent and reputed paramour the Countess Matilda, he stood, during three days, exposed to the rigours of the season, with his feet bare, his head uncovered, and a piece of coarse woollen cloth thrown over his person, and forming his only covering. On the fourth day he obtained an audience of the pontiff; and though the lordly Gregory was pleased to absolve him from the excommunication, he straitly charged him not to resume his royal rank and functions till the meeting of the Congress which had been appointed to try him. But the pontiff was humbled in his turn. Henry rebelling a second time, a furious war broke out between the monarch and the pontiff. The armies of the Emperor passed the Alps, besieged Rome, and Gregory, being obliged to flee, ended his days in exile at Salerno, bequeathing as a legacy to his successors the conflict in which he had been engaged, and to Europe the wars and tumults into which his ambition had plunged it.

Gregory was gone, but his principle survived. He had left the mantle of his ambition, and, to a large extent, of his genius also, to his successors, Urban II. and Paschal II. Urban maintained the contest in the very spirit of Gregory; the opposition of Paschal may deserve to be accounted as partaking of a higher character. A conviction that it was utterly incongruous in a layman to give admission to a spiritual office, seems to have mainly animated him in prosecuting the contest. He actually signed an agreement with Henry V. in 1110, whereby all the lands and possessions held by the Church in fief were to be given back to the Emperor, on condition that the Emperor should surrender the right of investiture. The prelates and bishops of Paschal's court, who saw little attractive in the episcopate save the temporalities, believed that their infallible master had gone mad, and raised such a clamour, that the pontiff was obliged to desist from his design. At length, in 1122, the contention was ended by a compromise between Henry and Calixtus II. According to this compact, the election of bishops was to be free, their investiture was to belong solely to ecclesiastical functionaries, while the Emperor was to induct them into their temporalities, not by the crozier and ring, as before, but by the sceptre.

It is not improbable that the sovereigns and barons of the age believed that this concordat left the substantial power in the election of bishops still in their own hands. With our clearer light it is not difficult to see that the advantage greatly preponderated in favour of the Church. It extricated the spiritual element from the control of the secular. It was a solemn ratification of the principle of spiritual independence, which, in the case of a church spurning co-ordinate jurisdiction, and claiming both swords, was sure speedily and inevitably to grow into spiritual supremacy. The temporalities might come in some cases to be lost; but in that age the risk was small; and granting that it was realized, the loss would be more than counterbalanced by the greatly enlarged spiritual action which was now secured to the Church. The election of bishops, in which the emperors had ceased to interfere, was now devolved, not upon the laity and clergy, whose suffrages had been deemed essential in former times, but upon the chapters of cathedral churches, which tended to enlarge the power of the pontiff and the higher clergy. In this way was the conflict carried on. The extent of supremacy involved in the principle *that the Pope is Christ's Vicar*, had been fully and boldly propounded to the world by Gregory; and, what was more, had been all but realized. Rome had tasted of dominion over kings, and was never to rest till she had securely seated herself in the lofty seat which she had been permitted for so brief a season to occupy, and which she only, as she believed, had a right to possess, or could worthily and usefully fill. The popes had to sustain many humiliations and defeats; nevertheless, their policy continued to be progressively triumphant. The power of the empire gradually sank, and that of the pontificate steadily advanced. All the great events of the age contributed to the power of the popedom. The ecclesiastical element was universally diffused, entered into all movements, and turned to its own purposes all enterprises. There never perhaps was an age which was so completely ecclesiastical and so little spiritual. Spain was reclaimed from Islamism, Prussia was rescued from Paganism, and both submitted to the authority of the Roman pontiff. The crusades broke out, and, being religious enterprises, they tended to the predominance of the ecclesiastical element, and silently moulded the minds and the habits of men to submission to the Church. Moreover, they tended to exhaust the resources and break the spirit of kingdoms, and rendered it easier for Rome to carry out her scheme of aggrandizement. The same effect attended the wars and convulsions which disturbed Europe, and which grew out of the struggles of Rome for dominion. These weakened the secular, but left the vigour of the spiritual element unimpaired. The deepening ignorance of the masses was exceedingly favourable to the pretensions of Rome. It formed a basis of power, not only over them, but, through them, over kings. Add to all this, that of the two principles between which this great contest was waged, the secular was divided, whereas the spiritual was one. The kings had various interests, and frequently pursued conflicting lines of policy. The most perfect organization and union reigned in the ranks of the Papacy. The clergy in all countries were thoroughly devoted to the papal see, and obeyed as one man the behests which came from the chair of St. Peter. It is also to be borne in mind, that in this conflict the emperors could contend with but secular weapons; whereas the popes, while they by no means disdained the aid of armies, fought with those yet more formidable weapons which the power of superstition furnished them with. Is it wonderful that with these advantages they triumphed in the contest, — that every successive age found Rome growing in influence and dominion, — and that at last her chief was seen seated, god-like, on the Seven Hills, with the nations, tribes, and languages of the Roman world prostrate at his feet? "After long centuries of confusion," says Ranke, — "after other centuries of often doubtful strife, — the independence of the Roman see, and that of its essential principle, was finally attained. In effect, the position of the popes was at this moment most exalted; the clergy were wholly in their hands. It is worthy of remark, that the most firm-minded pontiffs of this period, — Gregory VII. for example, — were Benedictines. By the introduction of celibacy, they converted the whole body of the secular clergy into a kind of monastic order. The universal bishopric now claimed by the popes bears a certain resemblance to the power of an abbot of Cluny, who was the only abbot of his order; in like manner, these pontiffs aspired to be the only bishops of the assembled Church. They interfered, without scruple, in the administration of every diocese, and even compared their legates with the pro-consuls of ancient Rome! While this closely-knit body, so compact in itself, yet so widely extended through all lands, — influencing all by its large possessions, and controlling every relation of life by its ministry, — was concentrating its mighty force under the obedience of one chief, the temporal powers were crumbling into ruin. Already, in the beginning of the twelfth century, the Provost Gerohus ventured to say, 'It will at last come to this, that the golden image of the empire shall be shaken to dust; every great monarchy shall be divided into tetrarchates, and then only will the Church stand free and untrammelled beneath the protection of her crowned high priest.'" Thus did Rome seize the golden moment when the iron of the German race, like that of the Carlovingian before it, had become mixed with miry clay, to complete her work of five centuries. She had watched and waited for ages; she had flattered the proud and insulted the humble; bowed to the strong and trampled upon the weak; she had awed men with terrors that were false, and excited them with hopes that were delusive; she had stimulated their passions and destroyed their souls; she had schemed, and plotted, and intrigued, with a cunning, and a malignity, and a success, which hell itself might have envied, and which certainly it never surpassed; and now her grand object was within her reach, — was attained. She had triumphed over the empire; she was lord paramount of Europe; nations were her footstool; and from her lofty seat she showed herself to the wondering tribes of earth, encompassed by the splendour, possessing the attributes, and wielding the power, not of earthly monarchs, but of the Eternal Majesty.

Accordingly, we are now arrived at the golden age of the Papacy. In A.D. 1197, Innocent ascended the papal chair. It was the fortune of this man, on whose shoulders had fallen the mantle of Lucifer, to reap all that the popes his predecessors had sowed in alternate triumphs and defeats. The traditions and principles of the papal policy descended to him matured and perfected. The man, too, was equal to the hour. He had the art to veil a genius as aspiring as that of Gregory VII. under designs less avowedly temporal and worldly. He affected to wield only a spiritual sceptre; but he held it over monarchs and kingdoms, as well as over priests and churches. "Though I cannot judge of the right to a fief," wrote he to the kings of France and England, "yet it is my province to judge where sin is committed, and my duty to prevent all public scandals." So lofty were his notions of the spiritual prerogative, and so much did he regard temporal rule as its inseparable concomitant, that he disdained to hold it by a formal claim. He exercised an omnipotent sway over mind, and left it to govern the bodies and goods of men. We find De Maistre comparing the Catholic Church in the days of Charlemagne to an ellipse, with St. Peter in one of the foci, and the Emperor in the other. But now, in the days of Innocent, the Church, or rather the European system, from being an ellipse, had become a circle. The two foci were gone. There was but one governing point, — the centre; and in that centre stood Peter's chair. The pontificate of Innocent was one continued and unclouded display of the superhuman glory of the popedom. From a height to which no mortal had before been able to climb, and which the strongest intellect becomes giddy when it contemplates, he regulated all the affairs of this lower world. His comprehensive scheme of government took in alike the greatest affairs of the greatest kingdoms, and the most private concerns of the humblest individual. We find him teaching the kings of France their duty, dictating to the emperors their policy, and at the same time adjudicating in the case of a citizen of Pisa who had mortgaged his estate, and to whom Innocent, by spiritual censures, compelled the creditor to make restitution of the goods on receiving payment of the money; and writing to the Bishop of Ferentino, giving his decision in the case of a simple maiden for whose hand two lovers contended. Thus the thunder of Rome broke alike over the heads of puissant kings and humble citizens. The Italian republics he gathered under his own sceptre, and, binding them in leagues, cast them into the political scale, to counterpoise the empire. The kings of Castile and Portugal, as they hung on the perilous edge of battle, were separated by a single word from his legate. The king of Navarre held some castles of Richard's, which his power did not enable him to retake. The pontiff hinted at the spiritual thunder, and the castles were given up. Monarchs, intent only on a present advantage, failed to see that, by accepting the aid of such a power, they were the abettors of their own future vassalage. The King of France had offended the Pope by repudiating his wife and contracting a new marriage. An interdict fell upon the realm. The churches were closed, and the clergy forbore their offices to both the living and the dead. The submission of the powerful Philip Augustus illustrated the boundless spirit and appeased the immeasurable pride of Innocent. After this great victory, we name not those which he gained over the kings of Spain and England, the latter of whom he excommunicated, placing his kingdom under interdict, and compelling him to hold his crown and realm as the vassal of the Roman see. But the coronation of the Emperor Otho IV., and the varied and substantial concessions included in the oath which Otho took on that occasion, are worthy of being enumerated among the trophies of this mighty pope. The terror of his name extended to distant lands, — to Bohemia, to Hungary, to Norway. The pontifical thunder was heard rolling in even the latter northern region, where it smote a certain usurper of the name of Swero. As if all these labours had been too little, Innocent, from his seat on the Seven Hills, guided the progress of those destructive tempests which swept along the shores of Syria and the Straits of the Bosphorus. Constantinople fell before the crusaders, and the kings of Bulgaria and Armenia acknowledged the supremacy of Innocent.

"His legs bestrid the ocean; his reared arm
Crested the world; his voice was propertied
As all the tuned spheres, and that to friends
And when he meant to quail and shake the orb,
He was as rattling thunder. . . . . . .
. . . . In his livery
Walked crowns and crownets."

But the mightiest efforts of Innocent were reserved for the extirpation of heresy. He was the first to discover the danger to the popedom which lurked in the Scriptural faith, and in the mental liberty of the Albigenses and Waldenses. On them, therefore, and not on eastern schismatics or recalcitrating sovereigns, fell the full storm of the pontifical ire. Assembling his vassal kings, he pointed to the peaceful and thriving communities in the provinces of the Rhone, and inflamed the zeal and fury of the soldiers by holding out the promise of immense booty and unbounded indulgence. For a forty days' service a man might earn paradise, not to speak of the worldly spoil with which he was certain to return laden home. The poor Albigenses were crushed beneath an avalanche of murderous fanaticism and inappeasable rapacity. To Innocent history is indebted for one of her bloodiest pages, — the European crusades; and the world owes him thanks for its most infernal institution, the Inquisition. He had for his grand object to bestow an eternity of empire upon the papal throne; and, to accomplish this, he strove to inflict an eternity of thraldom upon the human mind. His darling aim was to make the chair of Peter equally stable and absolute with its fellow-seat in pandemonium.

The noon of the Papacy synchronises with the world's midnight. Innocent III. was emphatically the Prince of the Darkness. There was but one thing in the universe which he dreaded, and that was light. The most execrable shapes of night could not appal him; — these were congenial terrors: he knew they had no power to harm him or his. But the faintest glimmer of day on the horizon struck terror into his soul, and he contended ceaselessly against the light, with all the artillery of anathemas and arms. During the whole century of his pontificate the globe was seen reposing in deep shadow, girdled round with the chain of the papal power, and corruscated fearfully with the flashes of the pontifical thunder. Like a crowned demon, Innocent sat upon the Seven Hills, muffled up in the mantle of Lucifer, and governed earth as Satan governs hell. At a great distance below, realizing by anticipation the boldest vision of the great poet, were the crowned potentates and mitred hierarchies of the world over which he ruled, lying foundered and overthrown, like the spirits in the lake, in the same degrading and shameful vassalage. Princes laid their swords, and nations their treasures, at the foot of the pontifical throne, and bowed their necks to be trodden upon by its occupant. Innocent might say, as Caesar to the conquered queen of Egypt, —

"I'll take my leave."

And the subject nations might reply with Cleopatra, —

"And may, through all the world: 'tis yours; and we

Your scutcheons, and your signs of conquest, shall

Hang in what place you please."

The boast better became his mouth than it did the proud Assyrian who first uttered it. "By the strength of my hand I have done it, and by my wisdom; for I am prudent: and I have removed the bounds of the people, and have robbed their treasures, and I have put down the inhabitants like a valiant man. And my hand hath found, as a nest, the riches of the people; and as one gathereth eggs that are left, have I gathered all the earth; and there was none that moved the wing, or opened the mouth, or peeped."

Thus have we traced the course of the papal power, from its feeble rise in the second century, to its full development in the thirteenth. We have seen how the infant pontiff was suckled by the imperial wolf (for the fables of heathen mythology find their truest realization in the Papacy, and, from being myths, become vaticinations), and how, waxing strong on the pure milk of Paganism, he grew to manhood, and, being grown, discovered all the genuine pagan and vulpine qualities of the mother that nursed him, — the passion for images and the thirst for blood. The Ethiopian cannot change his skin; and the world has now found out that the beast of the

Roman hill is but a wolf in sheep's clothing. How often have slaughter and carnage covered the fold which he professed to guard! Take it all in all, the story of the papal power is a dismal drama, — the gloomiest that darkens history! We look back upon the past; and, as we behold this terrible power growing continually bigger and darker, and casting fresh shadows, with every succeeding age, upon the liberty and religion of the world, till at last both came to be shrouded in impenetrable night, we are reminded of those tragedies and horrors with which the imagination of Milton has given grandeur to his song. To nothing can we liken the progress of the Papacy, through the wastes of the middle ages to the universal domination of the thirteenth and succeeding centuries, save to the passage of the fiend from the gates of pandemonium to the sphere of the newly-created world. The old dragon of Paganism, broken loose from the abyss into which he had been cast, sallied forth in quest of the world of young Christianity, as Satan from with the like fiendish intent of marring and subjugating it. He had no "narrow frith" to cross; but he held his way with as cautious a step and as dauntless a front as his great prototype. His path, more especially in its first stages, was bestrewn with the wrecks of a perished world, and scourged by those tempests which attend the birth of new states. On this hand he shunned the whirlpool of the sinking empire, and on that guarded himself against the fiery blast of the Saracenic eruption. There he buffeted the waves of tumultuous revolutions, and here he planted his foot on the crude consistence of a young and rising state. Now "the strong rebuff of some tumultuous cloud" hurried him aloft, and, "that fury stayed," he was anon "quenched in a boggy Syrtis." Now he was upborne on the shield of kings; and now his foot trode upon their necks. Now he hewed his way with the bloody brand; and now, in more crafty fashion, with the forged document. Sometimes he wore his own shape, and showed himself as Apollyon; but more frequently he hid the hideous lineaments of the destroyer beneath the fair semblance of an angel of light. Thus he maintained the struggle through the weary ages, till at last the thirteenth century saw

"His dark pavilion spread
Wide on the wasteful deep; with him enthroned
Sat sable vested night, eldest of things,
The consort of his reign; and by them stood
Orcus and Ades, and the dreaded name
Of Demogorgon."

The scheme of Rome, viewed simply as an intellectual conception, is the most comprehensive and gigantic which the genius and ambition of man ever dared to entertain. There is a unity and vastness about it, which, apart from its moral aspect, compels our admiration, and awakens a feeling of mingled astonishment and terror. The depth of its essential principles, the boldness of the design, the wisdom and talent brought into play in achieving its realization, the perseverance and vigour with which it was prosecuted, and the marvellous success with which it was at last crowned, were all equal, and were all colossal. It is at once the grandest and the most iniquitous enterprise in which man ever embarked. But, as we have shown in our opening chapter, we ought not to regard it as a distinct and separate enterprise, springing from principles and contemplating aims peculiar to itself, but as the full development and consummation of man's original apostacy. The powers of man and the limits of the globe do not admit of that apostacy being carried higher; for had it been much extended, either in point of intensity or in point of duration, the human species would have perished. A corruption so universal and a tyranny so overwhelming would in due time have utterly depopulated the globe. In the domination of the Papacy we have a glimpse of what would have been the condition of the world had no scheme of salvation been provided for it. The history of the Papacy is the history of the rebellion of our race against Heaven.

Before dismissing this subject, let us glance a moment at another and different picture. What became of Truth in the midst of such monstrous errors? Where was a shelter found for the Church during storms so fearful? To understand this, we must leave the open plains and the wealthy cities of the empire, and retire to the solitude of the Alps. In primitive times the members of the then unfallen Church of Rome had found amid these mountains a shelter from persecution. He who built an ark for the one elect family of the antediluvian world had provided a retreat for the little company chosen to escape the mighty shipwreck of Christianity. God placed his Church aloft on the eternal hills, in the place prepared for her. Nature had enriched this abode with pine forests, and rich mountain pastures, and rivers which issue from the frozen jaws of the glacier, and made it strong as beautiful by a wall of peaks that pierce the clouds, and look down on earth from amidst the firmament's calm, white with everlasting snows. Here it is that we find the true apostolic Church. Here, far from the magnificence of Dom, the fragrance of incense, and the glitter of mitres, holy men of God fed the flock of Christ with the pure Word of

Life. Ages of peace passed over them. The storms that shook the world, the errors that darkened it, did not approach their retreat. Like the traveller, amid their own mountains they could mark the clouds gather and hear the thunders roll far below, while they enjoyed the uninterrupted sunshine of a pure gospel. An overruling Providence made the same events which brought trouble to the world to minister peace to them. Rome was entirely engrossed with her battles with the empire, and had no time to think of those who were bearing a testimony against her errors by the purity of their faith and the holiness of their lives. Besides, she could see danger only in the material power of the empire, and never dreamt the while that a spiritual power was springing up among the Alps, before which she was destined at last to fall. By and by these professors of primitive Christianity began to increase, and to spread themselves over the surrounding regions, to an extent that is but little known. Manufactures were established in the valley of the Rhone, and in those provinces of France which border on the Mediterranean or lie contiguous to the Pyrenees; as also in Lombardy and the towns of northern Italy. In fact, this region of Europe became in those ages the depot of the western world as regards arts and manufactures of all kinds. Villages grew into cities, new towns sprung up, and the population of the surrounding districts were insufficient to supply the looms and forges of these industrial hives. The pious mountaineers descended from their native Alps to find employment in the workshops of the plains, just as at this day we see the population of the Highlands crowding to Glasgow and Manchester, and other great manufacturing centres; and, as they brought their intelligence and steadiness along with them, they made admirable workmen. The workshop became a school, conversions went on, and the pure faith of the mountains extended itself over the plains, like the dawn, first seen on the hill-tops, but soon to descend and gladden the valley. In the eleventh and twelfth centuries manufactures and Christianity, — the loom and the Bible — went hand in hand, and promised to achieve the peaceful conquest of Europe, and rescue it from the hands of those pontifical and imperial barbarians who were doing their best to convert it into an unbroken expanse of solitudes and ruins. These manufacturing and Christian societies took possession of the whole of the Italian and French provinces adjoining the Alps. The valley of the Rhone swarmed with these busy and intelligent communities. They covered with population, industry, and wealth, the provinces of Dauphine, Provence, Languedoc, and, in short, all southern France. They were found in great numbers in Lombardy.

Their factories, churches, and schools, were spread over all northern Italy. They planted their arts and their faith in the valley of the Rhine, so that a traveller might journey from Basle to Cologne, and sleep every night in the house of a Christian brother. In some of the dioceses in northern Italy there were not fewer than thirty of their churches with schools attached. These professors of an apostolic creed were noted for leading pure and peaceful lives, for the pains they took in the instruction of their families, for their readiness to benefit their neighbours both by good offices and religious counsel, for their gift of extempore prayer, and for the large extent to which their memories were stored with the Word of God. Many of them could recite entire epistles and gospels, and some of them had committed to memory the whole of the New Testament. The region which they occupied formed a belt of country stretching on both sides of the Alps and the Pyrenees, from the sources of the Rhine to the Garonne and the Ebro, and from the Po and the Adriatic to the shores of the Mediterranean. Monarchs found that this was the most productive and the most easily governed part of their dominions. Amid the wars and feudalism that oppressed the rest of Europe, in which towns were falling into decay, and the population in some spots were becoming extinct, and little appeared to be left, especially in France, "but convents scattered here and there amid vast tracts of forest," this Populous tract, rich in the marvels of industry and the virtues of true religion, resembled a strip of verdure drawn across the wastes of the desert. Will it be believed that human hands rooted out this paradise, which a pure Christianity had created in the very heart of the desert of European Catholicism? Rome about this time had brought to an end her wars with the empire, and her popes were reposing, after their struggle of centuries, in the proud consciousness of undoubted supremacy. The light had been spreading unobserved, and the Reformation was on the point of being anticipated. The demon Innocent III. was the first to descry the streaks of day on the crest of the Alps. Horror-stricken, he started up, and began to thunder from his Pandemonium against a faith which had already subjugated provinces, and was threatening to dissolve the power of Rome in the very flush of her victory over the empire. In order to save the one half of Europe from perishing by heresy, it was decreed that the other half should perish by the sword. The monarchs of Europe dared not disobey a summons which was enforced by the most dreadful adjurations and threats. They assembled their vassals, and girded on the sword, not to repel an invader or to quell insurrection, but to extirpate those very men whose industry had enriched their realm, and whose virtue and loyalty formed the stay of their power.

Lest the work of vengeance should slacken, Rome held out dazzling bribes, equally compounded of paradise and gold. She could afford to be prodigal of both, for neither cost her anything. Paradise is always in her gift for those who will do her work, and the wealth of the heretic is the lawful plunder of the faithful. With such a bank, and permission to draw upon it to an unlimited amount, Rome had no motive, and certainly would have had no thanks, for any ill-judged economy. The fanatics who mustered for the crusade hated the person and loved the goods of the heretic. Onward they marched, to earn heaven by desolating earth. The work was three centuries a-doing. It was done effectually at last, however. "Neither sex, nor age, nor rank, have we spared," says the leader of the war against the Albigenses; "we have put all alike to the sword." The churches and the workshops, the Christianity and the industry, of the region, were swept away by this simoom of fanaticism. Before it was a garden, behind it a desert. All was silent now, where the solemn melody of praise and the busy hum of trade had before been so happily blent. Monarchs had drained their exchequers to desolate the wealthiest and fairest portion of their dominions; nevertheless they held themselves abundantly recompensed by the assurance which Rome gave them of crowns and kingdoms in paradise.

Chapter V: Foundation and Extent of the Supremacy.

This is the favourable point for taking a view of the character of the Papacy, — its lofty pretensions and claims, and the foundation on which all these are based. The conflict waged by the seventh Gregory, and which ended in disaster to himself, but in triumph to his system, brings out in striking relief the essential principles, the guiding spirit, and the unvarying aims, of the popedom. When intelligently contemplated, the Papacy is seen to be a monarchy of a mixed kind, partly ecclesiastical and partly civil, founded professedly upon divine right, and claiming universal jurisdiction and dominion. The empire which Gregory VII. strove to erect was of this mixed kind; the dominion he arrogated and exercised extended directly or indirectly to all things temporal and spiritual; and this vast power he claimed *jure divino*. This it now becomes our business to show.

The Pope had now made himself absolute master in the Church. There was, in fact, but one bishop, and Christendom was his diocese. From this one man flowed all ecclesiastical honours, offices, acts, and jurisdiction. The pontiffs presided in all councils by their legates; they were the supreme arbiters in all controversies that arose respecting religion or church discipline. "Gregory VII.," remarks D'Aubigné, "claimed the same power over all the bishops and priests of Christendom that an abbot of Cluny exercises in the order in which he presides." And all this they claimed as the successor of St. Peter. But it is unnecessary to spend time on a point so universally admitted as that the popes now possessed ecclesiastical supremacy, and professed to hold it by divine right, that is, as the successors of St. Peter, the prince of the apostles. But the point to be demonstrated here is, that the popes, not content with being supreme rulers in the Church, and having all ecclesiastical persons and things subject to their absolute authority, claimed to be supreme in the State also; and, in the character of God's vicegerents presumed to dispose of crowns and kingdoms, and to interfere in all temporal affairs. The foundation of this power was laid when the popes claimed to be the successors of St. Peter and the vicars of Christ, which they did, as we have already shown, as early as the middle of the fifth century; but the universal and uncontrolled dominion implied in this claim they did not seek to wield till towards the times of Gregory VII., in the eleventh century. But that they did then arrogate this power in the most open and unblushing manner, does not admit of doubt or denial. There exists a vast body of proof to the effect that the popes of the eleventh and succeeding centuries attempted to prostrate beneath their feet the temporal as well as the spiritual power, and that they succeeded in their attempt. The history of Europe from the era of Hildebrand to that of Luther must be blotted out before the condemnatory evidence — for condemnatory of the Papacy it certainly is, as irreconcileably hostile to the liberties of nations and the rights of princes — can be annihilated or got rid of. It has put this claim into a great variety of forms, and attempted in every possible way to make it good. It taught this claim in its essential principles; and, when the character of the times permitted, it advanced it in plain and unmistakeable statements. It spent five centuries of intrigue in the effort to realize this claim, and five centuries more of wars and bloodshed in the effort to retain and consolidate it. It was promulgated from the doctor's chair, ratified by synodical acts, embodied in the instructions of nuncios, and thundered from the pontifical throne in the dreadful sentence of interdict by which monarchs were deposed, their crowns transferred to others, their subjects loosed from their allegiance, and their kingdoms not unfrequently ravaged with fire and sword.

Acts so monstrous may appear to be the mere wantonness of ambition, or the irresponsible doings of men in whom the lust of power had overborne every other consideration. The man who reasons in this way either does not understand the Papacy, or wilfully perverts the question. This was but the sober and logical action of the popedom; it was the fair working of the evil principles of the system, and no chance ebullition of the destructive passions of the man who had been placed at its head; and nothing is capable of a more complete and convincing demonstration. The foundation of our proof must of course be the constitution of the Papacy. As is the nature of the thing, — as are the elements and principles of which it is made up, — so inevitably must be the character and extent of its claims, and the nature of its action and influence. What, then, is the Papacy? Is it a purely spiritual society, or a purely secular society? It is neither. The Papacy is a mixed society: the secular element enters quite as largely into its constitution as does the spiritual. It is a compound of both elements in equal proportions; and, being so, must necessarily possess secular as well as spiritual jurisdiction, and be necessitated to adopt civil as well as ecclesiastical action. But how does it appear that the Church of Rome combines in one essence the secular and spiritual elements? for the point lies here. It appears from the fundamental axiom on which she rests. There are but a few links in the chain of her infernal logic; but these few links are of adamant; and they so bind up together, in one composite body, the two principles, the spiritual and the temporal, and, by consequence, the two jurisdictions, that the moment Rome attempts to cut in twain what her logic joins in one, she ceases to be the popedom. Her syllogism is indestructible if the minor proposition be but granted; and the minor proposition, be it remembered, is her fundamental axiom: — CHRIST IS THE VICAR OF GOD, AND, AS SUCH, POSSESSES HIS POWER; BUT THE POPE IS THE VICAR OF CHRIST; THEREFORE THE POPE IS GOD'S VICAR, AND POSSESSES HIS POWER. To Christ, as the Vicar of God, all power, spiritual and temporal, has been delegated. All *spiritual* power has been delegated to Him as Head of the Church; and all *temporal* power has been delegated to Him for the good of the Church. This power has been delegated a second time from Christ to the Pope. To the Pope all *spiritual* power has been delegated, as head of the Church, and God's vicegerent on earth; and all *temporal* power also, for the good of the Church. Such is the theory of the popedom. This conclusively establishes that the Papacy is of a mixed character. We but perplex ourselves when we think or speak of it simply as a religion. It contains the religious element, no doubt; but it is not a religion; — it is a scheme of domination of a mixed character, partly spiritual and partly temporal; and its jurisdiction must be of the same mixed kind with its constitution. To talk of the popedom wielding a purely spiritual authority only, is to assert what her fundamental principles repudiate. These principles compel her to claim the temporal also. The two authorities grow out of the same fundamental axiom, and are so woven together in the system, and so indissolubly knit the one to the other, that the Papacy must part with both or none. The popedom, then, stands alone. In genius, in constitution, and in prerogative, it is diverse from all other societies. The Church of Rome is a temporal monarchy as really as she is an ecclesiastic body; and in token of her hybrid character, her head, the Pope, displays the emblems of both jurisdictions, — the keys in the one hand, the sword in the other.

Pope Boniface VIII. was a much more logical expounder of the Papacy than those who now-a-days would persuade us that it is purely spiritual. In a bull "given at the palace of the Lateran, in the eighth year of his pontificate," and inserted in the body of the canon law, we find him claiming both jurisdictions in the broadest manner. "There is," says he, "one fold and one shepherd. The authority of that shepherd includes the two swords, — the spiritual and the temporal. So much are we taught by the words of the evangelist, 'Behold, here are two swords,' namely, in the Church. The Lord did not reply, It is too much, but, It is enough. Certainly he did not deny to Peter the temporal sword: he only commanded him to return it into its scabbard. Both, therefore, belong to the jurisdiction of the Church, — the spiritual sword and the secular. The one is to be wielded for the Church, — the other by the Church; the one is the sword of the priest, — the other is in the hand of the monarch, but at the command and sufferance of the priest. It behoves the one sword to be under the other, — the temporal authority to be subject to the spiritual power." Whatever may be thought of this pontifical gloss, there can be no question as to the comprehensive jurisdiction which Boniface founds upon the passage.

It cannot be argued, then, with the least amount of truth, or of plausibility even, that this claim was the result of a kind of accident, — that it originated solely in the ambition of an individual pope, and was foreign to the genius, or disallowed by the principles, of the Papacy. On the contrary, nothing is easier than to show that it is a most logical deduction from the fundamental elements of the system. It partakes not in the slightest degree of the accidental; nor was it a crotchet of Hildebrand, or a delusion of the age in which he lived; as is manifest from the fact, that its development was the work of five centuries, and the joint operation of many hundreds of minds who were successively employed upon it. It was the logical consequence of principles which had been engrafted in the Papacy, or rather, as we have just shown, which lie at the foundation of the whole system; and accordingly, it was steadily and systematically pursued through a succession of centuries, and engaged the genius and ambition of innumerable minds. As the seed bursts the clod and struggles into light, so we behold the principle of papal supremacy struggling for development through the slow centuries, and in its efforts overturning thrones and convulsing society. We can discover the supremacy in embryo as early as the fifth century, and can trace its logical development till the times of Hildebrand. We see it passing through the consecutive stages of the dogma, the synodical decree, the papal missive, and the interdict, which shook the thrones of monarchs, and laid their occupants prostrate in the dust. The gnarled oak, whose lofty stature and thick foliage darken the earth for roods around, is not more really a development of the acorn deposited in the soil centuries before, than were the arrogant pretensions and domineering acts of the Papacy in the age of Innocent the result of the principle deposited in the Papacy in the fifth century, that the Pope is Christ's vicar.

The Pope's absolute dominion over priests is not a more legitimate inference from this doctrine than is his dominion over kings. If the pontiffs have renounced the temporal supremacy, it is on one of two grounds, — either they are not Christ's vicars, or Christ is not a King of kings. But they have claimed all along, and do still claim, to be the vicars of Christ; and they have likewise held all along, and do still hold, that Christ is Head of the world as well as Head of the Church. The conclusion is inevitable, that it is not only over the Church that they bear rule, but over the world also; and that they have as good a right to dispose of crowns, and to meddle in the temporal affairs of kingdoms, as they have to bestow mitres, and to make laws in the Church. The one authority is as essential to the completeness of their assumed character as is the other.

The popes have understood the matter in this light from the beginning. Some writers of name are at present endeavouring to persuade the world that the pontiffs (some few excepted, who, they say, transgressed in this matter the bounds of Catholicism as well as of moderation) never claimed or exercised supremacy over princes; that this is not, and never was, a doctrine of the Roman Catholic Church; and that she repudiates and condemns the opinion that the Pope has been invested with jurisdiction over temporal princes. But we cannot grant to Rome the sole right to interpret history, as her members grant to her the right to interpret the Bible. We can examine and judge for ourselves; and when we do so, we certainly find far more reason to admire the boldness than to confess the prudence of those who disclaim, on the part of Rome, this doctrine. The proofs to the contrary are far too plain and too numerous to permit of this disclaimer obtaining the least credit from any one, save those who are prepared to receive without scruple or inquiry all that popish writers may be pleased to assert in behalf of their Church. Popes, canonists, and councils have promulgated this tenet; and not only have they asserted that the power it implies rests on Divine right, but they have inculcated it as an article of belief on all who would preserve the faith and unity of the Church. "We," says Pope Boniface VIII., "declare, say, define, and pronounce it to be necessary to salvation, that every human creature be subject to the Roman pontiff. The one sword must be under the other; and the temporal authority must be subject to the spiritual power: hence, if the earthly power go astray, the spiritual shall judge it." These sentiments are re-echoed by Leo X. and his Council of Lateran. "We," says that pope, "with the approbation of the present holy council, do renew and approve that holy constitution." To that doctrine Baronius heartily subscribes: "There can be no doubt of it," says he, "but that the civil principality is subject to the sacerdotal, and that God hath made the political government subject to the dominion of the spiritual Church."

"He who reigneth on high," says Pius V., in his introduction to his bull against Queen Elizabeth, "to whom is given all power in heaven and in earth, hath committed the one holy Catholic Church, out of which there is no salvation, to one alone upon earth, that is, to Peter, the prince of apostles, and to the Roman pontiff, the successor of Peter, to be governed with a plenitude of power. This one he hath constituted prince over all nations, that he may pluck up, overthrow, disperse, destroy, plant, and rear." The Italian priest, therefore, thunders against the English monarch in the following style: — "We deprive the Queen of her pretended right to the kingdom, and of all dominion, dignity, and privilege whatsoever; and absolve all the nobles, subjects, and people of the kingdom, and whoever else have sworn to her, from their oath, and all duty whatsoever in regard of dominion, fidelity, and obedience."

"Snatch up, therefore, the two-edged sword of Divine power committed to thee," was the address of the Council of Lateran to Leo X., "and enjoin, command, and charge, that a universal peace and alliance, for at least ten years, be made among Christians; and to that bind kings in the fetters of the great King, and firmly fasten nobles with the iron manacles of censures; for to thee is given all power in heaven and in earth."

So speak the popes and councils of Rome. Here is not only the principle out of which the supremacy springs enunciated, but the claim itself advanced. Not in words only have they held this high tone; their deeds have been equally lofty. The supremacy was not permitted to remain a theory; it became a fact. For several centuries together we see the popes reigning over Europe, and demeaning themselves in every way as not only its spiritual, but also its temporal lords. We see them freely distributing immunities, titles, revenues, territories, as if all belonged to them; we see them sustaining themselves arbiters in all disputes, umpires in all quarrels, and judges in all causes; we see them giving provinces and crowns to their favourites, and constituting emperors; we see them imposing oaths of fidelity and vassalage on monarchs; and, in token, of the dependence of the one and the supremacy of the other, we see them exacting tribute for their kingdoms in the shape of Peter's pence; we see them raising wars and crusades, summoning princes and kings into the field, attiring them in their livery, the cross, and holding them but as lieutenants under them. In fine, how often have they deposed monarchs, and laid their kingdoms under interdict? History presents us with a list of not less than sixty-four emperors and kings deposed by the popes. But it is improper to despatch in a single sentence what occupies so large a space in history, and has been the cause of so much suffering, bloodshed, and war to Europe. Nothing can convey a better or truer picture of the insufferable arrogance and pride of the pontiffs than their own language on these occasions.

"For the dignity and defence of God's holy Church" says Gregory VII. (Hildebrand), "in the name of the omnipotent God, Father, Son, and Holy Ghost, I depose from imperial and royal administration, Henry the king, the son of Henry, formerly emperor, who, too boldly and rashly, has laid hands on thy Church; and I absolve all Christians subject to the empire from that oath by which they were wont to plight their faith unto true kings; for it is right that he should be deprived of dignity who doth endeavour to diminish the majesty of the Church.

"Go to, therefore, most holy princes of the apostles, and what I said, by interposing your authority, confirm; that all men may now at length understand, if ye can bind and loose in heaven, that ye also can upon earth take away and give empires, kingdoms, and whatsoever mortals can have; for if ye can judge things belonging unto God, what is to be deemed concerning these inferior and profane things? And if it is your part to judge angels who govern proud princes, what becometh it you to do towards their servants? Let kings now, and all secular princes, learn by this man's example what ye can do in heaven, and in what esteem ye are with God; and let them henceforth fear to slight the commands of holy Church, but put forth suddenly this judgment, that all men may understand, that not casually, but by your means, this son of iniquity doth fall from his kingdom."

"We therefore," says Innocent IV. in the Council of Lyons (1245), when pronouncing sentence of excommunication upon the Emperor Frederick II., "having had previous and careful deliberation with our brethren and the holy council respecting the preceding and many other of his wicked miscarriages, do show, denounce, and accordingly deprive of all honour and dignity, the said prince, who hath rendered himself unworthy of empire and kingdoms, and of all honour and dignity; and who, for his sins, is cast away by God, that he should not reign nor command; and all who are bound by oath of allegiance we absolve from such oath for ever, firmly enjoining that none in future regard or obey him as emperor or king; and decreeing, that whoever yields him in these characters advice, assistance, or favours, shall immediately lie under the bond of excommunication."

The following bull of Sixtus V. (1585) against the King of Navarre and the Prince of Conde, — *the two sons of wrath*, — is conceived in the loftiest pontifical style. "The authority given to St. Peter and his successors by the immense power of the Eternal King, excels all the power of earthly princes; it passes uncontrollable sentence upon them all; and if it find any of them resisting the ordinance of God, it takes a more severe vengeance upon them, casting them down from their throne, however powerful they may be, and tumbling them to the lowest parts of the earth, as the ministers of aspiring Lucifer. We deprive them and their posterity of their dominions for ever. By the authority of these presents, we absolve and free all persons from their oath [of allegiance], and from all duty whatever relating to dominion, fealty, and obedience; and we charge and forbid all from presuming to obey them, or any of their admonitions, laws, or commands."

But it were endless to bring forward all that might be adduced on the point. The history of the middle ages abounds with instances of the exercise of this tremendous power, of the disgrace and disaster it entailed on monarchs, and the confusion and calamity it occasioned to nations. But instead of citing instances of these, — of which the history of Europe, not excepting that of our own country, is filled, — we think it of more consequence here to observe, that the most high-handed of these acts grew directly out of the fundamental principle of the Papacy, — that the Pope is Christ's vicar. If this be granted, the pontiff is as really the temporal as the spiritual chief of Europe; and in dethroning heretical kings, and laying rebellious kingdoms under interdict, he is simply exercising a power which Christ has lodged in his hands; he is doing what he is not only entitled, but bound to do. Nothing could display greater ignorance of the essential principles of the Papacy, or greater incompetence to deduce legitimate inferences from these principles, than to hold, as some do, that the supremacy was an accident, or had its origin in the ambition of Gregory, or in the superstitious and slavish character of the times. True, it was only at times that the Papacy dared to assert or to act upon this arrogant claim. In itself the claim is so monstrous, and so destructive of both the natural rights of men and the just prerogatives of princes, that the instinct of self-preservation overcame at times the slavish dictates of superstition, and princes and people united to oppose a despotism that threatened to crush both. When the state was strong the Papacy held its claims in abeyance; but when the sceptre came into feeble hands, that moment Rome advanced her lordly pretensions, and summoned both her ghostly terrors and her material resources to enforce them. She trampled with inexorable pride upon the dignity of princes; she violated without scruple the sanctity of oaths; she repaid former favours with insult; and treated with equal disdain the rights and the supplications of nations. Nothing, however exalted, nothing, however venerable, nothing, however sacred, was permitted to stand in her way to universal and supreme dominion. She became the lady of kingdoms. She was God's vicegerent, and could bind or loose, build up or pull down, as seemed good unto her. In disposing of the crowns of monarchs, she was disposing of but her own; and in assuming the supreme authority in their kingdoms, she was exercising a right inherent in her, and with which she could no more part than she could cease to be Rome.

Such is the principle viewed logically. The most arrogant acts of Gregory and Innocent did not exceed by a single hairbreadth the just limits of their power, judged according to the fundamental axiom out of which that power springs. But we are not to suppose that Romanists have all been of one mind respecting the nature and extent of the supremacy. On this, as on every other point, they have differed widely. By a curious but easily explained coincidence, the Romanist theory of the supremacy has been enlarged or contracted, according to the mutations which the supremacy itself, in its exercise upon the world, has undergone. The papal sceptre has been a sort of index-hand. Its motions, whether through a larger or a narrower space, have ever furnished an exact measure of the existing state of opinion in the schools on the subject in question. In fact, the risings and fallings of *theory* and *practice* on the head of the supremacy have been as coincident, both in time and space, as the turnings of the vane and the wind, or as the changes of the mercury and the atmosphere; furnishing an instructive specimen of that very peculiar infallibility which Rome possesses. We distinctly recognise three well-defined and different opinions, not to mention minute shades and variations, among Romish doctors on this important question. The first attributes temporal power to the Pope on the ground of express and formal delegation from God. We are, say they, Peter's representative, God's vicegerent, possessors of the two keys, and therefore the rulers of the world in both its spiritual and temporal affairs. This may be held, speaking generally, as the claim of the popes who lived from Gregory VII. to Pius V., as expressed in their bulls, and interpreted (little to the comfort of sovereigns) in their acts. They were the world's priest and monarch in one person. And, we repeat, this, which is the high ultra-montane theory, appears to us to be the most consistent opinion, strictly logical on Romanist principles, and, indeed, wholly impregnable if we but grant their postulate, that the Pope is Christ's vicar. Prior to the Reformation there was scarce a single dissentient from this view of the supremacy in the Romish Church, if we except the illustrious defenders of the "Gallican liberties." Theologians, canonists, and popes, with one voice claimed this prerogative. "The first opinion," says Bellarmine, when enumerating the views held respecting the Pope's temporal supremacy, "is, that the Pope has a most full power, *jure divino*, over the whole world, in both ecclesiastical and civil affairs." "This," he adds, "is the doctrine of Augustine Triumphus, Alvarus Pelagius, Hostiensis, Panormitanus, Sylvester, and others not a few." The same doctrine was taught by the "Angelical Doctor," as he is termed. Aquinas held, that "in the Pope is the top of both powers," and "by plain consequence asserting," says Barrow, "when any one is denounced excommunicate for apostacy, his subjects are immediately freed his dominion, and from their oaths of allegiance to him."

The second opinion is, that the Pope's *immediate* and *direct* jurisdiction extends to ecclesiastical matters only, but that he possesses a *mediate* and *indirect* authority over temporal affairs also. This opinion found its best expositor and its ablest champion in the redoubtable Cardinal Bellarmine. The Cardinal had sense to see, that the monstrous and colossal Janus, which turned a cleric or laic visage to the gazer, according to the side from which he viewed it, — which sat upon the seven hills, and was worshipped in the dark ages, — could no longer be borne by the world; and accordingly he set himself, with an adroitness and skill for which he had but little thanks from the reigning pontiff, — for the Cardinal narrowly escaped the *Expurgatorius*, — to show that the Pope had but one jurisdiction, the spiritual; and could exercise temporal authority only indirectly, that is, for the good of religion or the Church. The Pope, however, lost nothing, in point of fact, by the Cardinal's logic; for

Bellarmine took care to teach, that that *indirect* temporal power would carry the pontiff as far, and enable him to do as much, as the *direct* temporal authority. This *indirect* temporal power, the Cardinal taught, was supreme, and could enable the Pope, for the welfare of the Church, to annul laws and depose sovereigns. This was dexterous management on the part of the Jesuit. He professed to part the enormous power which had before centred in Peter's chair, between the kings and the pope, giving the temporal to the former and the spiritual to the latter; but he took care that the lion's share should fall to the pontiff. It was a grand feat of legerdemain; for this division, made with such show of fairness, left the one party with not a particle more power, and the other with not a particle less, than before. Bellarmine had not broken or blunted the temporal sword; he had simply muffled it. He had left the pope brandishing in his hand the spiritual mace, with the temporal stiletto slung conveniently by his side, concealed by the folds of his pontificals. He could knock monarchs on the head with the spiritual bludgeon; and, having got them down, could despatch them with the secular poignard. What was there then in Bellarmine's theory to prevent the great spiritual freebooter of Rome doing as much business in his own peculiar line as before? Nothing.

But Bellarmine's opinion has become antiquated in its turn. The papal sceptre now describes a narrower political circle, and the opinions of the Romish doctors on the subject of the supremacy have undergone a corresponding limitation. A third opinion is that of those who hold the pope's indirect temporal power in its most mitigated and attenuated form, — in so very attenuated a form, indeed, that it is all but invisible; and accordingly the authors of this opinion take leave to deny that they grant to the pope any temporal power at all. There are the views propounded by Count de Maistre and Abbe Gosselin on the Continent, and by Dr. Wiseman in this country, and now generally received by all Roman Catholics. De Maistre strongly condemns the use of the term *temporal supremacy* to indicate the power which the popes claim over sovereigns; and maintains that it is in virtue of a power *entirely and eminently spiritual* that they believe themselves to be possessed of the right to excommunicate sovereigns guilty of certain crimes, without, however, any temporal encroachment, or any interference with their sovereignty. He instances the case of the present Pope, who is possessed of so little temporal power, that he is compelled to submit to the ridicule of the Roman citizens. De Maistre conveniently forgets that the question is not what the popes possess, but what they claim, either directly or by implication. The matter is stated in almost precisely similar terms by Dr. Wiseman, in his "Lectures on the Doctrines and Practices of the Catholic Church." "The supremacy which I have described," says he, "is of a character purely spiritual, and has no connexion with the possession of any temporal jurisdiction. . . . Nor has this spiritual supremacy any relation to the wider sway once held by the pontiffs over the destinies of Europe. That the headship of the Church won naturally the highest weight and authority, in a social and political state, grounded on catholic principles, we cannot wonder. That power arose and disappeared with the institutions which produced or supported it, and forms no part of the doctrine hold by the Church regarding the papal supremacy." What sort of power, then, is it which these writers attribute to the Pope? A purely spiritual power, which, however, *may*, as they themselves admit, and *must*, as we shall show, carry very formidable temporal consequences in its train. A single term expresses the modern view of the supremacy, *direction*. It is not, according to this view, *jurisdiction*, but *direction*, which rightfully belongs to the pontiff. He sits upon the Seven Hills, not as the world's magistrate, but as the world's casuist. He is there to solve doubts and guide the consciences, not to coerce the bodies, of men. It is not as the dictator, but as the doctor of Europe that he occupies Peter's chair. But this is just Bellarmine's theory in a subtler form. The mode of action is changed, but that action in its result is the very same: we are led, in no long time, and by no very indirect path, to the full temporal supremacy. If the Pope be the director and judge of all consciences; if he be, as Romanists maintain, an infallible director and judge; must he not require submission to his judgment, — implicit submission, — seeing it is an infallible and supreme judgment? Suppose this infallible resolver had such a case of conscience as the following submitted to him, — it is no hypothetical case: — The Grand Duke of Tuscany solicits the papal see to direct his conscience as to whether it is lawful to permit his subjects to read the Word of God in the vernacular tongue, or to permit Protestant worship in the Italian language in his dominions; and he is told it is not. The Pope does not send a single *sbirri* to Florence; he simply directs the ducal conscience. But the Grand Duke, as an obedient son of the church, feels himself bound to act on the advice of infallibility. Immediately the *gens d'armes* appear in the Protestant chapel, the Waldensian ministers are banished, and a count of the realm, along with others, whose only crime is attendance at Protestant worship, and reading the Word of God in Italian, are thrown into the Bargello or common prison. The sentence of excommunication thundered from Gaeta against the Romans was the precursor of the French cannon which the Jesuits of the cabinet of the Elysee sent to Rome. The excommunication was a purely spiritual act; but the gaps in the Roman wall, filled with gory masses of Roman and French corpses, had not much of a spiritual character. Laws favourable to toleration and Protestantism, the succession of Protestant sovereigns, and all other acts of the same kind, must be condemned by this supreme spiritual judge, as hostile to the interests of religion. Of course, every Catholic conscience throughout the world is *directed* by the judgment of the pontiff, and must feel bound to carry that judgment out to the best of his power. Were the Catholics of Ireland to propound such a case of casuistry as this to the papal see, — whether it is for the good of the Church in Ireland that a heretic like Queen Victoria should bear sway over that island, — who can doubt what the reply would be? Nor can it be doubted that Irish Catholic consciences would take the direction which infallibility indicated, if they thought they could do so to good purpose. This autocrat of all consciences in and out of Christendom may disclaim all temporal power, and affect to be head of but a spiritual organization; but well he knows that, on the right and left of Peter's chair, as turnkey and hangman to the holy apostolic see, stand Naples and Austria. The knife of De Maistre, fine as its edge is, has but lopped off the branches of the tree of supremacy; the root is in the earth, fastened with a band of iron and brass. The artillery of Romanist logic plays harmlessly upon the fabric of the papal power. It veils it in clouds of smoke, but it does not throw down a single stone of the building. The spectator, because it is blotted from his sight, thinks it is demolished. Anon the smoke clears away, and it is seen standing unscathed, and strong as ever.

History is a great bar in the way of the reception of this theory, or rather of the general conclusion to which its authors seek to lead the public mind, namely, that the pontifical direction is not connected, either directly or consequentially, with temporal power; and that the popes simply pronounce judgment in abstract questions of right and wrong, leaving their award, as any other moral and religious body would do, to exercise its legitimate influence upon the opinion and action of the age. The reception of such a view of the supremacy as this is much impeded, we say, by the monuments of history. But what can be neither blotted out nor forgotten, it may be possible to explain away; and this is the task which De Maistre, and especially Gosselin and other modern Romanist writers, have imposed upon themselves. De Maistre admits, as it would be madness to deny, that the popes of a former age did depose sovereigns and loose subjects from their oath of allegiance; but to the amount to which these acts embodied temporal jurisdiction, or differed in their mode from *direction*, the adherents of the modern theory maintain that they grew out of the spirit and views of the middle ages, and that they were founded, not on divine right, but on public right, that is, on the general consent of the sovereigns and people of those days. Now, to this view of the subject there are many and insuperable objections. The popes themselves give quite a different account of the matter. When they pronounced sentence of excommunication on monarchs, in the middle ages, on what ground did they rest their acts? On the constitutional law of Europe? On rights made over to them by a convention, express or tacit, of sovereigns and people? No; but on the highest style of *divine right*. They gave and took away crowns, as the vicars of Christ and the holders of the keys. These popes did not act as casuists, but as rulers. They did not decide a point of morality, but a point of policy. One can easily imagine the measureless indignation of Gregory or Innocent, had any one then dared to propound such a theory, — how quickly they would have smelt heresy in it, and summoned the pontifical thunders to purge out that heresy. Jurisdiction they did claim then, and on the theory of infallibility they claim it still; nor does it mend the matter though one should grant that that jurisdiction is of a spiritual nature, with the *indirect* temporal power attached; for, as we have already shown, this is but adding one step more to the logic, without adding even a step more to the process by which the act becomes thoroughly temporal. Nay, it does not mend the matter though we should drop the attached indirect temporal power, and retain only the spiritual jurisdiction. That jurisdiction is infallible and supreme, and extends to all things affecting religion, that is, the Church, the popes being the judges. We have had a modern proof how little this would avail to curb the excesses of pontifical ambition. We have seen the Pope, solely by the force of the spiritual jurisdiction, endeavouring to compel Piedmont to alter its laws, and to restore the lands to monasteries, and again extend to the clergy immunity from the secular tribuinals. Even De Maistre grants the right of excommunicating sovereigns guilty of great crimes. But the Pope is to be the judge of what crimes do and do not merit this dreadful punishment; and the notions of pontiffs on this grave point are apt to differ from those of ordinary men. Innocent III. threatened to interrupt the succession to the throne of Hungary because his legate had been stopped in passing through that kingdom. Wherever duty is involved, there the Pope has the right to interfere. But what action is it that does not involve duty? There is nothing a man can do, — scarce anything he can leave undone, — in which the interests of religion are not more or less directly concerned, and in which the Pope has not a pretext for thrusting in his direction. He can prescribe the food a man is to eat, the person with whom he is to trade, the master whom he is to serve, or the menial whom he is to hire. One can marry only whom the priest pleases; and can send one's children to no school which the Pope has disallowed; he must be told how often to come to confession, and what proportion of his goods to give to the Church; above all, his conscience must be directed in the important matter of his last will and testament. He cannot bury his dead unless he is on good terms with the Church. Whether as a holder of the franchise, a municipal councillor, a judge, or a member of parliament, he must give an account of his stewardship to Rome. From his cradle to his grave he is under priestly direction. That direction is not tendered in the shape of advice, and so left to guide the man by its moral force: it is delivered as an infallible decision, the justice of which he dare not question, and to hesitate to obey which would be to peril his salvation. Thus, in every matter of life and business the Church comes in. But the Church can as thoroughly direct a whole kingdom as she can direct the individual man. The whole affairs of a nation, from the state secret down to the peasant's gossip, lie open before her eye. Her agents ramify everywhere, and can at a given signal commence simultaneously a system of opposition and agitation over the whole kingdom. Any decision in the cabinet, any law in the senate, unfriendly to the Church, is sure in this way to be met and crushed. In directing national affairs, Rome has dropt the bold, blustering tone of Hildebrand: she now intimates her will in blander accents and politer phrase, but in a manner not less firm and irresistible than before. She has only to hint at withholding the sacraments, as the Archbishop Franzoni lately did to the minister Rosa, and the threat generally is successful. Governments cannot move a step but they are met by this tremendous spiritual check. They cannot make laws about education or about church lands, — they cannot regulate monasteries or take cognizance of the clergy, — they cannot extend civil privileges to their subjects, or conclude a treaty with foreign states, — without coming into collision with the

Church. Every matter which they touch is Church, and before they can avoid her they must step out of the world. Under the plea of directing their consciences, their power, they find, is a nullity, and the real master of both themselves and their kingdom is the Bishop of Rome, or his cowled or scarlet-hatted representative at their court. Thus there is nothing of a temporal kind which is not drawn within the jurisdiction of the Pope's constructive empire; and the "purely spiritual power" is felt in practice to be an intolerable secular thraldom. Under Rome's scheme of infallible spiritual direction things sacred and civil are inseparably and hopelessly blended; and the attempt to separate the two would be as vain as the attempt to separate time from the beings that live in it, or space from the bodies it contains, or, as it is well expressed by a writer in the *Edinburgh Review*, to cut out Shylock's pound of flesh without spilling a drop of blood. The recent concordat between the Pope and the Spanish government shows what a powerful engine the "spiritual jurisdiction" is for the government of a nation in all its affairs, temporal and spiritual. That concordat puts both swords into the hands of Pius IX. as truly as ever Gregory VII. or Innocent III. held them. Let the reader mark its leading provisions, and see how it subjects the temporal to the spiritual power: —

"Art. 1 declares that the Roman Catholic religion, being the sole worship of the Spanish nation, to the exclusion of all others, shall be maintained for ever, with all the rights and prerogatives which it ought to enjoy, according to the law of God and the dispositions of the sacred canons.

"Art. 2 deposes that all instruction in universities, colleges, seminaries, and public or private schools, shall be conformable to Catholic doctrine; and that no impediment shall be put in the way of the bishops, &c. whose duty is to watch over the purity of doctrine and of manners, and over the religious education of youth, even in the public schools.

"Art. 3. The authorities to give every support to the bishops and other ministers in the exercise of their duties; and the government to support the bishops when called on, whether in opposing themselves to the malignity of men who seek to pervert the minds of the faithful and corrupt their morals, or in impeding the publication, introduction, and circulation of bad and dangerous books.'"

The 29th article provides for the establishment by the government of certain religious houses and congregations, specifying those of San Vicente Paul, San Felipe Neri, and "some other one of those approved by the Holy See;" the object being stated to be, that there may be always a sufficient number of ministers and evangelical labourers for home and foreign missions, &c., and also that they may serve as places of retirement for ecclesiastics, in order to perform spiritual exercises and other pious works.

Art. 30 refers to religious houses for women, in which those who are called to a contemplative life may follow their vocation, and others may follow that of assistance to the sick, education, and other pious and useful works; and directs the preservation of the institution of Daughters of Charity, under the direction of the clergy of San Vicente Paul, the government to endeavour to promote the same; religious houses in which education of children and other works of charity are added to a contemplative life also to be maintained; and, with respect to other orders, the bishops of the respective dioceses to propose the cases in which the admission and profession of noviciates should take place, and the exercises of education or of charity which should be established in them.

The 35th article declares that the government shall provide, by all suitable means, for the support of the religious houses, &c. for men; and that, with respect to those for women, all the unsold convent property is at once to be returned to the bishops in whose dioceses it is, as their representatives.

Here, then, is the supremacy, not as portrayed in the ingenious theories of De Maistre and Gosselin, but as it exists at this moment in fact. Stript of the sanctimonious phraseology with which it has always been the policy of Rome to veil her worst atrocities and her vilest tyrannies, the document just means that the Pope is the real sovereign of Spain, that his priests are to rule it as they list, and that the court at Madrid, and the other civil functionaries, are there merely to assist them. The first article of this concordat declares freedom of conscience eternally proscribed in the realm of Spain; the second decrees the extinction of knowledge and the perpetual reign of ignorance; the third takes the civil authorities bound and astricted to aid the clergy in searching for Bibles, hunting out missionaries, and burning converts; and the following articles grant license for the erection of sacerdotal stews, and the institution of clubs all over the country, the better to enable the clergy to coerce the citizens and beard the government. The concordat means this, and nothing else. It is as detestable and villanous an instrument as ever emanated from the gang of conspirators which has so long had its head-quarters on the Roman hill. It is meant to bind down the conscience and the manhood of Spain in everlasting slavery; and it shows that, despite all the recent exposures of these men, — despite all the disasters which have befallen them, and the yet more terrible disasters that lower over them, — their hearts are fully set upon their wickedness, and that they are resolved to present to the last a forehead of brass to the wrath of man and the bolts of heaven. This concordat has been shelved, meanwhile, — no thanks to the imbeciles who exchanged ratifications with Rome, but to the revolution which broke out at that moment in Portugal, and to the mutterings, not loud, but deep, which began to be heard in Spain itself, and which convinced its rulers that even a concordat with the Pope might be bought at too great a price.

Not in the high despotic countries of Italy and Spain only do we meet these lofty notions of the sacerdotal power: in constitutional and semi-Protestant Germany we find the bishops of the Church of Rome advancing the same exclusive and intolerant claims. The triumph of Austrian arms and of Austrian politics in the south of Germany has already made the Romish priesthood of that region predominant, and led them to aspire to the supremacy. Accordingly, demands utterly incompatible with any government, and especially constitutional and Protestant government, have been put forth by the bishops of the two Hesses, Wurtemberg, Nassau, Hamburg, Frankfort, — all Protestant States; and of Baden, a semi-Protestant State. The document in which these demands are contained is entitled, "The Assembled Bishops of the Ecclesiastical Province of the Haut-Rhin, to the several Governments." A copy has been sent over by our ambassador, Lord Cowley, and published by order of Parliament. Its leading claims are as follows:

"The repeal of all religious concessions made since March 1848.

"The free nomination to all ecclesiastical employments and benefices by the several bishops in their respective dioceses.

"The right of the bishops to subject their subordinates to a special examination, and to punish them according to the canon law.

"The abolition, in the exercise of the ecclesiastical penal jurisdiction, of the right of appeal to the secular tribunals. This shall extend from the simple remonstrance to the removal from office and the loss of emolument. Every attempt to appeal in these matters to the secular authority shall be looked upon as an act of disobedience to the legal authority of the Church, and shall be punished by *excommunicatio latae sententiae*.

"The establishment of seminaries for young boys.

"Episcopal sanction for the nomination of masters for religious education in the colleges and universities.

"Abolition of the right of *placet* of the secular authority as regards the publication of papal bulls, of briefs, and pastoral letters of the bishops to the members of the clergy.

Permission for the bishops to preach to the people in public, and to hold exercises for the instruction of priests.

"Permission to collect men and women for prayer, for contemplation, and for self-denial.

"The re-instatement of the bishops in the entire enjoyment of their ancient penal jurisdiction as against such of the members of the Church as shall manifest contempt for ecclesiastical ordinances.

"Free communication between the bishops and Rome.

"No interference of the secular power in questions of filling up the appointment to the chapter of canons.

"Independent administration of the property of the Church and of foundations."

Can any man peruse these two documents, appearing as they do at the same moment in widely-separated quarters of Europe, yet identical in their spirit and in the claims they put forth, and fail to see that the Papacy has plotted once more to seize upon the government of the world; and that its priests in all countries are working with dauntless audacity and amazing craft, on a given plan, to accomplish this grand object? In every country they insolently claim independence of the government and of the courts of law, with unlimited control of the schools. They would override all things, and be themselves controlled by no one. Rome, through her organs, bids Europe again crouch down beneath the infallibility. How strikingly also do these documents teach that Popery is as unchangeable in her character as in her creed. Amid the liberal ideas and constitutional governments of Germany she retains her exclusive and intolerant spirit, not less than amid the medieval opinions and barbaric despotism of Spain. The glacier in the heart of the Swiss valley lies eternally congealed in the midst of fruit, and flowers, and sunshine. In like manner, an eternal congelation holds fast the Papacy, let the world advance as it may. In the middle of the nineteenth century it starts up grizzly, ferocious, and bloodthirsty, as in the fifteenth. As a murderer from his grave, or a wild beast from his lair, so has it come back upon the world. The compilers of these documents breathe the very spirit of the men who, in former ages, covered Spain with inquisitions and Germany with stakes. They lack simply opportunity to revive, and even outdo, the worst tragedies of their predecessors. In Germany they attempt by a single stroke of the pen to sweep away all the guarantees which flowed from the treaty of Westphalia; and in southern Europe they strike down with the sabre the rights of conscience and the liberties of states. How long will princes and statesmen permit themselves to be misled by the wretched pretext that these men have a divine right to commit all these enormities and crimes, — that heaven has committed the human race into their hands, — and that neither the rights of man nor the prerogatives of God must come into competition with their sacerdotal will? How long is the world to be oppressed by a confederacy of fanatics and ruffians, who are only the abler to play the knave, that they rob under the mask of devotion, and tyrannize in the awful name of God?

But we have no need to go so far from home as to Spain and Germany, for an instance of "a purely spiritual jurisdiction" transmuting itself immediately and directly into temporal supremacy. Let us look across St. George's Channel. The British government, pitying the deep ignorance of the natives of Ireland, wisely resolve to erect a number of colleges in that dark land, in the hope of mitigating the wretchedness of its people. The priesthood discover that this scheme interferes with the Church, whose vested right in the ignorance of the natives it threatens to sweep away. The Pope does not throw down a single stone of any of these colleges. His interference takes a purely spiritual direction, but a direction that accomplishes his object quite as effectually as could be done by a physical intervention. He issues a bull, denouncing the Irish colleges as godless, and forbidding every good Catholic, as he values his salvation, to allow his child to enter them. This bull, given at the Quirinal, makes frustrate the intention of the Queen, and renders the colleges as completely useless to the Irish nation, — at least to that large portion of it for whose benefit they were specially intended, — as if an army had been sent to raze the obnoxious buildings, and not leave so much as one stone upon another. It matters wonderfully little whether we term the Pope the director of Ireland or the dictator of Ireland: while Ireland is Catholic, the pontiff is, and must be, its virtual sovereign. The British power is limited in that unhappy island to the work of imposing taxes, — imposing, not gathering, for the taxes are taken up by the priests and sent to Rome; while to us is left the duty of feeding a country which clerical rapacity and tyranny has made a country of beggars. Thus the Pope's yoke is not whit lighter that, instead of calling it temporal supremacy, we call it "spiritual jurisdiction," or even "spiritual direction." It would yield, we are disposed to think, wonderfully little consolation to the unhappy sovereign whose throne is struck from under him, and whose kingdom is plunged into contention and civil war, to be told that the Pope in this has acted, not by *jurisdiction*, but by *direction*; that he exercises this power, not as lord paramount of his realm, but as lord paramount of his conscience; that, in fact, it is his conscience, and not his territory, that he holds as a fief of the papal see; and that he is enduring this castigation from the pontifical ferula, not in his capacity of king, but in his capacity of Christian. The unhappy monarch, we say, would find but little solace in this nice distinction; and, even at the risk of adding to both his offence and his punishment, might denounce it as a wretched quibble.

These, then, are the two points between which the supremacy oscillates — *direction* and *divine right*. It never sinks lower than the former; it cannot rise higher than the latter. But it is important to bear in mind that, whether it stands at the one or at the other of these points, it is supremacy still. We have already indicated that the temporal and spiritual jurisdictions are co-ordinate. This, we believe, is the only rational, as it is undoubtedly the scriptural view of the subject. The liberties of society can be maintained only by maintaining the divinely-appointed equilibrium between the two. If we make the temporal preponderate, we have Erastianism, or the slavery of the Church. If we make the spiritual preponderate, we have Popery, or the slavery of the State. The popish element entered into the jurisdiction of the Church when spiritual independence was transmuted into spiritual supremacy. This happened about the sixth century, when the Bishop of Rome claimed to be Christ's vicar. From that time the popes began to interfere in temporal matters by *direction*; for it is curious to note, that the supremacy, as defined in the modern theory, has come back to its beginnings, to run, of course, the same career, should the state of the world permit. At the period of Gregory VII. it ceased to be *direction*, and became a *jurisdiction*, and so continued down till the Reformation. Since that time it has been slowly returning through the intermediate stages of *indirect temporal power*, — of *purely spiritual jurisdiction*, — to its original form of *direction*, at which it now stands. But the root of the matter is the claim to be Christ's vicar; and till that is torn up, the evil and malignant principle cannot be eradicated. The supremacy may change shapes; it may go into a nutshell, as some philosophers have held the whole universe may do; but it can develope itself as suddenly; and, let the world become favourable, it will speedily shoot up into its former colossal dimensions, overshadowing all earthly jurisdiction, and claiming equality with, if not supremacy above, divine authority. We repeat, according to the modern theory, to go no higher, all Christendom holds its conscience as a fief of the Roman see; and we trust pontifical dignities will forgive the homely metaphor by which we seek to show them the extent of their own power. The governing power in the world is conscience, or whatever else may occupy its place; and he who governs it governs the world. But the pontiff is the infallible and supreme director of conscience. He sits above it, like the driver of a railway train behind his engine. An ingenious apologist might make out a case of limited powers in behalf of the latter, showing how little he has to do with either the course or velocity of the train. "He does not drag the train," might such say; "he has not power enough to move a single carriage; he but regulates the steam." Here is the Pope astride his famous ecclesiastical engine, with all the Catholic states of Europe dragging at his heels, and careering along at a great rate. Here is the Bourbon family-coach, which upset so recently, pitching its occupant in the mud, looking as new as it is possible for an old battered vehicle to do by the help of fresh tri-colour paint and varnish; here is the old imperial car which Austria picked up for a trifle when the Caesars had no longer any need for it, — here it is, blazoned with the bloody beak and iron talons of the double-headed eagle; here is the Spanish state-coach, hurtling along in the tawdry and tattered finery of its better days, its wheels worn to their spokes, and its motion made up of but a succession of jerks and bounds; here is the Neapolitan vehicle and the Tuscan vehicle, and others lumbering and crazy; and here, in front, is the famous engine St. Peter, snorting and puffing away; and here is Peter himself as engineer, with superstition for a propelling power, and excommunication for a steam-whistle, and tradition for spectacles, to enable him to keep on the rails of apostolic succession, and prevent his being bogged in heresy. It would be very wrong to say that he drags along this great train. No; he only turns the handle, to let on or shut off the steam; shovels in coals, manages the valves, blows his whistle at times with eldrich screech, and catches at his three-storied cap, which the wind blows off now and then. It is not *jurisdiction*, but *direction*, with which he favours the members of his tail: nevertheless, it moves where, when, and as fast as he pleases.

But something in a somewhat more classic vein would doubtless be deemed more befitting the pure and lofty function of the pontiff. The Romanists have exalted their Father, as the Pagans did their Jove, into an empyrean, far above sublunary affairs. In that eternal calm he issues his infallible decisions, thinking, the while, no more of this little ball of earth, or of the angry passions that contend upon it, than if it had yet to be created. Or if at times the thought does cross the pontifical mind that there are such things in the world beneath him as cannon and sabres, and that these are often had recourse to to execute the determinations of infallibility, how can he help it? He must needs discharge his office as the world's spiritual *director*; he dare not refrain from pronouncing infallibly on those high questions of duty which are brought before him; and if others will have recourse to material weapons in carrying out his advice, he begs the world to understand that this is not his doing, and that he cannot be justly blamed for it. One cannot but wonder at the admirable distribution of parts among the innumerable actors by whom the play of the Papacy is carried on. From the stage-manager at Rome, to the lowest scene-shifter in Clonmel or Tipperary, each has his place, and keeps it too. When an unhappy monarch is so unfortunate as to incur the displeasure of mother church, the pontiff does not lay a finger upon him; he does not touch a hair of his head; no, not he; he only gives a wink to the bullies who, he knows, are not far off, and whose office it is to do the business; and thus the wretched farce goes.

Chapter VI: The Canon Law.

It would be bad enough that a system of the character we have described should exist in the world, and that there should be a numerous class of men all animated by its spirit, and sworn to carry into effect its principles. But this is not the worst of it. The system has been converted into a code. It exists, not as a body of maxims or principles, though in that shape its influence would have been great: it exists as a body of laws, by which every Romish ecclesiastic is bound to act, and which he is appointed to administer. This is termed CANON LAW. The canon law is the slow growth of a multitude of ages. It reminds us of those coral islands in the great Pacific, the terror of the mariner, which myriads and myriads of insects laboured to raise from the bottom to the surface of the ocean. One race of these little builders took up the work where another race had left it; and thus the mass grew unseen in the dark and sullen deep, whether calm or storm prevailed on the surface. In like fashion, monks and popes innumerable, working in the depth of the dark ages, with the ceaseless and noiseless diligence, though not quite so innocently as the little artificers to which we have referred, produced at last the hideous formation known as the canon law. This code, then, is not the product of one large mind, like the Code Justinian or the Code Napoleon, but of innumerable minds, all working intently and laboriously through successive ages on this one object. The canon law is made up of the constitutions or canons of councils, the decrees of popes, and the traditions which have at any time received the pontifical sanction. As questions arose they were adjudicated upon; new emergencies produced new decisions; at last it came to pass that there was scarce a point of possible occurrence on which infallibility had not pronounced. The machinery of the canon law, then, as may be easily imagined, has reached its highest possible perfection and its widest possible application. The statute-book of Rome, combining amazing flexibility with enormous power, like the most wonderful of all modern inventions, can regulate with equal ease the affairs of a kingdom and of a family. Like the elephant's trunk, it can crush an empire in its folds, or conduct the course of a petty intrigue, — fling a monarch from his throne, or plant the stake for the heretic. Like a net of steel forged by the Vulcan of the Vatican and his cunning artificers, the canon law encloses the whole of Catholic Christendom. A short discussion of this subject may not be without its interest at present, seeing Dr. Wiseman had the candour to tell us, that it is his intention to enclose Great Britain in this net, provided he meets with no obstruction, which he scarce thinks we will be so unreasonable as to offer. Seeing, then, it will not be Dr. Wiseman's fault if we have not a nearer acquaintance with canon law than we can boast at present, it may be worth while examining its structure, and endeavouring to ascertain our probable condition, once within this enclosure. Not that we intend to hold up to view all its monstrosities; the canon law is the entire Papacy viewed as a system of government: we can refer to but the more prominent points which bear upon the subject we are now discussing, — the supremacy; and these are precisely the points which have the closest connection with our own condition, should the agent of the pontiff in London be able to carry his intent into effect, and introduce the canon law, "the real and complete code of the Church," as he terms it. Here we shall do little more than quote the leading provisions of the code from the authorized books of Rome, leaving the canon law to commend itself to British notions of toleration and justice.

The false decretals of Isidore, already referred to, offered a worthy foundation for this fabric of unbearable tyranny. We pass, as not meriting particular notice, the earlier and minor compilations of Rheginon of Prum in the tenth century, Buchardus of Worms in the eleventh, and St. Ivo of Chartres in the twelfth. The first great collection of canons and decretals which the world was privileged to see was made by Gratian, a monk of Bologna, who about 1150 published his work entitled *Decretum Gratiani*. Pope Eugenius III. approved his work, which immediately became the highest authority in the western Church. The rapid growth of the papal tyranny soon superseded the *Decretum Gratiani*. Succeeding popes flung their decretals upon the world with a prodigality with which the diligence of compilers who gathered them up, and formed them into new codes, toiled to keep pace. Innocent III. and Honorius III. issued numerous rescripts and decrees, which Gregory IX. commissioned Raymond of Pennafort to collect and publish. This the Dominican did in 1234; and Gregory, in order to perfect this collection of infallible decisions, supplemented it with a goodly addition of his own. This is the more essential part of the canon law, and contains a copious system of jurisprudence, as well as rules for the government of the Church. But infallibility had not exhausted itself with these labours. Boniface VIII. in 1298 added a sixth part, which he named the *Sext*. A fresh batch of decretals was issued by Clement V. in 1313, under the title of *Clementines*. John XXII. in 1340 added the *Extravagantes*, so called because they extravagate, or straddle, outside the others. Succeeding pontiffs, down to Sixtus IV., added their extravagating articles, which came under the name of *Extravagantes Communes*. The government of the world was in some danger of being stopped by the very abundance of infallible law; and since the end of the fifteenth century nothing has been formally added to this already enormous code. We cannot say that this fabric of commingled assumption and fraud is finished even yet: it stands like the great Dom of Cologne, with the crane atop, ready to receive a new tier whenever infallibility shall begin again to build, or rather to arrange the materials it has been producing during the past four centuries. While Rome exists, the canon law must continue to grow. Infallibility will always be speaking; and every new deliverance of the oracle is another statute added to canon law. The growth of all other bodies is regulated by great natural laws. The tower of Babel itself, had its builders been permitted to go on with it, must have stopped at the point where the attractive forces of earth and of the other planets balance each other; but where is the canon law to end? "This general supremacy," says Hallam, "effected by the Roman Church over mankind in the twelfth and thirteenth centuries, derived material support from the promulgation of the canon law. The superiority of ecclesiastical to temporal power, or at least the absolute independence of the former, may be considered as a sort of key-note which regulates every passage in the canon law. It is expressly declared, that subjects owe no allegiance to an excommunicated lord, if after admonition he is not reconciled to the Church. And the rubric prefixed to the declaration of Frederick II.'s deposition in the Council of Lyons asserts that the Pope may dethrone the Emperor for lawful causes." "Legislation quailed," says Gavazzi, "before the new-born code of clerical command, which, in the slang of the dark ages, was called canon law. The principle which pollutes every page of this nefarious imposture is, that every human right, claim, property, franchise, or feeling, at variance with the predominance of the popedom, was *ipso facto* inimical to heaven and the God of eternal justice. In virtue of this preposterous prerogative, universal manhood became a priest's footstool; this planet a huge game-preserve for the Pope's individual shooting." We repeat, it is this law which Dr. Wiseman avows to be one main object of the papal aggression to introduce. Its establishment in Britain implies the utter prostration of all other authority. We have seen how it came into being. The next question is, What is it? Let us first hear the canon law on the subject of the spiritual and civil jurisdictions, and let us take note how it places the world under the dominion of one all-absorbing power, — a power which is not temporal certainly, neither is it purely spiritual, but which, for want of a better phrase, we may term pontifical.

"The constitutions of princes are not superior to ecclesiastical constitutions, but subordinate to them."

"The law of the emperors cannot dissolve the ecclesiastical law."

"Constitutions (civil, we presume) cannot contravene good manners and the decrees of the Roman prelates."

"Whatever belongs to priests cannot be usurped by kings."

"The tribunals of kings are subjected to the power of priests."

"All the ordinances of the apostolic seat are to be inviolably observed."

"The yoke which the holy chair imposes must be borne, although it may seem unbearable."

"The decretal epistles are to be ranked along with canonical scripture."

"The temporal power can neither loose nor bind the Pope."

"It does not belong to the Emperor to judge the actions of the Pope."

"The Emperor ought to obey, not command, the Pope."

Such is a specimen of the powers vested in the Pope by the canon law. It makes him the absolute master of kings, and places in his grasp all law and authority, so that he can annul and establish whatever he pleases. It is instructive also to observe, that this power he possesses through the spiritual supremacy; and, as confirmatory of what we have already stated respecting the *direct* and *indirect* temporal supremacy, that the two in their issues are identical, we may quote the following remarks of Reiffenstuel, in his textbook on the canon law, published at Rome in 1831: — "The supreme pontiff, or Pope, by virtue of the power immediately granted to him, can, in matters spiritual, and concerning the salvation of souls and the right government of the Church, make ecclesiastical constitutions for the whole Christian world. . . . . It must be confessed, notwithstanding, that the Pope, as vicar of Christ on earth, and universal pastor of his sheep, has indirectly (or in respect of the spiritual power granted to him by God, in order to the good government of the whole Church) a certain supreme power, for the good estate of the Church, if it be necessary, OF JUDGING

AND DISPOSING OF ALL THE TEMPORAL GOODS OF ALL CHRISTIANS." But we pursue our quotations.

"We ordain that kings, and bishops, and nobles, who shall permit the decrees of the Bishop of Rome in anything to be violated, shall be accursed, and be for ever guilty before God as transgressors against the Catholic faith."

"The Bishop of Rome may excommunicate emperors and princes, depose them from their states, and assoil their subjects from their oath of obedience to them."

"The Bishop of Rome may be judged of none but of God only."

"If the Pope should become neglectful of his own salvation, and of that of other men, and so lost to all good that he draw down with himself innumerable people by heaps into hell, and plunge them with himself into eternal torments, yet no mortal man may presume to reprehend him, forasmuch as he is judge of all, and is judged of no one."

This surely is license enough; and should the pontiff complain that his limits are still too narrow, we should be glad to know how they could possibly be made larger. But let us hear the canon law on the power of the Pope to annul oaths, and release subjects from their allegiance.

"The Bishop of Rome has power to absolve from allegiance, obligation, bond of service, promise, and compact, the provinces, cities, and armies of kings that rebel against him, and also to loose their vassals and feudatories."

"The pontifical authority absolves some from their oath of allegiance."

"The bond of allegiance to an excommunicated man does not bind those who have come under it."

"An oath sworn against the good of the Church does not bind; because that is not an oath, but a perjury rather, which is taken against the Church's interests."

We may glance next at the doctrine of the canon law on the subject of clerical immunities.

"It is not lawful for laymen to impose taxes or subsidies upon the clergy. If laics encroach upon cleric immunities, they are, after admonition, to be excommunicated. But in times of great necessity, the clergy may grant assistance to the State, with permission of the Bishop of Rome."

"It is not lawful for a layman to sit in judgment upon a clergyman. Secular judges who dare, in the exercise of a damnable presumption, to compel priests to pay their debts, are to be restrained by spiritual censures."

"The man who takes the money of the Church is as guilty as he who commits homicide. He who seizes upon the lands of the Church is excommunicated, and must restore four-fold."

"The wealth of dioceses and abbacies must in nowise be alienated. It is not lawful for even the Pope himself to alienate the lands of the Church."

Should the Romish priesthood ever come to be a twentieth of the male population of Britain, as is well nigh the case in Italy and Spain, it is not difficult to imagine the comfortable state of society which must ensue with so numerous a body withdrawn from useful labour, exempt from public burdens, paying their debts only when they please, committing all sorts of wickedness uncontrolled by the ordinary tribunals, and plying vigorously the ghostly machinery of the confessional and purgatory to convey the nation's property into the treasury of their Church; and once there, there for ever. It is useless henceforth, unless to feed "holy men," — the term by which Rome designates her consecrated bands of idle, ignorant, sorning monks, and vagabondising friars and priests. No wonder that Dr. Wiseman is so anxious to introduce the canon law, which brings with it so many sweets to the clergy.

There is but one other point on which we shall touch: What says the canon law respecting heresy? In the judgment of Rome we are heretics; and therefore it cannot but be interesting to enquire how we are likely to be dealt with should the canon law ever be established in Britain, and what means the agents of the Vatican would adopt to purge our realm from the taint of our heresy. There is no mistaking the means, whatever may be thought of them. The Church has two swords; and, in the case of heresy, the vigorous use of both, but especially the temporal, is strictly enjoined.

In the decretals of Gregory IX., a heretic is defined to be a man "who, in whatever way, or by whatever vain argument, is led away and dissents from the orthodox faith and Catholic religion which is professed by the Church of Rome." The circumstance of baptism and initiation into the Christian faith distinguishes the heretic from the infidel and the Jew. The fitting remedies for the cure of this evil are, according to the canon law, the following: —

It is commanded that archbishops and bishops, either personally, or by their archdeacons or other fit persons, go through and visit their dioceses once or twice every year, and inquire for heretics, and persons suspected of heresy. Princes, or other supreme power in the commonwealth, are to be admonished and required to purge their dominions from the filth of heresy.

This goodly work of purgation is to be conducted in the following manner: —

I. Excommunication. This sentence is to be pronounced not only on notorious heretics, and those suspected of heresy, but also on those who harbour, defend, or assist them, or who converse familiarly with them, or trade with them, or hold communion of any sort with them.

II. Proscription from all offices, ecclesiastical or civil, — from all public duties and private rights.

III. Confiscation of all their goods.

IV. The last punishment is DEATH; sometimes by the sword, — more commonly by fire.

Pope Honorius II., in his Decretals, speaks in a precisely similar style. Under the head *De Hereticis* we find him enumerating a variety of dissentients from Rome, and thus disposing of them: — "And all heretics, of both sexes and of every name, we damn to perpetual infamy; we declare hostility against them; we account them accursed, and their goods confiscated; nor can they ever enjoy their property, or their children succeed to their inheritance; inasmuch as they grievously offend against the Eternal as well as the temporal king." The decree goes on to declare, that as regards princes who have been required and admonished by the Church, and have neglected to purge their kingdoms from heretical pravity a year after admonition, their lands may be taken possession of by any Catholic power who shall undertake the labour of purging them from heresy.

We shall close these extracts from the code of Rome's jurisprudence with one tremendous canon.

"Temporal princes shall be reminded and exhorted, and, if need be, *compelled* by spiritual censures, to discharge every one of their functions; and that, as they would be accounted faithful, so, for the defence of the faith, they *publicly make oath that they will endeavour*, bona fide, *with all their might, to extirpate from their territories all heretics marked by the Church*; so that when any one is about to assume any authority, whether of a permanent kind or only temporary, he shall be held bound to confirm his title by this oath. And if a temporal prince, being required and admonished by the Church, shall neglect to purge his kingdom from this heretical pravity, the metropolitan and other provincial bishops *shall bind him in the fetters of excommunication*; and if he obstinately refuse to make satisfaction within the year, it shall be notified to the supreme pontiff, that then *he may declare his subjects absolved from their allegiance, and bestow their lands upon good Catholics*, who, the heretics being exterminated, may possess them unchallenged, and preserve them in the purity of the faith."

"Those are not to be accounted homicides who, fired with zeal for Mother Church, may have killed excommunicated persons."

We shall add to the above the episcopal oath of allegiance to the Pope. That oath contemplates the pontiff in both his characters of a temporal monarch and a spiritual sovereign; and, of consequence, the fealty to which the swearer binds himself is of the same complex character. It is taken not only by archbishops and bishops, but by all who receive any dignity of the Pope; in short, by the whole ruling hierarchy of the monarchy of Rome. It is "not only," says the learned annotator Catalani, "a profession of canonical obedience, but an *oath of fealty*, not unlike that which vassals took to their direct lord." We quote the oath only down to the famous clause enjoining the persecution of heretics: —

"*I. N., elect* of the church of N., *from henceforward will be faithful* and obedient *to St. Peter* the apostle, *and to the holy Roman Church, and to our Lord* the Lord N. *Pope N., and to his successors, canonically coming in. I will neither advise*, consent, *or do anything that they may lose life or member, or that their persons may be seized*, or hands anywise laid upon them, or any injuries offered to them, under any pretence whatsoever. *The counsel which they shall intrust me withal, by themselves*, their messengers, *or letters, I will not* knowingly *reveal to any to their prejudice. I will help them to defend and keep the Roman Papacy*, and the royalties of St. Peter, *saving my order, against all men. The legate of the apostolic see, going and coming, I will honourably treat and help in his necessities.* The rights, honours, privileges, and authority of the holy Roman Church, of our lord the Pope, and his foresaid successors, I will endeavour to preserve, defend, increase, and advance. I will not be in any council, action, or treaty, in which shall be plotted against our said lord, and the said Roman Church, anything to the hurt or prejudice of their persons, right, honour, state, or power; and if I shall know any such thing to be treated or agitated by any whatsoever, I will hinder it to my power; and, as soon as I can, will signify it to our said lord, or to some other, by whom it may come to his knowledge. The rules of the holy fathers, the apostolic decrees, ordinances, or disposals, reservations, provisions, and mandates, I will observe with all my might, and cause to be observed by others. *Heretics, schismatics, and rebels to our said lord, or his foresaid successors, I will to my power persecute and oppose.*"

Such is a sample of Rome's infallible code. The canon law cannot cease to be venerated while hypocrisy and tyranny bear any value among men. It is by this law that Rome would govern the world, would the world let her; and it is by this law that she is desirous especially to govern Britain. This explains what Rome understands by a spiritual jurisdiction. She disclaims the temporal supremacy, and professes to reign only by *direction*; but we can now understand what a direction, acting according to canon law, and working through the machinery of the confessional, would speedily land us in. The moment the canon law is set up, the laws of Britain are overthrown, and the rights and liberties which they confer would henceforth be among the things that were. The government of the realm would become priestly, and the secular jurisdiction would be a mere appanage of the sacerdotal. Red hats and cowls would fill the offices of state and the halls of legislation, and would enact those marvels of political wisdom for which Spain and Italy are so justly renowned. A favoured class, combining the laziness of Turks with the rapacity of Algerines, would speedily spring up; and, to enable them to live in idleness, or in something worse, the "tale of bricks" would be doubled to the people. Malefactors of every class, instead of crossing the Atlantic, as now, would simply tie the Franciscan's rope round their middle, or throw the friar's cloak over their consecrated shoulders. The Bible would disappear as the most pestiferous of books, and the good old cause of ignorance would triumph. A purification of our island on a grand scale, from three centuries of heresy, would straightway be undertaken. As Protestants (the worst of all heretics) our lives would be of equal value with those of the wolf or the tiger; and it would be not less a virtue to destroy us, only the mode of despatch might not be so quick and merciful. The wolf would be shot down at once; the Protestant would be permitted to edify the Catholic by the prolongation of his dying agonies. Our Queen would have a twelvemonth's notice to make her peace with Rome, or abide the consequences. Should she disdain becoming a vassal of the Roman see, a crusade would be preached against her dominions, and every soldier in the army of the Holy League would be recompensed with the promise of paradise, and of as much of the wealth of heretical Albion as he could appropriate. These consequences would follow the introduction of the canon law, as certainly as darkness follows the setting of the sun.

But these effects would not be realized in a day. This tremendous tyranny would overtake the realm as night overtakes the earth. First, the Roman Catholics in Britain would be habituated to the government of this code; and it is to them only that Dr. Wiseman, making a virtue of necessity, proposes meanwhile to extend it. Having formed a colony governed by the code of Rome in the heart of a nation under the code of Britain, the agent of the Vatican would be able thus to inaugurate his system.. His *imperium in imperio*, once fairly set up, would be daily extending by conversions. A Jesuit's school here, a nunnery and cathedral there, would enlarge the sphere of the canon law, and fasten silently but tenaciously its manacles upon the community. Give Rome darkness enough, and she can do anything, — govern by canon law, with equal ease, a family or the globe. We must look fairly at the case. Let us suppose that this law is put in operation in Britain, though confined at first to members of the Romish Church. Well, then, we have a colony in the heart of the country actually released from their allegiance to the sovereign. They are the subjects of canon law, and that teaches unmistakeably the supremacy of the pontiff, and holds as null all authority that interferes with his; and especially does it ignore the authority of heretical sovereigns. Should these persons continue to obey the civil laws, they would do so simply because there is an army in the country. Their real rulers would be the priesthood, whom they dared not disobey, under peril of their eternal salvation. All their duties as citizens must be performed according to ghostly direction. Their votes at the poll must be given for the priest's nominee. They must speak and vote in Parliament for the interests of Rome, not of England. In the witness-box they must swear *to* or *against* the fact, as the interests of the Church may require. And as a false oath is no perjury, so killing is no murder, according to canon law, when heresy and heretics are to be purged out. Thus, every duty, from that of conducting a parliamentary opposition down to heading a street brawl, must be done with a view to the account to be rendered in the confessional. Allegiance to the Pope must override all other duties, spiritual and temporal. Popery, a deceiver to others, is a tyrant to its own.

Should we, then, permit the introduction of the canon law, the Greek who opened the gates to the Trojan horse will henceforward pass for a wise and honest man. We must not have our understandings insulted by being told that this law is meliorated. It is the code of an infallible Church, and not one jot or tittle of it can ever be changed. Rome and the canon law must stand or perish together. Besides, it is only twenty years since it was republished in Rome, under the very eye of the Pope, without one single blasphemy or atrocity lopped off. Nor must we listen to the assurance that the laws of Britain will protect us from the canon law. We may have perfect confidence in the strength of our fortress, though we do not permit the enemy to plant a battery beneath its walls. But the trust is false; — the law of Britain will not be a sufficient protection in the long run. Dr. Wiseman demands permission to erect a hierarchy in order that he may govern the members of his Church in England by canon law. We refuse to grant him leave, and the doctor raises the cry of persecution, and prefers a charge of intolerance, because we will not permit him to give full development to the code of his Church, — a code, be it remembered, which teaches that the Pope can annul the constitutions of princes, — that it is damnable presumption in a lay judge to compel an ecclesiastic to pay his debts, — and that it is no crime to swear a false oath against a heretic, or even to kill him, if the massacre of his character or his person can in anywise benefit the Church. The doctor, we say, even now raises the cry of persecution against us, because we will not permit him to put this code into effect by erecting the hierarchy; and many Protestants profess to see not a little force in his reasoning. But suppose we should grant leave to erect the hierarchy, and so help Dr. Wiseman to put the canon law into working gear; what would be his next demand? Why, that we should subject the laws of England to instant revision, so as to conform them to the canon law. "You allowed me," would the doctor say, "to introduce the canon law, and yet you forbid me to give it full development. Here it is perpetually checked and fettered by your enactments. I demand that these shall be rescinded in all points where they clash with canon law. You virtually pledged yourselves to this when you sanctioned the hierarchy. Why did you allow me to introduce this law, if you will not suffer me to work it? I insist on your implementing your pledge, otherwise I shall brand you as persecutors." The Protestants who gave way in the former instance will find it hard to make good their resistance here. In this manner point after point will be carried, and a despotism worse than that of Turkey, and growing by moments, will be established in the heart of this free country. All lets and hindrances in its path will crumble into dust before the insidious and persistent attacks of this conspiracy. Its agents will act with the celerity and combination of an army, while the leaders will remain invisible. It will attack in a form in which it cannot be repelled. It will use the Constitution to undermine the Constitution. It will basely take advantage of the privileges which liberty bestows, to overthrow liberty: and it will never rest content till the mighty Dagon of co-mingled blasphemy and tyranny known as canon law is enthroned above the ruins of British liberty and justice, and the neck of prince and peasant is bent in ignominious vassalage.

Were Lucifer to turn legislator, and indite a code of jurisprudence for the government of mankind, he would find the work done already to his hand in the canon canon law. Surveying the labours of his renowned servants with a smile of grim complacency, — sorely puzzled what to alter, where to amend, or how to enlarge with advantage, — unwilling to run the risk of doing worse what his predecessors had done better, — he would wisely forgo all thoughts of legislative and literary fame, and be content to let well alone. Instead of wasting the midnight oil over a new work, he would confine his labours to the more useful, if less ambitious, task of writing a recommendatory preface to the canon law.

Chapter VII: That the Church of Rome Neither has Nor Can Change Her Principles on the Head of the Supremacy.

We have shown in the foregoing chapter, that nothing in all past history is better authenticated than the fact that the Papacy has claimed supremacy over kings and kingdoms. We have also shown that this claim is a legitimate inference from the fundamental principles of the Papacy, — that these principles are of such a nature as to imply a Divine right, and that the arrogant claim based on these principles Rome has not only asserted, but succeeded in establishing. Her doctors have taught it, her casuists have defended it, her councils have ratified it, the papal bulls have been based upon it, and her popes have reduced it to practice, in the way of deposing monarchs, and transferring their kingdoms to others. "Seeing it hath been current among their divines of greatest vogue and authority," reasons Barrow, "the great masters of their school, — seeing by so large a consent and concurrence, during so long a time, it may pretend (much better than divers other points of great importance) to be confirmed by tradition or prescription, — why should it not be admitted for a doctrine of the holy Roman Church, *the mother and mistress of all churches*? How can they who disavow this notion be the true sons of that mother, or faithful scholars of that mistress? How can they acknowledge any authority in that Church to be infallible, or certain, or obliging to assent. No man apprehending it false, seemeth capable, with good conscience, to hold communion with those who profess it; for, upon supposition of its falsehood, the Pope and his chief adherents are the teachers and abettors of the highest violation of Divine commands, and most enormous sins of usurpation, tyranny, imposture, perjury, rebellion, murder, rapine, and all the villanies complicated in the practical influence of this doctrine."

But does the fact, so clearly established from history, that the Church of Rome not only claimed, but succeeded in making good her claim, to universal supremacy, suggest no fears for the cause of public liberty in time to come? Has the Papacy renounced this claim? Has she confessed that it is a claim which she ought never to have made, and which she would not now make were she in the same circumstances? So far from this, it can be shown, that though Gosselin and other modern writers have attempted to apologise for the past usurpations of the Papacy, and to explain the grounds on which these acts were based, as being not so much definite principles as popular beliefs and concessions; and though they have written with the obvious intention of leading their readers to infer that the Papacy would not so act now were it placed in the same circumstances as before; yet it can be shown that the Papacy has not renounced this claim, — that it never can renounce it, — and that, were opportunity to offer, it would once more take upon itself the high prerogative of disposing of crowns and kingdoms. How does this appear? In the first place, if Rome has renounced this alleged right, let the deed of renunciation be produced. The fact is notorious, that she *did* depose monarchs. When or where has she confessed that in doing so she stopped out of her sphere, and was betrayed by a guilty ambition into an act of flagrant usurpation? The contrition must be as public as the crime is notorious. But there exists no such deed; and, in lieu of a public and formal renunciation, we cannot accept the explanations and apologies, the feeble and qualified denials, of modern writers. It is the interest of these writers to keep discreetly in the shade claims and pretensions which it would be dangerous meanwhile to avow. And even granting that these disavowals were more explicit than they are, and granting, too, that they were sincerely made, they carry no authority with them. They are merely private opinions, and do not bind the Church; and there is too much reason to believe that they would be repudiated by Rome whenever she found it safe or advantageous to do so. The case stands thus: — the Church of Rome, in violation of the principle of a co-ordinate jurisdiction in spiritual and civil affairs, and in violation of her own proper character and objects as a church, has claimed and exercised supremacy over kings and kingdoms; but she has not to this hour acknowledged that she erred in doing so, nor has she renounced the principles which led to that error; and so long as she maintains an attitude which is a virtual defence and justification of all her past pretensions, both in their theory and their practice, the common sense of mankind must hold that she is ready to repeat the same aggressions whenever the same occasions and opportunities shall occur.

It is also to be borne in mind, that though the Church of Rome is silent on her claims meanwhile, we are not warranted to take that silence for surrender. They are not claims renounced; they are simply claims not asserted. The foundation of these claims, and their desirableness, remain unchanged. Moreover, it is important to observe, that wherever the action of the Romish Church is restrained, it is restrained by a power from without, and not by any principle or power from within. Her prerogatives have sometimes been wrested from her, but never without the Church of Rome putting on record her solemn protest. She has declared that the authority of which she was deprived was rightfully hers, and that to forbid her to use it was an unrighteous interference with her just powers; which means, that she was purposed to reclaim these rights the moment she thought she could make the attempt with success. In those countries where she still bears sway, we find her giving effect to her pretensions to the very utmost which the liberty allowed her will permit; and it is certainly fair to infer, that were her liberty greater, her pretensions would be greater too, not in assumption only, but in practice also.

But, second, the Church of Rome cannot renounce this claim, because she is infallible. We shall afterwards prove that that Church does hold the doctrine of the infallibility, and that it is one of the fundamental principles on which her system is built. Meanwhile we assume it. Being infallible, she can never believe what is false, or practise what is wrong, and is therefore incapable in all time coming of renouncing any one doctrine she ever taught, or departing from any one claim she ever asserted. To say that such an opinion was taught as true ages ago, but is not now recognised as sound, or held to be obligatory, is perfectly allowable to Protestants, for they make no claim to infallibility. They may err, and they may own that their fathers have erred; for though they have an infallible standard, — the Word of God, — in which all the fundamental doctrines appertaining to salvation are so clearly taught, that there is no mistaking them on the part of any one who brings ordinary powers and ordinary candour, with a due reliance on the Spirit's promised aid, to their investigation, yet there are subordinate matters, especially points of administration, on which a longer study of the Word of God will throw clearer light. Protestants, therefore, may with perfect consistency amend their system, both in its theory and in its practice, and so bring it into nearer conformity with the great standard of truth. They have built up no wall of adamant behind them. Not so Rome. She is infallible; and, as such, must stand eternally on the ground she has taken up. It is a double thraldom which she has perpetrated: she has enslaved the human understanding, and she has enslaved herself. The dogma of infallibility, like a chain which mortal power cannot break, has tied her to the bulls of popes, and the decrees of councils and canonists; and it matters not how gross the error, how glaring the absurdity, or how manifest the contradiction, into which they may have fallen; the error is part of her infallibility, and must be maintained. The Church of Rome can never plead that she believed so and so, and acted agreeably thereto, six hundred years ago, but that she has since come to think differently on the point, — that a deeper knowledge of the Bible has corrected her views. Infallibility was infallibility six hundred years ago, as really as it is so to-day. Infallibility can never be either less or more. To an infallible Church it is all one whether her decisions were delivered yesterday or a thousand years ago. The decision of ten centuries since is as much a piece of infallibility as the decision of ten hours since. With Rome a day is as a thousand years, and a thousand years are but as a day.

Nor can the Church of Rome avail herself of the excuse, that such an opinion was held by her in the dark ages, when there was little knowledge of any sort in the world. There was infallibility in it, however, according to the Church of Rome. In those ages, that Church taught as infallible that the earth was stationary, while the sun rolled round it, and that the earth was not a globe, but an extended plain. The apology that this was before the birth of the modern astronomy, however satisfactory in the mouth of another, would in her mouth be a condemnation of her whole system. The ages were dark enough, no doubt; but infallibility then was still infallibility. Why, it is precisely at such times that we need infallibility. An infallibility that cannot see in the dark is not worth much. If it cannot speak till science has first spoken, but at the risk of falling into gross error, why, we think the world might do as well without as with infallibility. A prophet that restricts his vaticinations to what has already come to pass, possesses no great share of the prophetic gift. The beacon whose light cannot be seen but when the sun is above the horizon, will be but a sorry guide to the mariner; and that infallibility which cannot move a step without losing itself in a quagmire, except when science and history pioneer its way, is but ill fitted to govern the world. The infallibility has made three grand discoveries, — the first in the department of astronomy, the second in the department of geography, and the third in the department of theology. The first is, that the sun revolves round our earth; the second is, that the world is an extended plain; and the third and greatest is, that the Pope is God's vicar. If the Church of Rome be true, these three are all equally infallible truths.

To dwell a little longer on this infallibility, and the unchangeableness with which it endows the Church of Rome, — that Church is not only infallible as a church or society, but every separate article of her creed is infallible. In fact, Popery is just a bundle of infallible axioms, every one of which is as unalterably and everlastingly true as are the theorems of Euclid. How impossible that a creed of this character can be either amended or changed! Amended it cannot be, for it is already infallible; changed still less can it be, for to change infallible truth would be to embrace error. What would be thought of the mathematician who should affirm that geometry might be changed, — that though it was a truth when Euclid flourished, that the three angles of a triangle were together equal to two right angles, it does not follow that it is a truth now? Geometry is what Popery claims to be, — a system of infallible truths, and therefore eternally immutable. Between the trigonometrical survey of Britain in our own times, and those annual measurements of their fields which were wont to be undertaken by the early Egyptians on the reflux of the Nile, there is an intervening period of not less than forty centuries, and yet the two processes were based on the identical geometrical truths. The two angles at the base of an isosceles triangle were then equal to one another, and they are so still, and will be myriads of ages beyond the present moment, and myriads and myriads of miles away from the sphere of our globe. Popery claims for her truths an equally necessary, independent, universal, and eternal existence. When we talk of the one being changed, we talk not a whit more irrationally than when we talk of the other being changed. There is not a dogma in the bullarium which is not just as infallible a truth as any axiom of geometry. It follows that the canon law is as unchangeable as Euclid. The deposing power having been received by the Church as an infallible truth, must be an infallible truth still. Truth cannot be truth in one age and error in the next. The infallibility can never wax old. To this attribute has the Church of Rome linked herself: she must not shirk its conditions. Were she to confess that in any one instance she had ever adopted or practised error, — above all, were she to grant that she had erred in the great acts of her supremacy, — she would virtually surrender her whole cause into the hands of Protestants.

We find Cardinal Perron adopting this precise line of argument on a very memorable occasion. After the assassination of Henry IV. by the Jesuits, it was proposed, for the future security of government, to abjure the papal doctrine of deposing kings for heresy. When the three estates assembled in 1616, Cardinal Perron, as the organ of the rest of the Gallican clergy, addressed them on the subject. He argued, that were they to abjure the pope's right to depose heretical sovereigns, they would destroy the communion hitherto existing between them and other churches, — nay, even with the church of France before their own time: that seeing the popes had claimed and exercised this right, they could not take the proposed oath without acknowledging that the Pope and the whole Church had erred, both in faith and in things pertaining to salvation, and that for many ages the Catholic Church had perished from the earth: that they behoved to dig up the bones of a multitude of French doctors, even the bones of St. Thomas and St. Bonaventure, and burn them upon the altar, as Josiah burnt the bones of the false prophet. So reasoned the Cardinal; and we should like to see those who now attempt to deny the Pope's deposing power try to answer his arguments.

The infallibility is the iron hoop around the Church of Rome. In every variety of outward circumstances, and amid the most furious conflicts of discordant opinions, that Church is and must ever be the same. Change or amendment she can never know. She cannot repent, because she cannot err. Repentance and amendment are for the fallible only. Far more marvellous would it be to hear that she had changed than to hear that she had been destroyed. It will one day be told the world, and the nations will clap their hands at the news, that the Papacy has fallen; but it will never be told that the Papacy has repented. She will be destroyed, not amended.

But, in the third place, the Papacy cannot renounce this claim without denying its essential and fundamental principles. Between the dogma that the Pope is Christ's vicar and the claim of supremacy, there is, as we have shown, the most strict and logical connection. The latter is but the former transmuted into fact; and if the one is renounced, the other must go with it. On the assumption that the Pope is Christ's vicar is built the whole fabric of Popery. On this point, according to Bellarmine, hangs the whole of Christianity; and one of the latest expounders of the Papacy re-echoes this sentiment: — "Wanting the sovereign pontiff," says De Maistre, "Christianity wants its sole foundation." Anything, therefore, that would go to annihilate that assumption, would raze, as Bellarmine admits, the foundations of the whole system. The Papacy, then, has it in its choice to be the superior of kings or nothing. It has no middle path. *Aut Caesar aut nullus*. The Pope is Christ's vicar, and so lord of the earth and of all its empires, or his pretensions are unfounded, his religion a cheat, and himself an impostor.

It is necessary here to advert to the popular argument, — a miserable fallacy, no doubt, but one that possesses an influence that better reasons are sometimes found to want. The world is now so greatly changed that it is impossible not to believe that Popery also is changed. It is incredible that it should now think of enforcing its antiquated claims. We find this argument in the mouths of two classes of persons. It is urged by those who see that the only chance which the Papacy has of succeeding in its present criminal designs is to persuade the world that it is changed, and who accordingly report as true what they know to be false. And, second, it is employed by those who are ignorant of the character of Popery, and who conclude, that because all else is changed, this too has undergone a change. But the question is not, Is the world altered? — this all admit; but, Is the Papacy altered? A change in the one gives not the slightest ground to infer a change in the other. The Papacy itself makes no claim of the sort; it repudiates the imputation of change; glories in being the same in all ages; and with this agrees its nature, which shuts out the very idea of change, or rather makes change synonymous with destruction. It is nothing to prove that society is changed, though it is worth remembering that the essential elements of human nature are the same in all ages, and that the changes of which so much account is made lie mainly on the surface. The question is, Is the Papacy changed? It cannot be shown on any good ground that it is. And while the system continues the same, its influence, its mode of action, and its aims, will be identical, let the circumstances around it be what they may. It will mould the world to itself, but cannot be moulded by it. Is not this a universal law, determining the development alike of things, of systems, and of men? Take a seed from the tomb of an Egyptian mummy, carry it into the latitude of Britain, and bury it ill the earth; the climate, and many other things, will all be different, but the seed is the same. Its incarceration of four thousand years has but suspended, not annihilated, its vital powers; and, being the same seed, it will grow up into the same plant; its leaf, and flower, and fruit, will all be the same they would have been on the banks of the Nile under the reign of the Pharaohs. Or let us suppose that the mummy, the companion of its long imprisonment, should start into life. The brown son of Egypt, on looking up, would find the world greatly changed; — the Pharaohs gone, the pyramids old, Memphis in ruins, empires become wrecks, which had not been born till long after his embalmment; but amid all these changes he would feel that he was the same man, and that his sleep of forty centuries had left his dispositions and habits wholly unchanged. Nay, will not the whole human race rise at the last day with the same moral tastes and dispositions with which they went to their graves, so that to the characters with which they died will link on the allotments to which they shall rise? The infallibility has stereotyped the Papacy, just as nature has stereotyped the seed, and death the characters of men; and, let it slumber for one century, or twenty centuries, it will awake with its old instincts. And while as a system it continues unchanged, its action on the world must necessarily be the same. It is not more accordant with the law of their natures that fire should burn and air ascend, than it is accordant with the nature of the Papacy that it should claim the supremacy, and so override the consciences of men and the laws of kingdoms.

Nay, so far is it from being a truth that Popery is growing a better thing, that the truth lies the other way: it is growing rapidly and progressively worse. So egregiously do the class to which we have referred miscalculate, and so little true acquaintance do they show with the system on which they so confidently pronounce, that those very influences on which the rely for rendering the Papacy milder in spirit, and more tolerant in policy, are the very influences which are communicating a more defined stamp to its bigotry and a keener edge to its malignity. By an inevitable consequence, the Papacy must retrograde as the world advances. The diffusion of letters, the growth of free institutions, above all, the prevalence of true religion, are hateful to the Papacy; they threaten its very existence, and necessarily rouse into violent action all its more intolerant qualities. The most cursory survey of its history for the past six centuries abundantly attests the truth of what we now say. It was not till arts and Christianity began to enlighten southern Europe in the twelfth century, that Rome unsheathed the sword. The Reformation came next, and was followed by a new outburst of ferocity and tyranny on the part of Rome. Thus, as the world grows better, the Papacy grows worse. The Papacy of the present day, so far from being set off by a comparison of the Papacy of the middle ages, rather suffers thereby; for of the two, the latter certainly was the more tolerant in its actings. No thanks to Rome for being tolerant, when there is nothing to tolerate. No thanks that her sword rusts in its scabbard, when there is no heretical blood to moisten it. But let a handful of Florentines open a chapel for Protestant worship, and the deadly marshes of the Maremme will soon read them the lesson of the Papacy's tolerance; or let a poor Roman presume to circulate the Word of God, and he will have time in the papal dungeons to acquaint himself with Rome's new-sprung liberality; or let the

Queen's government build colleges in Ireland, to introduce a little useful knowledge into that model land of sacerdotal rule, and the anathemas which will instantly be hurled from every Popish altar on the other side of the Channel will furnish unmistakeable evidence as to the progress which the Church of Rome has recently made in the virtue of toleration. Assuredly Rome will not change so long as there are fools in the world to believe that she is changed.

At no former period, and by no former holder of the pontificate, was the primary principle of the Papacy more vigorously or unequivocally asserted, than it has been by the present pontiff. In his encyclical letter against the circulation of the Bible we find Pius IX. thus speaking: — "All who labour with you for the defence of the faith will have especially an eye to this, that they confirm, defend, and deeply fix in the minds of your faithful people that piety, veneration, and respect towards this supreme see of Peter, in which you, venerable brothers, so greatly excel. Let the faithful people remember that there here lives and presides, in the person of his successors, Peter, the prince of the apostles, whose dignity faileth not even in his unworthy heir. Let them remember that Christ the Lord hath placed in this chair of Peter the unshaken foundation of his Church; and that he gives to Peter himself the keys of the kingdom of heaven; and that he prayed, therefore, that his faith might fail not, and commanded him to confirm his brethren therein; so that the successor of St. Peter holds the primacy over the whole world, and is the true vicar of Christ and head of the whole Church, and father and doctor of all Christians." There is not a false dogma or a persecuting principle which Rome ever taught or practised, which is not contained, avowedly or implicitly, in this declaration. The Pope herein sets no limits to his spiritual sway but those of the world, — of course excommunicating all who do not belong to his Church; and claims a character, — "true vicar of Christ and head of the whole Church," — which vests in him temporal dominion equally unbounded and supreme.

The popes do not now send their *legates a latere* to the court of London or of Paris, to summon monarchs to do homage to Peter or transient tribute to Rome. The Papacy is too sagacious needlessly to awaken the fears of princes, or to send its messengers on what, meanwhile, would be a very bootless errand. But has the Pope renounced these claims? We have shown *a priori* that he cannot, and with this agrees the fact that he has not: therefore he must, in all fairness, be held as still retaining, though not actually asserting, this claim. No conclusion is more certain than this, that the essential principles of the system being the same, they will, in the same circumstances, practice the same evils and mischiefs in future which they have done in the past. What has been may be. In the sixth century, had any one pointed out the bearing of these principles, affirming that they necessarily led to supremacy over kings, one might have been excused for doubting whether practically this result would follow. But the same excuse is signally awanting in the nineteenth century. The world has had dire experience of the fact; it knows what the Papacy ispractically as well as *theoretically*. Moreover are not the modern chiefs of the Papacy as ambitious and as devoted to the aggrandizement of the Papacy as the pontiffs of the past? Is not universal dominion as tempting an object of ambition now as it was in the eleventh century? and, provided the popes can manage, either by craft or force, to persuade the world to submit to their rule, is any man so simple as to believe that they will not exercise it, — that they will modestly put aside the sceptre, and content themselves with the pastoral staff? There is nothing in that dominion, on their own principles, which is inconsistent with their spiritual character; nay the possession of temporal authority is essential to the completeness of that character, and to the vigour of their spiritual administration. Is it not capable of being made to subserve as effectually as ever the authority and influence of the Church? In times like the present, pontiffs may affect to undervalue the temporal supremacy; they may talk piously of throwing off the cares of State, and giving themselves wholly to their spiritual duties; but let such prospects open before them as were presented to the Gregories and the Leos of the past, and we shall see how long this horror of the world's pomps and riches, and this love of meditation and prayer, will retain possession of their breasts. The present occupant of the pontifical chair talked in this way of his temporal sovereignty; but the moment he came to lose that sovereignty, instead of venting his joy at having got rid of his burden, he filled Europe with the most dolorous complaints and outcries, and fulminated from his retreat at Gaeta the bitterest execrations and the most dreadful anathamas against all who had been concerned in the act of stripping him of his sovereignty. So far was Pius from betaking himself to the spiritual solace for which he had so thirsted, that he plunged headlong into the darkest intrigues and conspiracies against the independence of Italy, and sent his messengers to every Catholic court in Europe, exhorting and supplicating these powers to take up arms and restore him to his capital. The result, as all the world knows, was, that the young liberties of Italy were quenched in blood, and the throne of the triple tyrant was again set up. "The good shepherd giveth his life for the sheep," — so wrote they on the gates of Notre Dame; — "Pius IX. kills his." Accordingly, the doctrine now maintained by the pontiff and the advocates of the Papacy in every part of Europe is, that the sacerdotal and temporal sovereignties cannot be disjoined, and that the union of the two, in the person of the Pope, is indispensable to the welfare of the Church and the independence of its supreme bishop. But if it be essential to the good of the Church and the independence of its head that the Pope should be sovereign of the Roman States, the conclusion is inevitable, that it is equally essential for these objects that he should possess the temporal supremacy. Will not the same good, but on a far larger scale, flow from the possession of the temporal supremacy that now flows from the temporal sovereignty? and will not the loss of the former expose the Papacy to similar and much greater inconveniences and dangers than those likely to arise from the loss of the latter? When we confound the distinction between things civil and sacred, or rather, — for the error of Rome properly lies here, — when we deny the co-ordinate jurisdiction of the two powers, and subordinate the temporal to the spiritual, there is no limit to the amount of temporal power which may not be possessed and exercised by spiritual functionaries. If to possess any degree of temporal jurisdiction conduce to the authority of ecclesiastical rulers and the good of the Church, then the more of this power the better. The temporal supremacy is a better thing than the temporal sovereignty, in proportion as it is a more powerful thing. Thus, every argument for the sovereignty of the Pope is *a fortiori* an argument for the supremacy of the Pope. Why does he cling to the temporal sovereignty, but that he may provide for the dignity of his person and office, maintain his court in befitting splendour from the revenue of St. Peter's patrimony, transact with kings on something like a footing of equality, keep his spies at foreign courts in the shape of legates and nuncios, and by these means check heresy, and advance the interests of the universal Church? But as lord paramount of Europe, he will be able to accomplish all these ends much more completely than merely as sovereign of the Papal States. His spiritual thunder will possess far more terror when launched from a seat which rises in proud supremacy over thrones. The glory of his court, and the numbers of his returns, will be far more effectually provided for when able to subsidize all Europe, than when dependent simply on the limited and now beggared domains of the fisherman. With what vigour will he chastise rebellions nations, and reduce to obedience heretical sovereigns, when able to point against them the combined temporal and spiritual artillery! How completely will he purge out heresy, when at his powerful word every sword in Europe shall again leap from its scabbard! Will not bishops and cardinals be able to take high ground at foreign courts, when they can tell their sovereigns, "The Pope is as much your master as ours?" But this is but a tithe of the power and glory which the supremacy would confer upon the Church, and especially upon its head. To grasp the political power of Europe, and wield it in the dark, is the present object the Jesuits are striving to attain; and can any man doubt that, were the times favourable, they would exercise openly what they are now trying to wield by stealth? Never will the Papacy feel that it is in its proper place, or that it is in a position to carry out fully its peculiar mission, till, seated once more in absolute and unapproachable power upon the Seven Hills, it look down upon the kings of Europe as its vassals, and be worshipped by the nations as a God; and the turn that affairs are taking in the world appears to be forcing this upon the Papacy. A crisis has arrived in which, if the Church of Rome is to maintain herself, she must take higher ground than she has done since the Reformation. She has the alternative of becoming the head of Europe, or of being swept out of existence. A new era, such as neither the Pope nor his fathers have known, has dawned on the world. The French Revolution, after Napoleon had extinguished it in blood, as all men believed, has returned from its tomb, refreshed by its sleep of half a century, to do battle with the dynasties and hierarchies of Europe.

The first idea of the Papacy was to mount on the revolutionary wave, and be floated to the lofty seat it had formerly occupied. "Your Holiness has but one choice," Cicerovacchio is reported to have said to the Pope: "you may place yourself at the head of reform, or you will be dragged in the rear of revolution." The pontifical choice was fixed in favour of the former. Accordingly, the world was astonished by the unwonted sight of the mitre surmounted by the cap of liberty; the echoes of the Vatican were awakened by the strange sounds of "liberty and fraternity;" and the Papacy, wrinkled and hoar, was seen to coquette with the young revolution on the sacred soil of the Seven Hills. But nature had forbidden the banns; and no long time elapsed till it was discovered that the projected union was monstrous and impossible. The Church broke with the revolution; the harlot hastened to throw herself once more into the arms of her old Paramour the State; and now commenced the war of the Church with the democracy. It is plain that the issue of that war to the Papacy must be one of two things, — complete annihilation, or unbounded dominion. Rome must be all that she ever was, and more, or she must cease to be. Europe is not wide enough to hold both the old Papacy and the young Democracy; and one or other must go to the wall. Matters have gone too far to permit of the contest being ended by a truce or compromise; the battle must be fought out. If the Democracy shall triumph, a fearful retribution will be exercised on a Church which has proved herself to be essentially sanguinary and despotic; and if the Church shall overcome, the revolution will be cut up root and branch. It is not for victory, then, but for life, that both parties now fight. The gravity of the juncture, and the eminent peril in which the Papacy is placed, will probably spirit it on to some desperate attempt. Half-measures will not save it at such a crisis as this. To retain only the traditions of its power, and to practise the comparatively tolerant policy which it has pursued for the past half-century, will no longer either suit its purpose, or be found compatible with its continued existence. It must become the living, dominant Papacy once more. In order that it may exist, it must reign. We may therefore expect to witness some combined and vigorous attempt on the part of Popery to recover its former dominion. It has studied the genius of every people; it has fathomed the policy of every government; it knows the principles of every sect, and school, and club, — the sentiments and feelings of almost every individual; and with its usual tact and ability, it is attempting to control and harmonize all these various and conflicting elements, so as to work out its own ends. To those frightened by revolutionary excesses the Church of Rome announces herself as the asylum of order. To those scared and shocked by the blasphemies of Socialist infidelity she exhibits herself as the ark of the faith. To monarchs whom the revolution has shaken upon their thrones she promises a new lease of power, provided they will be ruled by her. And as regards those fiery spirits whom her other arts cannot tame, she has in reserve the unanswerable and silencing arguments of the dungeon and the scaffold. Popery is the soul of that re-action that is now in progress on the Continent, though, with her usual cunning, she puts the State in the foreground. it was the Jesuits who instigated and planned the expedition to Rome. It was the Jesuits who plotted the dreadful massacres in Sicily, who have filled the dungeons of Naples with thousands of innocent citizens, who drove into exile every Roman favourable to liberty and opposed to the Pope, who closed the clubs and fettered the press of France, Tuscany, Germany, and Austria; and, in fine, it was the Jesuits of Vienna who crushed the nationalities and counselled the judicial murders of Hungary. History will lay all this blood to the door of the Papacy. It has all been shed in pursuance of a plan concocted by the Church, — now under the government of Jesuitism, — to recover her former ascendancy. The common danger which in the late revolution threatened both Church and State, has made the two cling closely together. "I alone," — so, in effect, said the Church to the State, — "can save you. In me, and no where else, are to be found the principles of order and the centre of union. The spiritual weapons which it is mine to wield are alone able to combat and subdue the infidel and atheistic principles which have produced the revolution. Lend me your aid now, and promise me your submission in time to come, and I will reduce the masses to your authority." This reasoning was omnipotent, and the bargain was struck. Accordingly there is not a court of Catholic Europe where the Jesuit influence is not at this moment supreme. And it is happening at present, as it has happened at all former periods of confusion, that in proportion as the State loses the Church acquires strength. Although its companion in trouble, the Church is acting at this moment as the State's superior. She extends to the civil powers the benefit of her matchless policy and her universal organization. So stands the case, then. It must force itself upon the conviction of all, that this relation of the Church to the State is fraught with tremendous danger to the independence of the secular authority and the liberties of the world. In no fairer train could matters be for realizing all that Rome aspires to. And soon would she realize her aim, were it not that the present era differs from all preceding ones, in that there is an antagonist force in existence in the shape of an infidel Democracy. These two tremendous forces, — Democracy and Catholicism, — poise one another; and neither can reign so long as both exist. But who can tell how soon the equilibrium may be destroyed? Should the balance preponderate in favour of the Catholic element, — should Popery succeed in bringing over from the infidel and democratic camp a sufficient number of converts to enable her to crush her antagonist, — the supremacy is again in her hands. With Democracy collapsed, with the State exhausted and owing its salvation to the Church, and with a priesthood burning to avenge the disasters and humiliations of three centuries, wo to Europe! — the darkest page of its history would be yet to be written.

Book II: Dogmas of the Papacy.

Chapter I: The Popish Theology.

The Popish theology is based on the great fundamental truths of revelation. So far it agrees with the evangelical and Protestant scheme. Any attempt on the part of the Church of Rome to obscure or extinguish those doctrines which form the ultimate foundations of religion would have been singularly imprudent, and as futile as imprudent. By retaining these truths, and founding her system upon them, the Romish Church has secured to that system an authority and power which it never otherwise could have possessed. Building so far upon a divine foundation, she has been able to palm her whole system upon the world as divine. Had she come denying the very first principles of revealed truth, she would scarce have been able to obtain a hearing;-she would have been at once repudiated as an impostor. Popery saw and avoided the danger; and it has shown in this its usual dexterity and cunning. The system is not the less opposed to Scripture on that account, nor the less essentially superstitious. Paganism was essentially a system of idolatry, notwithstanding that it was founded on the great truth that there is a God. It has been a leading characteristic of Satan's policy from the beginning, to admit truth up to a certain point, but to pervert it in its legitimate applications, and turn it to his own use and purpose. So is it with Popery: it does not raze the great foundations of religion; but if it has left them standing, it has spared them, not for their own sake, but for the sake of what it has built upon them. The Popish theology includes the existence of a self-existent and eternal Jehovah, the Creator of the universe, of man, and of all things. It teaches that in the Godhead there are three distinct persons, Father, Son, and Holy Ghost, the same in substance, and equal in power and glory; that man was created in God's image, holy and immortal, but that he fell by eating the forbidden fruit, and became, in consequence, sinful in condition and life, and liable to death, temporal and eternal. It holds that the posterity of Adam shared in the guilt and consequences of his sin, and that they come into the world "children of wrath." It embraces the doctrine of man's redemption by Jesus Christ, who for this end became incarnate, and endured the cursed death of the cross, to satisfy the justice of God for the sins of his people. It teaches that he rose from the dead, ascended to heaven, and will return at the Last

Day. It teaches, farther, that Christ has set up a Church upon the earth, consisting of those who are baptized in his name and profess obedience to his law; that He has appointed ministers to instruct and govern his Church, and ordained ordinances to be dispensed in it. It embraces, in fine, the doctrine of a resurrection of the body, and or a general judgment, which will issue in the acquittal of the righteous, and their admission into "life eternal," and in the condemnation of the wicked, and their departure into "everlasting punishment."

We find these great and important truths lying at the foundation of the popish system. It will afterwards be apparent that they are permitted to occupy this place, not from any value which the Church of Rome puts upon them as connected with the glory of God and the salvation of man, but because they afford her a better foundation than any she could invent on which to rear her system of superstition. For certainly no system bearing to be a religious system would have obtained any credit with men, in the circumstances in which the Church of Rome was placed, which ventured on repudiating these great truths. But that Church has so overlaid these glorious truths, so buried them beneath a mass of mingled falsehood, absurdity, and blasphemy, and has so turned them from their peculiar and proper end, that they have become altogether inoperative for man's salvation or God's glory. In her hands they are the instruments, not of regenerating, but of enslaving the world. The only purpose they serve is that of imparting the semblance of a supernatural origin and a divine authority to what is essentially a system of superstition and imposture. It is as if one should throw down a temple to liberty, and on its foundations proceed to rear a dungeon. On the everlasting stones of truth Rome has built a bastile for the human mind. This will very plainly appear when we proceed briefly to state the leading tenets of the Popish theology.

In following out our brief sketch of Romanism, it may conduce somewhat to perspicuity and conciseness that we adopt the following order:-We shall speak first of the CHURCH; second, of her DOCTRINE; third, of her SACRAMENTS; and fourth, of her WORSHIP. This method will enable us to embrace all the more salient points in the system of Romanism. Our task is one mainly of statement. We are not to aim, save in an indirect and incidental way, either at a refutation of Popish error or a defence of Protestant truth; but must restrict ourselves to giving a concise, though tolerably complete,-and, above all, an accurate and candid, statement of what Popery is. Though this forbids that we should indulge in proofs, or illustrations, or arguments, yet it demands that we adduce from the standard works of the Roman Church the authorities on which we base our portraiture of her system. We shall mostly permit Popery to paint herself. We shall take care at least to adduce nothing which the Church of Rome may be able on good grounds to disavow. It also appears to us that this is the proper place for a distinct exhibition of the system of Popery. It is necessary to be shown the ingenuity, compactness, and harmony of her system of doctrine, before proceeding to point out the adroitness and vigour with which she made it the instrument of accomplishing her ambitious and iniquitous designs. The popish theology was the arsenal of Rome. Here hung the bows, and spears, and swords, wherewith she did battle against the armies of the living God. Here were stored up the weapons with which she combated religion and liberty, subjugated the understanding and conscience, and succeeded for a while in subjecting the world to her iron yoke. The system of Popery is worthy of being made the subject of profound study. It is no crude, ill-digested, and clumsily constructed scheme. It possesses an amazing subtlety and depth. It is pervaded by a spirit of fearful potency. It is the product of the combined intellects of many successive ages, acute, powerful, and crafty, intently occupied in its elaboration, and aided by Satanic cunning and power. Wo to the man who falls under its power! Its adamantine chain no weapon has an edge so keen as to be able to cut through, but the sword of the Spirit, which is the Word of God. Once subjected to its dominion, no power but Omnipotence can rescue the man. Its bitings, like those of Cleopatra's asp, are immortal. "There was in some of my friends," says Mr. Seymour, speaking of the priests whom he met at Rome, "an extraordinary amount of scientific attainment, of classical erudition, of polite literature, and of great intellectual acumen; but all seemed subdued, and held, as by an adamantine grasp, in everlasting subjection to what seemed to them to be the religious principle. This principle, which regarded the voice of the Church of Rome as the voice of God himself, was ever uppermost in the mind, and held such an influence and a mastery over the whole intellectual powers, over the whole rational being, that it bowed in the humility of a child before everything that came with even the apparent authority of the Church. I never could have believed the extent of this if I had not witnessed it in these remarkable instances." As a piece of intellectual mechanism Popery has never been equalled, and probably will never be surpassed. As the pyramids have come down to our day, and bear their testimony to the skill and power of the early Egyptians, so Popery, long after its day is over, will be seen towering across the interval of ages, a stupendous monument of the power for evil which lies in the human soul, and of the prodigious efforts the mind of man can put forth, when impelled to action by hatred to God and the desire of self-aggrandizement.

Chapter II: Scripture and Tradition.

Papists concur with Protestants in admitting that God is the source of all obligation and duty, and that the Bible contains a revelation of his will. But while the Papist admits that the Bible is *a* revelation of the will of God, he is far from admitting, with the Protestant, that it is the only revelation. He holds, on the contrary, that it is neither a sufficient rule of faith, nor the only rule; but that tradition, which he terms the *unwritten* word, is equally inspired and equally authoritative with the Bible. To tradition, then, the Papist assigns an equal rank with the Scriptures as a divine revelation. The Council of Trent, in its fourth session, decreed, "that all should receive with equal reverence the books of the Old and New Testament, and the traditions concerning faith and manners, as proceeding from the mouth of Christ, or inspired by the Holy Spirit, and preserved in the Catholic Church; and that whosoever knowingly, and of deliberate purpose, despised traditions, should be anathema." In the creed of the Council of Trent is the following article:-"I do most firmly receive and embrace the apostolical and ecclesiastical traditions, and other usages, of the Roman Church." "The Catholics," says Dr. Milner, "hold that *the Word of God in general, both written and unwritten*,-in other words, *the Bible and tradition taken together*,-constitute the rule of faith, or method appointed by Christ for finding out the true religion." "Has tradition any connection with the rule of faith?" it is asked in Keenan's Controversial Catechism. "Yes," is the answer, "because it is a part of God's revealed Word,-properly called the unwritten Word, as the Scripture is called the written Word." "Are we obliged to believe what tradition teaches, equally with what is taught in Scripture?" "Yes, we are obliged to believe the one as firmly as the other." We may state, that the traditions which the Church of Rome has thus placed on a level with the Bible are the supposed sayings of Christ and the apostles handed down by tradition. Of course, no proof exists that such things were ever spoken by those to whom they are imputed. They were never known or heard of till the monks of the middle ages gave them to the world. To apostolical is to be added ecclesiastical tradition, which consists of the decrees and constitutions of the Church. It is scarcely a true account of the matter to say that tradition holds an equal rank with the Bible: it is placed above it. While tradition is always employed to determine the sense of the Bible, the Bible is never permitted to give judgment on tradition. What, then, would the Church of Rome lose were the Bible to be set aside? Nothing, clearly. Accordingly, some of her doctors have held that the Scriptures are now unnecessary, seeing the Church has determined all truth.

In the second place, Papists make the Church the infallible interpreter of Scripture. The Church condemns all private judgment, interdicts all rational inquiry, and tells her members that they must receive the Scriptures only in the sense which she is pleased to put upon them. She requires all her priests at admission to swear that they will not interpret the Scriptures but according to the consent of the fathers,-an oath which it is impossible to keep otherwise than by abstaining altogether from interpreting Scripture, seeing the fathers are very far indeed from being at one in their interpretations. "How often has not Jerome been mistaken?" said Melancthon to Eck, in the famous disputation at Leipsic; "how frequently Ambrose! and how often their opinions are different! and how often they retract their errors!" The Council of Trent decreed, that "no one confiding in his own judgment shall dare to wrest the sacred Scriptures to his own sense of them, contrary to that which hath been held, and still is held, by holy Mother Church, whose right it is to judge of the true meaning and interpretation of the sacred writ." And they further enact, that if any disobey, they are to be denounced by the ordinaries, and punished according to law. In accordance with that decree is the following article in Pope Pius's creed:-"I receive the holy Scripture according to the sense which holy Mother Church (to whom it belongeth to judge of the true sense of the holy Scriptures) hath held and doth hold; nor will I ever receive and interpret it otherwise than according to the unanimous consent of the fathers." "Without the authority of the Church," said Bailly the Jesuit, "I would believe St. Matthew no more than Titus Livius." So great was the fervour for the Church, of Cardinal Hosius, who was appointed president of the Council of Trent, that he declared, in one of his polemical writings, that were it not for the authority of the Church, the Scriptures would have no more weight than the fables of Aesop. Such are the sentiments of modern Papists. Dr. Milner devotes one of his letters to show that "Christ did not intend that mankind in general should learn his religion from a book." "Besides the rule," says he, "he has provided in his holy

Church a living, speaking judge, to watch over it, and explain it in all matters of controversy."

Such is the rule of faith which Rome furnishes to her members,-the Word of God and the traditions of men, both equally binding. And such is the way in which Rome permits her members to interpret the Scriptures,-only by the Church. And yet, notwithstanding that the Church forbids her members to interpret Scripture, she, as a Church, has never come forward with any interpretation of the Word of God; nor has she adduced, nor can she adduce, the slightest proof from the Word of God that she alone is authorized to interpret Scripture; nor is the consent of the fathers, according to which she binds herself to interpret the Word of God, a consent that has any existence. Her claim as the only and infallible interpreter of Scripture implies, moreover, that God has not expressed, or was not able to express, his mind, so as to be intelligible to the generality of men,-that he has not given his Word to all men, or made it a duty binding on all to read and study it.

The Church of Rome has farther weakened the authority and polluted the purity of God's holy Word, by assigning to the Apocrypha a place in the inspired canon. The inspiration of these books was not made an article of the popish faith till the Council of Trent. That Council, in its fourth session, decreed the divine authority of the Apocrypha, notwithstanding that the books are not found in the Hebrew Bible, were not received as canonical by the Jews, are never quoted by Christ or by his apostles, were repudiated by the early Christian fathers, and contain within themselves manifold proofs that they are not inspired. At the same moment that the Church of Rome was exposing herself to the curse pronounced on those who shall add to the words of inspiration, she pronounced an anathema on all who should refuse to take part with her in the iniquity of maintaining the divine authority of the Apocrypha.

The Roman Catholic arguments in support of tradition as a rule of faith resolve themselves into three branches: first, *passages from scripture*; second, *the office of the Church to attest the authenticity and genuineness of the Bible*; and third, *the insufficiency of private judgment.*

First, we are presented with a few texts which seem to look with some favour upon tradition. These are either utterly inconclusive, or they are plain perversions. *"Hear the Church,"* from the frequency with which it is quoted, would seem to be regarded by Roman controversialists as one of their greatest strongholds. The words, as they stand by themselves, do look as if they inculcated submission to the Church in the matter of our belief. When we examine the passage in connection with its context, however, we find it refers to a supposed dispute between two members of the Church, and enjoins the appeal of the matter to the decision of the Church, that is, of the congregation, provided the offending party refuse to listen to the remonstrances of the offended; which is a different thing altogether from the implicit submission of our judgments in matters of doctrine. Common sense teaches every man that there is no comparison between a written and an oral account of a matter, as regards the degree of reliance to be placed on each. Every time the latter is repeated, it acquires a new addition, or variation, or corruption. It is inconceivable that the truths of salvation should have been conveyed to us through a medium so inaccurate, fluctuating, and doubtful. Was it not one main design of Christ and his apostles, in committing their doctrine to writing, to guard against the uncertainties of tradition? In places innumerable, are not traditions, as a ground of faith, explicitly and pointedly condemned, and the study of the Scriptures strenuously enjoined? Besides, why should the Church of Rome offer proofs from Scripture on this or any other point? Does she not act inconsistently in doing so, inasmuch as she at the same instant forbids and requires the exercise of private judgment?

But, in the second place, from the Church, say the Romanists, you received the Bible; she transmitted it to you, and you take her authority for its authenticity and genuineness. We admit the Church, that is, the universal Church, and not exclusively the Church of Rome, to be a main witness as to the authenticity and genuineness of the Scriptures, on the ground that they have come down to us through her; but that is another question altogether from her right to solely and infallibly interpret Scripture. The messenger who carries a letter may be a very competent witness as to its authenticity and genuineness. He had it from the writer; it has not been out of his possession since; and he can speak very confidently and authoritatively as to its expressing the will of the person whose signature it bears; but is he only, therefore, entitled to interpret its meaning? He may be a very competent authority on its authenticity, but a very incompetent authority on its sense. The Church of Rome has confounded the question of authenticity and the question of interpretation. Because the Church carried this divine letter to us, we will listen to what she has to say on its authenticity; but inasmuch as this letter is addressed to us, and touches questions which involve our eternal welfare, and contains not the slightest hint that it needs to be either interpreted or supplemented by the bearer, we will use the right and responsibility of interpreting it for ourselves.

As regards the insufficiency of private interpretation, it is hard to say whether Rome has conjured up more difficulties on the side of the Bible or on the side of man. She has made the most of the few difficult passages which the Bible contains, overlooking its extraordinary plainness and clearness on the great matters of salvation, and has laboured to show that, however the Bible may be fitted for a higher order of intelligences, it is really of no use at all to those for whom it was written. When a Romanist declaims on this topic, we cannot help fancying that we are listening to the pleadings of some acute, ingenious, and thoroughly in earnest infidel. And, as regards man, to believe Rome, one would think that reason and right understanding is a gift which has been denied the human family, or, at most, is confined to some scores of bishops and cardinals whom she denominates the Church. The Bible is to be subjected to the same rules of criticism and interpretation to which we daily subject the statements of our fellow-men and the works of human composition, and by which we search out the hidden principles and fundamental laws of physical and moral science. The faculties which can do the one can do the other. The moral obliquity which prevents the heart from receiving what the intellect can discover in the field of revelation, and which sheds darkness upon the understanding itself, is not to be overcome by papal infallibility, but by the promised assistance of the Divine Spirit. The Roman Catholic Church has also found a specious argument against the sufficiency of private judgment, in the differences of opinion on subordinate matters which exist among Protestants. These she has greatly magnified; but whatever they may be, she is not the party to reproach us, as we shall afterwards show. It is well known what a nest of diverse, unclean, and monstrous things is that over which the mighty Roman mother, Infallibility, sits brooding. Peter, it is maintained, frowned upon private interpretation, when he wrote as follows respecting the Epistles of Paul:-"In which are some things hard to be understood, which they that are unlearned and unstable wrest, as they do also the other Scriptures, unto their own destruction." Now, first, this shows that they who so wrested the Scriptures had free access to them; second, the statement is limited to the Epistles of Paul, and in these it is only *some* things that are hard to be understood, showing that the *many* are not so. But what preservative does the apostle recommend for this evil?

Does he blame those negligent pastors who allowed their people to read the Scriptures? Does he enjoin Christians to hear the living authority in the Church?-and there were then some really infallible men in her: no; he has recourse to no such expedient; but, seeing they were the unlearned and the unstable who so wrested the Scriptures, he enjoins them to "grow in grace, and in the knowledge of our Lord Jesus Christ." But how are men to grow in the knowledge of Jesus Christ?" Unquestionably by the study of that book that reveals him; agreeably to his own injunction, "Search the Scriptures; they are they which testify of me." "Prove all things; hold fast that which is good."

But the Church of Rome, in the very act of forbidding the exercise of private judgment, and demanding of men implicit submission to her own authority, requires of them the exercise of their faculties. She makes her appeal to those very faculties which she forbids them to use, and calls upon them to exercise their private judgment in order that they may see it to be their duty not to exercise their private judgment. The appeal of Rome is, that men should submit to her infallibility; but she herself shows that she is conscious that a rational being can submit to this appeal only in the use of reason, because she recommends her appeal with arguments. Why does she urge these arguments, if our reason be unfit to determine the question? Before we can submit to infallibility, we must first satisfy ourselves as to several things, such as the truth of Christianity, the vicarship of Peter, and the transmission of the supremacy down to the living pontiff; for on these grounds is the infallibility based. The private judgment that can determine these momentous points might, one should think, competently decide others. To affirm that the sound judgment of men can conduct them so far, but no farther, looks very like saying, that the moment men submit to the infallibility they take leave of their sound judgment. Their reason is unfit, says the Church of Rome; and yet they are required, with an unfit reason, to reason fitly out the unfitness of their reason. If they succeed in reasoning out this proposition, does not their very success disprove the proposition? and if they do not succeed, how can they know the proposition to be true? And yet the Church of Rome continues to exhort men to use their reason to discover that reason is of no use; which is just as sensible as to bid a man walk a few miles along the highway, in order to discover that his limbs are incapable of carrying him a single yard from his own door. This conclusion, that reason is of no use, is true, or it is false. If it is true, how came men to arrive at a sound conclusion with a reason that is altogether useless? and if it is false, what becomes of the dogma of Rome? To tell a man, "Your reason is useless, but here is infallibility for your guide, only you must reason your way to it," is very like saying to a man in a shipwreck, "True, friend, you cannot swim a single stroke; but there is a rock half a league off; you can take your stand on it."

The Protestant rule is the Scripture. "To the Scripture the Roman Catholic adds, first, the Apocrypha; second, traditions; third, acts and decisions of the Church, embracing numerous volumes of the Popes' bulls, ten folio volumes of decretals, thirty-one folio volumes of acts of councils, fifty-one folio volumes of the Acta Sanctorum, or the doings and sayings of the saints; fourth add to these at least thirty-five volumes of the Greek and Latin fathers, in which, he says, is to be found the *unanimous consent* of the fathers; fifth, to all these one hundred and thirty-five volumes folio add the chaos of unwritten traditions which have floated to us down from the apostolic times. But we must not stop here; for the expositions of every priest and bishop must be added. The truth is, such a rule is no rule; unless an endless and contradictory mass of uncertainties could be a rule. No Romanist can soberly *believe*, much less *learn*, his own rule of faith."

But even granting that all this infallibility is centred in the person of the pontiff, and that, practically, the guide of the Romanist is the *dictum* of the Pope; how is he to interpret its meaning, unless by an operation of judgment of the same kind with that by which the Protestant interprets the *dictum* of Scripture? Thus there is no scheme of infallibility which can supersede the exercise of private judgment, unless that of placing an infallibility in the head of every man, which shall guide him, not through his understanding, but in the shape of an unreasoning, unquestioning instinct.

Chapter III: Of Reading the Scriptures.

One would have thought that the Church of Rome had removed her people to a safe distance from the Scriptures. She has placed the gulf of tradition between them and the Word of God. She has removed them still farther from the sphere of danger, by providing an infallible interpreter, whose duty it is to take care that the Bible shall express no sense hostile to Rome. But, as if this were not enough, she has laboured by all means in her power to prevent the Scriptures coming in any shape into the hands of her people. Before the Reformation she kept the Bible locked up in a dead language, and severe laws were enacted against the reading of it. The Reformation unsealed the precious volume. Tyndale and Luther, the one from his retreat at Vildorfe in the Low Countries, and the other from amid the deep shades of the Thuringian forest, sent forth the Bible to the nations in the vernacular tongues of England and Germany. A thirst was thus awakened for the Scriptures, which the Church of Rome deemed it imprudent openly to oppose. The Council of Trent enacted ten rules regarding prohibited books, which, while they appeared to gratify, were insidiously framed to check, the growing desire for the Word of God. In the fourth rule, the Council prohibits any one from reading the Bible without a licence from his bishop or inquisitor; that licence to be founded on a certificate from his confessor that he is in no danger of receiving injury from so doing. The Council adds these emphatic words: — "That if any one shall dare to read or keep in his possession that book, without such a licence, he shall not receive absolution till he has given it up to his ordinary." These rules are followed by the bull of Pius IV., in which he declares that those who shall violate them shall be held guilty of mortal sin. Thus did the Church of Rome attempt to regulate what she found it impossible wholly to prevent. The fact that no Papist is allowed to read the Bible without a licence does not appear in the catechisms and other books in common use among Roman Catholics in this country; but it is incontrovertible that it forms the law of that Church. And, in accordance therewith, we find that the uniform practice of the priests of Rome, from the popes downwards, is to prevent the circulation of the Bible, — to prevent it wholly in those countries, such as Italy and Spain, where they have the power, and in other countries, such as our own, to all the extent to which their power enables them. Their uniform policy is to discourage the reading of the Scriptures in every possible way; and when they dare not employ force to effect this object, they scruple not to press into their service the ghostly power of their Church, by declaring that those who presume to contravene the will of Rome in this matter are guilty of mortal sin. No farther back than 1816, Pope Pius VII., in his bull, denounced the Bible Society, and expressed himself as "shocked" by the circulation of the Scriptures, which he characterizes as a "most crafty device, by which the very foundations of religion are undermined;" "a pestilence," which it behoves him, "to remedy and abolish;" "a defilement of the faith, eminently dangerous to souls." He congratulates the primate, to whom his letter is addressed, on the zeal he had shown "to detect and overthrow the impious machinations of these innovators;" and represents it as an episcopal duty to expose "the wickedness of this nefarious scheme," and openly to publish "that the Bible printed by heretics is to be numbered among other prohibited books, conformably to the rules of the index; for it is evident from experience, that the holy Scriptures, when circulated in the vulgar tongue, have, through the temerity of men, produced more harm than benefit." Thus, in the solemn judgment of the Church of Rome, expressed through her chief organ, the Bible has done more evil than good, and is beyond comparison the worst book in the world. There is only one other being whom Rome dreads more than the Bible, and that is its Author.

The same Pope issued a bull in 1819 on the subject of the circulation of the Scriptures in the Irish schools. He speaks of the circulation of the Scriptures in the schools as *a sowing of tares*; and that the children are thereby *infested with the fatal poison of depraved doctrines*; and exhorts the Irish bishops to endeavour to prevent the wheat being *choked by the tares*.

In 1824 Pope Leo XII. published an encyclical letter, in which he adverts to a certain society, vulgarly termed the BIBLE SOCIETY, as spreading itself throughout the whole world; and goes on to term the Protestant Bible the "Gospel of the Devil." The late Pope Gregory XVI., in his encyclical letter, after referring to the decree of the Council of Trent., quoted above, ratifies that and similar enactments of the Church:"Moreover, we confirm and renew the decrees recited above, delivered in former times by apostolic authority, against the publication, distribution, reading, and possession of books of the holy Scriptures translated into the vulgar tongue." That this hostility to the Word of God is not confined to the occupant of the Vatican, but pervades the entire body of the Romish clergy in all parts of the world, is evident from the recent well-authenticated instances of the burning of Bibles by priests in Belgium, in Ireland, and in Madeira. Not less significant is the fact, stated in evidence before the Commissioners of Education, that among the four hundred students attending the College of Maynooth, there were not to be found more than ten Bibles or Testaments; while every student was required to provide himself with a copy of the works of the Jesuits Bailly and Delahogue. Dr. Doyle, in his instructions to priests regarding Kildare Place Society, says, that if the parents sent their children to a Bible school, after the warning of the priest, "they would be guilty of *mortal sin* or if any of them suffered their children to go to an Hibernian school, he should think it proper "to withhold the sacrament from them when dying;" and he adds, "the Scriptures being read and got by heart, is quite sufficient in order to make the schools obnoxious to us." And to the use of the Bible without note or comment in these schools, Lord Stanley directly attributes their failure: the priests, says he, exerting "themselves with energy and success against a system to which they were *in principle* opposed." The hostility of the priests "does not appear to be against the versions of Protestants only, but against Scripture itself; as is manifest from their decided opposition to the Catholic version [the Douay], without note or comment, which the Bible Society proposed printing for the use of Catholics, but which was absolutely refused by their clergy?" Mr. Nowlan, in a debate with some Protestant clergymen in 1824, says, "If the Bible Society came to distribute copies of the Bible, even of that version which the Catholic Church approves of, on this principle [that of the Bible Society], we should still consider it our duty to oppose them." Since the 1st of June 1816, four pontiffs in succession, including Pius IX., have distinctly and formally intimated to the world, that by the distribution and reading of the holy Scriptures in the vulgar tongue, "*the very* FOUNDATIONS *of their religion are undermined.*"

In the face of these facts, — of their written creed plainly prohibiting the reading of the Scriptures without a licence, under pain of being held guilty of *mortal sin*; of anathemas against Bible Societies, thundered forth by the pontiffs; of the burning of the Bible by the hands of priests, as if it were "the book of heresy," as it was termed by the public prosecutor, when he pulled the New Testament from the sleeve of the "Vicar of Dollar;" in the face of the refusal of the sacrament to the dying, for the crime of sending their children to a school where the Bible was read; and the attempts both in Edinburgh, as in the case of the Ragged Schools, and in Ireland, as in the case of the Kildare Place Society schools, to defeat and overthrow schemes devised for the reclamation of the ignorant, the vicious, and the outcast, because these schemes included the reading of the Scriptures without note or comment, — it requires, assuredly, no small amount of hardihood to maintain, as we find priests of the Church of Rome doing, "that it is a great mistake, and, indeed, a calumny against the Catholic Church, to say that she is opposed to the full and unrestricted use and circulation of the Scriptures." We do not know that we have ever met with a more barefaced attempt of this kind than the following, made, too, in circumstances where, one would have thought, the most reckless audacity would have shrunk from such an attempt. The words we have quoted, charging it as a calumny on the Church of Rome to say that she is opposed to the "full and unrestricted use and circulation of the Scriptures," were uttered at Rome in the midst of millions sunk in the grossest ignorance of the sacred volume. They fell from the professor of dogmatic theology in the Collegio Romano, in a conversation held with the Rev. Mr. Seymour, a clergyman of the Church of England, who visited Rome a few years ago, and who has recorded his experience of Popery, as he found it existing in the metropolis of Roman Catholicism, in his work entitled "Mornings among the Jesuits at Rome." "The answer I made to this," says Mr. Seymour, "was, that having resided many years among a Roman Catholic population in Ireland, I had always found that the sacred volume was forbidden to them; and that since I came to Italy, and especially to Rome, I observed the most complete ignorance of the holy Scriptures, and that it was ascribed by themselves to a prohibition on the part of the Church.

"He at once stated that there must be some mistake, as the book was permitted to all who could understand it, and was, in fact, in very general circulation in Rome.

"I said that I had heard the contrary, and that it was impossible to procure a copy of the holy Scriptures in the Italian tongue in the city of Rome, — that I had so heard from an English gentleman who had resided there for ten years, — that I looked upon the statement as scarcely credible, — that I wished much to ascertain the matter for my own information, — that I had one day resolved to test this by visiting every bookselling establishment in the city of Rome, — that I had gone to the book-shop belonging to the Propaganda Fide, — to that patronized by his holiness the Pope, — to that which was connected with the Collegio Romano, and was patronized by the order of Jesuits, — to that which was established for the supply of English and other foreigners, — to those who sold old and second-hand books, — and that in every establishment, without exception, I found that the holy Scriptures were not for sale; I could not procure a single copy in the Roman language, of a portable size, in the whole city of Rome; and that when I asked each bookseller the reason of his not having so important a volume, I was answered, in every instance, *e prohibito*, or *non é permesso*, — that the volume was prohibited, or that it was not permitted to be sold. I added, that Martini's edition was offered to me in two places, but it was in twenty-four volumes, and at a cost of 105 francs (that is, £ 4 sterling); and that, under such circumstances, I could not but regard the holy Scriptures as a prohibited book, at least in the city of Rome.

"He replied by acknowledging that it was very probable that I could not find the volume in Rome, especially as the population of Rome was very poor, and not able to purchase the sacred volume; and that the real reason the Scriptures were not at the booksellers, and also were not in circulation, was, not that they were forbidden or prohibited by the Church, but that the people of Rome were too poor, to buy them.

"I replied that they probably were too poor, whether in Rome or in England, to give one hundred and five francs for the book; but that the clergy of Rome, so numerous and wealthy, should do as in England, namely, form an association for cheapening the copies of the Scriptures.

"He said, in reply, that the priests were too poor to cheapen the volume, and that the people were too poor to purchase it.

"I then stated, that if this was really the case, — that if there was no prohibition against the sacred volume, — that if they would be willing to circulate it, — and that really and sincerely there was no other objection than the difficulties arising from the price of the book, — that difficulty should at once be obviated: I would myself undertake to obtain from England, through the Bible Society, any number of Bibles that could be circulated; and that they should be sold at the lowest possible price, or given freely and gratuitously, to the inhabitants of Rome. I stated that the people of England loved the Scriptures beyond all else in this world; and that it would be to them a source of delight and thanksgiving to give for gratuitous circulation any number of copies of the sacred volume that the inhabitants of Rome could require.

"He immediately answered, that he thanked me for the generous offer; but that there would be no use in accepting it, as the people of Rome were very ignorant, were in a state of brutal ignorance, were unable to read anything; and therefore could not profit by reading the Scriptures, even if we supplied them gratuitously.

"I could not conceal from myself that he was prevaricating with me, — that his former excuse of poverty, and this latter excuse of ignorance, were mere evasions; so I asked him whose fault it was that the people remained in such universal and unaccountable ignorance. There were above five thousand priests, monks, and nuns, besides cardinals and prelates, in the city of Rome; that the whole population was only thirty thousand families; that thus there was a priest, or a monk, or a nun, for every six families in Rome; that thus there were ample means for the education of the people; and I asked, therefore, whether the Church was not to blame for this ignorance on the part of the people?

"He immediately turned from the subject, saying, that the Church held the infallibility of the Pope, to whom it therefore belonged to give the only infallible interpretation of the Scriptures.

But a more authoritative confirmation still of all that we have advanced against Popery on this head has lately appeared. It is the Encyclical Letter of Pius IX. (issued in January 1850). The document is such a compound of despotism and bigotry as Leo XII. might have conceived, and Gregory XVI. signed. It is in itself such an exposure, that we add not a word of comment. After condemning the "*new* art of printing," the Pope goes on to say, — "Nay, more; with the assistance of *the Biblical Societies*, which have long been condemned by the holy chair, they do not blush to distribute holy Bibles, translated into the vulgar tongue, without being conformed to the rules of the Church." . . . . "Under a false pretext of religion, they recommend the reading of them to the faithful. You, in your wisdom, perfectly understand, venerable brothers, with what vigilance and solicitude you ought to labour, that the faithful may fly with horror from this poisonous reading; and that they may remember that no man, supported by his own prudence, can arrogate to himself the right, and have the presumption, to interpret the Scriptures otherwise than as our holy mother the Church interprets them, to whom alone our Lord has confided the guardianship of the faith, judgment upon the true sense and interpretation of the divine books."

So much for the doctrine and practice of the Church of Rome on this vital point. The world does not contain to her a more dangerous book than the Bible, or one from which she recoils with more instinctive dread. She neither dare disavow its authority, nor venture an open appeal to it by putting it into the hands of her people. With all her impudence and audacity, she trembles at the thought of appearing before this tribunal, well knowing that she cannot "stand in the judgment." Thus Rome is constrained to do homage to the majesty of the Bible. She has done her utmost to exile that book from the world, with all the treasures it contains, — its thrilling narratives, its rich poetry, its profound philosophy, its sublime doctrines, its blessed promises, its magnificent prophecies, its glorious and immortal hopes. Were any being so malignant or so powerful as to extinguish the light of day, and condemn the successive generations of men to pass their lives amid the gloom of an unbroken night, where would words be found strong enough to execrate the enormity. Far greater is the crime of Rome. After the day of Christianity had broke, she was able to cover Europe with darkness, and, by the exclusion of the Bible, to perpetuate that darkness from age to age. The enormity of her wickedness cannot be known on earth. But she cannot conceal from herself that, despite her anathemas, her *indices expurgatorii*, her tyrannical edicts, by which she still attempts to wall round her territory of darkness, the Bible is destined to overcome in the conflict. Hence her implacable hostility, — a hostility founded, to a large extent, upon fear. We find her members at times making this unwilling confession. The Bible, said Richard du Mans, in the Council of Trent, "ought not to be made a study, because the Lutherans only gain those who read it." And in more modern times we find Mr. Shiel asserting, on a stage not less conspicuous than that of the Council of Trent, that "the reading of the Bible would lead to the subversion of the Roman Catholic Church." The Popish divine and the British senator, at an interval of three centuries, unite in declaring that Popery and the Bible cannot stand together. How like are these vaticinations to the words spoken to Haman by Zeresh his wife! — "Then said his wise men and Zeresh his wife unto him, if Mordecai be of the seed of the Jews, before whom thou hast begun to fall, thou shalt not prevail against him, but shalt surely fall before him." The world is not wide enough to contain both the Bible and the Pope. Each claims an undivided empire. To suppose that the two can live together at Rome, is to suppose an impossibility. The entrance of the one is the expulsion of the other. To

Popery a single Bible is more dreadful than an army of ten thousand strong. Let IT enter, and, as Dagon fell before the ark of old, so surely shall the mighty Dagon which has sat enthroned so long upon the Seven Hills fall prostrate and be utterly broken. Unseal this blessed page to the nations, and farewell to the inventions and the frauds, to the authority and the grandeur, of Rome. This is the catastrophe she already apprehends. And therefore, when she meets the Bible in her path, she is startled, and exclaims in terror, "I know thee, whom thou art: art thou come to torment me before the time?"

Chapter IV: Unity of the Church of Rome.

The Church is not the work of man: it is a special creation of God. Seeing it is wholly supernatural in its origin, we can look nowhere for information respecting its nature, its constitution, and its ends, but to the Bible. The New Testament declares that the Church is a spiritual society, being composed of spiritual, that is, of regenerated men; associated under a spiritual head, the Lord Jesus Christ; held together by spiritual bonds, which are faith and love; governed by spiritual laws, which are contained in the Bible; enjoying spiritual immunities and privileges, and entertaining spiritual hopes. This is the Church invisible; so called because its members, *as such*, cannot be discovered by the world. The Church, in this sense, cannot be bounded by any geographical limits, nor by any denominational peculiarities and distinctions. It is spread over the world, and embraces all, in every place and of every name, who believe in the Lord Jesus, and are united to him as their head, and to one another as members of the same body, by the bond of the Spirit and of faith. "By one spirit are we all baptized into one body, whether we be Jews or Gentiles, whether we be bond or free, and have been all made to drink into one spirit." Protestants willingly concede to the Church of Rome what, as we shall afterwards show, that Church will not concede to them, that even within the pale of Popery there may be found members of the Church of Christ, and heirs of salvation. But the Church may be viewed in its external aspect, in which respect it is called the Church visible, which consists of all those throughout the world who profess the true religion, together with their children. These are not two Churches, but the same Church viewed under two different aspects. They are composed, to a great degree, of the same individuals. The Church visible includes all who are members of the Church invisible; but the converse of this proposition is not true; for, in addition to all who are genuine Christians, the Church visible contains many who are Christians only in name. Its limits, therefore, are more extensive than those of the invisible Church. Such are the views generally held by Protestants on the subject of the Church. From these the opinions held by Papists on this important subject differ very materially. Papists hold that the Church of Rome is emphatically *the* Church; that she is the

Church, to the exclusion of all other communities or Churches bearing the Christian name. They hold that this Church is ONE; that she is CATHOLIC or universal; that She is INFALLIBLE; that the Roman pontiff, as the successor of Peter and the vicar of Christ, is her visible head; and that there is no salvation beyond her pale.

The Church, say the Papists, must possess certain great marks or characters. These must not be of such a kind as to be discoverable only by the help of great learning and after laborious search; they must be of that broad and palpable cast that enables them to be seen at once and by all. The Church must resemble the sun, to use Bellarmine's illustration, whose resplendent beams attest his presence to all. By these marks is the important question to be solved, — "Which is the true Church?" Papists hold, and endeavour to prove, that in the Church of Rome alone are these marks to be found; and therefore that she, to the exclusion of all other societies, is the holy Catholic Church.

The first indispensable characteristic of the true Church, possessed by the Church of Rome alone, as Papists hold, is UNITY. Bellarmine places the unity of the Church in three things, — the same faith, the same sacraments, and the same head, the Roman pontiff. This unity is defined by Dens to consist "in having one head, one faith, in being of one mind, in partaking of the same sacraments, and in the communion of the saints." With regard to the first, — the unity of the head, — Dens holds that the Church of Rome is signally favoured; for nowhere but in her do we find one visible head "under Christ," namely, the Roman pontiff, "to whom all bishops, and the whole body of the faithful, are subjected." In him, continues Dens, the Church has a "centre of union," and a source of "authority and discipline, which extends in its exercise throughout the whole Church." "What is the Church?" it is asked in Dr. Reilly's Catechism. It is answered, "It is the congregation of the faithful, who profess the true faith, and are obedient to the Pope." Romanists lay much stress likewise upon the fact, that the same creed, particularly that of Pope Pius IV., drawn up in conformity with the definitions of the Council of Trent, is professed by Roman Catholics in all parts of the world; that the same articles of faith and morality are taught in all her catechisms; that she has one rule of faith, viz. "Scripture and tradition;" and that she has "the same expositor and interpreter of this rule, — the Catholic Church." "Nor is it in her *doctrine* only," says Dr. Milner, "that the Catholic Church is one and the same: she is also uniform in whatever is essential in her *liturgy*. In every part of the world she offers up the same unbloody sacrifice of the holy mass, which is her chief act of divine worship; she administers the same seven sacraments." As regards the communion of saints, we find it defined in Reilly's Catechism to consist in the members of the Church "being partakers of the spiritual blessings and treasures that are to be had in it;" and these, again, are said to consist in "the sacraments, the holy sacrifice of the mass, the prayers of the Church, and the good works of the just." Generally, Papists, in deciding this point, discard altogether the graces and fruits of inward Christianity, and found entirely on outward organization. Bellarmine asserts that the fathers have ever reckoned communion with the Roman pontiff an essential mark of the true Church; but when he comes to prove this, he leaps at once over the apostles and inspired writers, and the examples of the New Testament, where we find numerous churches unquestionably independent, and owning no subjection to Rome, and comes to those writers who were the pioneers of the primacy. When one man only in the world is permitted to think, and the rest are compelled to agree with him, unity should be of as easy attainment as it is worthless when attained. Yet despite the despotism of force and the despotism of ignorance, which have been employed in all ages to crush free inquiry and open discussion in the Church of Rome, serious differences and furious disputes have broken out in her. When we name the Pope, we indicate the whole extent of her unity. Here she is at one, or has usually been so; on every other point she is disagreed. The theology of Rome has differed materially in different ages; so that her members have believed one set of opinions in one age, and another set of opinions in another age. What was sound doctrine in the sixth century, was heresy in the twelfth; and what was sufficient for salvation in the twelfth century, is altogether insufficient for it in our day. Transubstantiation was invented in the thirteenth century; it was followed, at the distance of three centuries, by the sacrifice of the mass; and that again, in our day, by the immaculate conception of the Virgin. In the twelfth century, the Lombardic theology, which mingled faith and works in the justification of the sinner, was in repute. This had its day, and was succeeded in about a hundred years after by the scholastic theology. The schoolmen discarded faith, and gave works alone a place in the important matter of justification. On the ruins of the scholastic divinity flourished the monastic theology. This system extolled papal indulgences, adoration of images, prayers to saints, and works of supererogation; and on these grounds rested the sinner's justification. The Reformation came, and a modified theology next became fashionable, in which the grosser errors were abandoned to suit the newly risen light. But now all these systems have given place to the theology of the Jesuits, whose system differs in several important points from all that went before it. On the head of justification the Jesuitical theology teaches that habitual righteousness is an infused grace, but that actual righteousness consists in the merit of good works. Here are five theologies which have successively been in vogue in the Church of Rome. Which of these five systems is the orthodox one? Or are they all orthodox? But not only do we desiderate unity between the successive ages of the Romish Church; we desiderate unity among her contemporary doctors and councils. They have differed on questions of ceremonies, on questions of morals, and they have differed not less on the questions of the supremacy and infallibility. Contrariety of opinion has been the rule; agreement the exception. Council has contended with council; pope has excommunicated pope; Dominican has warred with Franciscan; and the Jesuits have carried on ceaseless and furious battles with the Benedictines and other orders. What, indeed, are these various orders, but ingenious contrivances to allay heats and divisions which Rome could not heal, and to allow of differences of opinion which she could neither prevent nor remove? What one infallible bull has upheld as sound doctrine, another infallible bull has branded as heresy. Europe has been edified with the spectacle of two rival vicars of Christ playing at football with the spiritual thunder; and what we find one holy father, Nicholas, commending as an assembly of men filled with the Holy Ghost, namely, the Council of Basil, we find another holy father, Eugenius, depicting as "madmen, barbarians, wild beasts, heretics, miscreants, monsters, and a pandemonium." But there is no end of the illustrations of papal unity. The wars of the Romanists have filled history and shaken the world. The loud and discordant clatter which rose of old around Babel is but a faint type of the interminable din and furious strife which at all times have raged within the modern Babel, — the Church of Rome.

Such is the unity which the Romish Church so often and so tauntingly contrasts with what she is pleased to term "Protestant disunion." As a corporation, having its head at Rome, and stretching its limbs to the extremities of the earth, she is of gigantic bulk and imposing appearance; but, closely examined, she is seen to be an assemblage of heterogeneous materials, held together simply by the compression of force. It is a coercive power from without, not an attractive influence from within, that gives her being and form. The appearance of union and compactness which she puts on at a distance is altogether owing to her organization, which is of the most perfect kind, and of the most despotic character, and not to any spiritual and vivifying principle, whose influence, descending from the head, moves the members, and results in harmony of feeling, unanimity of mind, and unity of action. It is combination, not incorporation; union, not unity, that characterizes the Church of Rome. It is the unity of dead matter, not the unity of a living body, whose several members, though performing various functions, obey one will and form one whole. It is not the spiritual and living unity promised to the Church of God, which preserves the liberty of all, at the same time that it makes all ONE: it is a unity that degrades the understanding, supersedes rational inquiry, and annihilates private judgment. It leaves no room for conviction, and therefore no room for faith. It is a unity that extorts from all submission to one infallible head, that compels all to a participation in one monstrous and idolatrous rite, and that enchains the intellect of all to a farrago of contradictory, absurd, and blasphemous opinions. This is the unity of Rome. Men must be free agents before it can be shown that they are voluntary agents. In like manner, the members of the Church must have liberty to differ before it can be shown that they really are agreed. But Rome denies her people this liberty, and thus renders it impossible that it can ever be shown that they are united. She resolves all into absolute authority, which in no case may either be questioned or opposed. Dr. Milner, after striving hard, in one of his letters, to show that all Catholics are agreed as regards the "fundamental articles of Christianity," is forced to conclude with the admission, that they are only so far agreed as that they all implicitly submit to the infallible teaching of the Church. "At all events," says he, "the Catholics, if properly interrogated, will confess their belief in one comprehensive article, namely this, *I believe whatever the Holy Catholic Church believes and teaches.*" So, then, this renowned champion of Roman Catholicism, forced to abandon all other positions as untenable, comes at last to rest the argument in behalf of his Church's unity upon this, even the unreasoning and unquestioning submission of the conscience to the teaching of the Church. In point of fact, this "one comprehensive article" sums up the entire creed of the Papist: the Church inquires for him, thinks for him, reasons for him, and believes for him; or, as it was expressed by a plain-speaking Hibernian, who, making his last speech and dying confession at the place of execution, and resolved not to expose himself to purgatory for want of not believing enough, declared, "that he was a Roman Catholic, and died in the communion of that Church, and believed as the Catholic Church ever did believe, now doth believe, or ever shall believe." Put out the eyes of men, and there will be only one opinion about colour; extinguish the understandings of men, and there will be but one opinion regarding religion This is what Rome does. With her rod of infallibility she touches the intellect and the conscience, and benumbs them into torpor. There comes thus to reign within her pale a deep stillness, broken at times by ridiculous disputes, furious quarrels, and serious differences, on points termed fundamental, which remain unsettled from age to age, — the famous question, for instance, touching the seat of infallibility; and this profound quiescence, so like the repose of the tomb, accomplished by the waving of her mystic rod, she calls unity.

Chapter V: Catholicity of the Church of Rome.

Catholicity, apostolicity, and infallibility, are other marks, borne only, as Papists affirm, by the Church of Rome, and attesting her claim to be the true Church. Let us briefly state these marks in their Roman sense; and still more briefly inquire whether, in truth, they are to be found in that Church.

Finding numerous passages in the Psalms and the prophets promising universal and perpetual dominion to the Church, Papists infer that the Church must be catholic or universal, at least since the age of the apostles; and that any diminution of her numbers, or any contraction of her limits, so as to leave her in a minority, would invalidate her claim to be the true Church. "The Church," says the Catechism of the Council of Trent, "is rightly called Catholic, because, as St. Augustine saith, from the east even unto the west it has shed abroad the splendour of one faith. Nor is the Church confined to the commonwealths of men, or the conventicles of heretics; it is not bounded by the limits of a single kingdom, or composed of but one tribe; but it embraces all with the bond of love, whether they be Barbarian or Scythian, bond or free, male or female." "The term Catholic implies," says Dens, "that the Church is diffused over the world, or is universal in point of place, nation, and time;" and he quotes, in proof, the song of the redeemed in the Revelations, that is, according to the current of Protestant interpreters, the song of those who had triumphed over Antichrist: — "Thou hast redeemed us out of every tribe, and tongue, and people, and nation." "That this mark belongs to our Church," continues Dens, "appears from the circumstance that in all places and in every nation Catholics are found, who, although divided in respect of place, are joined under the government of the Roman pontiff. Moreover, there have been, and there will be, Catholics in all ages." The same writer, following Bellarmine, repudiates the claim of other bodies to rank as members of the Church, on the ground that they are limited to certain districts, — that the time when they took their rise is known, — and that they are diverse in name, taking their appellatives generally from their founders. "We trace our descent from Peter, the prince of the apostles, say the Romanists, and our Church has spread and flourished in the earth ever since the fisherman founded it at Rome: you come from Germany, and were not, till Luther gave you being." There is one question, which, according to the Rev. Stephen Keenan, will effectually gravel every Protestant. "Ask him," says he, "where the true Church was before the time of Luther and Calvin?" It is sufficient to ask in return, Where were the wells which Abraham had digged, before Isaac cleared out the rubbish with which the Philistine herdsmen had filled them? Rome, to show that she has existed in all ages since the apostolic era, appeals to history. It requires assuredly no little courage to look history in the face, deeply indented as it is with her bloody foot-prints. She delights to recall to her own and to others' recollection her palmy state in the twelfth, thirteenth, and fourteenth centuries, when, by the help of fire and sword, she had succeeded in suppressing all public profession of the truth; and to show that the savage spirit of vengeance which persecuted these men to the death still lives in certain members of the Roman Church in our day, we find the Rev. Stephen Keenan stigmatizing those confessors whom his Church compelled to inhabit the "dens and caves of the earth," and whom she slew with "the edge of the sword," as "hypocrites, dastardly traitors to their religion, utterly incapable of composing the holy, fearless body of the true Church of Christ."

We deny, in the first place, that the *promises* appropriated by the Church of Rome refer to her; we deny, in the second place, that that Church is catholic in point of *doctrine*; we deny, in the third place, that she is Catholic in point of *time*; and we deny, in the fourth place, that she is catholic in point of *place*.

First, as regards the promises applied to herself by the Church of Rome, we deny that it is anywhere foretold in Scripture that the Church, commencing with the apostolic era, would continue uninterruptedly to progress and triumph. We have several plain intimations to the contrary. We find the apostle Paul predicting the rise of a great apostacy, of which a temporary and comparative catholicity was to form one of the more obvious marks. In the one prophetic book of the New Testament it is expressly said of Antichrist, whose marks Rome, if she examine, will find written upon her forehead, "all the world wondered after the beast." What the passages in question foretell is, that after ages of conflict and oppression, and especially after the overthrow of that great system of error which was not only to arrest the progress of the Church, but actually to make her retrograde, she should surmount the opposition of her foes, and become triumphant and ascendant. Then would the prophet's words be fulfilled, "The Gentiles shall see thy light, and all kings thy glory." Rome has had her "lifetime," in which she has received her "good things," — glory, and dominion, and the worship of "all that dwell upon the earth, whose names are not written in the Book of Life." And whilst she clothed herself "in purple and fine linen, and fared sumptuously every day," the poor members of Christ's body lay at her gate, glad of such crumbs of toleration as she was pleased to let fall, and thankful when the dogs of her household licked their sores. It is meet, therefore, that when the one is tormented the other should be comforted.

But we deny that these promises refer to the Church of Rome. These promises were given to the Church of Christ; and the question, which is the Church of Christ, is to be determined, not by numbers, but by the fact of possessing the spirit of Christ and the doctrine of Christ. This brings us to the second point, that of *doctrine*, in which we deny catholicity to the Church of Rome. Though the Roman pontiff could show that every knee on earth is bent to him, that would prove nothing. He must show that he preaches the doctrines which Christ preached, and governs the Church by the laws which Christ instituted. Now Rome will not, and dare not, appeal this question to the Bible. Her invariable policy here is to raise a cloud of dust, by presenting a formidable list of the names and sects of the Protestant world, and in this way to cover her retreat. But, though she could prove that we are wrong, it does not follow that she is right. It is with the Bible alone that she has to do. And when tried by this test, — and we are entitled to do so, seeing Roman Catholics admit that the Bible is the Word of God, — when tried, we say, by this test, the Church of Rome is scriptural neither in her constitution, nor in her government, nor in her doctrine. Scriptural in her constitution she is not. The true Church is founded upon the doctrine of Christ's divinity, whereas the Church of Rome is founded upon the doctrine of Peter's primacy. The primacy, as Bellarmine says, is the very germ of Christianity; a sterling truth, if for *Christianity* we substitute *Catholicism*. Nor is she scriptural in her government. It is an undeniable historical fact, that neither in scriptural times nor in primitive times was she governed as she has been governed since the sixth century. Where in all the Bible do we find a warrant for placing the government of the Church in the hands of one man, possessed of both a temporal and a spiritual crown, governing according to a code of laws which virtually ignores the New Testament, and through a splendidly equipped and richly salaried hierarchy of cardinals, archbishops, and bishops, formed on the model of the empire, and exhibiting, at the best, but an impious travesty of the equality and simplicity of the New Testament Church? There is no mistaking the *lordship* of Rome for the *episcopate* of the Scriptures. The one is the exact counterpart of the other. Their stations are at the opposite poles of the ecclesiastical sphere. Nor is the Church of Rome scriptural in doctrine. This is the great test by which she must stand or fall. "They do not possess the inheritance of Peter who do not possess the faith of Peter," says Ambrose. The Church of Rome may wear the same name, occupy the same territory, possess continuity of descent and similarity of organization; — she may have every outward mark of apostolicity under heaven; but if she wants this mark, she wants all. And it is precisely here, in this the most vital point, that she comes most decidedly short. As the various branches of the Romish theology come successively under our view, it will be seen how far the church of Rome has erred from the faith of the apostles. At present we can only indicate the main directions in which her apostacy has lain. For the sacrifice of the cross the Church of Rome has substituted the sacrifice of the mass. For the one Mediator between God and man that Church has substituted innumerable mediators, — angels and saints. For the gospel method of justification, which is by grace, the Church of Rome has substituted justification by *works*. For the agency of the *Spirit* in the sanctification of men she has substituted the agency of the *Sacrament*. These are the four cardinal doctrines of Christianity, and on each of them the Church of Rome has grievously erred. She has erred as regards that grand fundamental truth on which the scheme of redemption is based, — the one all-meritorious sacrifice of Christ; she has erred as regards the way by which sinners have access into the presence of God; she has erred as regards the ground on which sinful men are made just in the sight of God; and she has erred as regards that divine agent by whom men are made holy, and prepared for the blessedness of heaven. There cannot be a doubt as to the teachings of the New Testament on these four heads; as little can it be doubted that the Church of Rome on all these points teaches the very opposite. The doctrine and its opposite cannot both be true. If the deliverances of the Bible are truths, the dogmas of the Romish Church must be errors. The Church of Rome, therefore, is unknown to the New Testament. She is the Church of the Pope, — not the Church of Christ.

But, in the third place, we deny that the Church of Rome is Catholic in point of *time*. It is indeed a foolish question, "Where was your Church before the time of Luther?" What though we should reply, She dwelt amid the eternal snows of the Alps; she lay hid in the caves of Bohemia? They were "hypocrites, dastardly traitors to their religion," for doing so, exclaims the Rev. Stephen Keenan. Ah! had they been hypocrites and dastardly traitors, they needed not have been wretched outcasts; they might have dwelt in palaces, and ministered in gorgeous cathedrals, like the kings and priests who persecuted them. Do those who put this question know that the "men of old, of whom the world was not worthy," inhabited "dens and caves of the earth;" and that the early apostolic, not apostate, Church of Rome, to save herself from the fury of the emperors, actually made her abode in the catacombs beneath the city? But the question to which we have referred, if it means anything, implies that Luther was the inventor of the doctrines now held by Protestants, and that these doctrines were never heard of in the world till he arose. This, indeed, is expressly taught in Keenan's Catechism : — "For fourteen hundred years," says the writer, "after the last of the apostles left this world, Protestant doctrines were unknown amongst mankind." The cardinal truth of Luther's teaching was "justification by faith alone." This truth Luther certainly did not invent: it was the very truth which Paul preached to Jew and Gentile. "Therefore we conclude," says Paul, writing to the Church at Rome, "that a man is justified by faith, without the deeds of the law." This was the truth which was revealed to the patriarchs, and proclaimed by the prophets. "And the Scripture, foreseeing that God would justify the heathen through faith, preached the gospel before unto Abraham." The doctrine of Protestants, then, is just Christianity, and Christianity is as old as the world. That Christianity Luther did not invent; he was simply God's instrument to summon it from the grave to which Popery had consigned it. But with what force may it be retorted upon the advocates of Roman Catholicism, "Where was your Church before the middle ages?" Where was transubstantiation before the days of Innocent III.? Where was the sacrifice of the mass before the Council of Trent? When we go back to the twelfth, eighth, and even the fifth century, we find palpable proofs of Popery; but when we pass much beyond that limit, we lose all trace of the system; and when we go as far down as the apostolic age, we find that we have passed utterly beyond the sphere of Romanism; — we find that there is, in fact, a well-defined middle region, to which Romanism is limited, and beyond which, on one side at least, it does not extend. We search in vain the pages of the earliest Christian fathers, and, above all, the pages of inspired men, for the peculiar doctrines of the Roman Church. Where, in these venerable documents of early Christianity, — where, in the inspired canon, — do we read of the mass, or of purgatory, or of the worship of the Virgin, or of the supremacy of the Bishop of Rome? When Paul indited his epistles, and Peter preached to the Gentiles "remission of sins," these doctrines were unknown in the world. They were the growth of a later age. Thus, in digging downwards, we find that we have come at last to the living and eternal rock of Christianity, and have fairly got through the superincumbent mass of rude, ill-compacted, and heterogeneous materials which have been deposited in the course of ages from the dark ocean of superstition. Protestantism is old truth, — Popery is medieval error.

If the Church of Rome takes her appeal to antiquity, even Paganism will carry it against her. Its rites were celebrated upon the Seven Hills long before Popery had there fixed its seat. The Roman Church has played off upon the world the same trick which was practised so successfully by the Gibeonites of old: she has put tattered garments upon her back, and clouted shoes upon her feet, and dry and mouldy bread into her sacks, and laid them upon the backs of her asses, and taken advantage of the obscurity of her origin to say, "We be come from a far country." It is not the number of years, but the weight of arguments, that must carry the point.

In fine, we deny that the Church of Rome is Catholic in point of *place*. Catholicity, in the absolute sense of the word, as Turrettin remarks, can be predicated only of that society that includes the Church triumphant in heaven, as well as militant on earth, — that society that comprehends all the elect, reaching back to the days of Abel, and onward to the last trumpet. But the great matter with Rome is to make it appear that she has achieved a terrestrial catholicity. Now certainly it is not Rome's fault if she have not done so. Her efforts to extend her dominion have been of no ordinary kind: they have been skilfully contrived and vigorously prosecuted. And if in this great work she has made but little use of the Bible, she has made abundant use of the sword. Her missionaries have been soldiers, who have pressed the pike and the musket into the service of Christianity, and spread the faith of Rome as Mahomet spread the religion of the Koran. The weapons she has wielded have been the false miracle, the forged document, the lying legend, the persecutor's brand. At no time has she been particularly nice as to the character of her converts, — receiving hordes within her pale who had nothing of Christianity but the name; and yet, after all, that empire which she calls catholic or universal is very far, in point of fact, from being so. She boasts that at this day she can count upwards of two hundred millions of subjects. We do not stay to inquire how many of these arc real Papists. The Pope has of late excommunicated *en masse* whole cities and provinces. Do these count as children of the Church? But the Church of Rome parades the number of her followers, and asks, is it possible that all these millions can be mistaken? She forbids her members to make use of their reason in judging of their religion, and then claims weight for their testimony, as if they had used their reason in the matter. This is simply to practise a delusion. The very smallest Protestant sect would furnish far more real witnesses in favour of Protestantism than the Roman Catholic Church could do in favour of Romanism. In a court of justice, the latter would be counted but as one witness. They have not examined the matter for themselves; they believe it on infallibility; their evidence, therefore, is simply hearsay, and in a court of law would be held as resolving itself into the evidence of but one man. If he be right, they are right; but if he be mistaken, they all are necessarily mistaken. But in a Protestant Church every member acts on his own judgment and belief. Such a body, therefore, contains as many independent, intelligent, and real witnesses as it does members. That Church, then, which boasts of catholicism and numbers is, as far as testimony goes, the smallest sect in Christendom.

But, giving her the matter her own way, she includes within her pale a decided minority of the human family. The one pagan empire of China alone greatly outnumbers her. The Greek Church, an older Church than that of Rome, never owned her supremacy; nor the other numerous Churches in Asia, nor the great and once famous Church in Africa, nor the Church in the Russian empire. And, considering how many kingdoms have broken off from her since the Reformation, the communion of Rome is now reduced to a very small part of the Christian Church. Around her limited and restricted territory, which includes, it is true, many a fair province in Europe, there extends a broad zone of Mahommedanism and Hinduism, which merges into another and a darker zone, which, as it stretches away towards the extremities of the earth, deepens into the unbroken night of heathenism. Surveyed from the Seven Hills, the empire of Rome does indeed seem ample, — alas! too ample for the repose and progress of the world; but to the eye that can take in the globe, it dwindles into an insignificant speck, lying embosomed in the folds of the pagan night. But the dominion promised to the Church is universal in a sense which cannot be affirmed of any dominion which Rome ever attained, or is likely ever to attain. It is a dominion from which no land or tribe under the cope of heaven is excluded. "Behold, the darkness shall cover the earth, gross darkness the people; but the Lord shall arise upon thee, and his glory shall be seen upon thee. And the Gentiles shall see thy righteousness, and all kings thy glory." "He shall have dominion also from sea to sea, and from the river unto the ends of the earth. They that dwell in the wilderness shall bow before him; and his enemies shall lick the dust. The kings of Tarshish and of the isles shall bring presents; the kings of Sheba and Seba shall offer gifts. Yea, all kings shall fall down before him; all nations shall serve him."

Chapter VI: Apostolicity, or Peter's Primacy.

Seated on the throne of the Caesars, and drawing the peculiar doctrines of their creed, and the peculiar rites of their worship, from the fount of the pagan mythology, the Roman pontiffs have nevertheless sought to persuade the world that they are the successors of the apostles, and that they wield their authority and inculcate their doctrines. Apostolicity is a peculiar and prominent claim of Rome. Protestants lay claim to apostolicity in the sense of holding the doctrines of the apostles; but the popes of Rome assert an uninterrupted lineal descent from the apostle Peter, and on the ground of this supposed lineal succession they sustain themselves the heirs of the powers and functions of Peter. The doctrine held by the Church of Rome on this head is briefly as follows: — That Christ constituted Peter the prince of the apostles and the head of the Church; that he raised him to this high dignity when he said to him, "Thou art Peter, and upon this rock I will build my Church." "Jesus saith unto him, feed my sheep;" that Christ in these words committed to Peter the care of the whole Church, pastors as well as people; that Rome was the seat of the bishoprick of Peter; that the popes succeeded him in his see, and, in virtue of this succession, inherited all the royalties and jurisdiction, the functions and virtues, with which Peter became invested when Christ addressed him in the words we have quoted; that this "mystic oil" has flowed down through the "golden pipes," — the popes, — to our day; that it resides in all its fulness in the present occupant of Peter's chair; and that it is thence diffused by innumerable lesser pipes, formed by the bishops and priests, to the remotest extremities of the Roman Catholic world, vivifying and sanctifying all its members, giving authority to all its priests, and validity and efficacy to all their official acts.

Bellarmine, as was to be expected, has entered at great length into this question. He lays it down as an axiom, that Christ has adopted for the government of his Church that particular mode which is the best; and then, having determined, that of the three forms of government, — *monarchy*, *aristocracy*, and *democracy*, — monarchy is the most perfect, he concludes that the government of the Church is a monarchy. This inference he bases not simply on general reasonings, but also on particular passages of

Scripture, in which the Church is spoken of as a house, a state, a kingdom. It is not enough that the Church has a head and king in heaven, with a code of laws on earth, — the Bible, to determine all causes and controversies. That king, says Bellarmine, is invisible; the Church must have an earthly and visible head. Having thus paved the way for the erection of the papal despotism, Bellarmine proceeds to show, from the passage quoted above, that Peter was constituted sole head and monarch of the Church under Christ. "Of that passage," remarks Bellarmine, "the sense is plain and obvious. Under two metaphors the primacy of the whole Church is promised to Peter. The first metaphor is that of a foundation and edifice; for what a foundation is in a building, that a head is in a body, a ruler in a state, a king in a kingdom, a father in a family. The latter metaphor is that of the keys; for he to whom the keys of a kingdom are delivered is made king and governor of that state, and has power to admit or exclude men at his pleasure." We merely state at present the interpretation of this fatuous passage given by the learned Jesuit: we shall examine it afterwards.

The two main reasons assigned by Dens why the Roman Church is termed apostolic are, *first*, That "the doctrine delivered by the apostles is the same which she has always held, and will continue to hold;" and, *second*, Because that Church "possesses a lawful and uninterrupted succession of bishops, especially in the chair of Peter." "Messiah founded the kingdom of his holy Church in Judea," says Dr. Milner, "and chose his apostles to propagate it throughout the earth, over whom he appointed Simon as the *centre of union and head pastor*, charging him to feed his whole flock, sheep as well as lambs, giving him the keys of the kingdom of heaven, and changing his name into that of PETER or ROCK; adding, 'On *this rock I will build my Church.*' Thus dignified, St. Peter first established his see at Antioch, the head city of Asia; whence he sent his disciple St. Mark to establish and govern the see of Alexandria, the head city of Africa. He afterwards removed his own see to Rome, the capital of Europe and the world. Here, having with St. Paul sealed the gospel with his blood, he transmitted his prerogative to St. Linus, from whom it descended in succession to St. Cletus and St. Clement." In Dr. Challoner's Grounds of the Catholic Doctrine, as contained in the profession of faith published by Pope Pius IV., it is asserted "that the Church of Christ must be apostolical by a succession of her pastors, and a lawful mission derived from the apostles;" and when it is asked, "how do you prove this?" it is answered; 1st, Because only those who can derive their lineage from the apostles are the heirs of the apostles! and, consequently, they alone can claim a right to the Scriptures, to the administration of the sacraments, or any share in the pastoral ministry: it is their proper inheritance, which they have received from the apostles, and the apostles from Christ." "Her [Catholic Church] pastors, says Keenan, are the only pastors on earth who can trace their mission from priest to bishop, and from bishop to pope, back through every century, until they trace that mission to the apostles." This is a vital point with Rome. The primacy of Peter is her corner-stone; and if that is removed, the whole fabric tumbles into ruin. It is reasonable, then, to ask some proof of that long chain of facts by which she attempts to link the humble fisherman with the more than imperial pontiffs. We are entitled to demand that the Church of Rome produce conclusive and incontrovertible proof of the following points: — That Christ constituted Peter prince of the apostles and head of the whole Church; that Peter went to Rome, and there established his see; that, dying at Rome, he transmitted to his successors in his charge the rights and prerogatives of his sovereignty; and that these have been handed down through an unbroken series of bishops, every one of whom possessed and exercised Peter's powers and prerogatives. If the Church of Rome fail in establishing any one of these points, she fails as regards the whole. The loss of one link in this chain is as fatal as the loss of all. But, doubtless, in a matter of such consequence, where not much *simply*, but *all*, is at stake, Rome is ready with her evidences, full, clear, and incontrovertible; with her proofs from Scripture so plain and palpable in their meaning; and with her documents from history all endorsed and countersigned by cotemporary writers and great collateral facts. It is her citadel, — the *arx causae pontifiae*, as Spanheim terms it,— for which she is to do battle: doubtless she has taken care to make it impregnable, and "esteemeth iron as straw, and brass as rotten wood. Darts are counted as stubble;" she "laugheth at the shaking of a spear." So one would have thought. But alas for Rome! Not one of the positions above stated has she proved to be true, and not a few of them can be shown to be false.

The words of our Lord to Peter, already quoted, are the anchor by which Rome endeavours to fasten the vessel of her Church to the rock of Christianity: "Thou art Peter, and upon this rock I will build my Church; and the gates of hell shall not prevail against it." As it happens that, in the original, the term Peter and the term *rock* closely resemble each other, the Church of Rome has taken advantage of this, dexterously, and by a kind of sleight of hand, to substitute the one for the other, and thus to read the passage substantially as follows: — *Thou art Peter; and upon thee, Peter, will I build my Church.* The reader who is just breaking ground in the popish controversy learns with astonishment that this is the sole foundation of the Papacy, and that if the Church of Rome fail to make good that this is the true meaning of the text, her cause is lost. In no other case has so slender a foundation been made to sustain so ponderous a structure; nor would it have sustained it for a single five minutes, had it not been more indebted for its support to credulity and superstition, to fraud and compulsion, than to either reason or Scripture. "If the whole system of the Roman Catholic Church be contained in this passage," remarks the Rev. J. Blanco White, "it is contained like a diamond in a mountain;" and, we may add, this diamond would have remained buried in the mountain till the end of time, had not the Romish alchymists arisen to draw it forth. We look upon such feats of interpretation much as we gaze upon the feats of the juggler. Who but the Roman doctors could have evolved from this plain passage a whole race of popes? But why did they not go farther, and infer that each of these pontiffs would rival the sons of Anak in stature, and Mathuselah in longevity? The passage would have borne this marvel equally well. After proceeding a certain length in interpreting Scripture, it is easy to go all lengths; for that interpretation that proceeds on no fixed principles, and is regulated by no known laws, may reach any conclusion, and establish the possibility of any wonder.

But the Protestant may ask an hundred questions on this point, which it will baffle the ingenuity and sophistry of all the doctors of Rome satisfactorily to answer. Why was so important a fact, so vital a doctrine, — for let it be borne in mind, that they who do not believe in the infallibility of the Pope cannot be saved, — why was so important a fact as the primacy of Peter revealed in so obscure a passage? Why is there no other passage corroborating its sense, and helping out its meaning? Why, even with the aid of papal spectacles, or tradition, which discovers so many wonderful things in Scripture never seen by the man who examines it simply with the eyes of his understanding, do we fail to make out this sense from the passage? For the opinion of the fathers on the words of our Lord to Peter is directly opposed to the interpretation which the Church of Rome has put upon them; and every priest swears at his ordination that he "will not interpret the Scriptures but, according to the unanimous consent of the fathers." Peter but a moment before had made his great confession, "Thou art the Christ, the Son of the living God." And, says Poole, in his examination of the Church's infallibility, "the fathers generally understood this rock to be, not Peter's person, but his confession, or Christ, as confessed by him. *Vide* St. Cyril, Hilary, Hierom, Ambrose, Basil, and Austin, who are proved by Moulins, in his discourse entitled 'The Novelty of Popery,' to have held this opinion." Of the same sentiments was Chrysostom, Theodoret, Origen, and others. Here, then, we leave the priests of Rome taking a solemn oath at their ordination that they will not interpret Scripture except with the unanimous consent of the fathers, and yet interpreting this passage in a sense directly contrary to the concurrent opinion of the fathers.

What, then, are we to understand by the "*rock*" on which Christ declared that he would build his Church? Whether are we to understand Peter, who afterwards thrice denied him, or the great truth which Peter had just confessed, even the eternal deity of Christ? The fathers, we have seen, interpreted "this rock" of Christ himself, or of the confession of his deity by Peter; and so will every man, we venture to affirm, who is competent to form an opinion, and has no object to serve but the discovery of truth. Our Lord and his disciples were now on a northward journey to Cesarea Philippi. They were already within its coasts; the snowy peaks of Lebanon gleamed full in their sight; and nearer to them, indenting the bottom of "the goodly mountain," the wooded glens where the Jordan has its rise. Our Lord, knowing the time of his death to be nigh, thought it well, as they journeyed onward, to direct the current of the conversation to topics relating to the nature and foundation of that kingdom which was so shortly to be visibly erected in the world. "Whom do men say that I, the Son of man, am?" said he to his disciples. To this interrogatory the disciples replied by an enumeration of the various opinions held respecting him by the people at large. "But," said he, directing his question specially to the disciples, — "But whom say ye that I am?" "And Simon Peter answered and said, Thou art the Christ, the Son of the living God." Pleased to find his true character so clearly understood, so firmly believed in, and so frankly avowed, our Lord turned to Peter and said, "Blessed art thou, Simon Bar-jona; for flesh and blood hath not revealed IT unto thee." What IT? Unquestionably the truth he had just acknowledged, that Jesus is "the Christ, the Son of the living God," — a truth which lay at the foundation of his mission, which lay at the foundation of all his reaching, and, by consequence, at the foundation of that system of truth, commonly called his kingdom, which he was to erect in the world, and which, therefore, was a fundamental truth, if any truth ever merited to be called such; for unless it be true that Jesus was "the Christ, the Son of the living God," there is nothing true in Christianity, — it is all a fable. We must bear in mind, then, in proceeding to the next clause, that it was on this truth, which both Papist and Protestant must confess to be the very *first* truth in Christianity, that the minds of our Lord and his disciples were now undividedly fixed. "And I say also unto thee," continues our Lord, "that thou art Peter; and upon this rock will I build my Church." Upon what rock? Upon Peter, say Romanists, grounding their interpretation upon the similarity of sound, "Tu es *Petrus*, et super hanc *petram*." Upon the truth Peter had just confessed, say Protestants, grounding their interpretation upon the higher principles of sense, and the reason of the thing. "Upon *this* rock, says our Lord, not upon *thee*, the rock, but upon *this* rock, namely, the truth you have now enunciated in the words, "the Christ, the Son of the living God," — a truth which has been matter of special revelation to thee, the belief in which has made you truly blessed, and a truth which holds a place so fundamental and essential in the gospel kingdom, that it may be well termed "a rock." What is the Church? Is it not an association of men holding certain truths? The members of the Church are united, not by their belief in certain men, but by their belief in certain principles. As is the building, so must be the foundation: the building is spiritual, and the foundation must be spiritual also. And where, in the whole system of supernatural truth, is there a doctrine that takes precedence, as a fundamental one, of that which Peter now confessed? Remove it, and nothing can supply its place; the whole of Christianity crumbles into ruin. This truth formed the foundation of our Lord's personal teaching; it was this truth which he nobly confessed when he stood upon his trial; this truth formed the sum of the sermons of the apostles and first preachers of Christianity; and this truth it was that constituted the compendious creed of the primitive Church. Thus, in opposition to an interpretation which has nothing but an agreement in sound to support it, we can set an interpretation which is strongly supported by the reason of the thing, by the constitution of the Church as revealed in the New Testament, and by the whole subsequent actings and declarations of the apostles and primitive believers. To choose between these two interpretations appears to us to involve little difficulty indeed, — at least to the man in quest of the single object of truth.

To make the meaning, as we have evolved it, still more undoubted, it is added in the following clause, "And I will give unto thee the keys of the kingdom of heaven." This power is manifestly given to Peter. But mark how our Lord points directly to him, — names him, — "I will give unto *thee* the keys of the kingdom of heaven." Had he, in the preceding clause, meant to intimate that he would build his Church on Peter, doubtless he would have said so as plainly and with as little circumlocution as now, when giving him the keys. As regards this last, we shall permit Peter himself to explain the authority and privilege implied in it. "Brethren," said he, addressing the meeting at Jerusalem, "ye know how that a good while ago God made choice among us, that the Gentiles by my mouth should hear the word of the gospel, and believe." On Peter this great honour was conferred, that he was the first to "open the door" of the gospel Church to both Jews and Gentiles. The power which Romanists assign to Peter over the apocryphal world of purgatory, founding upon this verse, and also his sole right to open or shut the gate of paradise, is a gross and palpable misapprehension of its meaning. Peter himself tells us it was "the door of faith" which he was honoured to open, by the discharge of an office which those who are the most forward to claim kindred with him are the least ready to fulfil, — the preaching of the gospel. It is not the man who sits as sentinel at the fabulous portal of purgatory that carries the key of Peter, but the man who, by the faithful preaching of the everlasting gospel, "opens the door of faith" to perishing sinners. He is the real successor of Peter; he holds his key, and opens and shuts, on a higher authority than Peter's, — even that of Peter's master. Farther, we must bear in mind that Christ spoke in the vernacular tongue of Judea; and that not only are the Vulgate and English versions translations, but the Greek of the evangelist is a translation also; but it is inspired, and therefore as authoritative as the very words that Christ uttered. Now, it is not difficult to show that the most literal and correct rendering of the Greek would run thus: — "Thou art a stone (*petros*), and on this rock (*petra*) I will build my Church." When Peter was called to be an apostle, his name was changed from Simon to Cephas. Cephas is a Syriac word, and synonymous with Peter. This is indubitable, from the account we have of his call: "When Jesus beheld him, He said, thou art Simon the son of Jona: thou shalt be called Cephas, which is by interpretation, a *stone*;" or, as it is in the original, *Peter*. Both names (÷çñáò and ðåôñïò) signify a stone, — a stone that may be rolled about, or shifted from place to place, and therefore very proper to be used in building, but altogether unsuitable for being built upon. But the word used in the second clause of the passage, and translated "rock," is the word that strictly signifies a rock, or some mass which, from its immobility, is fitting for a foundation. Two different words, then, are employed, each having its appropriate signification. Now, it may be asked, if one person only, namely, Peter, is meant, why is not the same word employed in both clauses? Why, in the first clause, employ that word which denotes the material used in building; and, in the second, that word which denotes the foundation on which the building is placed? There is a nice grammatical distinction in the verse which the Protestant interpretation preserves, but which the Romanist interpretation violates. As Turrettine remarks, the *petros* of the first clause is masculine; whereas the *petra* of the second clause is feminine, and cannot, therefore, denote the person of Peter. If our Lord did indeed intend that *petros*, the stone, should form the *rock* or foundation of his Church, he would undoubtedly have repeated the masculine *petros* in the second clause. Why obscure the sense and violate the grammar by using the feminine *petra*? or why not use *petra* in both clauses, and so call Peter a *rock*, instead of a *stone*, if such was his meaning, and so preserve at once the figure and the grammar? It is clear that there are two persons and two things in this verse. There is Peter, a *stone*, and there is "the Christ, the Son of the living God," a *rock*. The words insinuate, delicately yet obviously, a contrast between the two. The Papists have confounded them, and have built upon the *stone*, instead of the *rock*.

Even were the passage dubious, which we by no means grant, its sense would fall to be determined by the great principles taught in other and plainer passages, about which there is not, and cannot be, any dispute. In the New Testament we find certain great principles on this subject, which the papal interpretation of the verse violates and sets at nought.

It is impossible that in the New Testament, which was written to make known the existence and constitution of the Church, its foundation should not be clearly and unmistakeably indicated. And, in truth, it is so in numerous passages. In his first epistle to the Corinthians we find Paul discoursing on this very topic, in a way to leave no room for doubt or cavil. He calls himself a master builder, and says, "I have laid the foundation." What was that foundation? Was it Peter's primacy, — the true foundation, according to Rome? Paul himself, in terms which do not admit of being misunderstood, tells us what that foundation is: "Other foundation can no man lay than that is laid, which is Jesus Christ." The question at issue is, On what foundation is the Church, that is, Christianity, built? On Jesus

Christ, replies the apostle. If these words do not definitely settle that question, we despair of words being found capable of settling it. "It is here," says Calvin, "abundantly evident on what rock it is that the Church is built." Bellarmine, unable to meet this plain testimony, attempts to turn aside its force by saying, that it is granted that Christ is the primary foundation of the Church, but that Peter is the foundation of the Church in the room of Christ, or as Christ's vicar; and that it is proper to speak of the Church as immediately and literally built upon Peter. Now, no enlightened Protestant affirms that Romanists make Peter the sole and primary author of Christianity, or that they utterly ignore the person and work of the Saviour: the question, they admit, is regarding vicarship. But to make Peter the foundation of the Church in the room of Christ, or as Christ's vicar, is just to make him the foundation of the Church. To devolve upon a second party the immediate and literal government of the realm, would be a virtual dethronement of the real monarch, more especially if the party in question had no patent of investiture to exhibit. The more enlightened heathens willingly allowed the existence and supremacy of an infinite and invisible Being, only they put idols in his room. Romanists have dealt in the same way by the divine foundation of the Church: reserving the empty name to Christ, they have put him aside, and substituted another. The Bible furnishes not a tittle of evidence that the person of Peter can in any sense, or to any extent, be denominated the foundation. Nay, it explicitly asserts that Christ is that foundation, to the exclusion of all participation on the part of any one. "Other foundation can no man lay than that is laid, which is Jesus Christ."

To the same import is the passage, "And are built upon the foundation of the apostles and prophets, Jesus Christ himself being the chief corner-stone." Romanists sometimes quote this passage, as if it favoured their theory of Christ being the primary foundation and Peter the immediate foundation of the Church. The passage overthrows this view. Romanists must admit that there are but two senses which can be put upon the words "the foundation of the apostles and prophets;" they can mean only the persons of the apostles and prophets, or the doctrine of the apostles and prophets; but either sense is opposed to the Romanist theory. If it be said that by the words "the foundation of the apostles and prophets" is meant their *persons*, what then becomes of Peter's primacy? He appears here simply as one of the twelve; nay, his name is not seen at all; and no hint is given that one is superior to another. If *persons* are here meant, then all the twelve are foundations; and, on the doctrine of transmission, each of the twelve ought to have his representative; we ought to have not only a Peter, but a James, a John, and a Paul in the world. Nay, we ought to have an Isaiah, a Jeremiah, an Ezekiel, and others also; for with the apostles of the New are joined the prophets of the Old Testament. If it be said that by "the foundation of the apostles and prophets" we are to understand their doctrines, this is just what we maintain, and is but another way of stating that Christ is the foundation.

It is clear that when Paul wrote this passage he was ignorant of Peter's primacy; and it is equally undeniable that every other writer in the New Testament was as ignorant of it as Paul. Amazing, that Peter should have been the Church's foundation, the Church's head, and that his superangelic dignity should have been unknown and unsuspected by his brethren! Or, if any man affirms the contrary, he must have had his knowledge through inspiration; for not the slightest allusion to it has come from the apostles themselves. The prophets may be excused for being ignorant of it. Although Isaiah spoke of a foundation which God was to lay in Zion, — "a stone, a tried stone, a precious corner-stone, a sure foundation,"— there is nothing to lead us to suppose that he had the least idea that Peter was here meant. More marvellous still, Peter himself knew nothing of it; for we find him applying to another than himself these words just cited. And we find him, too, in his ignorance of his own primacy, misapplying another passage: — "The stone which the builders refused," said the Psalmist, "is become the head stone of the corner." So far was Peter from believing that himself was that stone, that we find him charging their rejection of Christ upon the chief-priest and his council as a fulfilment of the prophecy, "Jesus Christ of Nazareth, whom ye crucified, whom God raised from the dead, even by him doth this man stand here before you whole. This is the stone which was set at nought of you builders, which is become the head of the corner." Nay, more, our Lord himself knew not that the passage referred to Peter's primacy, otherwise he surely never would have claimed the honour to himself, as we find him doing. "Did ye never read in the Scriptures," said he to the representatives of those evil husbandmen who slew the Son, "the stone which the builders rejected, the same has become the head of the corner?" Thus, He who conferred the dignity, the person on whom that dignity was conferred, and those who were the witnesses of the act, all, on their own showing, were ignorant of the important transaction. The apostles preach sermons and write epistles, and omit all mention of the fundamental article of Christianity. They delivered to the world but a mutilated gospel. They kept back, through ignorance or through perversity, that on which, according to Bellarmine and De Maistre, hangs the whole of Christianity, and the belief in which is essential to salvation on the part of every human being. Paul preached "Christ crucified" when he ought to have preached "Peter exalted." He gloried in the "cross" when he ought to have gloried in the "infallibility." The profession of the Ethiopian eunuch to Philip ought to have run, not "I believe that Jesus Christ is the Son of God," but "I believe that Peter is prince of the apostles and Christ's vicar." The writer of the epistle to the Ephesians, when he enumerates apostles, prophets, evangelists, pastors, and teachers, and omits the pontiff, leaves out the better half of his list, and passes over an office-bearer who had much more to do with the perfecting of the saints and the unity of the Church than all the rest put together. And, in fine, when the survivor of the twelve, the beloved disciple, indited his epistles, exhorting to love and unity, recommending for this purpose an earnest attention to those things which they had heard from the beginning, he altogether mistook his object, and ought to have reminded those to whom he wrote that Peter's successor was reigning at Rome, and that the perfection of Christian duty was implicit obedience to the infallible dictates of the apostolic chair. But all the apostles went to their graves and carried this secret along with them. Peter's primacy was not so much as whispered in the world till Rome had bred a race of infallible bishops. Nevertheless, we have so much of the spirit of apostolical succession in us as to prefer being in error with the apostles to being in the right with the popes.

To help out the sense of this obscure passage, the Church of Rome has called in the assistance of other passages still more obscure, — obscure, we mean, not in themselves, but under the sombre lights of Rome's hermaneutics. Not a little stress has been laid upon the words that follow those on which we have been commenting, — "And I will give unto thee the keys of the kingdom of heaven; and whatsoever thou shalt bind on earth shalt be bound in heaven; and whatsoever thou shalt loose on earth shalt be loosed in heaven." We have already adverted to these words, and have here only to remark, that, even granting the affirmation of the Papists, that the keys of the kingdom of heaven were given to Peter, to the exclusion of the other apostles, his tenure of sole authority must have been brief indeed; for we find our Lord, after his resurrection, associating all the apostles in the exercise of these keys. "Receive ye the Holy Ghost:

whosesoever sins ye remit, they are remitted unto them; and whosesoever sins ye retain, they are retained." Here no primacy is conferred on Peter. He ranks with the other apostles, and receives but his own share of the gift now conferred by his Master on all. If, then, Peter ever had sole possession of the keys, which we deny, he must from this time forward have admitted his brother apostles to a participation with him in his power, or usurped what did not belong to him, and was in no degree more his right than it was the right of all. If the former, how could Peter transmit to his successors what himself did not possess? and if the latter, he transmitted a power that was unlawful, because usurped; and therefore the Popes are still usurpers. "I have prayed for thee, that thy faith fail not," said our Lord to the same apostle, when predicting that he should fall, but not finally apostatize; and Papists have built much upon the words, especially as regards the infallibility of the Pope. The words refer us back to a part of Peter's history which one would have thought those seeking to establish a primacy for him would have prudently avoided. They attest, as a historical fact, Peter's fallibility; and it does seem strange to found upon them in proof of the infallibility of the popes. If the ordinary laws which regulate the transmission of moral qualities operated in this case, and if Peter begot popes in his own likeness, how comes it that from a fallible man proceeded a race of infallible pontiffs? It is one of Rome's many mysteries, doubtless, which is to be believed, not explained. But to an ordinary understanding such arguments prove nothing but the desperate straits to which those are reduced who make use of them. And what, moreover, are we to think of the Council of Basil, which, by solemn canon, decreed that a pope might be deposed in case of heresy, — a most necessary provision, verily, against an evil which, on the principles of the papists, can never happen!

Once more, we are referred in proof of Peter's primacy to these words in John, — "Jesus saith unto him [Peter], feed my sheep." "At most, the words do only," as St. Cyril saith, "*renew the former grant of apostleship*, after his great offence of denying our Lord." But according to the Roman interpretation of these words, Peter was now constituted UNIVERSAL PASTOR of the Church. Now, certainly, as a doctor of the Sorbonne argues, if these words prove anything peculiar to Peter, they prove that he was *sole* pastor of the Church, and that there ought to be but one Church in the world, St. Peter's, and but one preacher, the Pope. "The same office," says Barrow, in his incomparable treatise on the supremacy of the Pope, "certainly did belong to all the apostles, who (as St. Hierom speaketh) were the princes of our discipline and chieftains of the Christian doctrine; they at their first vocation had a commission and command to go unto the lost sheep of the house of Israel, that were scattered abroad like sheep not having a shepherd; they, before our Lord's ascension, were enjoined to teach all nations the doctrines and precepts of Christ, to receive them into the fold, to feed them with good instruction, to guide and govern their converts with good discipline. Hence all of them (as St. Cyprian saith) were shepherds. But the flock did appear one, which was fed by the apostles with unanimous agreement. Neither could St. Peter's charge be more extensive than was that of the other apostles, for they had a general and unlimited care of the whole Church. They were ecumenical rulers (as St. Chrysostom saith), appointed by God, who did not receive several nations or cities, but all of them in common were entrusted with the world." The proofs of what is here asserted are not difficult to seek for. The very same charge here given by Christ to Peter, on which the Romanists have reared so stupendous a structure of exclusive and universal jurisdiction, does the Holy Ghost, through the instrumentality of Paul, give to the elders of the Church of Miletus. The apostle bids them "take heed to all the flock over which the Holy Ghost hath made them overseers, to feed the Church of God." Nay, we find Peter himself, the holder, according to the Roman idea, of this universal pastorate, writing to the Asiatic churches thus: — "The elders I exhort, who am also an elder: feed the flock of God." Nor can we mistake the import of the last solemn act of Christ on earth, which was to commit the evangelization of the world — to whom? To Peter? No; to all the apostles. "Go ye into all the world and preach the gospel to every creature." "And surely," says Poole, "Peter's diocese cannot be more extensive, unless perhaps Utopia be taken in, or that which is in the same part of the world, I mean purgatory."

On the supposition that Peter possessed the primacy, he must have exercised it; and if so, how comes it that not the slightest trace of such a thing is to be discovered, either in the New Testament or in Ecclesiastical History? The rest of the apostles were entirely ignorant of the fact. Even after the words on which we have been commenting were addressed to Peter, we find them raising the question, with no little warmth, "who should be the greatest" in their master's kingdom? — a question which Romanists believe had already been conclusively settled by Christ. Ardent in temper and fearless in disposition, Peter was on some occasions more prominent than the rest; but that was a pre-eminence springing from the man, not from the office. His whole intercourse with the other apostles does not furnish a single instance of official superiority. When "Judas by transgression fell," Peter did not presume to nominate to the vacant dignity; and yet, as prince of the apostles, and the fountain of all ecclesiastical dignity, he ought to have done so. We do not find him, as arch-apostle, appointing the ordinary apostles to their spheres of labour, or summoning them to his bar, to give an account of their mission, or reproving, admonishing, and exhorting them, as he might judge they required. In the synod holden at Jerusalem, to allay the dissensions which had sprung up on the subject of circumcision, it was James, and not Peter, that presided. Paul, in the matter of the Gentile converts, withstood Peter "to the face, because he was to be blamed." "We find," says Stillingfleet, "the apostles sending St. Peter to Samaria, which was a very unmannerly action, if they looked on him as head of the Church." Ministers do not send their sovereign on embassies. What would be thought should Cardinal Wiseman order Pius IX. on a mission to the United States? Nor, though very conspicuous, was this apostle the most conspicuous member in the small but illustrious band to which he belonged? Peter was overshadowed by the colossal intellect and prodigious labours of the apostle Paul. The great and indisputable superiority, in these respects, of this apostle, has been acknowledged by the popes themselves. The following may be cited as a curious sample of that unity which Rome claims as her peculiar attribute: — "He was better than all men," says Chrysostom, "greater than the apostles, and surpassing them all." Pope Gregory I. says of the apostle Paul, — "He was made head of the nations, because he obtained the principate of the whole Church."

Nor is it less unaccountable, on the supposition that Peter was head of the whole Church, that we fail to discover the remotest trace of this sovereignty in his epistles. Addressing the members of the Church on a variety of subjects, one would have thought that he must needs have occasion at times to remind them of his jurisdiction, and the duty and allegiance which they in consequence owed. But nothing of this sort occurs. "No critic perusing those epistles," remarks Barrow, "would smell a pope in them." Peter does not say, — "It is our apostolic will and command," as is now the style of the popes. The highest style he assumes is to speak in the common name of the apostles, — "Be mindful of the words which were spoken before by the holy prophets, and of the commandment of us the apostles of the Lord and Saviour."_A pontifical pen employed on these letters could not but have left traces of itself. The Epistles of Peter emit the sweet perfume of apostolic humility, — not the rank effluvia of papal arrogance.

Thus the primacy of Peter is without the least foundation, either in Scripture, in ecclesiastical history, or in the reason of the thing; and unless we are good enough to accept the word of the pontiff, given *ex cathedra*, in the room of all other evidence, this pretence of primacy must be given up as a gross delusion and imposture. The argument ends here of right; for all other reasons, urged from such considerations as that Peter was Bishop of Rome, are plainly irrelevant, seeing it matters not to the authority of the popes in what city or quarter of the world Peter exercised his office, unless it can be shown that he was primate of the apostles and head of the Church. But granting that that difficulty is got over, Papists are instantly met by other difficulties equally great. It is essential to the Roman scheme to establish as a fact, that Peter was Bishop of Rome. This no Romanist has yet been able to do. Now, in the first place, we are not prepared to deny that Peter ever visited Rome, any more than Papists are able to prove that he did. In the second place, the improbability of Peter having been Bishop of Rome is so exceedingly great, amounting as near as may be to an impossibility, that we would be warranted in denying it. And, in the third place, we do most certainly deny that Peter was the founder of the Church of Rome.

With regard to the averment that Peter was Bishop of Rome, it is as near as may be a demonstrable impossibility. To have been Bishop of Rome would have been in plain opposition to the great end of his apostleship. As an apostle, Peter had the world for his diocese, and was bound by the duty which he owed to Christianity at large, to hold himself in readiness to go wherever the Spirit might send him. To fetter himself in an inferior sphere, so that he could not fulfil his great mission, — to sink the apostle in the bishop, — to oversee the diocese of Rome and overlook the world, — would have been sinful; and we may conclude that Peter was not chargeable with that sin. Baronius himself confesseth that Peter's office did not permit him to stay in one place, but required him to travel throughout the whole world, converting the unbelieving and confirming the faithful. To have acted as the Romanists allege, would have been to desert his sphere and neglect his work; and it would scarce have been held a valid excuse for being "unfaithful in that which was much," that he was "faithful in that which was least." And if it would have been inconsistent on our principles, it would have been still more inconsistent on Romanist principles. On their principles, Peter was not only an apostle, — he was primate of the apostles; and, as Barrow observes, "it would have been a degradation of himself, and a disparagement to the apostolic majesty, for him to take upon him the bishoprick of Rome, as if the king should become mayor of London."

On other grounds it is not difficult to demonstrate the extreme improbability of Peter having been Bishop of Rome. Peter had the Jews throughout the world committed to him as his especial charge. He was the apostle of the circumcision, as Paul was of the Gentiles. This people being much scattered, their oversight was very incompatible with a fixed episcopate. His regard to the grand division of apostolic labour, to which we have just alluded, would have restrained him from intruding into the bounds of a brother apostle, unless to minister to the Jews; and at this time there were few of that people at Rome, a decree of the Emperor Claudius having, a little before, banished them from the metropolis of the Roman world; and, as Barrow remarks, "He was too skilful a fisherman to cast his net there, where there were no fish."

If Peter ever did visit Rome, of which there exists not the slightest evidence, his residence in that metropolis must have been short indeed, — by far too short to admit of his acting as bishop of the place. Paul passed several years at Rome: he wrote several of his epistles (the epistle to the Galatians, that to the Ephesians, that to the Philippians, that to the Colossians, and the second to Timothy) from that city; and though these abound with warm greetings and remembrances, the name of Peter does not once occur in them. In the epistle which he wrote to the Church at Rome, he sends salutations to twenty-five individuals, and to several whole households besides; but he sends no salutation to Peter, *their bishop*! It is plain, that when these epistles were written, Peter was not at Rome. "Particularly St. Peter was not there," argues Barrow, in his matchless treatise, "when St. Paul, mentioning Tychicus, Onesimus, Aristarchus, Marcus, and Justus, addeth, 'these alone my fellow-workers unto the kingdom of God, who have been a comfort unto me.' He was not there when St. Paul said, 'at my first defence no man stood with me, but all men forsook me.' He was not there immediately before St. Paul's death (when the time of his departure was at hand), when he telleth Timothy that all the brethren did salute him, and, naming divers of them, he omitteth Peter."

Nor have the Romanists been able to establish in Peter's behalf that he was the founder of the Church at Rome. It is no uncertain inference, that the apostle Paul, if not the first to carry Christianity within the imperial walls, was the first to organize a regular Church at Rome. When the epistle to the Romans was written, there was a small company of believers in that metropolis, partly Jews and partly Gentiles; but they had never been visited by any apostle. Of this we find a proof in the opening lines of his epistle, where he says, "I long to see you, that I may impart unto you some spiritual gift." To an apostle only belonged the power of imparting such gifts; and we may conclude that, had the Christians at Rome been already visited by Peter, these gifts would not have been still to bestow. That they had as yet been visited by no apostle is indubitable, from what Paul assigns as the cause of his great desire to visit them, namely, "that I might have some fruit among you also, as among other Gentiles." Now, it was Paul's wont never to gather where he had not first planted; for, resuming, in the end of his epistle, the subject of his long-cherished visit to Rome, he says, "Yea, so have I strived to preach the gospel, not where Christ was named, lest I should build upon another man's foundation." By the hand of Paul then, and not of Peter, was planted the Roman Church, — "a noble vine," whose natural robustness and vigour of stock was abundantly attested by the renown of its early faith, as well as by the magnitude of its later corruptions.

But though we should concede the question of Peters Roman bishoprick, as we formerly conceded the point of his primacy, the Romanist is not a whit nearer his object. He is immediately met by the question, Were the arch-apostolical sovereignties and jurisdiction of Peter of a kind such as he could bequeath to his successor, and did he actually so bequeath them? This is a point which can be determined only by a consideration of the nature of these powers, and of what is related in the New Testament respecting the institution of offices for the future government of the Church. In the first place, Romanists found the gift of primacy to Peter upon certain acts done by Peter, and upon certain qualities possessed by Peter; but it is abundantly clear that these acts and qualities Peter could not communicate to his successors; therefore he could not communicate the dignity which was founded upon them. His office was strictly personal, and therefore expired with the person who had been clothed with it. In the second place, the apostleship was designed for a temporary purpose: it was therefore temporary in its nature, and ceased whenever that purpose had been served. In the next place, no one could assume the apostleship unless invested with it directly by Christ. The first twelve were literally called by Christ. The appointment of Matthias was by an express intimation of the Divine will, through the instrumentality of the lot; and that of Paul, perhaps the most powerful intellect which has ever been enlisted in the service of Christianity, by the miraculous and glorious appearance of Christ to him as he travelled to Damascus. Hence it is, that on this proof the apostle so often rests the validity of his great office, — "Paul, an apostle, not of men, neither by man, but by Jesus Christ." In the last place, it was essential on the part of all who bore the apostleship, that they had seen the Lord. This renders it impossible that this office could have validly existed longer than for a certain number of years after the death of Christ. The popes have at no time been very careful to keep their pretensions within the bounds of credibility; but we are not aware that any of them have ever gone so far as to assert that they had received investiture directly from Christ, or that literally they had seen the Lord.

It may also be urged with great force against Papists, as Barrow does, that "if some privileges of St. Peter were derived to popes, why were not all? Why was not Pope Alexander VI. as holy as St. Peter? Why was not Pope Honorius as sound in his private judgment? Why is not every pope inspired? Why is not every papal epistle to be reputed canonical? Why are not all popes endowed with power of doing miracles? Why did not the Pope, by a sermon, convert thousands? [Why, indeed, do popes never preach?] Why doth he not cure men by his shadow? [He is, say they, himself his shadow.] What ground is there of distinguishing the privileges, so that he shall have some, not others? Where is the ground to be found?"

The practice of the apostles was in strict accordance with what we have now proved respecting the nature and end of the apostleship. They made no attempt to perpetuate an office which they knew to be temporary. They never thought of conveying to their contemporaries, or transmitting to their successors, prerogatives and powers which were restricted to their own persons, and which they knew would expire with themselves. They planted churches throughout the greater part of the then civilized world, and they ordained pastors in every place; but throughout the vast field which they covered with Christianity and planted with pastors and teachers, we do not find a single new apostleship created. One by one did these FATHERS of the Christian Church descend into the tomb; but the survivors took no steps to supply their place with men of equal rank and powers. It is not alleged that even Peter invested any with the apostleship; and yet no sooner does he breathe his last, than, lo! there springs from his ashes, as Romanists assure us, a whole race of popes. Most marvellous is it that the dead body of Peter should possess more virtue than the living man.

In fine, though we should concede this point, as we have conceded all that went before it, the difficulties of the Romanists are by no means at an end. Granting that Peter did possess this dignity, — granting that he made Rome its seat, — and granting, too, that he could and did transmit it to his successor when he died, — Romanists have still to show that this dignity has descended pure and entire to the present occupant of the pontifical throne. It is not enough that the mystic waters existed on the Seven Hills eighteen centuries ago; we must be able to trace the continuity of the channel which has conveyed them over the intervening period to our day. Pius IX. is the two hundred and fifty-seventh name on the pontifical list; and, in order to prove that in him resides the plenitude of pontifical power, the Romanist must show that every one of his predecessors was duly elected, — that none of them fell into heresy, or into simony, or into any other error which the Roman councils have declared to be inconsistent with being valid successors of Peter, or, indeed, members of the Church at all. But is there a man living who has the least acquaintance with history, who will undertake this, or who, on the question of genuineness, would stand surety for the one-half of those who have sat in the chair of Peter? Is it not notorious that that chair has been gained, in instances not a few, by fraud, by bribery, by violence, — that the election of a pope has often led to the deluging of Rome with blood, — that men who have been monsters of iniquity have called themselves the vicars of Him who was without sin, — that there have been violent schisms, numerous vacancies, and sometimes two, or even three, pretenders to the popedom, each of whom has endeavoured to establish his pretensions by excommunicating his rival, — thus affording a fine specimen of Catholic unity, as they have also done of Catholic infallibility, when, as in cases not a few, one pope has flatly contradicted another pope, and that in circumstances where it was quite possible that both popes might be wrong, but altogether impossible that both could be right? It is notorious also, that in many instances popes have fallen into what the Church of Rome accounts heresy, and have ceased, in consequence, not only to be genuine popes, but even members of the Church. What became of the apostolic dignity in these cases? How was it preserved, and how transmitted? Sometimes we find the chair of Peter vacant, at other times it is filled with a heretical pope, at other times it is claimed by two or more popes, each of whom is as like or as unlike Peter as his rival. So far is the line of succession from being continuous, that we find it broken, at short intervals, by wide gaps, through which, if there be any truth in Romanist principles, the mystic virtues must have lapsed, leaving the Church in a most deplorable state, her popes without pontifical authority, her priests without true consecration, and her sacraments without regenerating efficacy. The great geographical problems which have been undertaken in our day, in which mighty rivers have been traced up to their source, through tangled forests, and low swampy flats on which the miasma settles thick and deadly, and through the burning sands of the trackless desert, have been of easy achievement, compared with that of the man who would trace up to its source that mystic but powerful influence which is held to pervade the Church of Rome. And even when some bold spirit does adventure upon the onerous task, and pushes resolutely on through the moral wastes, the tangled controversies, and the perplexed and devious paths of the Papacy, and through the dense clouds of superstition and vice that overhang the pontifical annals, what is his disappointment to find that, instead of being conducted at last to the pellucid waters of the apostolic fount, he is landed on the mephitic shores of some black and stagnant pool, — some Acheron of the middle ages!

Thus have we examined, severally, the assumptions of Rome on this fundamental point. Some of them are utterly false, the rest are in the highest degree improbable, and not one of them has Rome been able to establish. This forms her foundation; and what is it but a quicksand? Though we should agree to concede the point to Rome on condition that she made good but one of these propositions, she would fail; and yet it is essentially necessary to the success of her cause that she should establish every one of them. If but one link be awanting in this chain, its loss forms an impassable gulf, which eternally divides Popery from Christianity, and the Church of Rome from the Church of Christ.

Chapter VII: Infallibility.

The crowning attribute claimed by the Church of Rome is infallibility. This forms a wide and essential distinction between that Church and all other societies. It is her crowning blasphemy, as Protestants hold; her peerless excellence, as Romanists maintain. These are the locks in which the great strength of this modern Sampson lies, and to which are owing, in no small degree, the prodigious feats that Rome has performed in enslaving the nations. If these locks are shorn, she becomes weak as others. Progression, and consequently change, which excludes the idea of infallibility, is an essential condition in the existence of all created beings. It is the law of the material universe: it is not less that of the rational creation. Man, whether as an individual or as formed into society, is ever advancing. In science he drops the crude, the vague, and the false, and rises to the certain and the true. In government he is gradually approximating what is best adapted to the constitution of society, the nature of the human mind, and the law of God. In religion he is dropping the symbolical, and rising to the spiritual; he is gradually enlarging, correcting, and perfecting his views. Thus he advanced from the Patriarchal to the Mosaic, — from the Mosaic to the Christian; and to this condition of his being the Bible is adapted. The Bible, like no other book in the world, remains eternally immutable, notwithstanding it is as completely adapted to each successive condition of the Church and of society as if it had been written for that age, and no other. Why so? Because that book is stored with great principles and comprehensive laws, adapted to every case that can arise, and capable of being applied to all the conditions and ages of the world. The Church, so far from having got beyond the Bible, is not yet abreast of it. Rome, on the other hand, is an iron circle, within which the human mind may revolve for ever without progressing a hairbreadth. That Church is the only society that never progresses. She never abandons a narrow view of truth for one more enlarged; she never corrects what is wrong or drops what is untrue; because she is infallible. Had she been able to render society as fixed as herself, it might have been safe to adopt, as her policy, immobility. But society is in motion; she can neither go along with the current nor arrest it, and therefore must founder at her moorings. Thus, in the righteous providence of God, that which was the source of her power will be the cause of her destruction.

We are fully warranted in affirming that the Church of Rome has claimed infallibility. If not directly and formally asserted, it is manifestly implied, in the decrees of general councils, in the bulls of popes, and in canons and articles of an authoritative character. The Catechism of the Council of Trent, after the assumptions we have already discussed, lays it down as a corollary, that "the Church cannot err in faith or morals." Infallibility is universally and formally claimed in behalf of their Church, by all Romanists; it is taught in all their Catechisms, and in all their text-books and systems of theology; and forms so prominent a point in all their defences of their system, that it is quite fair to assert that Papists hold and teach that their Church is infallible. Romanists do not hold that all persons and pastors in their Church are infallible, but only that the "Church" is infallible. To this extent Romanists are agreed on the question of infallibility, but no farther. The seat or locality of that infallibility remains to this hour undecided. The Jesuits and the Italian bishops hold that this infallibility resides in the Pope, as the head of the Church, and the organ through which she makes known her mind; the French bishops place it in general councils; while a third party exists which holds that neither popes nor councils separately are infallible, but that both conjointly are so. The Roman Catholics of England used anciently to side with the Italians on this question, but latterly they have gone over to the opinions of the French. Those who place infallibility in the Pope do not maintain that he is infallible either in his personal conduct or in his private opinions, but only when *ex cathedra* he pronounces on points of faith and decides controversies. Then he speaks infallibly, and every Roman Catholic is bound, at his peril, to receive and obey the decision. The compendious creed of the Romanist, according to Challoner, is as follows: — "I believe in all things, according as the Holy Catholic Church believes;" and he "promises and swears true obedience to the Roman bishops the successor of St. Peter, the prince of the apostles, and vicar of Jesus Christ; and professes and undoubtedly receives all things delivered, defined, and declared, by the sacred canons and general councils, and particularly by the holy Council of Trent; and condemns, rejects, and anathematizes all things contrary thereto, and all heresies whatsoever condemned and anathematized by the Church." "'A general council, rightly congregated,' says Alphonsus de Castro, 'cannot err in the faith.' 'Councils,' says Eccius and Tapperus, 'represent the Catholic Church, which cannot err, and therefore they cannot err.' Costerus says, 'The decrees of general councils have as much weight as the holy gospel.' 'Councils,' says Canus, 'approved and confirmed by the Pope cannot err.' Bellarmine seconds him. Tannerus alleges, that 'councils, being the highest ecclesiastical judicatories, cannot err.' And Stapelton says, 'The decrees of councils are the oracles of the Holy Ghost.'" That Rome receives from her members the entire submission which she claims on the ground of her infallibility, appears from the following description, given by Mr. Blanco White, of his state of mind while a member of that Church: — "I grounded my Christian faith upon the infallibility of the Church. No Roman Catholic pretends to a better foundation. . . . . I believed the infallibility of the Church, because the Scripture said she was infallible; while I had no better proof that the Scripture said so than the assertion of the Church that she could not mistake the Scripture."

The texts of Scripture on which Romanists rest the infallibility are mainly those we have already examined in treating of the supremacy. To these they add the following: — "Upon this rock I will build my Church, and the gates of hell shall not prevail against it." "I am with you always, unto the end of the world." "He that heareth you heareth me; and he that despiseth you despiseth me." "The Comforter, the Holy Ghost, shall abide with you for ever." But these passages fall a long way short of the infallibility. Fairly interpreted, they amount only to a promise that the Church, maugre the opposition of hell, shall be preserved till the end of time, — that the substance of the truth shall always be found in her, — and that the assistance of the Spirit shall be enjoyed by her members in investigating truth, and by her pastors in publishing it, and in exercising that authority with which Christ has invested them. But Romanists hold that it is not in the words, but in the sense of these passages that the proof lies; and that of that sense the Church is the infallible interpreter. They hold that the Scripture is so obscure, that we can know nothing of what it teaches on any point whatever, but by the interpretation of the Church. It was the saying of one of their distinguished men, Mr. Stapelton, "that even the Divinity of Christ and of God did depend upon the Pope."

This is a demand that we should lay aside the Bible, as a book utterly useless as a revelation of the Divine will, and that we should accept the Church as an infallible guide. It is a proposition which, in fact, puts the Church in the room of God. It is but reasonable that we should demand proof clear and conclusive of so momentous a proposition. Romanists, in their attempts to prove infallibility, commonly begin by alleging the necessity of an infallible authority in matters of faith. This Protestants readily grant. They, not less than Papists, appeal every matter of faith to an infallible tribunal. But herein they differ, that while the infallible tribunal of the Protestant is God speaking in the Bible, the infallible tribunal of the Papist is the voice of the Church. Now, even a Papist can scarce refuse to admit that the Protestant ground on this question is the more certain and safe. Both parties — Protestants and Papists — acknowledge the inspiration and infallibility of the Scriptures; while one party only, namely, the Papist, acknowledges the infallibility of the Church. But the Romanist is accustomed to urge, that Scripture is practically useless as an infallible guide, from its liability to a variety of interpretations on the part of a variety of persons; and he hence infers the necessity of a living, speaking judge, at any moment, to determine infallibly all doubts and controversies. The Bible, according to the Romanist, is the *written law*, — the Church is the *interpreter* or *judge*; and the example of England and other countries is appealed to as an analogous case, where the written laws are administered by living judges. The analogy rather bears against the Romanist; for while in England the law is above the judge, and the judge is bound to decide only according to the law's award, in the Church of Rome the judge is above the law, and the law can speak only according to the pleasure of the judge. But the argument by which it is sought to establish this living and speaking infallible tribunal is a singularly illogical one. From the great variety of interpretations to which the Scriptures are liable, such a living tribunal, say the Romanists, is necessary; and because it *is necessary*, therefore it *is*. Was there ever a more glaring *non sequitur*? If Romanists wish to establish the infallibility of the Church of Rome by fair reasoning, there is only one way in which they can proceed: they must begin the argument on ground common to both parties. What is that ground? It is not the infallibility, because Protestants deny that. It is the holy Scriptures, the inspiration and infallibility of which both parties admit. The Romanist cannot refuse an appeal to the Bible, because he admits it to be the Word of God. He is bound by clear and direct proofs drawn from thence to prove the infallibility of his Church, before he can ask a Protestant to receive it. But the texts advanced from the Bible, taken in their obvious and literal import, do not prove the infallibility of the Church; and the Romanist, who is unable to deny this, maintains, nevertheless, that they do amount to proofs of the Church's infallibility, because the Church, who cannot possibly mistake the sense of Scripture, has said so. The thing to be proved is the *Church's infallibility*; and this the Romanist proves by passages from Scripture which in themselves do not prove it, but become proofs by a latent sense contained in them, which latent sense depends upon the infallibility of the Church, which is the very thing to be proved. This famous argument has not inaptly been termed the "Labyrinth, or Popish Circle." "Papists commonly allege," says Dr. Cunningham, "that it is only from the testimony of the Church that we can certainly know what is the Word of God, and what is its meaning; and thus they are inextricably involved in the sophism of reasoning in a circle; that is, they profess to prove the infallibility of the Church by the authority of Scripture; while, at the same time, they establish the authority of Scripture, and ascertain its meaning, by the testimony of the Church, which cannot err."

We do not deny that God might have appointed an infallible guide, and that, had he done so, it would have been our duty to submit implicitly to him; but it is reasonable to infer, that in that case very explicit intimation would have been given of the fact. In giving such intimation, God would have acted but in accordance with his usual method. His own existence he has certified to us by great and durable proofs, — creation without us, and conscience within. He has attested the Bible as a supernatural revelation by many infallible marks stamped upon it. Analogy, then, warrants the conclusion that, had the Church of Rome been appointed the infallible guide of mankind, at least one very distinct intimation would have been given of the fact. But where do we find the slightest proof, or even hint, of such a, thing? Not in the Bible certainly. We may search it through and through without learning that there is any other infallible guide on earth but itself. If we believe the infallibility at all, it must be either because it is self-evident, or because it rests on proof. If it were self-evident, it would be vain to think of bringing proof to make it more evident, just as it would be vain to think of bringing evidence to prove that things that are equal to the same thing are equal to one another, or that the whole is greater than its part. But in that case there would be as little difference of opinion among rational men about the infallibility, as about the axioms we have just stated. But we find great diversity of sentiment indeed about the infallibility. Not one in ten professes to believe it. It is not, then, a self-evident truth; and seeing it is not self-evident, we must demand proof. It is usual with the Church of Rome to send us first to the Scriptures. We search the Scriptures from beginning to end, but can discover no proof of the infallibility; and when we come back to complain of our bad success, we are told that it was impossible we could fare otherwise; that we have been using our reason, than which we cannot possibly commit a greater crime, reason being wholly useless in discovering the true sense of Scripture; and that the sense of Scripture can be discovered only by infallibility. Thus the Romanist is back again into his circle. We are to believe the infallibility because the Scriptures bid us, and we are to believe the Scriptures because the infallibility bids us; and out of this circle the Romanist can by no means conjure himself.

An attempt at escape from an eternal rotation round the two foci of Scripture and infallibility the Romanist does make, by what looks like an appeal to reason. Of various possible ways, it is asserted, God always chooses the best; and as the best way of leading men to heaven is to appoint an infallible guide, therefore an infallible guide has been appointed. This is but another form of the argument of *necessity*, to which we have already adverted. But this cannot answer the purpose of the Roman Catholic Church. The Greek Church might employ this argument to prove its infallibility; or the professors of the Mahommedan faith might employ it. They might say, it is inconsistent with the goodness of God that there should not be an infallible guide; it is plain that there is no other than ourselves; therefore we are that infallible guide. But a better way still would have been to make every man and woman infallible; and we humbly submit that, according to the argument of the Romanist, this is the plan that God ought to have adopted. The theory of the Roman Catholic Church proceeds on the idea that there is but one man in the world possessed of his sound senses. Accordingly, he has charged himself with the safe keeping of all the rest; and for this benevolent end he has established a large asylum called Catholicism. The design of this establishment is not to restore the inmates to reason, but to keep them away from their reason. Here men are taught that never are they so wise as when most completely bereft of their faculties; nor do they ever act so rationally as when least aided by their senses. But by this line of argument the Roman Catholic Church undeniably falls into the deadly sin of requiring men to use their private judgment. Granting that the best way of leading men to heaven is to provide them with a living infallible guide; what have they to discover that guide but their reason? But if we may trust our reason when it tells us that an infallible guide is necessary, why may we not trust it when it tells us that the Bible is silent as to the Church of Rome being that infallible guide? Why is reason so useful in the one case, — why so useless in the other? Can our belief in anything be stronger than our belief in the reason that assures us of its truth? Can we possibly repose greater confidence in the findings of our reason than in our reason itself? But our reason is useless; therefore its finding that an infallible guide is necessary, and that that guide is the Roman Catholic Church, is also useless. If it is answered, that the Scriptures, rightly interpreted by the Church, bid us believe this guide, this, we grant, is renouncing the inconsistency of grounding the matter on private judgment; but it is a return to the circle within which the infallibility rests upon the Scriptures and the Scriptures upon the infallibility. If the Protestant cannot use his reason within that circle, it is plain the Romanist cannot use his out of it. He never ventures far from it, therefore, and on the first appearance of danger flies back to it. The argument would be greatly more brief, and its logic would be equally good, were it to run thus: "The Church of Rome is infallible because she is infallible;" and much unnecessary wrangling would be saved, were the Romanist, before commencing the controversy, to tell his opponent, that unless he conceded the point, he could not dispute with him.

Moreover, the boasted advantage of this infallible method of determining all doubts and controversies is a gross illusion. When the person closes the Bible, and sets out in quest of this infallible tribunal, he knows not where to seek it. To this day Romanists have not determined where that infallibility is lodged; and whether the person goes to the canon law, or to the writings of the fathers, or to the decrees of councils, or to the bulls of the popes, he is met by the very same difficulties, but on a far larger scale, which Romanists urge, though on no good ground, against the Bible as a rule of faith. These all have been, and still are, liable to far greater diversity of interpretation than the holy Scriptures; and if the objection be valid in the one case, much more is it so in the other. That the fathers are not only not infallible, but are not even exempt from the faults of obscurity and inconsistency, is manifest from the voluminous commentaries which have been written to make their meaning clear, as well as from the fact, that the fathers directly contradict one another, and the same father sometimes contradicts himself. We do not find one of them claiming infallibility, and not a few of them disclaim it. If they are right in disclaiming it, then they are not infallible; and if they are wrong, neither are they infallible, seeing they err in this, and may err equally in other matters. "The sense of all these holy men" [the fathers], says Melchior Canus, "is the sense of God's Spirit." "That which the fathers unanimously deliver," says Gregory de Valentia, "about religion, is infallibly true." So say the monks; but the fathers themselves give a very different account of the matter. "A Christian is bound," says Bellarmine, "to receive the Church's doctrine without examination." But Basil flatly contradicts him. "The hearers," says he, "that are instructed in the Scriptures must examine the doctrine of their teachers; they must receive the things that are agreeable to Scripture, and reject those things that are contrary to it." "Do not believe me saying these things," says Cyril, "unless I prove them out of the Scriptures." If, then, we appeal to the fathers themselves, — and those who believe them to be infallible cannot certainly refuse this appeal, — the infallibility of tradition must be given up.

But not a few Romanists, when hard pressed, give up the infallibility of the fathers, and take refuge in that of general councils. But whence comes the infallibility of these councils? The men in their individual capacity are not infallible: how come they to be so in their collective capacity? We do not deny that God might have preserved the councils of his Church from error; but the question is not what God might have done, but what He has done. Has He signified his intention to infallibly guide the councils of the Church? If so, in two ways only can this intention have been made known, — through the Bible, or through tradition. Not through the Bible, for it contains no promise of infallibility to councils; and Papists produce nothing from Scripture on this head beyond the texts on which they attempt to base the primacy, which we have already disposed of. Nor does tradition reveal the infallibility of general councils. No father has asserted that such a tradition has descended to him from the apostles; and not only did the fathers reject the notion of their own infallibility, but they also rejected the infallibility of councils, and demanded, as Protestants do, submission to the holy Scriptures. "I ought not to adduce the Council of Nice," says St. Augustine, "nor ought you to adduce the Council of Ariminum, for I am not bound by the authority of the one, nor are you bound by the authority of the other. Let the question be determined by the authority of the Scriptures, which are witnesses peculiar to neither of us, but common to both." Thus this father rejects the authority of fathers, councils, and churches, and appeals to the Scriptures alone. Unless, then, we are good enough to believe that councils are infallible simply because they say they are so, we must give up this infallibility of councils as a chimera and a delusion. It not unfrequently happens that councils contradict one another. How perplexing, in such a case, for the believer in their infallibility to say which to follow! Nor is this his only difficulty. It has not yet been decided what councils are, and what are not, infallible. It is only in behalf of general councils that infallibility is claimed; but the list of general councils varies in different countries. On the south of the Alps some councils are received as general and infallible, whose claim to rank as such is denied in France. "When the Popish priests," asks Dr. Cunningham, "of this country swear to maintain all things defined by the oecumenical councils, whether do they mean to follow the French or the Italian list?"

There are some Romanists who place this wonderful prerogative in the Pope and councils acting in conjunction. Bellarmine, an unexceptionable authority, though on the subject of the infallibility he delivers himself with some little inconsistency, says, "All Catholics constantly teach that general councils confirmed by the Pope cannot err;" and again, "Catholics agree that the Pope, with a general council, cannot err in establishing articles of faith, or general precepts of manners." "Doth the decree," asks Stillingfleet, when confuting this notion, "receive any infallibility from the council or not? If it doth, then the decree is infallible, whether the Pope confirm it or no. If it doth not, then the infallibility is wholly in the Pope." The decree, when presented to the Pope for his confirmation, is either true, or it is not. If it is true, can the pontifical confirmation make it more true? and if it is not true, can the Pope's confirmation give it truth and infallibility? When infallibility is lodged in one party, it is not difficult to conceive how decrees issued by that party become infallible; but when, like Mahommed's coffin, this infallibility is suspended betwixt two parties, — when, equally attracted by the gravitating forces of the Pope above and of the council below, it hangs in mid air, — it is more difficult to conceive in what way the decree becomes charged with infallibility. At what point in the ascent from the council to the Pope is it that the decree becomes infallible? Is it in the middle passage that this mysterious property infuses itself into it? or is it only when it reaches the chair of Peter? In that case the infallibility does not rest in a sort of equipoise between the two, according to the theory we are examining, but attaches exclusively to the pontiff.

This is the only part of the theory of infallibility, viz., that it resides in the Pope, which remains to be examined. This fleeting phantom, which we have pursued from fathers to councils and from councils to popes, we shall surely be able to fix in the chair of Peter. No, even here this phantom eludes our grasp. It is a shadow which the Romanist is destined ever to pursue, but never to overtake. That there is such a thing he never for a moment doubts, though no mortal has ever seen its form or discovered its dwelling-place.

The majority of Romanists agree that it haunts the Seven Hills, and is never far distant from the pontifical tiara. But, though it is impossible to fix the seat of this infallibility, it is not difficult to fix the period when it first came into existence. Infallibility was never heard of in the world till a full thousand years after Christ and his apostles. It was first devised by the pontiffs, for the purpose of supporting their universal supremacy and enormous usurpations. For about three hundred years after it was first claimed, it was tacitly acknowledged by all. But the unbounded ambition, the profligate lives, and the scandalous schisms and divisions of the pontiffs, came at last to shake the faith of the adherents of the Papacy in the pretensions of its head , and gave occasion to some councils, — as those of Basle and Constance, — to strip the popes of their infallibility, and claim it in their own behalf. Hence the origin of the war waged between councils and pontiffs on the subject of the infallibility, in which, as we have said, the Jesuits and the bishops south of the Alps take part with the successor of Peter. The Gallican Church generally has taken the side of councils in this controversy. Three or four councils have ascribed infallibility to the Pope, especially the last Lateranand *Trent*. At the last of these, the legates were charged not to allow the council to come to any decision on the point of infallibility, the Pope declaring that he would rather shed his blood than part with his rights, which had been established on the doctrines of the Church and the blood of martyrs. Now, in the Pope the infallibility is less diffused, and therefore, one should think, more accessible, than when lodged in councils; and yet Papists are as far as ever from being able to avail themselves practically of this infallibility for the settlement of their doubts and controversies. Before we can make use of the Pope's infallibility, there is a preliminary point. Is he truly the successor of Peter and Bishop of Rome? for it is only in so far as he is so that he is infallible. This, again, depends upon his being truly in orders, truly a bishop, truly a priest, truly baptized. And the validity of his orders depends, again, upon the intention of the person who administered the sacraments to him, and made him a priest or a bishop. For, according to the councils of Florence and Trent, the right intention of the administrator is absolutely necessary to the validity of these sacraments. So it is quite possible for some evil-minded priest, — some Jew, perhaps, in priests orders, of which there have been instances not a few in the Church of Rome, — to place a mere SHAM in Peter's chair, — to place at the head of the Roman Catholic world, not a genuine pope, but, as Carlyle would say, a Simulacrum. Not only is the Catholic world exposed to this terrible calamity, but, before the Romanist can avail himself of the infallibility, he must make sure that such a calamity has not actually befallen it in the person then occupying Peter's chair. He must assure himself of the right intention of the priest who admitted the Pope to orders, before he can be certain that he is a true Pope. But on such a matter absolute certainty is impossible, and moral assurance is the utmost that is attainable. But, granting that this difficulty is got over, there are twenty behind. Romanists do not hold that the Pope is infallible at all times and under all circumstances. He is not infallible in his moral conduct, as history abundantly testifies. Nor is he infallible in his private opinions, for there have been popes who have fallen into the worst heresies. In the theses of the Jesuits, in the college of Clermont, it was maintained, "that Christ hath so committed the government of his Church to the popes, that he hath conferred on them the same infallibility which he had himself, as often as they speak *ex cathedra*" "The Pope," says Bellarmine, "when he instructs the whole Church in things concerning the faith, cannot possibly err; and, whether he be a heretic himself or not, he can by no means define anything heretical to be believed by the whole Church;" a doctrine which has given occasion to some to remark, that it is no wonder that they can work miracles at Rome, when they can make apostacy and infallibility dwell together in the same person. We have the authority of the renowned Ligouri, that the Pope is altogether infallible in controversies of faith and morals. "The common opinion," says he, "to which we subscribe, is, that when the Pope speaks as the universal doctor, defining matters *ex cathedra*, that is, by the supreme power given to Peter of teaching the Church, then, we say, he is WHOLLY INFALLIBLE."

Mr. Seymour a few years ago was told by the Professor of Canon Law in the Collegio Romano at Rome, in a conversation he had with the Professor on the subject of Pope Liberius, who, the Professor admitted, had avowed the heresy of the Arians, that had he "proceeded to decide anything *ex cathedra*, the decision would then have been infallible." "A good tree bringeth forth good fruit," said our Saviour; but it appears that the soil of the Seven Hills possesses this marvellous property, that a bad tree will bring forth good fruit; and there men may gather grapes of thorns.

So, then, the case as respects the Pope's infallibility stands thus: — When he speaks *ex cathedra*, he speaks infallibly: when he speaks non *ex cathedra*, he speaks fallibly. This is the nearest approach any one can make to the seat of the oracle, and yet he is a long way short of it. For now arises the important question, How are we to ascertain an infallible bull from a fallible one, — a pope pronouncing *ex cathedra* from a pope pronouncing non *ex cathedra*? The process, certainly, is neither of the shortest nor the easiest, and we shall state it at length, that all may see how much is gained by forsaking the volume of the holy Scriptures for the volume of the papal bulls. The method of ascertaining an infallible from a fallible bull we give on the authority to which we have just referred, that of the Professor of Canon Law in the Collegio Romano at Rome, — a gentleman whose important position gives him the best opportunities of knowing, and who is not likely to represent the matter unfairly for Rome, or to make the process more difficult and intricate than it really is. Well, then, according to the statements of the Professor, who is one of the most learned and accomplished men at Rome, there are seven requisites or essentials by which a bull is to be tested before it is recognised as *ex cathedra* or infallible.

"1. It was necessary, in the first place, that before composing and issuing the bull, the Pope should have opened a communication with the bishops of the universal Church," in order to obtain the prayers of the bishops and of the universal Church, "that the Holy Spirit might fully and infallibly guide him, so as to make his decision the decision of inspiration.

"II. It was necessary, in the second place, that before issuing the bull containing the decision, the Pope should carefully seek all possible and desirable information touching the special matter which was under consideration, and which was to be the subject of his decision..........from those persons who were residing in the district affected by the decision called in question.

"III. That the bull should not only be formal, but should be authoritative, and should claim to be authoritative: that it should be issued not merely as the opinion or judgment of the Pope in his mere personal capacity, but as the decisive and authoritative judgment of one who was the head of that Church which was the mother and mistress of all Churches.

"IV. That the bull should be promulgated universally; that is, that the bull should be addressed to all the bishops of the universal Church, in order that through them its decisions might be delivered and made known to all the members or subjects of the whole Church.

"V. That the bull should be universally received; that is, should be accepted by all the bishops of the whole Church, and accepted by them as an authoritative and infallible decision.

"VI. The matter or question upon which the decision was to be made, and which was therefore to be the subject matter of the bull, must be one touching faith or morals, that is, it must concern the purity of faith or the morality of actions.

"VII. That the Pope should be free, — perfectly free from all exterior influence, — so as to be under no exterior compulsion or constraint."

By all these tests must every bull issued by the popes be tried, before it can be accepted or rejected as infallible. Assuredly the Protestant has no reason to grudge the Papist his "short and easy method" of attaining certainty in his faith. If the Romanist, in determining the infallibility of the papal bulls, shall get through his work at a quicker rate than one in every twenty years, he will assuredly display no ordinary diligence. Most men, we suspect, will account the solution of a single bull quite work enough for a lifetime, while not a few will prefer taking the whole matter on trust, to entering on an investigation which they may not live to finish, and which, granting they do live to finish it, is so little likely to conduct to a satisfactory result. Let us suppose that a pope's bull, containing a deliverance necessary to be believed in order to salvation, is put into the hands of a plain English peasant: it is written in a dead language; and he must acquire that language to make sure that he knows its real sense, or he must trust the translation of another, — the very objection on which Papists dwell so much in reference to the Bible. He must next endeavour to ascertain that the Pope has sought and obtained the prayers of the universal Church for the infallible guidance of the Holy Spirit in the matter. This he may possibly do, though not without a good deal of trouble. He has next to assure himself that the Pope has been at pains to obtain all possible and desirable information in regard to the subject of the bull, and more especially from persons living in the district to which that bull has reference. Now, unless he is pleased to take his information at second hand, he has no possible means of attaining certainty on this point, unless by leaving his occupation, and perhaps also his country, and making personal inquiries on the spot as to the Pope's diligence and discrimination in collecting evidence. Having satisfied himself as to this, he has next to assure himself that the bull has been universally accepted, that is, that all the bishops of the whole Church have received it as an authoritative and infallible decision. This opens up a wider sphere of inquiry even than the former. On nothing is it more difficult to obtain certain information, for on nothing are the bishops of the Roman Church so divided, as on the infallibility of particular bulls. It is a fortunate decision indeed which carries along with it the unanimous assent of the Romish clergy. A bull may be held to be orthodox in Britain, but accounted heretical in France; or it may be accepted as most infallible in France, but repudiated in Spain; or it may be revered as the dictate of inspiration by the Spanish bishops, but held as counterfeit by those of Italy. Not a few bulls are in this predicament. Thus the person finds that this infallibility, instead of being a *Catholic*, is a very *provincial* affair; that by crossing a particular arm of the sea, or traversing a certain chain of mountains, he leaves the sphere of the infallible, and enters into that of the fallible; that as he changes his place on the earth's surface, so does the pontifical decree change its character; and that what is binding upon him as the dictate of inspiration on the south of the Alps, he is at liberty to disregard as the effusion of folly, of ignorance, or of heresy, on the north of these mountains. What is the man to do in such a case? If he side with the French bishops, he finds that the Italians are against him; and if he takes part with the Italians, he finds that he has arrayed himself against the Iberian and Gallican clergy. Truly it may be said, on the subject of the *infallibility*, that "he that increaseth knowledge increaseth sorrow."

But granting the possibility of the man seeing his way through all these conflicting opinions, to something like a satisfactory conclusion: he finds he has come so far only to encounter fresh and apparently insuperable difficulties. He has, last of all, to satisfy himself in reference to the state of the pontifical mind when the decree was given. Did the Pope's judgment move in obedience to an influence from above, which guided it into the path of truth and infallibility? or was it drawn aside into that of error by some exterior and earthly influence — a desire, for instance, to serve some political end, a wish to conciliate some temporal potentate, or a fear that, should he decide in a certain way, he might cause a rent in the Church, and thus shake that infallible chair from which he was about to issue his decree? How any man can determine with certainty respecting the purity of the motives and influences which guided the pontifical mind in coming to a certain decision, without a very considerable share of that infallibility of which he is in quest, we are utterly at a loss to conceive. And thus, though the Romish doctrine of infallibility may do well enough for infallible men who can do without it, it is not of the least use to those who really need its aid.

We have imagined the case of a man engaged on a single bull, and attempting to solve the question of infallibility with an exclusive reference to it. But the foundation of a Papist's faith is not any one bull, but the Bullarium. This must necessarily form an important item in every estimate of the difficulties attending the question of infallibility. The Bullarium is a work in scholastic Latin, amounting to between twenty and thirty folio volumes. To every one of its many hundred bulls must these seven tests be applied. Now, if, as we have seen, it is so difficult, or indeed so impossible, to apply these tests to the bulls of the day, the idea of applying them to the bulls of a thousand years ago is immeasurably absurd. Would any man in his five senses take up the bulls of Pope Hildebrand, or of Pope Innocent, and proceed to test, by these seven requisites, whether they are or are not infallible? No man ever did so, — no man ever thought of doing so; and we may affirm with the utmost confidence, that while the world stands, no man who is not utterly bereft of understanding and sense will ever undertake so chimerical and hopeless a task. The twelve labours of Hercules were as nothing compared with these seven labours of the infallibility. And then we have to think what a monument of folly and inconsistency, as well as of arrogance and blasphemy, is the Bullarium. Not only is it in a dead language, and has never been translated into any living tongue, and therefore is utterly unfit to form the guide of any living Church, but it is wanting even in agreement with itself. We find that one bull contradicts another, or rescinds that other, or expressly condemns it. We find that these bulls are the source of endless disputes, and the subject of varied and conflicting interpretations, on the part of the Romish doctors. What a contrast does the simplicity, the harmony, and the conciseness of the Bible form to the twenty or thirty volumes of the Bullarium, the Bible of the Papist, but which few if any living Papists have ever read, and the authority and infallibility of which no living Papist certainly has ever verified according to the rules of his Church! And yet we are asked to renounce the one, and to submit ourselves to the guidance of the other, to abandon the straight and even path of holy Scripture, and to commit ourselves to the endless mazes and the inextricable labyrinths of the Bullarium. A modest request, doubtless, but one which it will be time enough to consider when Papists agree among themselves as to where this infallibility is placed, and how it may be turned to any practical end. Till then we shall hold ourselves fully warranted to follow the dictates of that book which Christ has commanded us to "search," which "is able to make wise unto salvation," and which Papists themselves acknowledge to be the Word of God, and therefore infallible.

We have examined at great length the two questions of the primacy and the infallibility, because they are fundamental ones in the Romish system. They are the Jachin and Boaz of the Papacy. If these two principal pillars are overthrown, not a single stone of the ill-assorted, heterogeneous, and grotesque fabric which Rome has built upon them can stand. We have seen how little foundation the primacy and infallibility have in Scripture, in history, or in reason. Romanism stands unrivalled alike for the impudence and the baselessness of its pretensions. To nothing can we compare it, unless to the famous system of Indian cosmogony. The sage of Hindustan places the earth upon the back of the elephant, and the elephant upon the back of the crocodile; but when you ask him on what is the crocodile placed? you find that his philosophy can conduct him no farther. There is a yawning gulph in his system, like that which opens right beneath the feet of the sorely burdened and somewhat insufficiently supported crocodile. The great props of the Papacy, like those fabled animals which support the globe, lack foundation. The Romanist places the Church upon the Pope, and the Pope upon the infallibility; but when you ask him on what does the infallibility rest? alas! his system provides no footing for it; and if you attempt to go farther down, you are landed in a gulph across whose gloom there has never darted any ray of light, and whose profound depths no plummet has ever yet sounded. Over this gulph floats the Papacy.

Chapter VIII: No Salvation out of the Church of Rome.

On all other Christian societies the Church of Rome pronounces a sentence of spiritual outlawry. She alone is the Church, and beyond her pale there is no salvation. She recognises but one pastor and but one fold; and those who are not the sheep of the Pope of Rome, cannot be the sheep of Christ, and are held as being certainly cut off from all the blessings of grace now, and from all the hopes of eternal life hereafter. In the hands of Peter's successor are lodged the keys of heaven; and no one can enter but those whom he is pleased to admit; and he admits none but good Catholics, who believe that a consecrated wafer is God, and that he himself is God's vicegerent, and infallible. All others are heathens and heretics, accursed of God, and most certainly accursed of Rome. This compendious anathema, it is true, gives Protestants no concern. They know that it is as impotent as it is malignant; and it can excite within them nothing but gratitude to that Providence which has made the power of this Church as circumscribed as her cruelty is vast and her vengeance unappeasable. God has not put in subjection to Rome either this world or the world to come; and the Pope and his Cardinals have just as much power to consign all outside their Church to eternal flames, as to forbid the sun to shine or the rain to fall on all who dare reject the infallibility.

But while it is a matter of supreme indifference to Protestants how many or how dreadful the curses which the pontiff may fulminate from his seat of presumed infallibility, it is a very serious matter for Rome herself. It is a truly fearful and affecting manifestation of Rome's own character. It exhibits her as animated by a malignity that is truly measureless and quenchless, and actually gloating over the imaginary spectacle of the eternal destruction of the whole human race, those few excepted who have belonged to her communion. Not a few Papists appear to be conscious of the odium to which their Church is justly obnoxious, on account of this wholesale intolerance and uncharitableness and accordingly they have denied the doctrine which we now impute to their Church. The charge, however, is easily substantiated. The tenet that there is no salvation out of the Church of Rome is of so frequent occurrence in the bulls of their popes, in their standard works, in their catechisms, and is so openly avowed by foreign Papists, who have not the same reason to conceal or deny this tenet which British Papists have, that no doubt can exist about the matter. Their own memorable argument, whereby they attempt to prove that the Romish method of salvation is the safer one, conclusively establishes the fact that they hold the doctrine of exclusive salvation, and that we do not. That argument is, in short, as follows: — That whereas we admit that men may be saved in the Church of Rome, and whereas they hold that men cannot be saved out of that Church, therefore it is safer to be in communion with that Church. Here the Romanist makes the doctrine of exclusive salvation the basis of his argument.

Equally explicit is the creed of Pope Pius IV. That creed embraces the leading dogmas of Romanism; and the following declaration, which is taken by every Popish priest at his ordination, is appended to it: — "I do at this present freely profess and sincerely hold this true Catholic faith, *without which no one can be saved*; and I promise most constantly to retain and confess the same entire and unviolated, with God's assistance, to the end of my life." To the same purport is the decree of Pope Boniface VIII.: — "We declare, assert, define, and pronounce, that it is necessary to salvation for every human being to be subject to the Pope of Rome." Nor is there any mistaking the condition of those to whom the bull *in Coena Domini* has reference. This is one of the most solemn excommunications of the Romish Church, denounced every year on Maunday Thursday against heretics, and all who are disobedient to the Holy See. In that bull is the following clause, which has been inserted since the Reformation: — "We excommunicate and anathematize, in the name of God Almighty, Father, Son, and Holy Ghost, and by the authority of the blessed apostles Peter and Paul, and by our own, all Hussites, Wickliffites, Lutherans, Zuinglians, Calvinists, Huguenots, Anabaptists, Trinitarians, and apostates from the faith, and all other heretics, by whatsoever name they are called, and of whatsoever sect they be." If the words of the bull are not sufficient to indicate, with the requisite plainness, the fearful doom that awaits all Protestants, the action that follows certainly does so: a lighted candle is instantly cast on the ground and extinguished, and the spectators are thus taught by symbol, that eternal darkness is the portion which awaits the various heretical sects specified in the bull. The ceremony is concluded with the firing of a cannon from the castle of St. Angelo, which the Roman populace believe (or rather did believe) makes all the heretics in the world to tremble.

The very children in the popish schools are taught to lisp this exclusive and intolerant doctrine. "Can any one be saved who is not in the true Church?" it is asked in Keenan's Catechism; and the child is taught to answer, "No ; for those who are not in the true Church, — that is, for those who are not joined at least to the soul of the Church, there can be no hope of salvation." The true Church the writer afterwards defines to be the Roman Catholic Church. "Are all obliged to be of the true Church?" it is asked in Butler's Catechism. "Yes; no one can be saved out of it." Thus has the Church of Rome made provision that her youth shall be trained up in the firm belief that all Protestants are beyond the pale of the Church of Christ, are the objects of the divine abhorrence, and are doomed to pass their eternity in flames. An ineradicable hatred of Protestants is thus implanted in their breasts, which often, in after years, breaks out in deeds of violence and blood.

Papists who live in Britain, though they really hold this doctrine, are careful how they avow it. They know the danger of placing so intolerant a doctrine in contrast with the true catholic charity of Protestant Britain. Accordingly they endeavour, by equivocal statements, by jesuitical evasions and explanations, and sometimes by the fraudulent use of the phrase "fellow-Christians," addressed to Protestants, to conceal their true principles on this head; but foreign Papists, being under no such restraint, avow, without equivocation or concealment, that the doctrine of exclusive salvation is the doctrine of the Church of Rome. We cannot quote a more authoritative testimony as to the opinions held and taught on this important question by leading Romanists, than the published lectures of the Professor of Dogmatic Theology in the Collegio Romano at Rome. We find M. Perrone, in a series of ingenious and elaborately reasoned propositions, maintaining the doctrine of non-salvability beyond the pale of his own Church. On the assumption that the Church of Rome has maintained the unity of faith and government which Christ and his apostles founded, he lays down the proposition, that "the Catholic Church alone is the true Church of Christ," and that "all communions which have separated from that Church are so many synagogues of Satan." A following proposition pronounces "heretics and schismatics without the Church of Christ." M. Perrone then proceeds to argue that this character belongs to Protestants, and that it is plain that their faith is false, from their recent origin, and the little success which has attended their missions among the heathen. He then closes the discussion with the proposition, that "those who culpably fall into heresy and schism [i.e. into Protestantism], or into unbelief, can have no salvation after death." This is very appropriately followed by a short dissertation, showing that "religious toleration is impious and absurd." The same sentiments which he has given to the world in his published prelections, we find M. Perrone reiterating in language if possible still more plain, in a conversation with Mr. Seymour. "The truth of the Church was," said the reverend Professor, "that no man could be saved unless he was a member of the Church of Rome, and believed in the supremacy and infallibility of the popes as the successors of St. Peter." "I said," replied Mr. Seymour, "that that was going very far indeed; for, besides requiring men to be members of the Church of Rome, it required their belief in the supremacy and infallibility of the popes."

"He [the Professor] reiterated the same sentiment in language still stronger than before; adding, that every one must be damned in the flames of hell who did not believe in the supremacy and infallibility of the Pope."

"I could not but smile at all this," says Mr. Seymour, "while I felt it derived considerable importance from the position of the person who uttered it. He was the chief teacher of theology in the Collegio Romano, — the University of Rome. I smiled, however, and reminded him that his words were consigning all the people of England to the damnation of hell."

"He repeated his words emphatically."

From a statement which dropped at the same time from the learned Professor, it would seem that those even within the pale of Rome who deny this doctrine of the Church, do so at the risk of being disowned by her, and incurring the doom of heretics. Mr. Seymour was urging that the Roman Catholics of England and Ireland do not hold that doctrine, when his assertion was met by a decided negative. "He [the Professor] said that it was impossible my statement could be correct, as no man was a true Catholic who thought any one could find salvation out of the Church of Rome. They could not be true Catholics."

The solemn judgment of Rome, that no one can be saved who does not swallow an annual wafer, and live on eggs in Lent, gives us no more serious concern than if the head of Mahommedanism should decree that no one can enter paradise who does not wear a turban and suffer his beard to grow. It is equally valid with the dictum of any society among ourselves that might claim infallibility and so forth, and adjudge damnation to all who did not choose to conform to the fashion of buttoning one's coat behind. What ideas can those have of the Almighty, who can believe that he will determine the eternal destinies of his creatures according to such ridiculous niceties and trifles? "God so loved the world," says the apostle, "that he gave his only begotten Son, that whosoever believeth in him should not perish;" but perish you must, says the Church of Rome, unless you believe also that a wafer and a little wine, consecrated by a priest, are the real flesh and blood of Christ. When we ask the reason for this compendious destruction of the whole human race save the fraction that belongs to Rome, we can get no answer beyond this, that the Pope has said it (for certainly the Bible has nowhere said it), and therefore it must be so. This may be an excellent reason to the believer in infallibility, but it is no reason to any one else. It may be possible that this half-foundered craft named Peter, with its riven sails, its tangled cordage, its yawning scams, and its drunken crew, may be the one ship on the ocean which is destined to ride out the storm and reach the port in safety; but before beginning the voyage, one would like to have some better assurance of this than the mere word of a superannuated captain, never very sound in the head, and now, partly through age and partly through the excesses of his youth, to the full as crazy as his vessel.

It is fair to mention, that Romanists are accustomed to make an exception in the matter of non-salvability beyond the pale of their Church, in favour of those who labour under *"invincible ignorance."* The Professor in the Collegio Romano, when pressed by Mr. Seymour on the subject of his own personal salvation, gave him the benefit of this exception; and we doubt not that all Protestants will be made abundantly welcome to it. How far it can be of any use to them is another question. The hopes it holds out are of the slenderest; for, so far as Romish writers have defined this *invincible ignorance,* none can plead the benefit of it save such as have had no means of knowing the faith of Rome, but who, if they had, would willingly embrace it. This exception of "invincible ignorance" may include a few heathens, so benighted as never to have heard of the Church of Rome and her peculiar dogmas; and it may comprehend also those Protestants who are absolutely idiots; but it can be of no use to any one else. Such is the whole extent of Rome's charity.

But though sectarian in her charity, Rome is truly catholic in her anathemas. What sect or party is it which she has not pronounced accursed? What noble name is it which she has not attempted to blast? What generous art which she has not laboured to destroy? What science or study fitted to humanize and enlarge the mind on which she has not pronounced an anathema? Those men who have been the lights of their age, — the poets, the philosophers, the orators, the statesmen, who have been the ornaments and the blessings of their race, — she has confounded in the same tremendous doom with the vilest of mankind. it mattered not how noble their gifts, or how disinterested their labours: they might possess the genius of a Milton, the wisdom of a Bacon, the science of a Newton, the inventive skill of a Watt, the philanthropy of a Howard, the patriotism of a Tell, a Hampden, or a Bruce; they might be firm believers in every doctrine, and bright examples of every virtue, inculcated in the New Testament; but if they did not believe also in the supremacy and infallibility of the Pope, all their wisdom, all their philanthropy, all their piety, all their generous sacrifices and noble achievements, though, like another Wilberforce, they may have struck from the arm of millions the chain of slavery, or, like another Cranmer or another Knox, conquered spiritual independence for generations unborn, all, all went for nothing. Rome could recognise in them no character now but the odious one of *the enemies of God*; and she could afford to allow them no portion hereafter but the terrible one of eternal torments. And while she closed the gates of Paradise against these lights and benefactors of the world, she opened them to men whose principles and actions were alike pernicious, — to men who were the curses of their race, and who seemed born to no end but to devastate the world, — to fanatics and desperadoes, whose fierce zeal and fiercer swords were ever at the service of the Church.

Chapter IX: Of Original Sin.

We have examined the rock on which the Church of Rome professes to be built, and find that it is a quicksand. The infallibility is in the same unhappy predicament with the crocodile in the Indian fable, — it has not only to support itself, but all that is laid upon it to boot. Having disposed of it, we might be held, in point of form, as having disposed of the whole system. But our object being, first of all, to exhibit, and only indirectly to confute, the system of Popery, we proceed in our design, and accordingly now pass to the DOCTRINE of the Church. And, first, to her doctrine on the head of Original Sin.

The doctrine of original sin was one of the first points to be debated in the Council of Trent; and the discord and diversity of opinion that reigned among the fathers strikingly illustrates the sort of unity of which the Roman Catholic Church boasts. In discussing this doctrine, the council considered, first, the nature of original sin; second, its transmission; and, third, its remedy. On its *nature* the fathers were unable to come to any agreement. Some maintained that it consists in the privation of original righteousness; others, that it lies in concupiscence; while another party held that in fallen man there are two kinds of rebellion, — one of the spirit against God; the other, of flesh against the spirit; that the former is unrighteousness, and the latter concupiscence, and that both together constitute sin. After a lengthened debate, in which the fathers, not the Scriptures, were appealed to, and which gave abundant room for the display of that scholastic erudition which is so fruitful in casuistical subtleties and distinctions, the council wisely resolved to eschew the danger of a definition, and, despairing of harmonizing their views, promulgated their decree without defining its subject. "Whoever shall not confess," said the council, "that the first man, Adam, when he broke the commandment of God in Paradise, straitway fell from the holiness and righteousness in which he was formed, and by the offence of his prevarication incurred the wrath and indignation of God, and also the death with which God had threatened him, ... let him be accursed."

The council was scarce less divided on the subject of the transmission of original sin. Wisely avoiding to determine the manner in which this sin is

conveyed from Adam to his posterity, the council decreed as follows: —
"Whoever shall affirm that the sin of Adam injured only himself, and not
likewise his posterity; and that the holiness and justice which he received
from God he lost for himself only, and not for us also; and that, becoming
polluted by his disobedience, he transmitted to all mankind corporal death
and punishment only, but not sin also, which is the death of the soul; let
him be accursed"

The council, then, were at one as regards the penalty of sin, which is
death eternal; they were not less at one as regards the remedy, which is
baptism. And so efficacious is this remedy, according to the Council of
Trent, that in baptism — "the laver of regeneration," as they termed it, —
all sin is washed away. In the regenerate, that is, in the baptized, there
remains no sin. The council admitted that concupiscence dwells in all men,
and in true Christians among the rest; but it also decided that
concupiscence, which is a certain commotion and impulse of the mind,
urging to the desire of pleasures which it does not actually enjoy," is not
sin. On this part of the subject the council decreed as follows: —
"Whoever shall affirm that this sin of Adam can be taken away, either by
the strength of human nature, or by any other means than by the merit of
our Lord Jesus Christ, the one Mediator, . . . or shall deny that the merit of
Jesus Christ is applied both to adults and infants by the sacrament of
baptism, administered according to the rites of the Church, let him be
accursed." And again, — "Whoever shall deny that the guilt of original sin
is remitted by the grace of our Lord Jesus Christ, bestowed in baptism, or
shall affirm that that wherein sin truly and properly consists is not wholly
rooted up, but is only cut down, or not imputed, let him be accursed."

The doctrine of the Fall must necessarily be a fundamental one in every
system of theology: it formed the starting point in those meagre systems
which existed in the pagan world. But it is not enough that we give it a
place in our scheme of truth; — it must be rightly and fully understood,
otherwise all will be wrong in our system of religion. Should we fall into
the mistake of supposing that the injury sustained by man when he fell was
less than it really is, we will, in the same proportion, underrate the extent to
which he must be dependent upon the atonement of Christ, and
overestimate the extent to which he is able to help himself. It may be seen,
then, that an error here will vitiate our whole scheme, and may lead to fatal
consequences. It becomes important, therefore, to state accurately, though
succinctly, the opinions held by modern writers in the Church of Rome on

the doctrines of the Fall and Divine Grace. The authors of those systems of theology which are used as text-books in the training of the priesthood have not very distinctly stated in what they conceive original sin to consist. In this they have followed the example of the Council of Trent. Dens defines it simply to be disobedience. Bailly cites the opinions which have been held on this question by various sects, and more especially the doctrine of the Standards of the Presbyterian Church, which make "the sinfulness of that estate whereinto man fell" to consist "in the guilt of Adam's first sin, the want of original righteousness, and the corruption of his whole nature, which is commonly called original sin;" and though he condemns all these opinions, he offers no definition of his own, but takes farewell of the subject with some observations on its abstruseness, and the inutility of prying too curiously into the qualities of things. We know of no writer of authority in the Roman Catholic Church, since the days of Bellarmine at least, who has spoken so frankly out on the doctrine of the Fall as the present occupant of the chair of theology in the University at Rome. We shall state the opinions of M. Perrone as clearly and accurately as we are able; and this will put the reader in possession of the Roman Catholic doctrine on this important subject. M. Perrone, in his published prelections, teaches that the first man was exalted to a supernatural state by the sanctifying grace of his Creator; that this integrity or holiness of nature was not due to man, but was a gift freely conferred on him by the divine bounty; so that God, had he pleased, might have created man without these endowments. Accordingly, man, by his sin, says M. Perrone, lost only those superadded gifts which flowed from the liberality of God; or, what is the same thing, man by his sin reduced himself to that state in which he would actually have been created had not God added other gifts, both for this life and for the other.

M. Perrone fortifies his statement by an appeal to the opinions of Cardinals Cajetan and Bellarmine, both of whom have expressed themselves on the subject of the Fall in terms very similar to those employed by the Professor in the Collegio Romano. The difference, says Cajetan, between fallen nature and pure nature, — not nature as it existed in the case of Adam, who was clothed with supernatural gifts, but nature, as the Romish divines phrase it, *in puris naturalibus*, — may be expressed in one word. The difference is the same as that which exists between the man who has been despoiled of his clothing, and the man who never had any. "We do not distinguish between the two," argues the Cardinal, "on the ground that the one is more nude than the other, for that is not the case. In like manner, a nature *in puris naturalibus*, and a nature despoiled of original grace and righteousness, do not differ in this, that the one is more destitute than the other; but the great difference lies here, that the defect in the one case is not a fault, or punishment, or injury; whereas in the other, — that of a fallen nature, — there is a corrupt condition, and the defect is to be regarded as both a fault and punishment." When the Cardinal uses the phrase, "a corrupt condition," he means to express an idea, we apprehend, which Protestants would more fittingly designate by the terms "denuded condition;" for certainly the Cardinal intends to teach that the constitution of man has not suffered more seriously by his fall than would the body of man by being stript of its clothing. The same doctrine is taught by Bellarmine, who holds, that the nature of fallen man, the original fault excepted, is not inferior to a human nature *in puris naturalibus*.

This point is an important one, and we make no apology for dwelling a little longer upon it. We would fain present our readers, in a few words, with a view of what the Church of Rome holds on the doctrine of grace as opposed to the sentiments of Protestant divines, premising that absolute accuracy is not easily attainable, Popish writers not having expressed themselves either very definitely or very consistently. In the following summary we take M. Perrone as our chief authority and guide, using almost his very words: — 1st, The Roman Catholic Church teaches, in respect of the integrity of man, and the supernatural state to which he was raised, that he fell from that condition by sin, and lost his original righteousness, with all the gifts connected therewith. 2d, In respect of the supernatural state and the sanctifying grace bestowed on man, the Church of Rome teaches, that by his fall the soul of man came into a state of death, and that in respect of his integrity, both his soul and his body were changed for the worse. 3d, That by the fall the free will of man was weakened and biassed. 4th, With respect to those privileges and gifts of grace which were added to man's nature, and which are accidental to it, the doctrine of the Roman Catholic Church is, that fallen man has been denuded of these privileges and gifts, and has come into that state in which, not reckoning his fault, he would have been had God not willed to exalt him to a supernatural position, and to confer upon him uprightness and other endowments; and has, moreover, sunk into that state of feebleness which is incident to human nature of itself. 5th, Hence the Church teaches, says M. Perrone, that man is unable, by any strength, or effort, or wish of his, to raise himself to his former supernatural state; and that for his recovery the grace of the Saviour is altogether necessary. 6th, This grace is wholly free, and is conferred on man, by the goodness of God, on account of the merits of Christ. 7th, Since, however, in man fallen, the free will, such as human nature viewed in itself demands, has been preserved, nor otherwise debilitated but as respects that state of uprightness from which he was cut off, the Church teaches that man is able freely to co-operate, either in the way of complying with God, exciting and calling Him by his grace, or in the way of resisting Him, if he chooses. The Church, therefore, rejects the doctrine of irresistible grace. 8th, From the same principle, that man by his fall has not become bereft of the power of will, flows the doctrine of the Church, that man is able to wish what is good, and to do works morally right, and that works performed without grace are not so many sins. 9th, The Roman Catholic Church teaches likewise, that in difficult duties, and when assailed by strong temptations, fallen man stands in need of "medicinal" grace, to enable him to fulfil the one and overcome the other, just as some assistance would have been necessary to unfallen man, had God not conferred upon him the faculty of uprightness, and elevated him to a supernatural condition.

Unless we greatly mistake, we have now reached the fountainhead of the errors of Popery. We stand here beside its infant source. Thence those waters of bitterness go forth to collect the tributaries of every region through which they flow, till at last, like the river seen by the prophet in vision, from being a narrow and shallow stream, which one might step across, they become "waters to swim in, — a river that could not be passed over." How near to each other are situated the primal fountains of truth and error! Like twin sources on the summit of some Alpine chain, which a few yards only divide, yet lying on opposite sides of the summit, the flow of the one is determined towards the frozen shores of the north, — the current of the other to the aromatic climes and calm seas of the south; so between the Popish and the Protestant ideas on the doctrine of the Fall there is no very great or essential difference which strikes one at first sight. The sources of the two systems lie close beside each other; but the line that divides truth from error runs between them. From the first, therefore, they take opposite directions; and what was scarce perceptible at the outset becomes plain and palpable in the issue: the one results in the Roman papacy; the other is seen to be apostolic Christianity.

The divines of the Church of Rome conceive of humanity as existing, or capable of existing, in three states. The first is that of fallen man, in which we now exist; the second is that of simple humanity, or, as they term it, *puris naturalibus*, in which man, they affirm, *might* have been made; the third is that of supernatural humanity, or man clothed with those special gifts with which God endowed Adam. By his fall man brought himself down from the third or highest state to the first or lowest. But the theologians of the Roman school teach that man's condition now is in no respect worse than if he were in the middle state, or *inpuris naturalibus*, except that he once was in a higher, and has fallen from it. His nature is not injured thereby: he has lost the advantages which he enjoyed in his higher condition; he is to blame for having thrown away these advantages; but as to any injury, or disorder, or ruin of nature, by the Fall, that he has not sustained; — he has come scathless out of the catastrophe of Eden. Of two men totally destitute of clothing, — to use Cardinal Cajetan's illustration, — the one is not more nude than the other; but the difference lies here, — the one never had clothing, — the other had, but has lost it, and therefore suffers a want he did not feel originally, and has acted very foolishly, or, if you will, very sinfully, in stripping off his vestments. But the loss of raiment is one thing, — the injury of his person is another; and just as a man may be deprived of his raiment, and yet his body remain sound, vigorous, and active as ever, so our deprivation of the supernatural gifts we enjoyed in innocence, in consequence of the Fall, has left our mental and moral nature as whole and sound as before. God might have made us *in puris naturalibus* at the beginning. And what has the Fall done? just brought us into that state in which God might have created us; except it be (and it is in this that *original sin* consists, according to the only consistent interpretation of the popish scheme) that it is our own fault that we are not in that higher state still. Whatever powers we would have had *in puris natralibus* of loving God, of obeying his will, and resisting evil, we have in our fallen state. We need assisting grace in our more difficult duties and temptations now, and we would have needed it *in puris naturalibus*. Thus we have fallen, and yet we have not fallen; for we are now what God might have made us at the beginning. On this point, as on every other, Rome requires us to believe contradictions and absurdities: her doctrine of the Fall is a denial of the Fall.

God might have made man, say the divines of the Roman Church, in a state of simple nature. We will not answer for the idea which Romanists may attach to this state; but it is not difficult to determine what only that state can be. A state of positive corruption it cannot be; for Romanists refuse this in the case even of fallen man. Neither can it be a state of positive grace, for this is the supernatural condition to which God raised him. It can only be a state of indifference, in which man is equally attracted or equally repelled by good and evil. We do not stay to enquire whether it was due to the Divine character to make man in this state, — equally ready to engage himself to God or to Satan; but we ask, was it possible? According to this theory, man's faculties are entire in their number and perfect in their functional action; and yet they are utterly useless. They cannot act, — they cannot make a choice; for if the man inclines to either side, it is because he is *not* in a state of indifference. If he chooses good, it is because he prefers it; if he chooses evil, it is because he prefers it to good, and so is not indifferent. But it may be objected that the idea is, that till the object is put before the man he is indifferent. But till the object be put before the man, how can it be known that he is in a state of indifference or no? Besides, existence is but a series of volitions; and to say that the man is in a state of indifference till he begins to will, is just to say that he is in a state of indifference till he becomes a man. We are again called upon to believe contradictions. The scheme of *indifference* supposes a man with a conscience able to discriminate between good and evil, and yet not able to discriminate between them, — with the faculty of will, and yet not able to will, — with the affection of love, and yet able neither to love nor hate; which is just as rational as to speak of a human frame exquisitely strung to pleasure and pain, and yet incapable of either sensation. There is only one way of placing a man in a state of indifference, and that is, by striking conscience and will dead in his breast. While the constitution of things is what it is, and while the powers of man are what they are, a *state of indifference* is an impossibility. God cannot make impossibilities.

We repeat, the Roman Catholic doctrine of the Fall is a repudiation of the Scripture doctrine of the Fall. This must necessarily affect the whole of the theology of that Church. It must necessarily alter the complexion of her views on the subject both of the work of the Son and the work of the Spirit. *First,* If man has not fallen in the Scripture sense, neither has he been redeemed in the Scripture sense. Our redemption is necessarily the counterpart of our loss; and in the proportion in which we diminish the one do we also diminish the other. Our natures have escaped uninjured, the Romish divines teach. We can still do all which we could have done *in puris naturalibus*, had we been created in that state. Man, if he but give himself to the work in earnest, may almost, if not altogether, save himself. He needs only divine grace to help him over its more difficult parts. The atonement, then, was no such great work after all. Instead of presenting that character of unity and completeness which the Scriptures attribute to it, — instead of being the redemption of lost souls from hopeless and irremediable bondage, by the endurance in their room of infinite vengeance due to their sins, — the work of Christ wears altogether the character of a supplementary performance. Instead of being a display of unbounded and eternal love, and of power also unbounded and eternal, it dwindles into a very ordinary manifestation of pity and good-will. Nay, it would not be difficult to show that it might have been dispensed with, with some not inconsiderable advantages; that it has stood much in man's way, and prevented the exercise of his own powers, knowing that he had this to fall back upon. May not this help us to understand why Romanists can so easily associate Mary with the Son of God in the act of redemption, and can speak of her sufferings as if they had been the better half of the world? May it not account, too, for the case with which the Church of Rome can find the *material* of satisfaction for sin in the works of those whom she calls saints? May it not account also for the thoroughly *scenic* character which the death of Christ bears, as exhibited in the Church of Rome? And may it not likewise account for the extent to which that Church has undervalued Christ in his character of Mediator, by associating with Him in that august office so many of mortal origin? For if man's nature be not inferior in its condition to that in which God righteously might have made it, the work of mediating between God and man is not so pre-eminently onerous and dignified.

But, in the *second* place, if man is not fallen in the Scripture sense, neither does he need to be regenerated in the Scripture sense. Our regeneration is likewise the necessary counterpart of our fall. We have sustained, say the Romish divines, no radical derangement or injury of nature by the Fall; we have been stript merely of those superadded gifts which God bestowed; and all that we need, in order to occupy the same vantage ground as before, is just the restoration of these lost accomplishments. Regeneration, then, in the Romish acceptation of the term, must mean a very different thing indeed from what it does among Protestants. With us it is a change of nature so thorough, that we can find no term to express it but that employed in the New Testament, — "a new creation." We believe that man has not only been stript of his raiment, — to use the metaphor which Romish rhetoric has supplied; — he has been wounded, he has bled to death, and he needs to be made alive again. But no such regeneration can be necessary in the view of those who believe that man has suffered no internal injury, and that he has lost only what he might have wanted from the beginning without prejudice to the soundness of his constitution. Now, may not this help us to understand the marvellous efficacy, as it appears to us, which Romanists ascribe to the sacrament of baptism? We believe them to hold that baptism can *regenerate* the man; but we are misled by their abuse of the term *baptismal regeneration*. Theycannot hold this doctrine, for man needs no regeneration. Their error lies deeper than baptismal regeneration. It is not so much an error on the function of the baptismal rite, as an error on the yet more fundamental point of man's state. They cannot realize man as fallen, and therefore they cannot realize him as regenerated. All the regeneration he needs is not the *creating* of him anew, but the *clothing* of him anew, — the impartation of those superadded gifts which he has lost; and this, they believe, the sprinkling of a little water by the hands of a priest can effect. Baptism, then, restores man to the state in which he existed before the Fall. By baptism, the Church of Rome holds, original sin is taken away, and sanctifying grace, of which the Fall denuded man, is restored. Every man who is baptized, according to this doctrine, begins life with the same advantages with which Adam began it, — he begins it in a state of spotless and perfect innocence. At this early stage, then, even that of the Fall, do the Popish and Protestant theologies diverge, — diverge never more to meet. The one flows backward into the dead sea of Paganism, — the other expands into the living ocean of Christianity.

In the course of the debates in the Council of Trent, a momentous question was raised touching the conception of the Virgin. If, as the council had decreed, Adam had transmitted his sin to all his posterity, did it not follow that the Virgin Mary was born in sin? It is well known that since the twelfth century at least the Church of Rome has leaned to the doctrine of the "immaculate conception," according to which the humanity of the Virgin is as untainted by sin, and as holy, as is the humanity of the Saviour. Conflicting parties have always existed within the Church on this subject. Many and furious have been the wars they have waged with one another. The Franciscans have violently maintained the immaculate conception, and the Dominicans have as violently denied it. The most delicate management and the most skilful manoeuvring of the Pope have sometimes been unable to maintain the peace between these hostile parties, or to avert from the Church the flagrant scandal of open schism. In the seventeenth century, the kingdom of Spain was so violently convulsed by this question, that embassies were sent to Rome to implore the Pope to put an end to the war, and restore peace to the kingdom, by a public bull. The conduct of the Pope on this occasion illustrates the species of juggling by which he has contrived to keep up the idea of his infallibility. He issued no bull, because he judged it imprudent in the circumstances; but he declared that the opinion of the Franciscans had a high degree of probability in it, and must not be opposed publicly by the Dominicans as erroneous; while, on the other hand, the Franciscans were forbidden to treat the doctrine of the Dominicans as erroneous. The Council of Trent, though they debated the question, would come to no decision, but left the matter undetermined. To this day the question remains undetermined, proving a fertile source of fierce polemical wars, which break out every now and then, and rage with great violence. The revolution at Rome having set free the Pope from the cares of government, he employed his leisure at Gaeta in attempts to settle this great question, which so many renowned popes and so many learned councils had left undecided. He took the regular course to obtain the prayers of the Church and the suffrages of the bishops, in order to promulgate his bull. The Pope was engrossed by these deep theological inquiries when the success of Oudinot before the walls of Rome recalled him from the study of the fathers to the not less grateful work of issuing incarcerations and signing death-warrants. Should a second period of exile intervene, which is not improbable, the pontiff may even yet gather up the broken thread of his thoughts, and elaborate the bull which is to crown the blasphemies and idolatry of Rome, by decreeing that the Virgin Mary was as wonderfully conceived as was the Saviour, and that her humanity was as free from sin, as holy and undefiled, as is the humanity of our Lord. "Neither repented they of their idolatries."

Thus have we come to a leading characteristic of the system of Popery, — one that is already sufficiently distinct, but which will become more fully developed as we proceed, — the disposition to substitute the ordinances of the Church for the gospel, — the symbol for the truth, — the form for the principle, — the sacraments for Christ. The great doctrine of salvation through faith in the free grace of God is set aside, and the *opus operatum* of a sacrament is put in its room. "That it is faith that worketh in the sacrament, and not the sacrament itself," say the Romanists, "is plainly false; baptism giving grace, and faith itself, to the infant that had none before."

Chapter X: Of Justification.

Of all questions, by far the most important to a fallen man, obnoxious to death, is, "How may I be reconciled to God, and obtain a title to eternal glory?" The Bible answers, "By faith in the righteousness of Christ." It is here that the Church of Rome wholly misleads her members. She gives the wrong answer; and therefore she is most fatally in error, where it behoved her, above all things, to be in the right.

The doctrine of "justification through faith alone" is the oldest theological truth in the world. We can trace it, wearing the very form it still bears, in the patriarchal age. The apostle tells us that God preached this truth unto Abraham. It was preached by type and shadow to the Old Testament Church; and when the altars and sacrifices of the legal economy were no more, this great truth was published far and wide throughout the world by the pens and tongues of apostles. After being lost by all, save a chosen few, during many centuries, it broke out with a new and glorious effulgence upon the world in the preaching of Luther. It is the grand central truth of Christianity: it is, in short, the gospel. Now it is on this vital point, we affirm, that the teaching of Rome is erroneous, and that, so far as that teaching is listened to and followed, it must needs destroy, not save, her members. The point of all others on which the Bible has spoken out with most emphatic plainness is, that Christ is the one only Saviour, and that his atonement upon the cross is the sole and exclusive ground of eternal life. There are parts of revelation about which we may entertain imperfect or erroneous views, and yet be saved; but this truth is the chief corner-stone of the gospel, and an error here must necessarily be fatal. We forsake the one only foundation; we go about seeking to establish a righteousness of our own; we trust in a refuge of lies; and cannot be saved. "For other foundation can no man lay than that is laid, which is Jesus Christ."

Herein we may trace the essential and eternal difference between the Gospel and Popery, — between the Reformation and Rome. The Reformation ascribed all the glory of man's salvation to God, — Rome ascribed it to the Church. Salvation of God and salvation of man are the two opposite poles around which are ranged respectively all true and all false systems of religion. Popery placed salvation in the Church, and taught men to look for it through the sacraments; the Reformation placed salvation in Christ, and taught men that it was to be obtained through faith. "By grace are ye saved, through faith, and that not of yourselves, — it is the gift of God." The development of the grand primordial truth, — salvation of grace, — has constituted the history of the Church. This truth gave being to the patriarchal religion; it formed the vital element in the Mosaic economy; it constituted the glory of primitive Christianity; and it was it that gave maturity and strength to the Reformation. With one voice, Calvin, Luther, and Zuingle, did homage to God as the author of man's salvation. The motley host of wrangling theologians which met at Trent made man his own Saviour, by extolling the efficacy and merit of good works.

The decree of the council by which the doctrine of the Church of Rome on the subject of justification was finally settled, partakes of not a little vagueness. On this, as on most other points that engaged the attention of the council, there existed a variety of conflicting opinions, which long and warm debates failed to reconcile. The somewhat impossible object of faithfully reflecting all the sentiments of the fathers was aimed at in the decree, at the same time that it was intended pointedly to condemn the doctrine of the Protestants. But we believe the following will be found a fair statement of what the Romish Church really holds on this important subject.

The Council of Trent defines justification to be "a translation from that state in which the man is born a son of the first Adam, into a state of grace and adoption of the sons of God by the second Adam, Jesus Christ, our Saviour; which translation cannot be accomplished under the gospel, without the laver of regeneration, or the desire of it; as it is written, 'Unless a man be born again of water and of the Holy Ghost, he cannot enter the kingdom of heaven.'" The definition given by Dens is in almost the very same words. Justification, says Perrone, is not the forensic remission of sin, or the imputation of Christ's righteousness; but it consists in the renovation of the mind by the infusion of sanctifying grace. The Council of Trent teaches the same doctrine in almost the same words, and enforces it with its usual argument, — an anathema. "Justification," says Bailly, "is the acquisition of righteousness, by which we become acceptable to God." It is important to observe, that by the "laver of regeneration," the Roman Catholic Church means baptism. It is important also to observe, that this definition confounds justification with sanctification. But to this we shall afterwards advert. We proceed to state the way in which this justification is received. The Roman Catholic Church teaches that there is a preparation of the mind for its reception, and in that preparation the man who is to be justified has an active share. "Justification springs," the Romish Church holds, "from the preventing grace of God." That grace excites and helps the man, who, by the power of his free will, agrees and co-operates therewith. Excited and aided by divine grace, men are disposed for this righteousness; they are drawn to God, and encouraged to hope in him, by the consideration of his mercy; they begin to love him as the fountain of all righteousness, and consequently to hate sin, that is, "with that penitence which must necessarily exist before baptism; and, finally, they resolve to receive baptism, to begin a new life, and to keep the divine commandments." This constitutes the disposition or preparation of the mind for the reception of justification. Similar is the account which Dens has given of the matter. He states that the Council of Trent requires seven acts of mind in order to the justification of the adult through baptism. The first is divine grace, by which the sinner is excited and aided; the second is faith; the third is fear; then hope, then love, then contrition, and lastly, a desire for the sacrament. Perrone mentions much the same graces, though in a slightly different order. "Besides faith," says he, "which all agree is required in order to justification, there must be fear, hope, love, at least begun, penitence, and a purpose of keeping the divine commandments." The faith that precedes justification, according to the Church of Rome, is not of a fiducial character, or a trust in the divine mercy exhibited in the promise, but a belief of all things taught in the Scriptures, that is, by the Church; and approaches very closely to what Protestants term a *historical faith*. We are said to be "justified freely by his grace," says the Church of Rome, inasmuch as the grace of God aids the sinner by these acts. She holds, moreover, that these acts are meritorious. She does not hold that they possess the merit of *condignity*, as do the good works of the justified man; but she holds that these acts of faith and love, which prepare and dispose the mind for justification, possess the merit of *congruity*, that is, they merit a divine reward, not from any obligation of justice, but out of a principle of fitness or congruity.

The disposition for justification being thus wrought, the justification itself follows. This satisfaction, say the fathers of Trent, "is not remission of sin merely, but also sanctification, and the renovation of the inner man by the voluntary reception of grace and of gifts, so that the man, from being unrighteous, is made righteous." The decree then goes on to describe the cause of justification. The final cause is the glory of God; the efficient cause is the mercy of God; the meritorious cause is Jesus Christ, "who merited justification for us by his most holy passion on the cross;" the instrumental cause is the "sacrament of baptism, which is the sacrament of faith," says the Council of Trent, "without which no one can ever obtain justification." The formal cause is the righteousness of God; "not that by which he himself is righteous, but that by which he makes us righteous; with which, to wit, being endued by him, we are renewed in the spirit of our mind, and are not only reputed righteous, but truly are called, and do become righteous, receiving righteousness in ourselves, each according to his measure."

Such is the doctrine of justification as taught by the Church of Rome. It is diametrically opposed to the method of justifying sinners described in the epistles of Paul, and more especially in his Epistle to the Romans. It is diametrically opposed to the doctrine of the reformers, and to the confessions of all the reformed Churches. All sound Protestant divines receive the term "justification" in a forensic sense. Nothing is changed *by justification viewed in itself* but the man's state, which, from being that of a criminal in the eye of the law, and obnoxious to death, becomes that of an innocent man, entitled to eternal life. The source of justification they regard as being the grace of God; its meritorious cause, the righteousness of Christ imputed to the sinner; and its instrumental cause, faith, by which the sinner receives the righteousness which the gospel offers. Thus nothing is seen in this great work but the grace of God. To Him is all the glory. The sinner comes into the possession of profound peace, because he feels that he is resting, not on his own good qualities, but on the righteousness of the Saviour, which "has magnified the law and made it honourable;" and he abounds in works of righteousness, being now become "dead unto the law, but alive unto God;" and these good fruits are at once the proofs of his justification and the pledges of his glory. But all this is reversed according to the Romish method. It is clear, according to the Church of Rome, that the ground of a sinner's justification is not without him, but within him. He is justified, not because Christ has satisfied the law in his room, but because the man himself has become such as the law requires; or, as Romish divines are accustomed to say, the *formal* cause of justification is *inherent* or *infused* righteousness. The death of Christ has to do with our justification only in so for as it has merited the infusion of those good dispositions which are the formal cause of our justification, and whereby we perform those good works which are meritorious of an increase of grace and eternal life. And, as regards faith, "we are not," says Bailly, "justified by faith alone;" and its admitted connection with justification he states to be, not that of an instrument, but of a good work, or part of infused righteousness. The Roman Catholic scheme, therefore, is very clearly one of salvation by good works.

This is the "first justification," as the Roman Catholic divines are accustomed to speak, and in this justification the sinner has no absolute merit, but only that of congruity. It is different in the "second justification," which is thus defined: — "By the observance of the commandments of God and the Church, faith co-operating with good works, they gain an increase of that righteousness which was received by the grace of Christ, and are the more justified." In this "second justification," the man rises to the merit of *condignity*, his works being positively meritorious and deserving of heaven. It is here that the Romish doctrine of good works is most clearly seen. For though there is a loose reference to the merits of Christ, yet if our good works be meritorious, as is affirmed, there must be a positive obligation, in respect of justice, on God to bestow heaven upon us, and thus salvation is of works. "The merits of men," says Bellarmine, "are not required because of the insufficiency of those of Christ, but because of their own very great efficacy. For the work of Christ hath not only deserved of God that we should obtain salvation, but also that we should obtain it by our own merits." But the thirty-second canon of the sixth session of the Council of Trent puts the matter beyond controversy. "If any one shall say that the good works of a justified man are the gift of God in such a sense that they are not also the good merits of the justified man himself, or that a justified man, by the good works which are done by him through the grace of God, and the merit of Christ, of whom he is a living member, does not truly deserve increase of grace, eternal life, and the actual possession of eternal life if he die in grace, and also an increase of glory, let him be ANATHAMA."

The Roman Catholic Church teaches that the justified man has no certainty of eternal life. He may fall, she holds, from a state of grace, and finally perish. Should he so fall, however, that Church has made provision for his recovery, and that recovery is through the sacrament of penance, — the "second plank after shipwreck," as the fathers term it. "Be mindful, therefore, from whence thou art fallen, and do penance." Agreeably with this, that Church teaches that "no one can certainly and infallibly know that he has obtained the grace of God." To stand in doubt on this important point she enjoins as a duty, and anathematizes the doctrine of "assurance" as a Protestant heresy.

Thus the fact is incontrovertible, that the scheme of the Church of Rome is one of salvation by works. And the question is shortly this, — Is this scheme agreeable to Scripture, or is it not? Papists cannot refuse the authority of Scripture on this, or on any point, seeing they admit it to be the Word of God. Now, while the Scriptures speak of a reward of grace, they utterly repudiate, both by general principles and positive statements, what Papists maintain, — a reward of merit. If, then, we allow the Bible to decide the controversy, the Church of Rome errs in a point where error is necessarily fatal. Her scheme of *salvation by works* is a scheme which robs God of his glory, and man of his peace now and his salvation hereafter.

Chapter XI: The Sacraments.

It has pleased God, in condescension to our weakness, to confirm his promises by signs. The bow of heaven is a divinely-appointed token, confirmatory to the world of the promise that there shall be no second deluge. The world has but one sign of its safety; the Church has two of her perpetuity. The sacraments of Baptism and the Lord's Supper, — like two beauteous bows bestriding the heavens of the Church, — are seals of the covenant of grace, and give infallible certainty to all who really take hold of that covenant, that they shall enjoy its blessings. But the Church of Rome has accounted that these two signs are not enough, and, accordingly, she has increased them to the number of seven. These seven sacraments are baptism, confirmation, the eucharist, penance, extreme unction, orders, and matrimony. That Church is accustomed to boast with truth that most of these sacraments are unknown to Protestants: she might have added, with equal truth, that they are unknown to the New Testament. The institution of Baptism and the Supper is plainly to be seen upon the inspired page; but where do we find the institution of these five supplementary sacraments? Not a trace of them can be discovered in Scripture; and the attempt to adduce Scripture in their support is so hopeless, that it has seldom been made. But what is it that Roman infallibility will not attempt? Dens proves in the following notable way from Scripture, that the sacraments must be seven in number. He quotes the passage, "Wisdom hath builded her house; she hath hewn out her seven pillars." "In like manner," says he, "*seven* sacraments sustain the Church." He next refers to the *seven* lamps on one candlestick, in the furniture of the tabernacle. These *seven* sacraments are the *seven* lamps that illuminate the Church. The Jesuit would have rendered his argument irresistible, had he but added, there were seven evil spirits that entered the house that was swept and garnished. These seven sacraments are the seven spirits whose united power and wisdom animate the Roman Catholic Church. The Council of Trent rested the proof of these sacraments mainly on tradition, and a supposed hidden and mystical meaning in the number seven. And, in truth, there sometimes is a mystic meaning in that number; as, for instance, when the seer of Patmos saw seven hills propping up the throne of the apocalyptic harlot. Protestants most willingly yield up to the Roman Catholic Church the entire merit of discovering these sacraments, as they also yield up to her the entire benefit flowing therefrom. The first two, baptism and penance, confer grace; the rest increase it. The first, therefore, are sometimes called the sacraments of the *dead*; the others, the sacraments of the living.

The Roman Catechism defines a sacrament as follows: — "A thing subject to the senses, which, in virtue of the divine institution, possesses the power of signifying holiness and righteousness and of imparting these qualities to the receiver." There was considerable difference of opinion in the Council of Trent as to the way in which grace is conveyed along with the sacraments; but the fathers were unanimous in holding that it *is* so conveyed, and in condemning the reformers, who denied the power of the sacraments to confer grace. Accordingly, in their decree they speak of "the holy sacraments of the Church, by which all true righteousness is first imparted, then increased, and afterwards restored if lost." "The Catholic doctrine," says Dens, "is, that the sacraments of the new law contain grace, and confer it *ex opera operato*." And in this he is borne out by the Council of Trent, who declare, "If any one shall say that these sacraments of the new law cannot confer grace by their own power [*ex opera Operato*], but that faith alone in the divine promise suffices to obtain grace, let him be accursed." Three of these sacraments, — baptism, confirmation, and orders, — confer an indelible impression, and therefore they are not, and cannot be, repeated. As to the seat of this indelible stamp or impression, the Romish divines are not agreed, — some fixing on the mind, others on the will, while a third party make this wondrous virtue to reside in the hands and the tongue; which gave occasion to Calvin to say, that "the matter resembled more the incantations of the magician than the sound doctrine of the gospel." Not only do the sacraments infuse grace at first, but they confer an increase of grace, and all that divine aid which is necessary to gain their end. This grace is contained in the sacraments, say the Romanists, "not as the accident in its subject, or as liquor in a vase (as Calvin has vilely insinuated), but it is conferred by the sacraments as the instrumental cause."

One very important point remains, and that is, the validity of the sacrament. In order to this, it is not enough that the forms of the Church be observed in the administration of the sacrament; the *right direction* of the intention of the administrator is an essential requisite. "If any one shall say," says the Council of Trent, "that in ministers, while they form and give the sacraments, intention is not required, at least of doing what the Church does, let him be anathema." Any flaw here, then, vitiates the whole proceeding. If the priest who administers baptism or extreme unction be a hypocrite or an infidel, and does not intend what the Church intends, the baptized man lives without grace, and the dying man departs without hope. The priest may be the greatest profligate that ever lived; this will not in the least affect the validity of the sacrament; but should he fail to direct aright his intention, the sacrament is null, and all its virtue and benefit are lost, — a calamity as dreadful as the difficulty of providing against it is great. For as the intention of another cannot be seen, it can never be known with certainty that it exists.

It is not difficult to imagine the tremendous evil to which a single invalid act may lead. Take the case of a child whose baptism is invalid from the want of intention on the part of the priest. This child grows to manhood; he takes orders; but he is no priest. Every priestly act he does is null. Those he ordains are in the same predicament with himself; they neither possess nor can transmit the true apostolic ichor. Every host they consecrate, and which is first adored, then eaten, by the worshippers, is but a simple wafer. They cannot absolve; they cannot give the viaticum. But even this is not the whole of the mischief. It may happen, that of these pseudo-priests, one may be chosen to fill Peter's chair. He wants, of course, the infallibility; and so the Church loses her head, and becomes a corpse. There is no Romanist who can say with certainty, on his own principles, that there is a true catholic and apostolic Church on the earth at this day.

Roman Catholics are accustomed to grant that the sacraments in general, and baptism in particular, administered by Protestants or by other heretics, are valid and efficacious as regards their effects. This is a stretch of charity quite unusual on the part of that Church; and we may be sure that Rome has good reasons for being so very liberal on this point. Good reasons she verily has. She grants that baptism administered by heretical hands is valid, in order that when these children grow up she may have a pretext to seize upon them, and compel them to enter the Roman Catholic Church. And in the fourteenth canon of the seventh session of the Council of Trent, she pronounces an anathema on all who shall say that such children, when they grow up, are to be "left to their own choice, and not to be compelled to lead a Christian life," that is, to become Roman Catholics. Thus has the Pope converted an ordinance which was designed to represent our being delivered from the yoke of Satan, and made the freedmen of Jesus Christ, into a brand of slavery. As in the feudal times the lords of the soil were accustomed to put collars, with their names inscribed, upon the necks of their slaves, so baptism is the iron collar which Rome puts upon the necks of her slaves, that she may be able to claim her property wherever she may chance to find it. "Heretics and schismatics," says the Catechism of Trent, "are excluded because they have departed from the Church; for they no more belong to the Church than deserters to the army they have left. *Yet it is not to be denied that they are under the power of the Church, as those who may be called by her to judgment, punished, and condemned by an anathema.*" In short, like deserters from the army, on being retaken they may be shot. And thus, as Blanco White remarks, "the principle of religious tyranny, supported by persecution, is a necessary condition of Roman Catholicism: he who revolts at the idea of compelling belief by punishment is severed at once from the communion of Rome." If we may believe Bellarmine, the apostles would have burned all they failed to convert, had they had the use of the civil power. Their time would have been divided betwixt directing Christians in their faith and morals, and drawing up rules for the trial and execution of pagans and heretics, had they seen the least chance of being permitted to act upon their plan. Think of Paul writing some such sentence as this: — "Now abideth faith, hope, charity, these three; but the greatest of these is charity," — and laying down his pen, and going straight to assist at an *auto da fe*!

Chapter XII: Baptism and Confirmation.

Having considered the leading characteristics which belong to sacraments in general, according to the idea of the Roman Catholic Church, it only remains that we state the peculiarities proper to each.

Nothing could be more simple as a rite, or more significant as a symbol, than baptism administered according to Scripture; nothing could be more foolish, ridiculous, or superstitious, than baptism administered according to the forms of the Roman Catholic Church. Water sprinkled on the body is the divinely-appointed sign; but to the Scripture form a great many absurd additions have been made. The water is prepared and consecrated with "the oil of mystic unction;" certain words and prayers are muttered over the child, to exorcise the devil; salt is put into the mouth, to intimate the relish acquired by baptism for "the food of divine wisdom," and the disposition communicated to perform good works. On the forehead, the eyes, the breast, the shoulders, the ears, is put the sign of the cross, to block up the senses against the entrance of evil, and to open them for the reception of good and the knowledge of divine things. The responses being made at the font, the child is next anointed with the oil of catechumens; first on the breast, that his bosom may become the abode of the Holy Ghost and of the true faith; next on the shoulders, that he may become strong and active in the performance of good works; the assent is then given, either personally or by sponsor, to the apostle's creed; after which baptism is administered. The crown of his head is then anointed with chrism, to signify his engrafting into Christ. A white napkin is given to the infant, to signify that purity of soul and that glory of the resurrection to which he is born by his baptism. A lighted taper is put into his hand, to represent the good works by which his faith is to be fed and made to burn. And finally, a name is given, which is usually selected from some distinguished saint in the calendar, whose virtues he is to imitate, and by whose prayers he is to be shielded and blessed.

The Roman Catholic Church teaches that participation in this rite is essential to salvation. "Is baptism necessary to salvation?" it is asked in Butler's Catechism. "Yes," is the reply; "without it we cannot enter into the kingdom of God." "Without baptism," says Liguori, "no one can enter heaven." Dens states two exceptions, — that of the martyr, and that of the man labouring under invincible ignorance. The effects of baptism are great and manifold. The compilers of the Roman Catechism have enumerated seven of the more notable ones. It cleanses from the guilt both of original sin and actual transgression; and nothing remains in the person but the infirmity of concupiscence. All punishment due on account of sin is discharged; justification and adoption, and other invaluable privileges, are bestowed; it implants the germ of all virtues; it engrafts into Christ; it stamps with an ineffaceable character; and it constitutes the person an heir of heaven.

Next in order to baptism comes the sacrament of confirmation. Baptism is the spiritual birth; but the Roman Catholic Church, like a tender mother, desires and delights to see her children wax in stature and in strength; and this they do mainly through the mystic influence of confirmation, in which the grace of baptism is perfected. By baptism they become Christians; by confirmation they become strong Christians. The one is the gate by which they enter the Christian state; the other clothes them with the armour of a Christian soldier. None are to be confirmed till they have attained at least the age of seven years. Its rites are simpler than those of baptism, but they are equally without warrant in Scripture, and therefore equally superstitious. This rite is to be administered by a bishop, who, making the sign of the cross upon the forehead of the person with chrism, compounded of oil and balsam, says, "I confirm thee, in the name of the Father, and of the Son, and of the Holy Ghost." He next slaps the person on the cheek, to signify that, as a soldier of the cross, he must be prepared bravely to endure hardships; and, lastly, he bestows the kiss of peace, to denote the impartation of that "peace that passeth all understanding." With the chrism the person enjoys a mystic anointing. He is no longer a child; he is now a perfect man, equipped for performing the labours and fighting the battles of the Church. In this sacrament the Roman Catholic Church holds that the seven gifts of the Spirit are bestowed. These gifts are, — wisdom, understanding, counsel, fortitude, knowledge, piety, and the fear of the Lord. Like baptism, the sacrament of confirmation confers an ineffaceable character, and is never to be repeated.

Rome has a fine histrionic genius. She has eclipsed all other actors that ever appeared in the world. What is the Papacy but a mighty melo-drama, which, according to the vein of the hour, runs out into the humours and fooleries of comedy, or deepens into the horrors of tragedy. All the persons and verities of eternal truth pass in shadow before the spectator in Rome's scenic exhibition. She affects to play over again the grand drama, of which the universe is the stage, and eternity the development, — redemption. And for what end? That she may hide from man the reality. Her system is essentially counterfeit, and all she does is pervaded by a spirit of imposture and juggling. But in some of her rites she lays aside her usual disguise, thin enough at the best, and reveals her art to all as but a piece of naked witchcraft. If those are not spells which she commends her priests to operate with on certain occasions, Hecate herself never used incantation or charm. We open her missals, and find them but books of sorcery: they are filled with recipes or spells for doing all manner of supernatural feats, — exorcising demons, working miracles, and infusing new and extraordinary qualities into things animate and inanimate. She has her cabalistic words, which, if uttered by a priest in the appropriate dress, will bind or loose men, send them to paradise or shut them up in purgatory! What is this but magic? What is the Church of Rome but a company of conjurors? and what is her worship but a system of divination? Has she not an order of exorcists, specially and formally ordained to the somewhat dangerous office of fighting with and overcoming hobgoblins and devils? Has she not her regular formulas, by which she can change the qualities of substances, control the elements of air, earth, and water, and compel spirits and demons to do the bidding of her priests? Can any man of plain understanding take this for religion? What is her grand rite, but an incantation, which combines in more than the foulness of ancient sorcery with more than the blasphemy of modern atheism? And yet do not kings, presidents, and statesmen, countenance its celebration? and, while themselves practising this foul sorcery, and leading others by their influence to practise it, they affect to be shocked at the impieties of modern socialism! We excuse not Voltaire and the other high priests of infidelity; but it is indisputable that they treated the human understanding with more respect than do the stoled and mitred sorcerers, who first create, then eat their god. What are the rubrics of the Romish Church, but recipes for the manufacture of holy salt, holy mortar, holy ashes, holy incense, holy bells, holy oil, holy water, and we know not how many other things besides? And the instructions regarding this unearthly kind of manufacture are plentifully mixed with exorcisms for driving the devil out of oil, out of buildings, and out of infants. For, with striking but characteristic inconsistency, while, according to the theory of original sin, as we have explained it, man's nature is entire and sound, according to the formula of baptism he is possessed by a demon. "Come out of this body, unclean spirit!" So runs the summons uttered by priestly lips, and addressed to the supposed occupant of every infant brought to the baptismal font. According to the dogmatic view, man has no corrupt element in his constitution; according to the ritual, he is a demoniac, and remains a demoniac till the baptismal water restores him to his right mind. What, in form or essence, is awanting in the following scene, to entitle it to be regarded as a piece of genuine witchcraft? It is the exorcism of water in order to its being used in baptizing. Following the classic model which the words of Hecate to the three weird sisters furnish, —

"Your vessels and your spells provide,

Your charms, and everything beside," —

the rubric proceeds: —

"First, let the vessel be washed and cleansed, and then filled with clear water; then let the sacrificing priest, in his surplice (or alb) and stole, with the clerks or other priests, if they be at hand, with the cross, two wax candles, the censor and incense, the vessels of the chrism, and the oil of the catechumens, solemnly advance to the font, and there, or at the altar of the baptistery, if there be one, say the following litany" [in Latin].

That litany consists of an invocation of all the saints in the Roman calendar; for it is fitting that such an incantation should open with the names of the "three hundred gods" of Rome in whose honour these rites are performed. After this comes the EXORCISM.

"I exorcise thee, thou creature of water,

By the living †, by the true †,

By the holy † person who,

By a word, without a hand,

Parted thee from the dry land;

Who did brood upon thy face,

In the void and formless space;

Who did order thee to go,

And from Paradise to flow,

In four goodly rivers forth,

Towards the south, cast, west, and north."

"Here let him with his hand divide the water, and then pour some of it outside the edge of the font, toward the four parts of the world.

"Who, when bitter was thy flood,

By the prophet's branch of wood,
Made thee sweet; who from the stone,
In the desert parch'd and lone,
Fainting Israel's thirst to cure,
Brought thee forth . . . . .
. . . . . I thee conjure;
Be thou holy water, blest;
Cleanse the foul and guilty breast;
Wash away the filth of sin;
Make the bosom pure within.
And ye devils, every one,
Let what I prescribe be done.
Where this water sprinkled flies,
Thence eradicate all lies;
Every phantasm put to flight;
Every dark thing bring to light.
Let it be of life eternal,
Fountain salient and supernal;
Laver of Regeneration
For a chosen favoured nation.
In the name, &c. — Amen."

Then follow certain ceremonies, such as blowing three times into the water, incensing the font, and pouring in oil in the form of a cross; after which the incantation is concluded as follows: —

"Mingle, O thou holy chrism;
Blessed oil, I mingle thee;
Mingle, water of baptism,
Mingle, all ye sacred three;
Mingle, mingle, mingle ye,
In the name of †, and of †, and of †."

Now this appears to us to embody the very soul of magic. The only two spiritual agencies known to man, — the moral and supernatural agency of the Divine Spirit, and the intellectual and natural agency of truth, — are here set aside, and a third sort of agency, that of spells and incantations, is called into requisition. Is not this witchcraft? Of whom, then, are the priests of Rome the successors? Manifestly of the ancient diviners and wizards. Nor could anything be finer, as a piece of the histrionic, than the scene just described. The ancient models have been carefully studied, and their forms as well as spirit preserved. The obscurity produced by the incense and the tapers, — the mystic dresses, with their Hieroglyphical signs, — the crossings and blowings, — the mixing and mingling of various substances, — the intoned incantations, — the dread names employed to conjure with, — all combine to form a scene such as might have been beheld in the observatory of some ancient Chaldean astrologer, or in the cell of some Egyptian soothsayer; or such as the poor infatuated monarch witnessed in the sorceress's cot at Endor; or, to come nearer home, such as the great Hecate and her three bedlamite attendants celebrated at midnight on the bleak heath of Forres, so powerfully painted by the genius of Shakspeare. The one set of rites are equally important and dignified as the other; and both occupy the mind with precisely the same feeling, — that feeling being one of vague, hurtful, and demoralizing awe.

Chapter XIII: The Eucharist — Transubstantiation — The Mass.

We now come to speak of the Eucharist. This rite, as practised by the Church of Rome, forms the centralization of Popish absurdity, blasphemy, and idolatry. The mass, in short, is Superstition's masterpiece. It takes precedence of all other idolatries that ever existed in this fallen world. It is without a rival among the polytheisms of ancient times. The groves of Greece, the temples of Egypt, witnessed the celebration of no rite at once so revolting and so impious is that which is daily enacted in the temples of the Roman Catholic Church. What the priests of pagan Rome would have blushed to perform, the priests of papal Rome glory in, as that which imparts a peculiar lustre to their office, and a peculiar sanctity to their persons. As the polytheisms of the past have produced nothing that can equal the mass, so we may safely affirm that, while the world stands, this rite will remain unsurpassed by anything which the combined folly and impiety of man is able to invent.

The same place which the Pope occupies in the scheme of papal government does the host occupy in the scheme of papal worship. Each forms in its own department the culminating point of Rome's idolatry. Both are transformed into divinities. A mortal and fallible man, when seated in the chair of Peter, and crowned with the tiara, is straightway endowed with the attribute of infallibility, and is addressed and obeyed as God. Bread and wine, when placed upon the altars of the Romish Church, with a few prayers mumbled over them by the priest, and a few muttered words of consecration, are straightway changed into the real flesh and blood of Christ, and are commanded to be adored with the worship that is due to God. What a difference between the Eucharist of the primitive Church and the mass of the popish Church! And yet the latter is but the former disguised and metamorphosed by the evil genius of Popery. In nothing perhaps do we find a more striking illustration of the sad change that Romanism works on all that is pure, simple, and holy! How completely has it succeeded in changing the character and defeating the end of the ordinance of the Supper! A memorial at once affecting and sublime, designed to commemorate the most wonderful event the world ever saw, it has transformed into a rite which revolts by its absurdity and shocks by its impiety, and which robs of all its value and efficacy that death which it was designed to commemorate, and which, on the ground of its efficacy alone, was worthy of being commemorated.

The sum of what the Church of Rome holds under this head is, that the bread and wine in the Eucharist are changed into the real flesh and blood of Christ the moment the priest pronounces the words, "This is my body;" that the host is to be adored with the adoration usually given to God, and, in fine, is to be offered up to God by the priest, as a true propitiatory sacrifice for the sins of the quick and the dead. The subject then resolves itself as follows: *first*, the dogma of transubstantiation; *second*, the adoration of the host; and *third*, the sacrifice of the mass.

The origin of the term *mass* is involved in obscurity. The more common opinion is, that it signifies "a sending away." It was the custom anciently, at the conclusion of the sermon, and before proceeding to celebrate the Supper, for the officiating deacon to pronounce aloud, "*Ite, missa est,*" in order that catechumens and strangers might retire. From this circumstance the service that followed was called "mass." It required several centuries to give to the rite its present form. Transubstantiation was broached as early as the ninth century, but it was not formally established till the Council of Lateran, 1215, under the pontificate of Innocent III.; nor was it till three centuries later that the Council of Trent decreed it to be a true propitiatory sacrifice. It is on the dogma of transubstantiation that the whole of the mass is founded. The Council of Trent thus defines transubstantiation: — "If any one shall deny that in the sacrament of the most holy Eucharist there are contained truly, really, and substantially, the body and the blood, together with the soul and divinity, of our Lord Jesus Christ, and therefore whole Christ, and shall say that he is in it only by sign, or figure, or influence, let him be accursed." Still more explicit are the terms of the next canon: — "If any one shall say, that in the sacrament of the most holy Eucharist there remains the substance of bread and wine along with the body and blood of our Lord Jesus Christ, and shall deny the wonderful and singular conversion of the whole of the substance of the bread into the body, and the whole of the substance of the wine into the blood, there remaining only the appearances of bread and wine, which conversion the Catholic Church most appropriately calls transubstantiation, let him be accursed." Rome is careful to mark the complete and thorough character of the change effected by the consecrating words of the priest. There is no mixing of the bread and the wine with the body and the blood of Christ. The substance of the bread and the wine is annihilated; and the very body and blood of Christ, — "that very body," Rome is careful to state, which was born of the Virgin, and which now sits at the right hand of God," — that body which did all the miracles, uttered all the words, and endured all the agonies, which the evangelists record, — that very body it is which the priest reproduces, places upon the altar, and puts into the hands and into the mouths of the worshippers. Do the annals of the world contain another such wonder? Nay, with a particularity that sinks into the most offensive grossness, the authorized books of Rome are careful to explain that "the bones and sinews" of the body of Christ are contained in the host. There is nothing to indicate to the senses the stupendous change which the creating fiat of the priest has accomplished. To the eye it still appears as bread and wine; it smells as bread, it tastes as bread, and it can be eaten as bread; yet it is not bread: it is flesh; it is blood; it is the very body that eighteen centuries ago sojourned on earth, and that now sits enthroned in heaven. Christ has again returned to earth, not in glory, as he promised, and attended by his mighty angels; but summoned thither by the terrible power, or spell, or whatever it be, which the priest possesses, and for the purpose of undergoing a deeper humiliation than at first. Then he appeared as a man, but now he is compelled to assume the form of an inanimate thing, and under that form he is again broken, and again offered in sacrifice and so his humiliation is not yet over, — his days of suffering and sacrifice are still prolonged: so eager has Rome been to identify herself with that Church predoomed in the Apocalypse, and marked with this brand, "where also our Lord was crucified."

It is scarce possible to state the many revolting consequences involved in the popish doctrine of transubstantiation, without an appearance of profanity. But the dread of this charge must not unduly deter us. Rome it is that must bear the responsibility. The awful profanation is theirs, not ours. The priests of the Church of Rome have the power not only of creating the body of our blessed Lord, together with his divinity, as often as they will, but of multiplying it indefinitely. Every time mass is performed *two Christs* at least are created. There is a whole Christ in the host, or bread; and there is a whole Christ in the chalice, or cup — "It is most certain," says the Council of Trent, "that all is contained under either species, and under both; for Christ, whole and entire, exists under the species of bread, and in every particle thereof, and under the species of wine, and in all its parts." "The *body*," says Perrone, "cannot be separated from the blood, and soul, and divinity; nor can the *blood* be separated from the body, and soul, and divinity; therefore, under each species a whole Christ must of necessity be present." It follows that there are as many whole Christs as there are consecrated wafers. It follows also, that should we divide the wafer, there is a whole Christ in each part; should we divide it again, the same thing will take place; and how many soever the times we divide it, or the parts into which we divide it, a whole Christ is contained in every one of the parts. The same thing is true of the cup. Should we pour it out drop by drop, in every one of the drops there is a whole Christ. But we are also to take into account that the mass is being celebrated at many thousand altars at the same time. At each of these altars the body of our blessed Lord is reproduced. The priest whispers the potent word; the bread and wine are annihilated; the flesh and blood of Christ, the bones and nerves, — to use Rome's phrase, — together with his divinity, take their place, are immolated in sacrifice, and then eaten by the worshippers. That body is locked up in sacraria, is carried about in mass-boxes, is put into the pockets of priests, is produced at the beds of the sick, is liable to be lost, to be trodden upon, to be devoured by vermin, to — but we forbear; the enormity and blasphemy of the abomination sickens and revolts us.

But on what ground does Rome rest this doctrine? She rests it simply on these words, spoken by Christ at the first supper, — "This is my body." She holds that by these words Christ changed the bread and wine into his flesh and blood, and has transmitted the same power to every priest, in the celebration of the Eucharist, grounding this delegation of power upon the words, "This do in remembrance of me." To assail such a position by grave argument were a waste of time. We have nowhere met with so clear and beautiful an exposition of the true meaning of these words, "This is my body," and of the absurdity of the sense which Rome puts upon them, as in the life of Zwingle. The mass was about to be abolished in the canton of Zurich, and the reformer had been engaged all day in debating the question before the great council. Am-Grutt, the under Secretary of State, did battle in behalf of the impugned rite, and was opposed by Zwingle, the substance of whose reasoning, as stated by D'Aubigné, was, "that (is) is the proper word in the Greek language to express *signifies*, and he quoted several instances in which this word is employed in a figurative sense."

"Zwingle," continues the historian, "was seriously engrossed by these thoughts, and, when he closed his eyes at night, was still seeking for arguments with which to oppose his adversaries. The subjects that had so strongly occupied his mind during the day presented themselves before him in a dream. He fancied that he was disputing with Am-Grutt, and that he could not reply to his principal objection. Suddenly a figure stood before him, and said, 'Why do you not quote the eleventh verse of the twelfth chapter of Exodus, — *Ye shall eat it* (the lamb) *in haste: it is the Lord's passover?*' Zwingle awoke, sprung out of bed, took up the septuagint translation, and there found the same word, (is), which all are agreed is synonymous with *signifies* in this passage.

"Here, then, in the institution of the paschal feast under the old covenant, is the very meaning that Zwingle defends. How can he avoid concluding that the two passages are parallel?"

The canon of interpretation by which Rome finds transubstantiation in the Bible, is, that the words "This is my body" must be taken literally. No one is so great an adept as herself at mystical and figurative interpretation; but here it suits her purpose to insist on the literal sense. But are we bound to follow Rome's canon? Certainly not. Should we do so, there is no book in the world which is so fraught with absurdity and unintelligibility as the Bible. There is no figure more common, whether in Scripture or in ordinary speech, than that by which we give to the sign the name of the thing signified. "The seven kine are seven years," "I am the door," and a hundred other instances, which the memory of every reader can supply, — What would we make of these sayings on the literal principle?" "This is Calvin," say we, meaning it is his portrait. The veriest simpleton would scarce take us to mean that the lines and paint on the canvas are the flesh and blood, the soul and spirit, of Calvin. But, say the Romish doctors, these phrases occur in dreams and parables, where a figurative mode of speech is allowable; while the words "This is my body" form part of a plain narrative of the institution of the Supper. Well, let us take the corresponding narrative in the Old Testament, — the institution of the Passover, — and see whether a mode of speech precisely identical does not there occur. "It (the lamb) is the Lord's Passover;" that is, it is the token thereof. No one was ever so far bereft of understanding and reason as to hold that the lamb was transubstantiated into the Passover; that is, into the Lord's passing over the houses of the Israelites. The lamb, when eaten in after ages, was, and could but be, the *memorial*, and nothing more, of an event long since past. In these two analogous passages, then, we find a mode of speech precisely similar; and yet Rome interprets them according to two different canons. She applies the figurative rule to the *lamb*, the literal to the bread. But we need not go so far as to the Old Testament to convict Rome of violating her own canon; we have only to turn to the second clause of the same text, — "He took the cup,…saying,…this is my blood." Was the cup his blood? Yes, on the literal principle. But, says Rome, the "cup" is here, by a trope or figure of speech, put for what it contains. Undoubtedly so; but it is a trope or figure of the same kind with that in the first clause, — "This is my body;" and Rome pays her canon but a poor compliment, when it is no sooner enacted than abandoned. We cannot be blamed, surely, if we follow her example, and abandon it likewise, along with the monstrous dogma she has built upon it.

But, leaving canons of interpretation, let us betake ourselves to the use of our reason and our senses. Alas! the mystery is as insoluble as ever. Like those stars so immensely remote from our earth, that the most powerful telescope cannot assign their parallax, this mystery moves in an orbit so immeasureably beyond the range of both our mental powers and our bodily senses, that these make not the smallest perceptible approach to its comprehension. Reason and transubstantiation are quantities which have no relation to one another. The bread and the wine, say the Romish theologians, are transubstantiated into the flesh and blood of Christ. Had, then, our Lord two bodies? Was he dead and alive at the same instant? Did he break himself? Did he eat himself? Was he sacrificed in the upper room; and was his death on the cross but a repetition of his decease the evening before? Yes; on Rome's principle, all this, and more, is true. He rose to die no more, and yet it is not so. He rose to die many times every day. He is in heaven; and yet he is not in heaven, for he is on earth. He is here on this altar; and yet he is not here; he is there on that altar: he is in neither place; and yet he is in both places. He is broken; and yet he is not broken, for in each part is a whole Christ. From the whole wafer he passes into the fractured part; and yet he does not pass into it, for a whole Christ remains in the part from which it was disjoined. Here is motion and rest, existence and non-existence, predicated of the same body at the same instant. Rome has good reason for exhorting her devotees to qualify themselves for the reception of this doctrine by the following abjuration: — "Herein I utterly renounce the judgment of my senses, and all human understanding;" which is just a statement, in Rome's peculiar way, of what we are contending for, that transubstantiation is a proposition which no man in his senses can believe.

Reason, we have seen, grapples hopelessly with this mystery. It is equally baffling and confounding to the senses. To the sight, the touch, and the taste, the bread and wine are bread and wine still. It is our senses that mislead and deceive us, says the infallible Church. The *substance* of the bread is gone, — the *accidents*, that is, the colour, the smell, the taste of bread, remain. The substance gone and the accidents remain! This is the one instance in the universe where *accidents* exist apart from their SUBJECT. In no other instance did we ever see whiteness but in a white body; but here we see where there is nothing to be seen, we touch where there is nothing to be touched, and taste where there is nothing to be tasted. For this ingenious discovery a French physician was so unreasonable as to say, that the holy fathers of Trent ought to be doomed to live all their days after on the accidents of bread. In that case, we fear, both subject and accidents would have speedily gone the way of all the earth. The newest theory on the subject, as given by Dens, is, that the *accidents* exist in the air and in our senses, as in their *subject*. But behind this wonder rises another. While in the one case, that of the bread, the *accidents* exist apart from the *subject*, in the other, that of the body of our Lord, the subject exists without the *accidents*. That body is there, but it possesses none of the properties of a body. It is not extended; it cannot be seen; it cannot be touched nor tasted. We touch and taste only the accidents of bread; for the host, we are taught, is received under the appearance of bread. But it were bootless farther to pursue a mystery which Romanists candidly tell us falls not within the scope of reason or sense. Rome is unquestionably in the right when she assures us that the judgment of the Church on this head cannot be believed till the judgment of the understanding has been renounced.

One word more as regards the testimony of the senses. Rome knows perfectly that her doctrine cannot stand this test, and therefore she has straitly forbidden its application. If men will be so wicked as to use their senses in connection with this mystery, they will be justly punished by being landed in dreadful impiety; that is, they will learn to deride transubstantiation as an impious and iniquitous juggle.

"First of all," says the Catechism of Trent, "inculcate on the faithful the necessity of using their utmost endeavour to withdraw their minds and understandings from the dominion of the senses; for should they allow themselves to be led by what the senses tell them respecting this mystery, they will be drawn into the extreme of impiety." Rome, in this way, may save the dogma of transubstantiation; but, like those creatures which launch their stings and their life together in the effort of self-defence, she saves transubstantiation at the expense of Christianity. Her principle is one that would land us in universal disbelief. How know we that Christ existed? We know it on the testimony of men who had simply the evidence of their senses for the fact, — of men who saw, and heard, and handled him. In the same way do we believe in his miracles: we receive them on the testimony of men who tasted the wine into which the water was converted, or spake with Lazarus after he was raised. How know we that there is a God? The evidence of his works and of his Word, communicated through the senses, assures us that He exists. In fine, we have no evidence of anything which does not come through the senses; and if we distrust them, we can believe in nothing. We cannot believe that there is a universe, or indeed anything at all. We can stop short only at Hume's principle, that there is neither body nor spirit beyond our own minds, and that all is ideal.

Thus Rome, when she brings us before the shrine of her idol, insists on blindfolding us. We must submit to have our eyes put out in order that we may be able to worship! Why is this? Is it a God, or a monster, before whom she conducts us? Does she drop this dark veil to temper the glory, or to hide the deformity, of her divinity? The answer is not far to seek. The mass, like another great deity,

Is a monster of such frightful mein,

That, to be hated, needs but to be seen.

How differently does the Bible treat us! It addresses us through the powers God has endowed us with, and calls on us to exercise these powers. The faith of the Bible is the perfection of reason: the faith of Rome is based on the prostitution and extinction of all those faculties which are the glory of man.

Considering that the dogma of transubstantiation lacks footing in both Scripture and reason, one might think that Rome would have shown great moderation in pressing it. Quite the reverse. The belief of it was enforced with a rigour which would not have been justifiable although it had been the plainest, instead of the most confounding, of propositions. Rome endeavoured to make it plain by the help of racks and faggots. Transubstantiation defied belief notwithstanding; and the consequence was the effusion of blood in torrents. Rome has inaugurated her leading dogmas, as the heathen did their idols, by hecatombs of human beings. So many confessors have been called to die for the mass, that it has come to be known as Rome's "burning article."

The monstrous juggle of transubstantiating the elements is immediately followed by an act of gross idolatry. The host being consecrated, the officiating priest kneels and adores it; he next elevates it in the sight of the people, who likewise kneel and adore it. The Church distinctly teaches that it is to be worshipped with that worship which is rendered to God himself; because it is God. "It is therefore indubitable," say the fathers of Trent, "that all true Christians, according to the uniform practice of the Catholic Church, are bound to venerate this most holy sacrament, and to render to it the worship of *latria*, which is due to the true God. Nor is it the less to be worshipped that it was instituted by Christ the Lord, as has been stated; for we believe the same God to be present in it, of whom the eternal Father, when he introduces him into the world, thus speaks: — 'And let all the angels of God worship him.'" The same decree goes on to enact that the host shall be carried in public procession through the streets, that the faithful may adore it, and that heretics, seeing its "great splendour," may be smitten and die, or may be ashamed and repent.

The host, then, is to be worshipped; and how? Not as images are worshipped; not as saints are worshipped; but as the eternal Creator himself is worshipped. The Church of Rome does not teach that God is *worshipped through* the host: she teaches that the host *is* God, — is the flesh, the blood, the soul and divinity of Christ, — and therefore the worship is given to the host, and terminates on the host. If that Church can prove conclusively, by fair argument, that what appears to us to be bread and wine is not bread and wine at all, but the body and divinity of Christ, we will at once admit that she does right, and at once acquit her of idolatry, in rendering it divine honours; but till she irrefragably establish this, we must hold her guilty of the grossest idolatry. It is no answer to say, that the Papist believes that the wafer which he worships is God, and that if he did not believe it to be God he would not worship it. His so believing does not make it God; nor can his mistake alter the nature of the act, which is that of giving to a wafer that worship and homage which is due to God alone. The question is, Is it, or is it not, God? We deny that it is God, and challenge Rome to the proof; and till proof clear and conclusive is adduced, we shall hold, that in worshipping the bread and wine of the Eucharist, she is guilty of one of the foulest and most monstrous forms of idolatry ever practised on the earth.

Nor do the absurdity and impiety of the mass stop here. The priests of Rome not only create the body and divinity of Christ, — they actually offer it in sacrifice. The Church of Rome teaches that the mass is a true propitiatory sacrifice for the sins of the quick and the dead. So was it decreed to be by the Council of Trent. "The holy council teaches that this sacrifice is really propitiatory, and made by Christ himself. . . . . Assuredly God is appeased by this oblation, and grants grace and the gift of penitence, and discharges the greatest crimes and iniquities. For it is one and the same sacrifice which is now offered by the priests, and which was offered by Christ upon the cross, only the mode of offering is different. . . . . Wherefore it is rightly offered, according to the tradition of the apostles, not only for the sins, punishments, satisfactions, and other necessities of living believers, but also for the dead in Christ, who are not yet completely purified." The fathers of Trent establish this doctrine by the very peculiar logic with which they establish all the more unintelligible of their dogmas, that is, they present it to the understanding, and drive it home with an anathema. "Whoever shall affirm," say the fathers, "that the sacrifice of the mass is nothing more than an act of praise and thanksgiving, or that it is simply commemorative of the sacrifice offered on the cross, and not also propitiatory, or that it benefits only the person who receives it, nor ought to be offered for the living and the dead, for sins, punishments, satisfactions, and whatever besides may be requisite, let him be accursed." The practice of the Church is in full accordance with the decree of Trent. The following prayer accompanies the oblation of the host: — "Accept, O Holy Father, Almighty and Eternal God, this unspotted host, which I thy unworthy servant offer unto thee, my living and true God, for my innumerable sins, offences, and negligences, and for all here present; as also for all faithful Christians, both living and dead; that it may avail both me and them to everlasting life. — Amen." It is the doctrine of the Church of Rome, then, as taught by her great council, that in the sacrifice of the mass atonement is made for sin. But we think that we can discover a disposition on the part of the Papists of the present day to explain away the doctrine of Trent on this head. In their modern catechisms they no doubt state that the mass is a true propitiatory sacrifice, for otherwise they would impugn their Church's infallibility; but when they come to describe its effects, they state in a cursory way, "the remission of sins," and dwell largely on its efficacy in applying to us the merits and benefits of the sacrifice of Christ. But, not to speak of the absurdity of supposing that the merits of one sacrifice are applied to us by another sacrifice, the attempt to limit the nature and design of the mass to this is utterly inconsistent with all their other statements and reasonings respecting it. Why not also call baptism a "propitiatory sacrifice," seeing the benefits of Christ's death are applied to us by it? The very same flesh and blood, Papists hold, are offered in the mass which were offered on the cross: it is the same person who offers, even Christ, who is represented by the priest: it is one and the same sacrifice, the Church of Rome teaches, which was offered on the cross, and is now offered in the mass; the inference is therefore inevitable, that its design and effects are the same. It made a real atonement in the first instance; and, if still the same sacrifice, must still be, what the authorized expositors of the Romish creed declare it to be, a true propitiatory sacrifice.

The Council of Trent pronounces an anathema against the man who shall affirm that the sacrifice of the mass blasphemes or derogates from the sacrifice of Christ upon the cross. But despite its anathema, we maintain that the mass is in the highest degree derogatory to the sacrifice of Christ, — is so derogatory to it as virtually to supersede it altogether. The glory of the cross lies in its efficacy, and the mass makes void that efficacy. Rome here is emphatically the enemy of the cross. As oft as this sacrifice is offered, Rome emphatically declares that the cross has failed to accomplish the end which God proposed by it; that, though Christ has suffered, sin remains unexpiated; and that what he has failed to do by the pains of his body and the agonies of his soul, her priests are able to do by their *unbloody* sacrifice. It is theirs to offer for the sins of the world, — theirs to mediate between earth and heaven. And thus the dignity of the priesthood of Christ is completely eclipsed by the priesthood of Rome, and the glory of his cross by Rome's great sacrifice of the mass.

Moreover, the doctrine of the mass traverses all the leading principles and statements of the Bible on the subject of Christ's offering. The Bible teaches that the office and functions of priesthood are for ever at an end; the sacrifice of the mass implies that they are still in being. The Bible teaches that the sacrifice of Christ was offered "once for all," and is never to be repeated; but in the mass, Christ continues to be offered in sacrifice every day at the thousand altars of Rome. The great law of the Bible on the subject of satisfaction is, that "without shedding of blood there is no remission." This law the mass contradicts, inasmuch as it teaches that there is "remission" by its *unbloody* sacrifice, and so virtually affirms that the blood of Christ was uselessly shed.

While on this subject, we may be permitted to remark, that the man who assumes to be a priest is chargeable with a blasphemy next to that of the man who assumes to be God. Priesthood is the next sacred thing to Deity. There is only one priest in the universe; there never was, and there never will be, any other; for the circumstances of our world render it impossible that priesthood, in the true sense of the term, should be borne by any mere creature. The priests of the former economy were but types and figures, And as there is but ONE priest, so there is but ONE sacrifice. The sacrifices of the Mosaic dispensation were typical, like the priests; and now both are for ever at an end. Accordingly, in the New Testament, the term *priest* does not once occur, save in relation to a priesthood now abolished. The claim of priesthood, then, is sacrilegious and blasphemous, and the man who makes it is inferior in guilt only to the man who lays claim to Deity.

There are several practices connected with the celebration of the mass, which our limits may permit us to indicate, but forbid us to dwell upon. The Council of Trent, which was the first to decree that the mass is a true propitiatory sacrifice, also enacted that the cup should be denied to the laity. The King of France is (or rather was) the only layman in Christendom who, by virtue of a pontifical permission, is allowed the privilege of communicating in both kinds. Priests only were present at the first communion, say the Papists, and therefore the laity have no right to the cup. But this proves too much, and therefore proves nothing; for if this warrants the exclusion of the laity from the cup, it equally warrants their exclusion from the bread, — from the sacrament altogether. Sensible that this ground would not sustain her practice of giving the cup to no one but the officiating priest, the Roman Catholic Church has had recourse to tradition, but with no better success. It does not admit of doubt, that in early times the people were allowed the cup equally with the bread. But the practice has now come to be extremely common in the Church of Rome for the priest alone to partake sacramentally; so that, in point of fact, the people, in all ordinary cases, are debarred from both kinds. The writer has seen mass celebrated in most of the great cathedrals out of Italy; but in no instance did he ever see the worshippers permitted to partake. Attendance, however, on such occasions, is earnestly enjoined; and the people are taught that their benefit is the same whether they partake or no.

It is also a frequent practice of the priests of Rome to celebrate mass in their own closets, where not a single spectator is present. This custom is directly at variance with one leading end of the institution of the Supper, which, as a public memorial, was designed to commemorate a great public event. The priest, in this case, can apply the benefit of the mass to whomsoever he will; that is, he can apply it to any one who chooses to hire him with his money. The ghostly necromancer, shut up in his own closet, can operate by his spells upon the soul of the person he intends to benefit, with equal effect, whether he is in the next room or a thousand miles off. Nay, though he should be beyond "this visible diurnal sphere," in the gloomy regions of purgatory, the mysterious and potent rites of the priest can benefit him even there. No magician in his cave ever wrought with spells and incantations half so powerful as those wielded by the priests of Rome. The mysteries of ancient sorcery and the wonders of modern science are here left far behind. The electric telegraph can transmit intelligence with the speed of lightning across a continent, but the Romish priest can convey instantaneously the virtue of his spiritual divinations across the gulf that divides worlds. But we might write volumes on the mass, and not exhaust its marvels.

How all this goes to enrich, and almost to deify, the Romish priesthood, will be seen when we come to speak of the genius of Popery.

Chapter XIV: Of Penance and Confession.

In baptism all sin is washed away, and more particularly the guilt of original sin. For the remission of sins done after baptism, the Roman Catholic Church has invented the sacrament of penance. That mystic machinery by which Rome perfects men for heaven, without any trouble or pains of their own, is complete in all its parts. Holiness is conferred by one sacrament and maintained by another; and thus a mutual benefit is conferred. The people are enriched by the spiritual gifts of the Church, and the Church is amply recompensed and endowed with the temporal wealth of the people. "Penance is the channel through which the blood of Christ flows into the soul, and washes away the stains contracted after baptism," says the Catechism of Trent. It might have added with equal truth, that it is a main channel by which the gold of the people flows into the treasury of Rome, and repairs the havoc which the luxury and ambition of the clergy are daily making in the possessions of the Church.

Penance Dens defines to be "a sacrament of the new law, by which those who have been baptized, but have fallen into sin, upon their contrition and confession obtain absolution of sin from a priest having authority." The Council of Trent requires all to believe, under pain of damnation, that "the Lord specially instituted the sacrament of penance when, after his resurrection, he breathed on his disciples, saying, "Receive ye the Holy Ghost: whosesoever sins ye remit, they are remitted unto them; and whosesoever sins ye retain, they are retained." The fathers go on to argue, that the power of forgiving sins, which Christ undoubtedly possessed and exercised, was communicated to the apostles and their successors, and that the Church had always so understood the matter. Of this last, however, the council adduces no proof, unless we can regard as such the anathema with which it attempts to terrify men into the belief of this dogma. None can be saved, the Roman Catholic Church holds, without the sacrament of penance. It is "as necessary to salvation," says the Council of Trent, "for those who have sinned after baptism, as baptism itself for the unregenerate." "Without its intervention," says the Trent Catechism, "we cannot obtain, or even hope for, pardon." This sacrament, as regards its form, consists in the absolution pronounced by the priest; and as regards its matter, it consists in contrition, confession, and satisfaction, which are the acts of the penitent. These are the several parts which are held to constitute the whole. Let us speak briefly of each of these.

Contrition is defined by Dens to be "sorrow of mind and abhorrence of the sin, with a full purpose not to sin any more." This differs little from what Protestant divines are accustomed to call godly sorrow; and had the matter rested here, we might have congratulated Rome on retaining at least one portion of truth; but she has spoilt all by the distinction which immediately follows of *perfect* and *imperfect* contrition. Perfect contrition flows from love to God; and the penitent mourns for his sin chiefly because it has dishonoured God. This kind of contrition, the Council of Trent teaches, may procure reconciliation with God without confession and absolution; but then perfect contrition, according to that Council, includes a desire for the sacrament, and without that desire contrition cannot procure pardon. Imperfect contrition, or attrition, as it is called, does not arise, according to Dens, from the love of God, or any contemplation of his goodness and mercy, but from the desire of pardon and the fear of hell. Attrition of itself cannot procure justification. It fails of its end unless it be followed by the sacrament; that is, unless it lead the person to confession and absolution. It was attrition which the Ninevites showed on the preaching of Jonah, and which led them to do penance, and ultimately to share in the divine mercy. Perfect contrition, the Church of Rome admits, may justify without the intervention of the priest. But such is the infirmity of human nature, that contrition is seldom or never attained, according to that Church. The sorrow of the sinner in rare cases, if in any, rises above attrition; and therefore the doctrine of Rome on the head of penance is, in point of fact, briefly this, — that without auricular confession and priestly absolution no one can hope to escape the torments of hell.

The next act in the sacrament of penance is, confession. The Bible teaches the sinner to acknowledge his guilt to that Majesty against whom the offence has been done, "who is rich in mercy, and ready to forgive:" Rome requires all to make confession to her priests; and if any refuse to do so, she sternly denies them pardon, and shuts against them the gates of paradise. It is "incumbent on every penitent," says the Council of Trent, "to rehearse in confession all mortal sins which, after the most rigid and conscientious scrutiny of himself, he can recollect; nor ought he to conceal even the most secret." Perrone lays it down as a proposition, that "the confession of every mortal sin committed after baptism is of divine institution, and necessary to salvation." The confession of venial sins, "by which we are not excluded from the grace of God, and into which we so often fall," the Church of Rome has not made obligatory; nevertheless she recommends the practice as a pious and edifying one. For the confession of sins to man not even the shadow of proof can be produced from Scripture. But the Church of Rome proves to her own satisfaction the duty of auricular confession, by that convenient logic of which she makes such abundant use, and by which all her more difficult and extraordinary positions are established: she first lodges in the priest the power to pardon sin, and argues from that, that it is necessary to confess to the priest, in order to obtain the pardon he is authorized to bestow. He is a judge, says Dens; he sits there to decide the question whether such a sin is to be remitted or retained. But how can a judge pronounce sentence without hearing the case? and he can hear the case only by the confession of the sinner, to whom alone the sin is known.

Those sins only that are confessed can be pardoned. Concealment is held to be mortal sin. And thus the sinner conceals his offences at the peril of his salvation. How Rome, consistently with this doctrine, provides for the pardon of those sins which the memory of the penitent does not enable him to recollect, she does not explain. Nor is it only the bare fact the penitent is bound to mention: he must state all the circumstances and peculiarities of his sin, whether these aggravate or extenuate it. Nor is the penitent to be left to his own discretion: the confessor is bound to interrogate and cross-question, and, in doing so, is at liberty to suggest new crimes and modes of sinning hitherto unthought of, and, by sowing insidiously the seeds of all evil in the mind, to pollute and ruin the conscience he professes to disburden. There is no better school of wickedness on earth. History testifies, that for every offender whom the confessional has reclaimed, it has hardened thousands; — for one it may have saved, it has destroyed millions. And what must be the state of that one mind, — the confessor's, — into which is daily poured the accumulated filth and vice of a neighbourhood? He cannot decline the dreadful office although he were willing. He must be the depository of all the imagined and of all the acted wickedness around him. To him it all gravitates, as to its centre. Every purpose of lust, every deed of vengeance, every piece of villany, flows thither, forming a fresh contribution to the already fearful and fathomless mass of known wickedness within him. This black and loathly mass he carries about with him, — he carries within him. His bosom is a very sepulchre of rottenness and stench, — "a closet lock and key of villanous secrets." Wherever he is, alone or in society, or at the altar, he is chained to a corpse. The rank effluvia of its putrescence encompasses him like an atmosphere. Miserable doom! He cannot rid himself from the corruption that adheres to him. His efforts to fly from it are in vain.

"Which way I fly is hell; myself am hell."

To his mind, we say, this mass of evil must be ever present, mingling with all his feelings, polluting all his duties, and tainting at their very spring all his sympathies. How ghastly and foul must society appear to his eye! for to him all its secret wickedness is naked and open. His fellow-men are lepers foul and loathsome, and he sniffs their horrid effluvia as he passes them. An angel could scarce discharge such an office without contamination; but it is altogether inconceivable how a man can discharge it and escape being a demon. The lake of Sodom, daily fed by the foul and saline springs of the neighbourhood, and giving back these contributions in the shape of black and sulphurous exhalations, which scathe and desolate afresh the surrounding region, is but a faint emblem of the action and reaction of the confessional on society. It is a moral malaria, — a cauldron from which pestiferous clouds daily ascend, which kill the very souls of men. Hell itself could not have set up an institution more ingeniously contriven to demoralize and destroy mankind.

But the crowning point in the blasphemy here is the pardon which the priest professes to bestow. Protestants grant that Christ has committed to the office-bearers in his house the power of "binding and loosing," in the sense of excluding from or admitting to the communion of the Church visible. But it is a very different thing to maintain that ministers have the power, authoritatively and as judges, to pardon sin. This is the power which Rome claims. There is no sin which her priests may not pardon; only the remission of the more heinous offences she reserves to the higher orders of the clergy; while the most aggravated of all, namely, those done against the persons and property of ecclesiastics, can be forgiven only by the Pope. Nevertheless, lest any true son of the Church should die in mortal sin, and so perish, the Church has given power to all her priests to administer absolution to persons *in articulo mortis*. But it is only in the article of death that they have such power; and then it is absolute, extending to all censures and crimes whatsoever.

To pardon sin is the prerogative of God alone; and it must needs be awfully criminal in a poor mortal to mount the tribunal of heaven's justice, and affect the high prerogatives of mercy and of condemnation. Of what avail is it that man forgives, if still we underlie the condemnation of heaven? Will the fiat of a man like ourselves, standing in the same need of pardon with us, release us from the claims or shield us from the penalty of a violated law? It is with God we have to do; and if he condemn, alas! it matters little that the whole world absolve. The pardon of Rome it is equally impious to bestow or to receive. It is hard to determine whether the priest or the penitent acts the more guilty part. Rome's scheme of penance entirely reverses that of the gospel. In the one case pardon is free; in the other it must be bought. It is not of grace, but of merit; for the penitent has complied with all the requirements of the Church, and is entitled to demand absolution. There is no discovery of the rich grace of God, nor of the boundless efficacy of a Saviour's blood, nor of the sovereign power of the Spirit; all these are carefully veiled from the sinner, and he sees nothing but his own merit and the Church's power. In the holy presence of God the true penitent discovers at once his own and his sin's odiousness; and he goes away with the steadfast purpose that, as he has done iniquity, so, by the Spirit's help, he will do so no more for ever. In the impure atmosphere of the confessional the person is morally incapable of discerning either his own or his sin's enormity. He confesses, but does not repent; is absolved, but not pardoned; and departs with a conscience stupified, but not pacified, to resume his old career. He returns after a certain interval, laden with new sins, which are remitted on as easy terms, and to as little purpose, as before. Thus is he deluded and cheated through life, till all opportunity of obtaining the pardon which the Bible offers, and which alone is of any value, is gone for ever.

Chapter XV: Of Indulgences.

To dispense a gift so inestimable as the pardon of sin, and derive no benefit therefrom on her own account, was not agreeable to the usual manner of the Papacy. At the beginning, Rome scattered with a liberal hand the heavenly riches, without reaping, in return, the perishable wealth of men. But it was not to be expected that a liberality so extraordinary and unusual should last always. In the thirteenth century Rome began to perceive how the power of absolution might be turned to account as regards the mammon of unrighteousness. Formerly men had earned forgiveness by penance, by fasting, by pilgrimage, by flagellation, and other burdensome and painful performances; but now Rome fell upon the happy invention by which she contrives at once to relieve her votaries and to enrich herself; in short, she proclaimed the doctrine of indulgences. The announcement spread joy throughout the Catholic world, which had long groaned under the yoke of self-inflicted penances. The scourge was laid aside, the fast was forborne, and money substituted in their room. The theory of indulgences is as follows: — Christ suffered more than was required for the salvation of the elect; many of the saints and martyrs likewise have performed more good works than were requisite for their own salvation; and these, to which it is not uncommon to add the merits of the Virgin, have been all thrown into a common fund, which has been entrusted to the keeping of the Church. Of this treasury the Pope keeps the key, and whoever feels that his merits are not enough to carry him to heaven, has only to apply at this ghostly depot, where he may buy, for a reasonable sum, whatever he needs to supplement his deficiencies.

In this market, which Rome has opened for the sale of spiritual wares, money is not less indispensable than it is in the emporiums of earthly and perishable merchandise. The price varies, being regulated by the same laws which govern the price of earthly commodities. To cover a crime of great magnitude, a larger amount of merit is of course required, and for that it is but reasonable that a larger sum should be given. The Roman Catholic Church teaches, that by the sacrament of penance the guilt of sin and its eternal punishment are remitted, but that the temporal punishment is still due, and must be borne either in this life or in purgatory. This is the doctrine of Trent, in support of which the fathers bring their usual proof, an anathema, "Whoever shall affirm that God always remits the whole punishment, together with the fault, let him be accursed." The same is taught by the modern theological writers of Rome. It is in this way that indulgences are useful. They procure remission of the temporal punishment, either in whole or in part, that is, the calamities inflicted in this life are alleviated, and the sojourn in purgatory is very much shortened. Some modern Papists, such as Bossuet, ashamed of the doctrine of indulgences, have sought to disguise it, or deny it altogether, by representing it as nothing more than a remission of ecclesiastical penances or censures. This is shown incontrovertibly to be a fraud; first, by the fact that indulgences are held to benefit the dead, whom they release from purgatory; and, second, because this account of indulgences is in plain opposition to the decrees of Trent on this subject, to the deliverances of the Roman Catechism, and to the doctrine taught in Dens and Perrone. The latter remarks, that "the power of forgiving every kind of sin by the sacrament of penance resides in the Church; and consequently the absolving priest truly reconciles sinners to God by a *judicial power* received from Christ." He repudiates the idea that it is a mere power of *declaring* that the sin has been forgiven that the priest exercises. The man, says he, who heals a wound or unties a chain does not merely pronounce the patient to be whole or the captive to be free; he actually makes him so. So the absolution of the Church is not the mere declaring the sin to be forgiven; it is the remitting or retaining of the sin. The statement of Bossuet is in plain opposition, moreover, to the notorious practice of the Church of Rome, which, before the Reformation especially, kept open market in Europe, in which, for a little money, men might purchase the remission of all sorts of enormities and crimes. This scandalous traffic Rome unblushingly carried on till it was denounced by Luther. Since that time she has exercised a little more circumspection. She no longer sends trains of mules and waggons across the Alps, laden with bales of pardons. This branch of her business is now carried on by her ordinary bishops. The trade is too shameful to be openly avowed, but too gainful to be given up. Her hawkers have ceased to perambulate Europe; but her indulgences still circulate throughout it.

The doctrine of indulgences, as explained by Leo. X., is, "That the Roman pontiff may, for reasonable causes, by his apostolic authority, grant indulgences out of the superabundant merits of Christ and the saints, to the faithful who are united to Christ by charity, as well for the living as for the dead. . . . . All persons, whether living or dead, who really obtain any indulgences of this kind, are delivered from so much temporal punishment, due, according to divine justice, for their actual sins, as is equivalent to the value of the indulgence bestowed and received." We might quote, did our space permit, numerous bulls of succeeding popes to the same effect, all showing that the Church of Rome holds that the matter of indulgences is the merits of Christ and the saints, and that they confer remission of sin and release from purgatory. We might quote the bull of Pius VI., published in 1794; the bull of Benedict XIII. in 1724; and that of Benedict XIV. in 1747; and the bull of "Indiction for the Universal Jubilee in 1825," which grants, upon certain conditions, "a plenary indulgence, remission, and pardon of all their sins, to all the faithful of Christ." The Council of Trent strongly recommended indulgences as "salutary to Christian people," and anathematized all who should assert the contrary. But as the scandal of Tetzel was still fresh in the recollection of Europe, the council recommended no less strongly, discretion in the distribution of indulgences, and forbade all "wicked gains" accruing therefrom, — a decree that was to little purpose, seeing no priest would be forward to own that his gains, however great, were of the kind to which the Tridentine prohibition had reference. The Romish authorities, from the Council of Trent downwards, have been careful how they defined indulgences. Indeed, they have studiously involved the subject in obscurity. Their explanations remind us of the lucid reply given by a monk at Rome to a visitor in the eternal city, who asked him what an indulgence was. "An indulgence," said the friar, crossing himself, — "an indulgence is a great mystery!"

Still, no reader of the least discrimination can fail to discover, through all the ambiguities and generalities by which Popish writers seek to conceal the grosser features of this most demoralizing system, that indulgences carry all the power we have attributed to them. Such is the virtue ascribed to them by Dens, who tells us that they not only stay the censures of the Church, but avert the wrath of God, and redeem the spirit from the fires of purgatory. The same is the doctrine of those books which have been compiled by the Church for the instruction of her members. It is asked in Butler's Catechism, — "Q. Why does the Church grant indulgences? A. To assist our weakness, and to supply our insufficiency in satisfying the divine justice for our transgressions. — Q. When the Church grants indulgences, what does it offer to God to supply our weakness and insufficiency, and in satisfaction for our sins? *A*. The merits of Christ, which are infinite and superabundant; together with the virtues and good works of his Virgin Mother, and of all the saints." We have alluded to the open and shameless manner in which this traffic in sin was carried on before the Reformation; and to that period must we go back, in order to see the awful lengths to which the doctrine of indulgences has been, and still may be, carried; and that, in point of fact, whatever distinctions Popish writers in modern times may make, it is an assumption of power on the part of the priests to pardon all sins, past and present, — to remit all punishment, temporary and eternal, — in short, to act in the matter of pardoning men with the full absolute authority of God. The preachers of indulgences at the beginning of the sixteenth century knew none of the distinctions of modern casuists, and for this reason, that they spoke before the Reformation.

"Indulgences," said Tetzel, "are the most precious and the most noble of God's gifts. This cross [pointing to the red cross, which he set up wherever he came] has as much efficacy as the very cross of Jesus Christ. Come and I will give you letters, all properly sealed, by which even the sins that you intend to commit may be pardoned.

"I would not exchange my privileges for those of St. Peter in heaven; for I have saved more souls by my indulgences than the apostle by his sermons.

"There is no sin so great that an indulgence cannot remit; and even if any one [which is doubtless impossible] had offered violence to the blessed Virgin Mary, Mother of God, let him pay, — only let him pay well, — and all will be forgiven him.

"But more than this," said he; "indulgences avail not only for the living, but for the dead. For that repentance is not even necessary.

"Priest! noble! merchant! wife! youth! maiden! do you not hear your parents and your other friends who are dead, and who cry from the bottom of the abyss, 'We are suffering horrible torments; a trifling alms would deliver us: you can give it, and you will not?'

"At the very instant," continued Tetzel, "that the money rattles at the bottom of the chest, the soul escapes from purgatory, and flies liberated to heaven."

And even since the Reformation, and more especially in Countries where its light has not penetrated, we find this trade as actively carried on as ever, though without the extravagance and grossness of Tetzel. "I was surprised," says the authoress of "Rome in the Nineteenth Century," "to find scarcely a church in Rome that did not hold up at the door the tempting inscription of 'Indulgenzia *Plenaria*!' Two hundred days' indulgence I thought a great reward for every kiss bestowed upon the great black cross in the Colosseum; but that is nothing to the indulgences for ten, twenty, and even thirty thousand years, that may be bought at no exorbitant rate in many of the churches; so that it is amazing what a vast quantity of treasure may be amassed in the other world with very little industry in this, by those who are avaricious of this spiritual wealth, into which, indeed, the dross or riches of this world may be converted with the happiest facility imaginable."

"You may buy as many masses as will free your souls from purgatory for twenty-nine thousand years, at the church of St. John Lateran, on the festa of that saint; at Santa Bibiana, on All Souls' day, for seven thousand years; at a church near the Basilica of St. Paul, and at another on the Quirinal Hill, for ten thousand and for three thousand years, and at a very reasonable rate. But it is in vain to particularize, for the greater part of the principal churches in Rome and the neighbourhood are spiritual shops for the sale of the same commodity."

The writer may be permitted to state, that on the cathedral gates in the south of France, particularly at Lyons, he has seen handbills posted, announcing certain *fêtes*, and promising to all who should take part in them, and repeat so many *Ave Marias*, a plenary indulgence; that is, a full remission of all their sins up to the time of the *fête*. Adrian VI. decreed a plenary indulgence of all his sins to whomsoever should depart out of this life grasping in his hand a *hallowed wax candle*! The same inestimable blessing did the pontiff promise to the man who should say his prayers on Christmas day in the morning in the church of Anastasia at Rome. Sixtus IV. granted an indulgence of twelve thousand years to every man who should repeat the well-known salutation of the Virgin, "Hail, Mary, &c.; deliver me from all evils, and pray for my sins." Burnet mentions that he had seen an indulgence for ten hundred thousand years. In other cases, indulgences have been granted to the person and his kindred of the third generation; so that it might be handed down to his posterity like an estate or other property. Nobles have obtained indulgences, including their retinue as well as themselves, — much as a wealthy man now-a-days, in travelling by steamer or rail, buys a ticket for himself and all the members of his suite. Such companies one should think, must have had a jovial journey to the other world, seeing, however many the debts of sin which they might contract by the way, they were sure of finding all scores clear at the end. Others have had blank indulgences given them, with power to fill in what names they pleased. The holders of such indulgences exercised a patronage of a very uncommon kind. They could appoint their friends and dependents to a place in paradise; in which, it would seem, there are *reserved seats*, just as in terrestrial shows, to which the holders of the proper tickets are admissible, however late they may arrive. There are also *defunct* indulgences, — the comfort of the dead, as well as of the living, having been studied. The process in this case is an extremely simple one. The name of the *deceased* isentered on the indulgence, and straightway a *plenary remission* is accorded him, and he is instantly discharged from the torments of the purgatorial fire. Indulgences have been affixed also to such things as medals, scapularies, rosaries, crucifixes. Of this we have a notable instance in the bull of indulgence granted by Pope Adrian VI. to certain beads which he blessed. This bull was afterwards confirmed by Gregory XIII., Clement VIII., Urban VIII., and ran in the following terms: — "Whosoever has one of these beads, and says one Pater Noster and one Ave Maria, shall on any day release three souls out of purgatory; and reciting them twice on a Sunday or holiday shall release six souls. Also reciting five Pater Nosters and five Ave Marias upon a Friday, to the honour of the five wounds of Christ, shall gain a pardon *of seventy thousand years, and the remission of all his sins.*" These are mere gleanings. With a little industry one might collect as many facts of this sort as would fill volumes.

So lucrative a trade has not been left to regulate itself. An apostolic tariff was framed, so that all who frequented this great market of sin might know at what price to purchase the spiritual wares there exposed. A book was published at Rome, entitled "TAXES OF THE APOSTOLIC CHANCERY," in which the price of absolution from every sin is fixed. Murder may be bought for so much; incest for so much; adultery for so much; and so on through the long catalogue of abominations which it would pollute our page to quote. Sins unheard of and unthought of are here put up for sale, and generally at prices so moderate, that few can say they are beyond their reach. This book, the most atrocious and abominable the world ever saw, sets forth and commends the wares in which Rome deals, and of which she claims a monopoly. Herein she unblushingly advertises herself to the whole world as a *trafficker* in murders, parricide, incests, adulteries, thefts, perjuries, blasphemies, sins, crimes, and abominations of every kind and degree. Come hither, she says to the nations, and buy whatever your soul lusteth after. Let no fear of hell, or of the anger of God, restrain you: I will secure you against that. *"Take, eat; ye shall not surely die."* So spoke the serpent to our first parents beneath the boughs of the interdicted tree; and so does Rome speak to the nations. "Ye shall not surely die." He was indeed a true limner who drew Rome's likeness in the Apocalypse, "THE MOTHER OF HARLOTS AND ABOMINATIONS OF THE EARTH."

In some indulgences the Church exercises the power of *absolution*, and in others of simple *loosing*. The first has respect to the living; the second to the dead, whom the indulgence looses from purgatory, or strikes off so many days or years from the allotted period of suffering there. Indulgences are also divided into *plenary* and *partial*. The indulgence is plenary when the whole temporal punishment due for sins committed prior to the date of the indulgence is remitted. In a partial indulgence, part only of the temporal punishment is discharged: in this case the period is generally stated, and ranges from a day to some hundreds of thousands of years; which means that the person's future sojourn in purgatory will be less by the period fixed in the indulgence.

Romanists have affected a virtuous indignation at the charge which has not unfrequently been preferred against them, that their Church has established a system of selling licenses to commit sin. They have denounced this as a calumny, because, forsooth, their Church does not take money beforehand, but allows the sinner first to gratify his passions, and then receives the stipulated price. But where is the difference? If Rome tells the world, as she does, that for a certain sum, — which is generally a small one, — she will grant absolution for any sin which any one may choose to commit, and if the person finds that he has the requisite sum in his pocket, has he not as really a license to commit the sin as if the indulgence were already in his possession? Besides, what does Rome say to those indulgences which extend over some hundreds of thousands of years? How easy would it be to buy a few such indulgences, and so cover the whole period allotted for suffering in purgatory; and not only so, but to have a balance in one's favour. In such a case, let the person live as he lists; let him commit all manner of sins, in all manner of ways; is he not as sure as Rome can make him, that they are all pardoned before they are committed? Here is a license to sin with a vengeance. Could the evil heart of man, greedy on all wickedness, desire an ampler toleration, or could larger license be granted by the author of evil himself? The foulest of the ancient polytheisms were immaculate and holy compared with Rome. Their principles tended to relax the restraints of virtue, and generally to debase human nature; but when did they proclaim to the world an unbounded liberty of sinning? When did they trade in sin? All this Rome has done. Although hell were to empty itself upon the earth, it could not inflict a worse pollution than this spawn of Rome. Though fiends were to walk up and down in the world, and with serpent tongue and hissing accents to prompt and solicit mortals, they could not lure and destroy more effectually than Rome's pardonmongers. When Rome took her way among the benighted nations, who could resist her offers? A paradise of sin on earth, and a paradise of happiness hereafter, and all for a little money! Yes; of all the evil systems which have arisen to affront God, to mock man, and to do the work of hell, Rome is entitled to rank foremost. Others have done viciously, but she has excelled them all. She has invented sin, taught sin, acted sin, and traded in sin; and so has made good, beyond the possibility of doubt or question, her title to the name which stood on the page of prophecy as at once the ominous harbinger and the compendious description of a system afterwards to arise, — "THE MAN OF SIN."

There is not a day in the year in which indulgences for any sin, and to any amount, may not be obtained; but the year of jubilee is marked in the calendar of Rome as a year of special grace. The jubilee was instituted in the year 1300 by Boniface VIII. It was to return every hundredth year, in imitation of the secular games of the Romans, which were celebrated once in an age. "*A most plenary pardon*" of all their sins was promised to those who should visit the churches of St. Peter and St. Paul at Rome. The same reward was to belong to such as, unable to undertake so long a pilgrimage, should pay a certain sum, and to such as might die by the way. He who sat on the Seven Hills gave commandment to the angels to carry their souls direct to the glory of paradise, since they were absolved from the pains of purgatory. To the priests it was indeed a jubilee. The multitude of pilgrims filled Rome to overflow; their wealth replenished the coffers of the pontiff. The most notorious sinners were transformed by the pontifical magic into saints, and sent away as pure as they came. From their long journey, which had taxed alike the limbs and the purse, they reaped, as Rome had promised they should, "*a plentiful harvest of penitence.*" But most of all, it grieved the popes to think that a century must pass away before such another year should come round. It was not fit that the Church should so hoard her treasures, and afford to her sons only at long intervals, opportunities of evincing their gratitude by the liberality of their gifts. Considerations of this sort moved Clement VI. to reduce the term of jubilee to fifty years. It was found still to be too long, and was shortened by Urban VI.. to thirty-three, and finally fixed by Sixtus V. at twenty-five. Thus every quarter of a century does a whole shower of indulgences descend upon the papal world. The last return of "the year of expiation and pardon, of redemption and grace, of remission and indulgence," to use the terms of the bull of Leo XII., was 1850. The result is told by Gavazzi. "The late effort of Pio Nono to get up a pious enthusiasm, after the fashion of his predecessors, on the recurrence of the semi-secular year of 1850, had utterly failed throughout the Italian peninsula; and though he held forth one hand filled with indulgences, the other was too palpably armed with the cudgel of the Croat to attract the approach of his countrymen."

But is not the prodigality with which Rome scatters indulgences among all who need or will receive them, a dangerous one? In these evil times, a great deal must be flowing out of this treasury, and very little flowing in. Is there no risk of emptying it? Day and night there rolls a river of indulgences ample enough to supply the necessities of the Roman Catholic world; yet century after century finds the source of this mighty stream undiminished. Here is another of Rome's wonders! The ocean itself would in time become dry, were it not fed by the rivers. Where are the rivers that feed this spiritual reservoir? Where are the eminent living saints of the Roman Catholic Church, whose supererogatory virtues maintain a balance against the infidels, socialists, formalists, and evil characters of all kinds which, it is now confessed, abound within the pale of Rome? We see all coming with their pitchers to draw, but none bringing contributions hither. We are reminded of those natural phenomena which have exercised and baffled the ingenuity of naturalists. We have here a phenomenon exactly the reverse of the Dead Sea, into which the floods of the Jordan are hourly poured, but from whose dark confine there issues no stream. And we have a direct resemblance in the Mediterranean, out of which a stream is ceaselessly flowing through the Straits of Gibraltar into the capacious bosom of the Atlantic, yet the shores of the former are ever full and undiminished. Doubtless in both cases there is a compensatory process going on, though invisibly. And perhaps Rome may hold, in like manner, that the rivers that feed her ocean of merit roll in secret, unseen and unheard. At all events, she teaches that it is wholly INEXHAUSTIBLE. A time will come when the mines of Peru and California shall be exhausted, and their last golden grains dug up. But a time will never come when the treasury of Rome shall be exhausted, and not a grain of merit more remain to be doled out to the faithful. What has she not already drawn from that exhaustless treasury! Not to speak of the kings, nobles, priests, and the countless millions of people of all conditions whom she has delivered out of purgatory, she has carried on with its help numerous crusades, waged mighty wars, raised sumptuous palaces, and built magnificent temples. The dome of St. Peter's remains an imposing monument of the exhaustless mine of wealth which the indulgences opened to Rome. Those magnificent Gothic structures that cover papal Europe, — what are they? The

monuments of the piety of former ages? No: love did not place a stone in any one of them. The power which raised these noble piles, full of grandeur and beauty though they be, was that of superstition acting on a guilty conscience. Every stone in them expresses so much sin. Their beautiful marbles, their rich mosaics, their gorgeous paintings, their noble columns and towers, bespeak the remorse of the dying sinner, who vainly strove by these expiatory gifts to relieve a conscience which felt sorely burdened by the manifold crimes of a lifetime. Again Rome has been compelled, by the necessities of these latter times, to betake herself to a resource which very shame had forced her to abandon. There are Italian exiles in London which she would have rewarded with a dungeon in their own country, but for whom she builds a church in ours. And with what? With the sins of papal Europe. An indulgence of a hundred days, and a plenary indulgence of one day, are offered by the pontiff to all who shall contribute an alms for its erection. A temple of piety! Faugh! The structure will be redolent of abominations of all kinds. So profitable does Rome find this California of hers. After all that Rome has drawn out of the treasury of the Church, she declares with truth that this treasury is every whit as full as it ever was; and she might add with truth, that when centuries more shall have passed away, and their unnumbered wants shall have been supplied, it will not be a whit more empty than it is at this moment.

Chapter XVI: Of Purgatory.

Papists have mapped out the other world into four grand divisions. The lowest is hell, the region of the damned. There are the ever-burning fires; there are Lutherans, and all other Protestant heretics; and, in fine, there are all who have died beyond the pale of the Roman Catholic Church, with the exception of a few heathens, and a few Christian, — whose narrow intellects scarcely served to distinguish between their right hand and their left, and who have escaped on the ground of "invincible ignorance." The next region in order is purgatory, of which we shall have occasion to speak more fully immediately. Immediately above purgatory is *limbus patrum*, where the souls of the saints who died before our Saviour's time were confined till released by Him, and carried with Him to heaven at his ascension, when this region was abolished, and heaven substituted in its room. The last and remaining region is *limbus infantum*. To this receptacle the souls of children dying unbaptized are consigned; it being a settled point among the doctors of the Romish Church, that such as die unbaptized are excluded from heaven.

It is the lowest save one of these four localities of which we are to speak — purgatory. It is filled with the same fires, and is the scene of the same torments, as the region immediately beneath it, but with this important difference, that those consigned to it remain here only for a while. It is the doctrine of the Church of Rome, that no one enters heaven immediately on his departure. A short purgation amid the fires of purgatory is indispensable in the case of all, unless perhaps of those who are protected by a *very special and most plenary indulgence*. Even the pontiffs themselves, infallible though they be, must take purgatory in their way, and pass a certain period amid its fires, before being worthy to appear at those gates at which St. Peter keeps watch. All who die in mortal sin, — and of all mortal sins, heresy and the want of money to buy an indulgence are the most mortal, — are at once consigned to hell. Those who die in a state of grace, with the remission of the guilt of all their mortal sins, go to purgatory, where they are purified from the stain of venial sins, and endure the temporary punishment which remains due for their mortal offences. For it is a doctrine of the Roman Catholic Church, that even after God has remitted the guilt and the eternal punishment of sin, a temporary punishment remains due, which may be borne either in this life or in the next. Without this doctrine it would scarce be possible to maintain purgatory; and without purgatory, who would buy indulgences and masses? and without indulgences and masses, how could the coffers of the Pope be replenished? The sojourn is longer or shorter in purgatory, according to circumstances, being dependent mainly upon the amount of satisfaction to be given. But the period may be much shortened by the efforts made in behalf of the deceased by his friends on earth; for the Church teaches that souls detained in that state are helped by the suffrages of the faithful, that is, by the prayers and alms offered for them, and principally by the indulgences and masses purchased for their benefit.

The existence of purgatory is authoritatively taught and most surely believed among Roman Catholics. The doctrine respecting it decreed by the Council of Trent, and taught in the catechism of that council, as well as in all the common catechisms of the Church of Rome, is that which we have just stated. The Council of Trent decreed, "that there is a purgatory," and enjoined all bishops to "diligently endeavour that the wholesome doctrine of purgatory" be "everywhere taught and preached," — an injunction which has been carefully attended to. And so important is the belief of purgatory, that Bellarmine affirms that its denial can be expiated only amid the flames of hell. One would naturally expect that Rome would be prepared with very solid and convincing grounds for a doctrine to which she assigns such prominence, and which she inculcates upon her people under a penalty so tremendous. These grounds, such as they are, we shall indicate, and that is all that our limits permit. The first proof is drawn from the Apocrypha; but as this is an authority that possesses no weight with Protestants, we shall not occupy space with it, but pass on to the second, which is drawn from Scripture, and which is made to support the chief weight of the doctrine, — with what justice the reader will judge. The following is the passage in which Papists unmistakeably discover purgatory: — "Whosoever speaketh against the Holy Ghost, it shall not be forgiven him, neither in this world, neither in the world to come." Here, says the Papist, our Lord speaks of a sin that shall not be forgiven in the world to come; which implies that there are sins that *shall be* forgiven in the world to come. But sins cannot be forgiven in heaven, nor will they be forgiven in hell; therefore there must be a third place where sins are forgiven, which is purgatory. The answer which the Rev. Mr. Nolan has given to this is much to the point, and is all that such an argument deserves. "Let me suppose," says he, "a person committed a most enormous offence against the laws of this country, and that the Lord Lieutenant said, it shall not be forgiven, neither in this country nor in England; would any one be so irrational as to argue that the Lord Lieutenant meant to insinuate from this mode of expression that there was a middle place where the crime might be forgiven?" That our Lord meant simply to indicate the unpardonable character of the sin against the Holy Ghost, and not to teach the doctrine of purgatory, is incontrovertible, from the parallel passage in Luke, where it is said, "Whosoever shall speak a word against the Son of Man it shall be forgiven him; but unto him that blasphemeth against the Holy Ghost, it shall not be forgiven." Other passages have been adduced, which yield, if possible, a still more doubtful support to purgatory, and on which it were a waste of time here to dwell. The practice of the fathers, some of whom prayed for the dead, has been pled in argument, as if the unwarrantable customs of men lapsing into superstition could support a doctrine still more gross and superstitious. And, still farther to fortify an opinion which stands in need of all the aid it can obtain from every quarter, and finds all too little, the vision of Perpetua, a young lady of twenty-two, has been employed to silence those who refuse on this head to listen to the fathers. But if there be indeed a purgatory, and if the belief of it be so indispensable, that all are damned who doubt it, as Papists teach, why was it not clearly revealed? and why is the argument in its favour nought but a miserable patch-work of perverted texts, visions of young ladies, and the dotard practices of men whose Christianity had become emasculated by a nascent superstition? We can trace a purgatory nowhere but in the writings of the pagan philosophers and poets. The great father of poetry makes some not very obscure allusions to such a place: Plato believed in a middle state: it formed one of the compartments of Virgil's Elysium; and there souls were purified by their own sufferings and the sacrifices of their friends on earth, before entering the habitation of joy. From this source did the Roman Catholic Church borrow her purgatory.

But we have a sure word of prophecy. The world beyond the grave has been made known to us, so far as we are able to receive it, by One who knew it better than either popes or fathers, because He came from it. When he lifts the veil, we discover only two classes and two abodes. And while we meet with nothing in the New Testament that countenances the doctrine of purgatory we meet with much that expressly contradicts and confutes it. All the statements of the Word of God respecting the nature of sin, and the death and satisfaction of Christ, are condemnatory of purgatory, and conclusively establish that there neither is nor can be any such place. The Scripture authorizes no such distinction as Papists make between venial and mortal sins. It teaches that all sin is mortal, and, unless blotted out by the blood of Christ, will issue in the sinner's eternal ruin. It teaches, that after death there is neither change of character nor of state; that God does not sell his grace, but bestows it freely; that we are not redeemed with corruptible things, as silver and gold; that no man can redeem his brother, whether by prayers or by offerings; that the law of God demands of every man, every moment of his being, the highest obedience of which his nature and his faculties are capable, and that since the foundation of the world a single work of supererogation has never been performed by any of the sons of men; and that therefore the source whence this imaginary fund of merit is supplied has no existence, and is, like the fund itself, a delusion and a fable; it teaches, in fine, that God pardons men only on the footing of the satisfaction of his Son, which is complete and sufficient, and needs not to be supplemented by works of human merit; and that when he pardons, he pardons all sin, and forever.

But the grand criterion by which Rome tests all her doctrines is not their truth, nor their bearing on man's benefit and God's glory, but their value in money. How much will they bring? is the first question which she puts. And it must be confessed, that in purgatory she has found a rare device for replenishing her coffers, of which she has not failed to make the very most. We need go no farther than Ireland as an instance. For a poor man, when he dies, a private mass is offered, for which the priest is paid from two-and-sixpence to ten shillings. For rich men there is a HIGH or chanted mass. In this instance, a number of priests assemble, and each receives from seven-and-sixpence to a pound. At the end of the month after the death, mass is again celebrated. The same number of priests again assemble, and receive payment over again. Anniversary or annual masses are also appointed for the rich, when the same routine is gone through, and the same expenses are incurred. There are, moreover, in almost every parish in Ireland, purgatorial societies. The person becomes a member on the payment of a certain sum, and the subscription of a penny a-week; and the funds thus raised are given to the priest, to be laid out for the deliverance of souls from purgatory. There is, besides, ALL SOUL'S

DAY, which falls on the 2d of November, on which an extraordinary collection is taken up from all Catholics for the same purpose. In short, there is no end of the expedients and pretences which purgatory furnishes to an avaricious priesthood for extorting money. Popery, says the author of Kirwan's Letters, meets men "at the cradle, and dogs them to the grave, and beyond it, with its demands for money." The writer was told in Belgium, by an intelligent English Protestant, who had resided many years in that country, that it is rare indeed for a man of substance to die without leaving from thirty to fifty pounds to be laid out in masses for his soul. No sooner is the fact known, than the priests of the district flock to the dead man's house, as do rooks to carrion, and, while a centime of the sum remains, live there, singing masses, and all the while feasting like ghouls.

Another of the innumerable frauds connected with purgatory is the doctrine of intention. By this is meant that the priest offers his mass according to the intention of the person paying. The price varies, according to the circumstances of the person, from half-a-crown to five shillings. These intentions, in many instances, are never discharged. Mr. Nolan mentions the case of the Rev. Mr. Curran, parish priest of Killuchan, in the county of Westmeath, an intimate acquaintance of his own, who at his death bequeathed to the Rev. Dr. Cantwell of Mullingar, three hundred pounds, to be expended on masses (at two-and-sixpence each) for such intentions as he (Mr. Curran) had neglected to discharge. It thus appears that Mr. Curran died owing twenty four hundred masses, most of them, doubtless, for souls in purgatory. "The frauds," says Dr. Murray of New York, addressing Bishop Hughes, "which your Church has practised on the world by her relics and indulgences are enormous. If practised by the merchants of New York in their commercial transactions, they would send every man of them to state-prison." "In Roman Catholic countries," says Principal Cunningham "and in Ireland among the rest, the priests make the people believe that by the sacrifice of the mass, that is, by their offering up to God the body and blood of Christ, they can cure barrenness, heal the diseases of cattle, and prevent mildew in grain; and much money is every year spent in procuring masses to effect these and similar purposes. Men who obtain money in such a way, and upon such pretences (and this is a main source of the income of popish priests), should be regarded and treated as common swindlers."

Chapter XVII: Of the Worship of Images.

Two things are here to be determined; *first*, the practice of the Church of Rome as regards images; and, *second*, the judgment which the Word of God pronounces on that practice.

Her practice, so far as pertains to its outward form, is as incapable of being misunderstood as it is of being defended. She sets up images which are representations of saints, or of angels, or of Christ; and she teaches her members to prostrate themselves before these images, to burn incense, and to pray before them, to undertake pilgrimages to their shrine, and to expect a more than ordinary answer to the intercessions offered before them. There is not a church in any Roman Catholic country throughout the world where this manner of worship is not every day celebrated; and, being open to all, no concealment is possible, and none is sought. The worshipper enters the cathedral, he selects the image of the saint whom he prefers, he kneels, he counts his beads, he burns his candle, and, it may be, presents his votive offering. As regards the letter of the practice of the Church of Rome, there is not, and there cannot be, any dispute. These facts being admitted, the controversy might here take end. This is what the Word of God denounces as image-worship; this it strictly prohibits; and this is enough to substantiate the charge which Protestants have brought against the Church of Rome as guilty of idolatry. Her practice in this point is manifestly a revival of the pagan worship in one of its grossest and most offensive forms. She, as really as the ancient idolators, "worships the creature more than the Creator." But let us hear what Rome has to say in her own behalf.

She introduces the element of INTENTION, and on this mainly rests her defence. She pleads that she does not believe these images to be inspired with the Divinity, — she does not believe them to be gods. She pleads also, that she does not believe that the wood, or stone, or gold, of which they are composed, can hear prayer, or that the image of itself can bestow the blessings supplicated for; that she believes them to be only images, and therefore directs her worship and prayers past or beyond them, to the saint or angel whom the image represents. The Papist does not pray *to*, but *through*, the image. We accept this as a fair statement of what is the theoretic practice of the Church of Rome on the subject of images, but we reject it as a statement of what that practice is in, fact, and especially do we reject it as a defence of that practice. We do so for the following reasons.

In the first place, if the Papist is acquitted of idolatry on this ground, there is not an idolater on the face of the earth who may not on the same ground demand an acquittal. None but the most ignorant and brutish ever mistook the stock or stone before which they kneeled for the Creator. This representative principle, on which the image-worshipper of the Popish Church founds his justification, pervaded the whole system of the pagan worship. It was this which led the world astray at first, and covered the earth with a race of deities of the most revolting character. Whether it was the heavenly bodies, as in Chaldea, or a class of demigods, as in Greece and Rome, it was the great First Cause that was professedly adored through these symbolizations and substitutes. The vulgar, perhaps, failed to grasp this distinction, or steadily to keep it before them, just as the mass of worshippers in the Roman Catholic Church fail practically to apprehend the difference between praying *to* and praying *before*, or rather *beyond*, the image; but such *was* the system, and that system the Bible denounced as idolatry; and the same system stands equally condemned when found in a popish cathedral as when found in a pagan temple.

But , in the second place, it is not true that these images are simple helps to devotion, or mere *media* for the conveyanee of the worship offered before them to the object whom they represent. The homage and honour are given to the image *immediately*, and to the object represented *mediately*, the worshipper assuming the power, by an act of volition or intention, of transferring the honour from the image to the object. But the image is honoured, and is commanded to be so on no less an authority than the Council of Trent. "Moreover," says the Council, "let them teach that the images of Christ, and of the Virgin, mother of God, and of other saints, are to be had and retained, especially in churches, and due honour and veneration rendered to them." And the decree goes on to say, that the person is to prostrate himself before the image, to uncover his head before it, and kiss it, no doubt under the pretence, that by these marks of honour to the image he is honouring those whose likeness it bears. This decree reduplicates on a former decree of the second Council of Nice, held in A.D. 787, at which the controversy respecting images was finally settled. The Council of Nice decreed that the images of Christ and his saints are to be venerated and adored, though not with "*true latria*," or the worship exclusively due to God. The same doctrine is taught in the Catechism of the Council of

Trent. There such acts of worship as we have already specified are recommended to be performed to images, for the sake of those whom they represent; and it is declared that this is highly beneficial to the people, as is also the practice of storing churches with images, not for instruction simply, *but for worship*. If, therefore, we find the divines of the Romish Church not adhering to their own theory, but blending the image and the object in the same acts of adoration, if we find them expressly teaching that images are to be worshipped, though not with the same supreme veneration that is due to God, — how can we expect that this distinction should be observed by the people? By the mass of the people this distinction is neither understood nor observed: the image is worshipped, and nothing more. That is their deity; and in not one in a thousand cases do the thoughts or intentions of the worshipper go beyond it. Why, out of several images of the same saint, does the worshipper prefer one to the others? Why does he make long pilgrimages to its shrine? Why, but because he believes that a peculiar virtue or divinity resides in this his favourite image. This shows that it is more to him than simple wood and stone. There could not be grosser or more wholesale idolatry than the festival of the Bambino at Rome, as described by Seymour. When the priest on the summit of the Capitol elevates the little wooden doll which represents the infant Saviour, the thousands that cover the slope and bottom of the mount fall prostrate, and nothing is heard but the low sounds of prayer addressed to the image. The Rome of the Caesars never witnessed a more idolatrous spectacle. It is firmly believed that the image possesses miraculous powers; the priests take care to encourage the delusion; and not a day passes without an application for a cure. There are numerous images at Rome believed to possess the power of working miracles. Among the rest is that of Mary in S. Maria Maggiore. This picture was carried in procession through the streets of Rome to suppress the cholera, the Pope (Gregory XVI.) joining barefooted in the procession. And what, we may ask, is the change which the Papist believes passes upon the image in the act of consecration? Is it not this, that where. as before it was simply a piece of dead and inefficacious matter, it has now become filled or inspired with the virtue or divinity of the object it represents, who is now mysteriously present in it or with it?

But, in the third place, though this distinction were one that could be easily drawn, and though it could be shown that it always is clearly drawn by the worshipper, and though it could be shown also, that all the good effects which have been alleged do in point of fact flow from this practice, all this would make nothing as a defence. The Word of God denounces the practice as idolatrous, and plainly forbids it. The condemnation and prohibition of this practice form the subject of one entire precept of the Decalogue. "Thou shalt not make unto thee any graven image, or any likeness of anything that is in heaven above, or that is in the earth beneath, &c.; thou shalt not bow down thyself to them, nor serve them; for I the Lord thy God am a jealous God." Till these words are revoked as plainly and solemnly as they were promulgated, — till the same mighty voice shall proclaim in the hearing of the nations that the second precept of the Decalogue has been abrogated, — the practice of Rome must stand condemned as idolatrous. The case, then, is a plain one, and resolves itself into this, Whether shall we obey Rome or Jehovah? The former, speaking from the Seven Hills, says, "Thou mayest make unto thee graven images, and bow down thyself to them, and serve them:" the latter, speaking in thunder from Sinai, says, "Thou shalt not make unto thee any graven image…thou shalt not bow down thyself unto them and serve them." Rome herself has confessed that these two commands, — that from the Seven Hills and that from Sinai, — are eternally irreconcileable, by blotting from the Decalogue the second precept of the law. Alas! Will this avail her aught so long as that precept stands unrepealed in the law of God? May God have merey upon her poor benighted people, whom she leads blindfold into idolatry; and may He remember this extenuation of their guilt when he arises to execute judgment upon those who, knowing that they who do such things are worthy of death, not only do them, but teach others to do the same!

Chapter XVIII: Of the Worshipping of Saints.

The next branch of the idolatry of the Roman Catholic Church is her worship of dead men. These she denominates saints. Of this numerous and miscellaneous class some unquestionably were saints, as the apostles and others of the early Christians. Others may be accounted, in the judgment of charity, to have been saints; but there are others which figure in the calendar of Roman apotheosis, whom no stretch of charity will allow us to believe were saints. They were unmistakeable fanatics; and their fanaticism was far indeed from being of a harmless kind. It drew in its wake, as fanaticism not unfrequently does, gross immorality and savage and unnatural cruelty. In the list of Romish divinities we find the names of persons whose very existence is apocryphal. There are others whose incorrigible stupidity, laziness, and filth, rendered them unfit to herd even with brutes; and there are others who, little to the world's comfort, were neither stupid nor inactive, but who made themselves busy, much as a fiend would, in inventing instruments of torture, and founding institutions for destroying mankind and devastating the earth, — St. Dominic, for instance, the founder of the Inquisition. Prayers offered to such persons, and directed to heaven, run some risk of missing those of whom they are in quest. But the question here is, granting all the individuals of this promiscuous crowd to have been saints, is it right to pray to them?

We do not charge the Church of Rome with teaching that the saints are gods, or are able by their own power to bestow the blessings for which their votaries pray. The Church of Rome distinguishes between the worship which it is warrantable to offer to the saints, and the worship that is due to God. The former are to be worshipped with *dulia*; the latter with *latria*. God is to be worshipped with supreme veneration; the saints are to be venerated in an inferior degree. They occupy in heaven, — that Church teaches, — stations of dignity and influence; and on this ground, as well as on account of their eminent virtues while they lived, they are entitled to our esteem and reverence. It may be reasonably supposed, moreover, that they have great influence with God, and that, moved partly by pity for us, and partly by the homage we render to them, they are inclined to use that influence in our behalf. We ought therefore, says that Church, to address prayers to them, that they may pray to God for us. This, then, is the function which the Church of Rome assigns to departed saints. They present the prayers of suppliants to God, and intercede with God in their behalf They are intercessors of mediation, though not of redemption.

But the Church of Rome has been little careful accurately to state her theory on this head, — little careful to impress upon the minds of her people, that the only service they are to expect at the hands of the saints is that of intercession. She has used expressions of a vague character, if not purposely designed, yet obviously fitted, to seduce into gross idolatry; nay, she allows and sanctions idolatry, by teaching that saints may be the objects of a certain sort of veneration, namely, *dulia*, and instituting a distinction which is utterly beyond the comprehension of the common people; so that, in point of fact, there is no difference between the worship which they offer to the saints, and the worship which they offer to God, unless, perhaps, that the former is the more devout and fervent, as it is certainly the more customary of the two. In the Papal Church, millions pray to the saints who never bow a knee to God.

The Council of Trent teaches that "the saints who reign together with Christ offer their prayers to God for men;" and that "it is a good and useful thing suppliantly to invoke them, and to flee to their prayers, help, and assistance;" and that they are "impious men" who maintain the contrary. The caution of the council will not escape observation. It teaches the dogma, but does not expressly enjoin the practice. It is usual for Papists to take advantage of this in arguing with Protestants, and to affirm that the Church has not enjoined or commanded prayers to saints." This may be true in theory, but not in practice. Prayers to saints form part and parcel of her liturgy; so that no man can join in her worship without joining in these prayers; and thus she practically compels the thing. Moreover, they are obliged, under the penalty of being guilty of mortal sin, to celebrate certain fetes, — those, for instance, of the assumption of the Virgin, and All Saints' Day. The Catechism of Trent teaches that we may pray to the saints *to pity us*; and if we join this with the "assistance and help" on which we are encouraged to cast ourselves, and if we add the grounds on which we are taught to look for such help, namely, that the saints occupy stations of dignity and influence in heaven, we will feel perfectly satisfied that the Church of Rome is very willing that her people should believe that the function of the saints goes a very considerable way beyond *simple intercession*, and that the worship of which they are the objects should be regulated accordingly. This idea is strengthened by the fact, that the Roman Missal teaches that there are blessings bestowed upon us for the merits of the saints. Of such sort is the following prayer: — "O God, who, to recommend to us innocence of life, wast pleased to let the soul of thy blessed Virgin Scholastica ascend to heaven in the shape of a dove, grant by her merits and prayers that we may lead innocent lives here, and ascend to eternal joys hereafter!" We add another example from the Missal: — "May the intercession, O Lord, of Bishop Peter thy apostle render the prayers and offerings of thy Church acceptable to Thee, that the mysteries we celebrate in his honour may obtain for us the pardon of our sins!"

But it matters little what is the exact amount of influence and power attributed to the saints by Roman Catholics, or what the refinements and distinctions by which they attempt to justify the worship they pay to them. Their practice is undeniable. In the same place where God is worshipped, and with the same forms, do Roman Catholics pray to the saints to pray to God in their behalf. M. Perrone distinctly says that the saints, on the ground of their excellence, are the just objects of religious worship; and that if we reserve sacrifices, vows, and temples to God, we may approach the saints with prostration and prayer. Images and relics, he says, receive an improper worship and adoration, which passes through them to their prototypes; not so the veneration paid the saints, which is not relative, but absolute. Tried by the implicit principles and the express declarations of the Bible, this is idolatry. There is not, either in the Old or in the New Testament, a solitary instance of such a worship; nay, on those occasions on which we find worship attempted to be offered to the saints, it was promptly and indignantly rejected. No doubt we are commanded to pray *with* and *for* one another, as is often pleaded by Papists; but there a is a wide difference between this and praying *to the dead*. The vision in the Apocalypse of the elders with the "vials full of odours," which are said to be "the prayers of saints," though often paraded by Roman Catholics as an unanswerable proof, has no bearing upon the point. Commentators on the Revelations have shown by very conclusive reasonings, that the vision has no relation to heaven, but to the church on earth; and Papists must overthrow this interpretation before the passage can be of any service to their cause. Right reason and the express declarations of Scripture combine in testifying that God alone is the object of worship, and that we cannot offer prayer or perform an act of adoration to any other being, however exalted, without incurring the highest criminality. "Thou shalt have no other gods before me." The reply of our Lord to the tempter seems purposely framed so as to include both *latria* and *dulia*. "Thou shalt WORSHIP the Lord thy God, and Him only shalt thou SERVE." On the principles of the Roman Catholic Church, it is quite possible for a man to be saved without having performed a single act of devotion to God in his whole life. He has simply to entrust the saints with his case, who will pray for him, and with better success than he himself could obtain. And the tendency, not to say the design, of the Romish system is to withdraw our hearts and our homage altogether from God, and, under an affectation of humility, to banish us for ever from the throne of God's grace, and sink us in the worship of stocks and of dead men.

Manifestly the popish divinities are but the resuscitation of the gods of the pagan mythology. Venus still reigns under the title of Mary, and Jupiter under that of Peter; and so as regards the other gods and goddesses of the heathen world; — their names have been changed, but their dominion is prolonged. The same festivals are kept in commemoration of them; the same rites are celebrated in their honour — slightly altered to suit the modern state of things; and the same powers are ascribed to them. Like their pagan predecessors, they have their shrines; and, like them too, they have their assigned limits within which they exercise jurisdiction, and their favourites and votaries over whom they keep special guard.

Papists have been often asked to explain how it is that the saints in heaven are able to hear the prayers of mortals on earth. They do not affirm that the saints are either omnipotent or omniscient; and yet, unless they are both, it is difficult to understand how they can know what we feel, or hear what we say, at so great a distance. Thousands are continually praying to them in all parts of the earth; — they have suppliants at Rome, at New York, at Pekin: and yet, though but men and women, they are supposed to hear every one of these petitions. The difficulty does indeed seem a formidable one; and, though often pressed to explain it, Roman Catholics have given as yet no solution but what is utterly subversive of the idea on which the system is founded. They usually tell us that the saints acquire the knowledge of these supplications through God. According to this theory, the prayer ascends first to God, God tells it to the saints, and the saints pray it back again to God. But what becomes of the boasted advantage of praying to the saints? and why not address our prayers directly to God? Why not go to God at once, seeing it turns out that He alone can hear us in the first instance, and that, but for his subsequent revelation of our prayers, they would be dissipated in empty space, and those powerful intercessors the saints would know nothing at all of the matter? "You," said Mr. Seymour, to a priest at Rome, who had favoured him with this notable solution of the difficulty, "make the Virgin Mary and the saints mediators of prayer. According to this system, God is our mediator to the saints, and not the saints our mediators to God." The path is strangely circuitous, — far too circuitous to be the right one. Nothing could be happier than the illustration of Coleridge, with special reference to the Virgin. It is that of an individual of whom we wish to obtain a favour, and whose mother we employ to intercede for us. The man hears well enough himself, but his mother is deaf; so we tell him to tell her that we wish her to pray to him to bestow on us the favour we desire.

Chapter XIX: The Worship of the Virgin Mary.

There seems to be on the part of fallen man an inherent sense of his need of a man-God. The patriarch of Uz gave expression to this feeling, when he intimated his wish for a "days-man," who "might lay his hand upon us both." Our intellectual facilities and our moral affections are unable to traverse the mighty void between ourselves and the Infinite, and both unite in seeking a resting-place midway in One combining in himself both natures. The spirituality of God places Him beyond our grasp, and removes Him, in a manner, from the sphere of our sympathy. We are dazzled by his majesty and glory; his holiness overawes us; his greatness, seen from afar, and incomprehensible by us, seems to repel rather than invite confidence, and to chill the heart rather than expand it into love. "Is there no resting-place for our affections and sympathies," we instinctively ask, "nearer than the august throne of the Infinite?" We need to have the divine attributes reduced to a scale, so to speak, which corresponds more nearly with our intellectual and moral range, and exhibited in One who to the nature of God adds that of man. This feeling has received numerous and varied manifestations; and the effort to meet it has formed a prominent feature in every one of the great systems of idolatry which have arisen in the earth. The nations of antiquity had their race of demi-gods or deified men. In the modern idolatries it has operated not less powerfully. The Mahommedans have their PROPHET, and the Roman Catholics have their VIRGIN. "Here," says Popery, "is a being who may be expected to be more indulgent to your failings than Deity can be, — who will be more easily moved to answer your prayers, — and whom you may approach without any overwhelming awe;" and thus the false is substituted for the true Mediator. It is in the religion of the Bible alone that this instinct of our nature has received its full gratification. The wish breathed of old by the patriarch, and expressed with singular emphasis in all the idolatries that successively arose on the earth, is adequately met only in the "mystery of godliness, — God manifest in the flesh." But what we are here to speak of is the abuse of this principle, in the idolatrous worship of the Virgin.

Papists may make a shift to prove that it is a mitigated worship which they offer to the saints, — that they allow them no rank but that of mediators, and no function but that of intercession, — though even this worship, both in its principles and in its forms, the Bible denominates idolatry. But the worship of the Virgin is capable of no such defence; — it is direct, undisguised, rank idolatry. Roman Catholics give the same titles, perform the same acts, and ascribe the same powers, to Mary as to Christ; and in doing so they make her equal with God.

To Mary are given names and titles which can be lawfully given to no one but God. She is styled "Mother of God;" "Queen of Seraphim, of Saints, and of Prophets;" "Advocate of Sinners;" "Refuge of Sinners;" "Gate of Heaven;" "Morning Star;" "Queen of Heaven." In Roman Catholic countries she is commonly addressed as the "Most Holy Mary." She is often styled the "Most Faithful," and the "Most Merciful." In what other terms could Christ himself be addressed? The Papist alleges that he still regards her as but a creature; nevertheless he addresses her in terms which imply that she possesses divine perfections, power, and glory. The whole psalter of David has been transformed by Bonaventura to the invocation of Mary, by erasing the name of Jehovah, and substituting that of the Virgin. We give an example of the work: — "In thee, O Lady, have I put my trust: let me never be ashamed: in thy grace uphold me." "Unto thee have I cried, O Mary, when my heart was in heaviness; and thou hast heard me from the top of the everlasting hills." "Come unto Mary, all ye that labour and are heavy laden, and she shall refresh your souls."

In the second place, the same worship is rendered to Mary as to Christ. Churches are built to her honour; her shrines are crowded with devotees, enriched with their gifts, and adorned with their votive offerings. To her prayers are offered as to a divine being, and blessings are asked as from one who has power to bestow them. Her votaries are taught to pray, "Spare us, good Lady," and "From all evil, good Lady, deliver us." Five annual festivals celebrate her greatness, and keep alive the devotion of her worshippers. In Roman Catholic countries the dawn is ushered in with hymns to her honour; her praises are again chanted at noon; and the day is closed with an Ave Maria sung to the lady of heaven. Her name is the first which the infant is taught to lisp; and the dying are directed to entrust their departing spirits into the hands of the Virgin. In health and in sickness, in business and in pleasure, at home or abroad, the Virgin is ever first in the thoughts, the affections, and the devotions of the Roman Catholic. The soldier fights under her banner, and the bandit plunders under her protection. Her deliverances are commemorated by public monuments erected to her by cities and provinces. In 1832, the cholera desolated the country around Lyons, but did not enter the city. A pillar, erected in the suburbs, commemorates the event, and ascribes it to the interposition of the Virgin. When the pontiffs would bless with special emphasis, it is in the name of Mary; and when they threaten most terribly, it is her vengeance which they denounce against their enemies. In short, the Roman Catholic is taught that none are so miserable but she can succour them, none so criminal but she will pardon them, and none so polluted but she can cleanse them.

There is scarce an act which it is lawful to perform towards God which the Roman Catholic is not taught to perform towards the Virgin. One of the most solemn acts of worship a creature can perform is to give himself in covenant to God, — to make over himself to Jehovah, — for time and for eternity. The Papist is taught to make this solemn surrender of himself to the Virgin. "Entering into a solemn covenant with holy Mary, to be for ever her servant, client, and devotee, under some special rule, society, or form of life, and thereby dedicating our persons, concerns, actions, and all the moments and events of our life, to Jesus, under the protection of his divine mother; choosing her to be our adoptive mother, patroness, and advocate; and entrusting her with what we are, have, do, or hope, in life, death, or through eternity." Some of the most sublime and devotional passages of the Bible are applied to the Virgin Mary. From the work quoted above we may give the following illustrations, in which a strain of mingled prayer and praise suitable to be offered only to God, is addressed to the Virgin: —

"Vers. Open my lips, O mother of Jesus.

Resp. *And my soul shall speak forth thy praise.*

Vers. Divine lady, be intent to my aid.

Resp. *Graciously make haste to help me.*

Vers. Glory be to Jesus and Mary.

Resp. *As it was, is, and ever shall be.*"

To the Virgin Mary is likewise applied the eighth Psalm thus: —

"Mary, mother of Jesus, how wonderful is thy name, even unto the ends of the earth!

"All magnificence be given to Mary; and let her be exalted above the stars and angels.

"Reign on high as queen of seraphims and saints; and be then crowned with honour and glory," &c.

"Glory be to Jesus and Mary," &c.

It is true, the theologians of the Church of Rome profess to distinguish between the worship offered to Mary and the worship offered to Christ. The saints are to be worshipped with *dulia*, the Virgin with *hyperdulia*, and God with *latria*. But this is a distinction which has never yet been clearly defined: in practice it is utterly disregarded; it seems to have been invented solely to meet the Protestant charge of idolatry; and the mass of the common people are incapable of either understanding it or acting upon it. We not unfrequently find them praying in the very same words to God, to the Virgin, and to the saints. We may instance the well-known prayer to which, in 1817, an indulgence of three hundred days was annexed. It is as follows: —

"Jesus, Joseph, Mary, I give you my heart and soul;

Jesus, Joseph, Mary, assist me in my last agony;

Jesus, Joseph, Mary, I breathe my soul to you in peace."

According to the theory of lower and higher degrees of worship, three kinds of worship ought to have been here employed, — *latria* for God, *hyperdulia* for Mary, and *dulia* for Joseph; but all three, without the least distinction, or the smallest alteration in the words or in the form, are worshipped alike.

In the third place, the same works are ascribed to Mary as to Christ. She hears prayer, intercedes with God for sinners, guides, defends, and blesses them in life, succours them when dying, and receives their departing spirits into paradise. But passing over these things, the great work of Redemption, the peculiar glory of the Saviour, and the chief of God's ways, is now by Roman Catholics, plainly and without reserve, applied to Mary. The Father who devised, the Son who purchased, and the Spirit who applies, the salvation of the sinner, must all give place to the Virgin. It was her coming which prophets announced; it is her victory which the Church celebrates. Angels and the redeemed of heaven ascribe unto her the glory and honour of saving men. She rose from the dead on the third day; she ascended to heaven; she has been re-united to her Son; and she now shares with Him power, glory, and dominion. "The eternal gates of heaven rolled back; the king's mother entered, and was conducted to the steps of his royal throne. Upon it sat her Son. . . . . 'A throne was set for the king's mother, and she sat upon his right hand.' And upon her brow he placed the crown of universal dominion; and the countless multitude of the heavenly hosts saluted her as the queen of heaven and earth." All this Romanists ascribe to a poor fallen creature, whose bones have been mouldering in the dust for eighteen hundred years. We impute nothing to the Church of Rome, in this respect, which her living theologians do not teach. Instead of being ashamed of their Mariolatry, they glory in it, and boast that their Church is becoming every day more devoted to the service and adoration of the Virgin. The argument by which the work of redemption is ascribed to Mary we find briefly stated by Father Ventura, in a conversation with M. Roussel of Paris, then travelling in Italy.

"The Bible tells us but a few words about her" [the Virgin Mary], said M. Roussel to the Padre, "and those few words are not of a character to exalt her."

"Yes," replied Father Ventura, "but those few words express every thing! Admire this allusion: Christ on the cross addressed his mother as *woman*; God in Eden declared that the *woman* should crush the serpent's head; the woman designated in Genesis must therefore be the woman pointed out by Jesus Christ; and it is she who is the Church, in which the family of man is to be saved."

"But that is a mere agreement of words, and not of things," responded the Protestant minister.

"That is sufficient," said Father Ventura.

Not less decisive is the testimony of Mr. Seymour, as regards the sentiments of the leading priests at Rome, and the predominating character of the worship of Italy. The following instructive conversation passed one day between him and one of the Jesuits, on the subject of the worship of the Virgin.

"My clerical friend," says Mr. Seymour, "resumed the conversation, and said, that the worship of the Virgin Mary was a growing worship in Rome, — that it was increasing in depth and intenseness of devotion, — and that there were now many of their divines — and he spoke of himself as agreeing with them in sentiment — who were teaching, that as a woman brought in death, so a woman was to bring in life, — that as a woman brought in sin, so a woman was to bring in holiness, — that as Eve brought in damnation, so Mary was to bring in salvation, — and that the effect of this opinion was largely to increase the reverence and worship given to the Virgin Mary."

"To prevent any mistake as to his views," says Mr. Seymour, "I asked whether I was to understand him as implying, that as we regard Eve as the first sinner, so we are to regard Mary as the first Saviour, — the one as the author of sin, and the other as the author of the remedy."

"He replied that such was precisely the view he wished to express; and he added, that it was taught by St. Alphonso de Liguori, and was a growing opinion."

But we can adduce still higher authority in proof of the charge that Rome now knows no other God than Mary, and worships no other Saviour than the Virgin. In the Encyclical Letter of Pius IX., issued on the 2d of February 1849, soliciting the suffrages of the Roman Catholic Church, preparatory to the decree of the pontiff on the doctrine of the immaculate conception, terms are applied to the Virgin Mary which plainly imply that she is possessed of divine fulness and perfection, and that she discharges the office of Redeemer to the Church, "The most illustrious prelates, the most venerable canonical chapters, and the religious congregations," says the Pope, "rival each other in soliciting that permission should be granted to add and pronounce aloud and publicly, in the sacred Liturgy, and in the preface of the mass to the blessed Virgin Mary, the word 'immaculate;' and to define it as a doctrine of the Catholic Church, that the conception of the blessed Virgin Mary was entirely immaculate, and absolutely exempt from all stain of original sin." The document then rises into a strain of commingled blasphemy and idolatry, in which the perfections of God and the work of Christ are ascribed to the Virgin, who *"is raised, by the greatness of her merits, above all the choirs of angels, up to the throne of God; who has crushed under the foot of her virtues the head of the old serpent.* The foundation of our confidence is in the Most Holy Virgin, since *it is in her that God has placed the plenitude of all good, in such sort, that if there be in us any hope, — if there be any spiritual health, — we know that it is from her that we receive it,* — because it is the will of Him who hath willed that we should have all by the instrumentality of Mary." We need no other evidence of Rome's idolatry. The document, it is true, is not a formal deed of the Church; but the difference is one of form only; for the pontiff assures us that the sentiments it contains are not his own only, but those of "the most illustrious prelates, venerable canonical chapters, and religious congregations;" and of course the sentiments are shared in by a vast majority of the members of the Church. The document fully installs Mary in the office of Saviour, and exalts her to the throne of God; for, *in the first place*, it expressly applies to her the prophecy in Eden, and ascribes to her the work then foretold, — crushing the head of the serpent;

and, *in the second place*, it applies to Mary the ascription of Paul to Christ, — "In him dwells all the fulness of the Godhead bodily," and in doing so, exalts her to the throne of mediatorial power and blessing. The pontifical decree on the subject of the immaculate conception may after this be spared. Already Rome has consummated her idolatry, and its evidence is complete. That Church has installed Mary in the office of Redeemer, and exalted her to the throne of Deity.

To raise Mary to an equality with God, is virtually to place her above Him; for God can have no rival. But Roman Catholic writers teach, in express terms, that she is superior. In invoking her, they hold it warrantable to ask her to lay her commands upon her Son, which implies her superiority in power to Him to whom, the Bible teaches, "all power in heaven and in earth has been committed." And, second, they teach that she is superior in mercy, and that she hears prayer, and pities and delivers the sinner, when Christ will not. This doctrine has not only been taught in words, but has been exhibited in symbol, and that in so grotesque a way, that for the moment we forget its blasphemy. In the dream of St. Bernard, — which forms the subject of an altar-piece in a church at Milan, — two ladders were seen reaching from earth to heaven. At the top of one of the ladders stood Christ, and at the top of the other stood Mary. Of those who attempted to enter heaven by the ladder of Christ, not one succeeded, — all fell back. Of those who ascended by the ladder of Mary, not one failed. The Virgin, prompt to succour, stretched out her hand; and, thus aided, the aspirants ascended with ease.

Chapter XX: Faith Not to be Kept with Heretics.

There remains yet another matter, — a matter not strictly theological, it is true, yet one that enters deeply into the morality of the Church of Rome, and which is of vital moment as regards society. The question we are now to discuss discloses to our sight a very gulph of wickedness. It is as the opening of pandemonium itself. One wonders that the earth has borne so long a society so atrociously wicked, or that the lightnings of heaven have so long forborne to consume it. This doctrine of enormous turpitude is the dispensing power. The Church of Rome has adopted as a leading principle of her policy, that *faith is not to be kept with heretics when its violation is necessary for the interests of the Church*. This abominable doctrine papists have disclaimed. This does not surprise us. *A priori*, it was to be expected that any society that was wicked enough to adopt such a principle would be base enough to deny it. Besides, to confess to this policy would be the sure way of defeating its end. Who would contract alliances with Rome, if told beforehand that she would keep to them not a moment longer than it suited her own purposes? Who would entrust himself to her promise, if he saw it to be the net in which he was to be caught and destroyed? Were living Papists prepared publicly to avow this doctrine, they would be prepared also to abandon it, for it would manifestly be useless a moment longer to retain it. Besides, they are not prepared to brave the odium which the avowal of a maxim so abhorrent and detestable would be sure to provoke. This is the very mark of hell. Rome may wear this mark in her right hand, where its partial concealment is possible; but were that mark to be imprinted on her forehead, she dare not hold up her face before the world, knowing that the damning evidence of her guilt was visible to every eye. The living writers and priests of the Church of Rome are plainly inadmissible as witnesses here. We appeal the matter to her canons and her history, — a tribunal to which she can take no exception. At this bar do we sist her; and here she stands condemned as the CAIN of the human family, — the world's OUTLAW.

The proof, — and nothing is more capable of easy and complete demonstration, — is briefly as follows: — The doctrine that no faith is to be kept with heretics, when to do so would militate against the interests of the Church, was promulgated by the third Lateran Council, decreed by the Council of Constance, confirmed by the Council of Trent, and is sworn to by all priests at their ordination, when they declare on oath their belief of all the tenets taught in the sacred canons and the general councils; and it has been practised by the Church of Rome, both in particular cases of great flagrancy, and in the general course of her actings. The proof is as clear as the charge is grave and the crime enormous.

The third Lateran Council, which was held at Rome in 1167 under the pontificate of Alexander III., and which all Papists admit to be infallible, decreed in its sixteenth canon, that "oaths made against the interest and benefit of the Church are not so much to be considered as oaths, but as perjuries." The fourth or great Lateran Council absolved from their oath of allegiance the subjects of heretical princes.

The Council of Constance, which was holden in 1414, expressly decreed that no faith was to be kept with heretics. The words of this decree, as preserved by M. L'Enfant, in his learned history of that famous council, are, that "by no law, natural or divine, is it obligatory to keep faith with heretics, to the prejudice of the Catholic faith." This fearful doctrine the council ratified in a manner not less fearful, in the blood of John Huss. It is well known that this reformer came to the council trusting in a safe-conduct, which had been given him under the hand of the Emperor Sigismund. The document in the amplest terms guaranteed the safety of Huss, in his journey to Constance, in his stay there, and in his return home. Notwithstanding, he was seized, imprisoned, condemned, and burnt alive, at the instigation of the council, by the very man who had so solemnly guaranteed his safety.

When the Council of Trent assembled in the sixteenth century, it was exceedingly desirous of obtaining the presence of the Protestants at its deliberations. Accordingly, it issued numerous equivocal safe-conducts, all of which the Protestants, mindful of the fate of Huss, rejected. At last the council decreed, that *for this time*, and *in this instance*, the safe-conduct should not be violated, and that no "authority, power, statute, or decree, and especially that of the Council of Constance and Siena," should be employed against them. In this enactment of the Council of Trent, canons, decrees, and laws, to the prejudice of safe-conducts to heretics, are expressly recognised as already existing. These decrees are not revoked or abjured by the council; they are only suspended *for the time*, — "pro hac vice." This is a plain declaration, that on all other occasions Rome means to act upon them, and will, whenever she has the power. There has been no general council since; and as no decree of the Pope has repudiated the doctrine of these decrees and canons, they must be regarded as still in force.

The instances are innumerable in which popes and Roman Catholic writers have asserted and recommended this odious doctrine. It was promulgated by Hildebrand in the eleventh century. The cruel persecutions of the eleventh and twelfth centuries were based on this doctrine. Pope Martin V., in his letter to the Duke of Lithuania, says, *Be assured that thou sinnest mortally if thou keep faith with heretics.* "Gregory IX. made the following law: — 'Be it known unto all who are under the jurisdiction of those who have openly fallen into heresy, that they are free from the obligation of fidelity, dominion, and every kind of obedience to them, by whatever means or bond they are tied to them, and how securely soever they may be bound.' On which Bishop Simanca gives this comment: — 'Governors of forts and all kinds of vassals are by this constitution freed from the bond of the oath whereby they had promised fidelity to their lords and masters. Moreover, a Catholic wife is not obliged to perform the marriage contract with an heretical husband. If faith is not to be kept with tyrants, pirates, and other public robbers who kill the body, much less with obstinate heretics who kill the soul. Ay, but it is a sad thing to break faith. But, as saith Merius Salomonius, faith promised against Christ, if kept, is verily perfidy. Justly, therefore, were some heretics burnt by the most solemn judgment of the Council of Constance, although they had been promised security. And St. Thomas also is of opinion, that a Catholic might deliver over an untractable heretic to the judges, notwithstanding he had pledged his faith to him, and even confirmed it by the solemnity of an oath.' 'Contracts,' saith Bonacina, 'made against the canon law are invalid, though confirmed by oath; and a man is not bound to stand to his promise, though he had sworn to it.' 'Pope Innocent VIII., in his bull against the Waldenses in 1487, by his authority apostolical declares, that all those who had been bound and obliged by contract, or any other way whatever, to grant or pay anything to them, should not be under any manner of obligation to do so for the time to come.'"

When Henry of Valois was elected to the throne of Poland in 1573, Cardinal Hosius laboured ineffectually to prevent the newly-elected monarch confirming by his oath the religious liberties of Poland. He next openly recommended to him to commit perjury, maintaining "that an oath given to heretics may be broken, even without absolution." In the letter which he despatched to the King, he desired him to "reflect that the oath was not a bond of iniquity, and that there was no necessity for him to be absolved from his oath, because, according to every law, all that he had inconsiderately done was neither binding nor had any value." But Solikowski, a learned Roman Catholic prelate, gave Henry more dangerous advice still. He counselled him to submit to the necessity, and promise and swear everything demanded of him, in the hope that, as soon as he ascended the throne, he would find himself in a condition to crush without violence the heresy he had sworn to maintain. Thus have the councils, the popes, and the casuists of the Roman Catholic Church enacted, defended, and promulgated this horrible doctrine. It is as undeniable as the sun at noon-day, that that Church holds it as a tenet of her faith, that it *is unlawful to keep faith with heretics, when the good of the Church requires that it should be violated.*

The practice of the Church of Rome has been in strict accordance with her doctrine. Faith she has not kept with heretics, whenever it could serve her purpose to break it. Compacts framed with the highest solemnities, and sanctioned by the holiest oaths, she has violated, without the least scruple or compunction, when the interests of Protestantism were concerned. What, we ask, is her history, but one long unvaried tale of lies, frauds, perfidies, broken vows, and violated oaths? Every party that has trusted her she has in turn betrayed. It mattered not how awful the sanctions with which she was bound, or how numerous and sacred the pledges and guarantees of sincerity which she had given: these bonds were to Rome but as the green withes on the arm of Samson. Her wickedness is without parallel in the annals of human treachery. Perfidies which the most abandoned of pagan governments would have shuddered to commit, Rome has deliberately perpetrated and unblushingly justified. In the case of others, these enormities have been the exceptions, and have formed a departure from the generally recognised principles of their action; but in the case of Rome they have formed the rule, and have sprung from principles deliberately adopted as the guiding maxims of her policy. We question whether an instance can be adduced of so much as one engagement that has been kept in matters involving the conflicting interests of Protestantism and Popery, when it could be advantageously broken. We do not know of any such. But time would fail, and space is wanting, to narrate even a tithe of the instances in which the most solemn engagements were most perfidiously violated, nay, made to be violated, — framed to entrap the confiding victims. The cases are innumerable, we say, in which Roman Catholics have made promises and oaths to individuals, to cities, to provinces, with the most public and solemn forms; and the moment they obtained the advantage these oaths were intended to secure, they delivered over to slaughter and devastation those very men to whom they had sworn in the great name of GOD. Ah! could the soil of France disclose her slaughtered millions, — could the snows of the Alps and the vales of Piedmont give up the dead which they cover, — these confessors could tell how Rome kept her oaths and covenants. Their voice has been silent for ages; but history pleads their cause: it has preserved the vows solemnly made, but perfidiously violated; and, pointing to the blood of the martyr, it cries aloud to heaven for vengeance on the perfidy that shed it. In the Albigensian war, Louis of France having besieged the town of Avignon for a long time, and lost twenty-three thousand men before it, was on the point of raising the siege, when the following stratagem was successfully resorted to. The Roman legate swore before the city gates, that if admission were granted, he would enter alone with the prelates, simply for the purpose of examining the faith of the citizens. The gates were opened, the legate entered, the army rushed in at his back, hundreds of the houses were razed, multitudes of the inhabitants were slaughtered, and of the rest, a great part were carried away as hostages.

In the long and bloody war against the Waldenses in the thirteenth century, Rome never scrupled to employ treachery when the sword was unsuccessful; and it may be affirmed that that noble people were crushed rather by perfidy than by arms. They had much more to dread from the oaths than from the soldiers of Rome. Again and again did the house of Savoy pledge its faith to these confessors; but every new treaty was followed by new dishonour to the one party and new calamities to the other. The power of France itself would never have subdued these hardy mountaineers, but for the arts with which the arms of their powerful foe were seconded. Pacifications were framed with them, purposely to throw them off their guard, and pave the way for another crusade and another massacre. In this way did they perish from those vales which their piety had sanctified, and from those mountains which their struggles had made holy. They fell unlamented and unavenged. The throne of the crafty Bourbon still stood, and the sway of the triple tyrant was still prolonged; but in the silent vales where these martyrs had lived no trace of them now remained, save the ashes that blackened the site of their dwelling, and the bones that whitened the rocks by which it was overhung. Their names were unhonoured, and their deeds were unpraised, by a world which knew not how to estimate the greatness of their virtues or the grandeur of their cause. But not in vain did they offer themselves upon the altar of their faith. In the stillness that reigned throughout Europe, a solitary voice from a distant isle was heard saying, "Avenge, O Lord, thy slaughtered saints!" — the first utterance of a prayer in which a world shall yet join, and the first prophetic anticipation of a vengeance which, after the lapse of three centuries, God is now beginning to inflict upon the blood-stained dynasties and thrones which slew his saints.

It was the same in all the countries of Europe. Wherever Protestants existed they were assailed by arms and by treachery, and the latter weapon was a hundred times more fatal than the former. The butcheries of Alva in the Low Countries were preceded by promises and treaties of peace and conciliation oft and solemnly ratified. Philip II. pledged the honour of Spain to his subjects in Flanders; and the dungeons, the scaffolds, and the sanguinary troops by which that country was immediately thereafter inundated show how he redeemed the faith he had plighted. In the great struggle in Poland, in which for a while it seemed an even chance which of the two faiths should acquire the ascendancy, the Popish party kept their oaths only so long as they lacked opportunity of breaking them. When the struggle was at its height, Lippomani, the papal legate, arrived in Poland, and unscrupulously advised the sovereign, Sigismund Augustus, who pled that the laws of the kingdom forbade violence, to employ treachery and bloodshed to extirpate heresy. To this policy is to be ascribed the ultimate triumph of the Jesuitical party in Poland. "As the laws of the country," says Krasinski, "did not allow any inhabitant of Poland to be persecuted on account of his religious opinions, they [the Jesuits] left no means untried in order to evade those salutary laws; and the odious maxim that *no faith should be kept with heretics* was constantly advocated by them, as well as by other advocates of Romanism in our country." In most of the southern German States the Protestant cause was overthrown by the same arts. In truth, this maxim of Rome, that faith is not to be kept when to keep it would tend to the advantage of Protestantism or the detriment of Popery, kept Germany in the flames of war, with short intervals, for upwards of a century. The advantages which the Protestants had secured by their arms, and which they had compelled their enemies to ratify by solemn treaty, were perfidiously denied and infringed; they were thus forced again and again to take up arms; and the successive wars in which Europe was involved, and which occasioned so great an expenditure of blood and treasure, grew out of Rome's maxim, which in almost all these particular cases was directly applied and enforced by pontifical authority, that such oaths and treaties "were from the very beginning, and for ever shall be, null and void; and that no one is bound to observe them, or any of them, even though they have been often ratified and confirmed by oath."

But the guiltiest land and throne in Europe, in respect of violated oaths, is France. In point of perfidy, the house of Bourbon has far exceeded the ordinary measure, we do not say of pagan governments, but of Roman Catholic governments. The kings of France were the eldest sons of the Church, and bore most of the paternal likeness. Every one of their acts proclaimed them to be of their father the Pope, who was a liar from the beginning. Did the poor Huguenots ever trust them but to be betrayed by them? Of the numerous engagements into which they entered with their Protestant subjects, was there one which they ever honestly fulfilled? What were these treaties, with their ample appendages of oaths and ratifications, but crafty devices for ensnaring, disarming, and then massacring the Protestants? The first edict, guaranteeing them the exercise of their religion, was granted in 1561. It was soon violated, and a worse persecution befell them. They were forced to take up arms, for the first time, to save their lives and vindicate their rights. They triumphed; and their success obtained for them a new pacification. This was violated in like manner. "They [the Court] restrained," says Mezeray, "every day their liberty, which had been granted them by the edicts, until it was reduced almost to nothing. The people fell upon them in the places where they were weakest. In those where they could defend themselves the governors made use of the authority of the king to oppress them. Their cities and forts were dismantled; there was no justice for them; in the parliaments or king's council they were massacred with impunity; they were not reinstalled in their goods and charges. In fine, they had conspired their ruin with the Pope, the house of Austria, and the Duke of Alva." Six times was the public faith of France plighted to the Protestants, in solemn treaty, ratified and sanctioned by solemn oath; six times was the plighted faith of France openly dishonoured and violated; and six times did civil war, the direct fruit of these broken vows, waste the treasure and the blood of that nation.

The act of unparalleled crime which brought to an end the fourth pacification, that of 1570, merits our particular notice. Two years of profound dissimulation and hypocrisy paved the way for that awful tragedy, — the greatest of the crimes of Rome, — perhaps the most fearful monument of human wickedness which the history of the world contains, — the MASSACRE OF ST. BARTHOLOMEW. The chiefs of the Protestant party were invited to Court, caressed, and loaded with honours. The Protestants generally seemed to be taken into special favour, and now shared the same privileges with the Catholics. So bright was the deceitful gleam that heralded the dismal storm! Not only were the fears of the Protestants laid at rest, but those of Rome were awakened, thinking that either the King of France meant not to keep his engagement in the matter, or that he was overacting his part. But the cruel issue did more than make amends. In a moment the bolt fell. For three days and nights the work of human slaughter went on, and France became a very shambles. At length the dreadful business had an end. Seventy thousand corpses covered the soil of France. Paris shouted for joy, and the cannon of St. Angelo, from beyond the Alps, returned that shout. The Pope had some reason to rejoice. The blow struck at Paris decided the fortunes of Protestantism in Europe for two centuries. The Protestant faith was on the point of gaining the ascendancy both in Poland and France. The sagacious and patriotic Coligny meditated the project of a grand alliance between these two countries, and of giving thereby a powerful centre and a uniform action to the Protestant cause, and humbling the two main props of the Papacy, Spain and Austria. As matters then stood, the project would have been completely successful. The other Protestant states of Europe would have joined the alliance; but, in truth, France and Poland combined could have easily made head against the Popish powers, and could have shaken the dominion of Rome. But the massacre of St. Bartholomew was fatal to this great scheme. The venerable Coligny, as is well known, was its first victim; and his project, big with the fortunes of Protestantism, perished with him. The Protestants were panic-struck in France, and disheartened in other countries. The victory which had long trembled in the balance between the Reformation and Rome now inclined decidedly to the latter; and from that day the Protestant influence declined in Europe. The two centuries of dominion which have been added to Rome she owes to her grand maxim, that no dissimulation is too profound, and no perfidy too gross, to be employed against Protestants.

The last great national act of treachery on the part of France was the revocation of the Edict of Nantes. "Never was an edict, law, or treaty more deliberately made, more solemnly ratified, more *irrevocably* established, more repeatedly confirmed; nor one whereof policy, duty, or gratitude, could have more ensured the execution; yet never was one more scandalously or absolutely violated. It was the result of three years' negotiation between the commissioners of the king and the deputies of the Protestants, — was the termination of forty years' wars and troubles, — was merited by the highest services, sealed by the highest authority, registered in all the parliaments and courts of Henry the Great, — was declared in the preamble to be perpetual and irrevocable." It was confirmed by the Queen-mother in 1610, and repeatedly ratified by succeeding monarchs of France; yet all the while the purpose of overturning it was secretly entertained and steadily and craftily prosecuted. The rights it conferred and the privileges it guaranteed were gradually encroached upon: oppressions cruel and manifold, contrary to the spirit and to the letter of the edict, were practised on the Protestants; and at last, in 1685, it was publicly revoked. When the old Chancellor Tellier, the Jesuit, signed the edict of revocation, full of joy at this consummation of the intrigues and labours of his party, he cried out, — *"Lord, now lettest thou thy servant depart in peace, for mine eyes have seen thy salvation."* The proscriptions, the banishments, the massacres, which followed, and which were second only to the St. Bartholomew horror, are well known to every reader of history.

This act consummated the woes of French Protestantism and the guilt of the house of Bourbon. Tellier, in signing the Revocation, had signed the death-warrant of France. A chain of causes, extending from 1685 to 1785, and which it requires but a slight study of the history of that gloomy period clearly to trace, links together the Huguenot proscriptions and massacres of the one period with the revolutionary horrors of the other. Rome's favourite maxim, faithfully acted out by the bigoted court of France, introduced at last the Reign of Terror. How could it possibly be otherwise? Great part of the trade of the kingdom was in the hands of the Protestants; and when they were driven away, industry was paralyzed. The numerous and expensive wars waged against the Huguenots had exhausted the national exchequer, and new taxes had to be imposed, which pressed heavily on a crippled trade and a languishing agriculture. With religion had been extinguished the elements of morality and order. A new and powerful element, engendered by the Romish idolatry, was next introduced, —

infidelity, which passed, in numerous instances, into atheism. These terrible elements, which had their rise in the Huguenot persecutions, gathered apace; and at last, in little more than a century from the revocation of the Edict of Nantes, they burst over France in unexampled and desolating fury. All things were now changed, but so changed as to bear stamped upon them the awful mark of retributive vengeance. The Jesuit cabal was exchanged for the democrats' club. Rome's sanctified dagger was set aside for the guillotine of the Revolution. The Bourbon was gone, and Robespierre reigned in his room; bloodthirsty and revengeful, doubtless, but not more so than the tyrant he had succeeded, and certainly not so perfidious and hypocritical. Crowds of wretched fugitives were again seen on the frontier; but this time it was the priesthood and the noblesse of France. By and by foreign war drew off into a new channel the energies of the Revolution; but soon they returned to their former sphere, descended on France, as eagles on the carcase, or as the fires on the sacrifice; and now again are they seen preying with consuming fierceness upon that devoted country. Nor will they ever be quenched till the land of violated oaths and blood unrighteously shed has become the Gomorrah of the nations. Read thus, the history of France is an awful demonstration of God's moral government. Nations unborn will peruse her story, and learn to avoid her crimes and her woes. The persecutor of the past will be the beacon of the future.

But, it may be objected, these dreadful crimes and perjuries are to be attributed to the bad faith and despotic tendencies of governments, and not to the evil principles of the Church of Rome. Not so. It is Rome that must confront the appalling charge. She it was that broke all these vows and shed all this blood. She has associates in crime, doubtless, but she must not roll over on them the guilt she taught them to perpetrate. All the dreadful proceedings we have so briefly surveyed, — and they form scarce a tithe of the woes which constitute the history of Europe, — sprang directly out of the detestable doctrine which the councils, pontiffs, and casuists of the Roman Church inculcated. In the abyss of her councils were these plots hatched. France and the other Catholic powers did but follow the policy which the Court of Rome chalked out for them. All their enterprizes were undertaken with the Church's sanction, often at her earnest solicitation; and assuredly they were all undertaken in the Church's behalf, — for the extirpation of heresy and the aggrandisement of the priesthood. At her door, then, must be laid all this accumulated perfidy. The facts we have adduced undeniably prove that the doctrine that no *faith is to be kept with heretics* is regarded by the Church of Rome, not simply as a speculative theory, but as a maxim to which practical effect is to be given on all occasions, and to all the extent which the opportunities and the power of Rome will allow.

The recent history of Europe has furnished a fearful commentary on the Pope's "dispensing power." The sovereigns of southern Europe have of late been acting on this maxim, and, as a consequence, filling their dungeons with the most virtuous of their subjects; only this time the doctrine has been put in force, not against the confessors of religion solely, but also against the liberals in politics. A catechism, in which it is avowedly taught that "the head of the Church has authority to release consciences from oaths when he judges there is suitable cause for it," has been compiled by an ecclesiastic, is circulated by ecclesiastics, and taught to the youth in the schools of Naples. King Ferdinand, the bosom friend of Pio Nono, has taken the full benefit of this doctrine, by revoking the Constitution to which he solemnly swore in "the awful name of Almighty God," and has told his terror-stricken kingdom, that what he did he had a right to do, — that sovereignty is divine, — that an oath infringing on sovereignty possesses no obligation, — and that he alone is judge when the Constitution encroaches on his rights. The same "doctrine of devils" is taught by Liguori, who teaches that men may swear with any amount of equivocation or mental reservation, — that "any reasonable reason is enough" for violating an oath, — that an oath contrary to the rights of superiors or the interests of the Church is not to be kept with any party or on any occasion, and therefore, *a fortiori*, not to be kept with heretics. All this is taught by the "infallible" Liguori.

What, then, are we to say of the strong disclaimers of this doctrine by some modern Papists in behalf of their Church? These disclaimers, it is manifest, possess not the smallest weight, when we put in opposition to them the vast body of evidence by which the charge is supported, — the decrees of councils, the bulls and rescripts of popes, the public and uniform actings of the Church for well nigh three hundred years, and the deliverances of modern writers in the Church of Rome, — of Dens, Liguori, and others. That this was the doctrine of the Church, no one can deny; that it was also her practice so long as she possessed the power, is equally undeniable. If she has renounced it, let it be shown *when* and *where*. Renounced it she has not, and cannot, without overthrowing the infallibility, on which her whole system is founded. In truth, when popish divines abjure the doctrine *that no faith is to be kept with heretics*, they are guilty of practising a wretched quibble. Their meaning is, that so long as the oath exists it must be kept; but the Pope, in virtue of his dispensing power, may declare, on just grounds, — of which *"the necessity and utility of the Church"* is one, — that the oath is null, and does not exist, and consequently is not to be kept. They then triumphantly ask, How can an oath be said to be violated that does not exist? Were it their object to release the subjects of Great Britain from their oaths of allegiance, the procedure adopted would be as follows: the people would be taught, that so long as the oath existed, it must be respected; but then nothing is easier than to put it out of existence! The Pope has only, on some *"just ground,"* to declare our Queen no longer sovereign, and the oath would no longer exist. We know not which is the more astonishing, — the impiety of those who can juggle in this way, or the simplicity of those who can be deceived by such juggling. If those statesmen who are so desirous to form relations with Rome, can find comfort in this very peculiar mode of keeping faith, they are abundantly welcome to it. But plain it is, that when Romish priests disclaim on oath the lawfulness of the doctrine of not keeping faith with heretics, so plainly taught in those canons to which they have sworn, they are just exhibiting, as Dr. Cunningham strikingly remarks, "in its most aggravated form, the very enormity which they profess to abjure."

This doctrine strikes at the foundation of society. If oaths do not bind, — if vows and treaties possess force only so far as it accords with the will and interests of one of the parties, — there is an end of society, and men must return to the condition of savages. And if saved from falling into this state, it can only be by one man getting the start of the others, and making his will a law to the rest; for men must have some standard of faith, — some ground of mutual action; and if they do not find it in the eternal equity of things, they may find it in the necessity of a universal and infallible despotism. This Rome attempted to establish, and in no other way could the ultimate disorganization of the world have been averted. But this does not hinder our perceiving the heinous sin and the ruinous tendency of her maxim; and it by no means surprises us, that some of the great masters of ethical and moral science should have held that a community that contravenes the first and most essential conditions of society should be denied the first and most essential of social rights. "If there were in that age," says Macaulay, "two persons inclined by their judgment and by their temper to toleration, these persons were Tillotson and Locke. Yet Tillotson, whose indulgence for various kinds of schismatics and heretics brought on him the reproach of heterodoxy, told the House of Commons from the pulpit, that it was their duty to make effectual provision against the propagation of a religion more mischievous than irreligion itself, — of a religion which demanded from its followers services directly opposed to the first principles of morality. In his judgment, pagans who had never heard the name of Christ, and who were guided only by the light of nature, were more trustworthy members of civil society than men who had been formed in the schools of the popish casuists. Locke, in his celebrated treatise, in which he had laboured to show that even the grossest form of idolatry ought not to be prohibited under penal sanctions, contended that the Church which taught men not to keep faith with heretics had no claim to toleration.

Book III: Genius and Influence of the Papacy

Chapter I: Genius of the Papacy.

Volumes would scarce suffice to enable us to do justice to the incomparable genius of the Papacy. Thoroughly to explore and fully to unfold it would form a life-long task to the man of profoundest intellect. Such an one might expend all his strength and all his days in the study, and leave it at last with the confession that there are depths here which he has not fathomed, and mysteries which he must leave to be solved by his successors. Our limits are of the narrowest; and truly it would be a bootless undertaking to attempt a full elucidation of so vast a subject within the stinted space of a few pages. Nevertheless, we may indicate the more salient points of the system. If unable here fully to trace out the sources of its strength, we may be permitted to point out the direction in which they lie. Nor shall we have done so in vain, if we succeed in impressing any one with the singular interest and surpassing importance, as well as the great difficulty, of the study. Elements of great power there must have been in a system which has stood so long, and has exercised so great an influence; and if we can but succeed in rescuing these from the wreck, so to speak, we might employ them with advantage in the re-construction of society and the re-edification of the Church of God. Whole cities have sometimes been built from the ruins of colossal structures which time or violence had thrown down: in like manner, we may take the stones and timber of the Papacy, and consecrate them anew to the good of society and the service of God. A new solution may be awaiting the ancient riddle, — "Out of the cater came forth meat, and out of the strong came forth sweetness."

There is scarce a department of human knowledge on which the study of the Papacy does not throw light. It affords an amazing insight into the policy of Satan, its real author. It lays bare the innate depravity and the deceitful workings of the human heart; for Popery is but the religion of fallen human nature. It shows what an amount of mischief may grow out of a single evil principle, or out of a good one misapplied. It discloses to us the springs of error, and enables us to trace to the same source all errors, however deep their disguises, various their names, or diverse their forms; and it teaches by contrast the simplicity, consistency, grandeur, and substantial oneness of the truth. It shows, too, that no false system can be eternal; that it carries within itself the seeds of death; and that neither the defences of external power nor the sanctions of a venerable antiquity can save it from the death to which from its birth it is doomed. It has no self-renovating power; and, granting even that it should be let alone from without, the atrophy within would in due time consign it to its grave. But the immorality which falsehood wants truth possesses. Its seeds, sown in the world by the author of Christianity, are indestructible; and though all should perish, and but one survive, that one seedling would in time burst the clod and renovate the world. One atom of truth has more power in it than a whole system of error. We live too near the Papacy to see all the ends why God has permitted this evil system to exist. Some are already known, but the more important are still veiled in mystery; but we cannot doubt that ends there are, great, wise, and beneficent, and that what is dark to us will be clear to posterity. Nor can we doubt that, when these ends are disclosed, they will be found to be such as we have indicated, namely, a demonstration of the necessity of bringing the principles on which society is framed into harmony with those on which the divine government is carried on, in order that society may be saved, in its future stages, from the errors which have misled it hitherto, and the calamities which have overwhelmed it.

Popery we have described pretty fully in its leading principles and aspects; and we now pass from the subject of Popery, strictly considered, to that of the Papacy. We distinguish between Popery and the Papacy, and on just grounds, as we believe. Popery is the principle or error which may be defined to be *salvation of man*, in opposition to the truth of the gospel, which may be defined *salvation of God*. The Papacy is the secular organization by which the principle or error became as it were incarnate. This organization formed the body in which it dwelt, — the framework by which it sought to establish itself and reign in the world. The political system of Europe, as it has existed for the past thousand years and upwards, has been this framework. The soul that animated this system was Popery. It was the mind that guided it, and the powerful though invisible bond that gave it unity. Its head sat upon the Seven Hills; and there was not a priest in Europe, from the scarlet cardinals of the Eternal City, down to the wandering Capuchin, with his dress of serge and his girdle of rope, nor was there a king in Europe, from the monarchs of France down to the petty dukes of Germany, who was not a part of that system. All strove together with one heart and soul for the same iniquitous object, namely, the exaltation of the priesthood, and especially of the high priest of Rome, to the dishonour of the High Priest in the heavens. Such was the Papacy. It was the labour of a million of minds, and the growth of a thousand years. For we hold it impossible that the genius of one man, however powerful, could have contriven such a system; nay, we hold it impossible that the intellect of Satan himself, vast as it is, could have conceived beforehand so perfect and comprehensive a scheme. The entire plan, order, and government of the kingdom of heaven, that is, the Church, were sketched out from the beginning, and revealed in the New Testament. Thus, when the apostles began to build, they knew both how their work was to proceed, and to what it was to grow. But the author of the Papacy acted strictly on the development theory. The general outline of his system he plagiarised manifestly from the Scripture-revelation of the gospel kingdom. It is equally manifest, that the more fundamental principles of his scheme he obtained by a process of perversion; that is, he made counterfeits of the leading doctrines of the gospel, and on these proceeded to build. But as the work went on, he introduced novelties both of principle and of form, according as the spirit of the age and the circumstances of the times allowed or suggested. With a rare genius, the exigencies of the times were ever understood, and the modifications and amendments which they required were executed at the proper moment and in the happiest way. Working in this manner, Satan at last produced his masterpiece, — the Papacy.

The Papacy is the most wonderful of all human systems. It stands alone, unrivalled and unapproached, throwing all former systems of error into the shade, and challenging alike the power of man and the cunning of Satan to produce anything in after times that shall surpass it. The ancient polytheisms were comparatively simple in their plan and tolerant in their spirit. Not so the Papacy. It selects the worst passions of our nature, — the sensuality of the appetites, the idolatry of the heart, the love of wealth, the lust of dominion, pride, ambition, the desire to dictate to the faith of others. It gives to these passions the largest development of which they are capable; it combines and arranges them with exquisite skill, and thus enables them to act with the greatest effect. It is the most powerful organization that ever existed on the side of error and against the truth. When perfected, the once humble pastor of Rome occupied a seat which rose not merely above the thrones of earth, but above the throne of the Eternal. In *his* exaltation Satan recognised his *own* exaltation. The reign of the servant was the reign of the master. The Pope was Satan's vicar, and Satan therefore had withheld nothing that could strengthen his power or enhance his magnificence. He enthroned him on the wealth and dominion of Europe; he commanded kings to obey him, and all nations to serve him; he did more for him than he had done for the greatest of his servants before; he did more for him than he will ever be able to do again for the best beloved of his servants; he literally did his all, because the emergency was great. Let us take this into account when we contemplate the surpassing state and dazzling magnificence of these masters of the world. It is the very utmost which even Lucifer can do for a mortal. Like Judas, the pontiff had betrayed his lord, and behold the reward! — all the kingdoms of the world and the glory of them.

In speaking of the genius of the Papacy, it is necessary to distinguish between the real though invisible author of Popery, which is Satan, and the secondary and visible author, that is, the Pope. Viewing the system as emanating from Satan, its genius is of course that of its invisible author. He has thrown into it his whole intellect. Just as the work of redemption is an exhibition of the character of God, and comes stamped with the glorious perfections of His nature, so the Papacy is an exhibition of the character of Satan: it is stamped with the great qualities of his mind; and in studying the Papacy, we are just contemplating those powerful but malignant attributes with which this mysterious spirit is endowed. We gaze into the abyss of the satanic soul. But, to speak more strictly, the key of the Papacy, viewed as an emanation from Satan, is to be sought for in the history of the reduction of our first parents. Satan's policy has been substantially the same from the beginning. Of course, that policy has been modified by circumstances, and adapted in a masterly manner to each successive emergency. Its front of opposition has been more or less extended, according as it stood arrayed against but a single truth or a whole system of truths; but it has employed substantially the same policy throughout. The general may employ the same rule of military tactics in the preliminary skirmish as in the more complicated manoeuvres of the battle that succeeds. In like manner, Satan employed the identical policy in the assault in the Garden which he developed more fully in the secular and ecclesiastical domination which he set up in an after age in Western Europe. The study of the simpler event, then, furnishes a key for the solution of the greater and more complicated.

What, then, was his policy in the Garden? It may be summed up in one word: it was a dexterous substitution of the *counterfeit* for the *real*. The real in this case was, that life was to come to our first parents through the tree as the *symbolic cause*; thecounterfeit which Satan succeeded in palming upon them was, that life was to come to them through that tree as the *efficacious cause*. They were to have this life not *from*, but *by* the tree. The life was not in the tree, but beyond it, — in God, from whom they were to receive it, in the way of submitting to his ordinance. But by a train of subtle and fallacious argument, — not more subtle and fallacious, however, than that which Rome still employs, — the woman was brought to regard the tree as the *efficacious cause* of the life which she had been promised, and to which she had been bidden aspire; she was brought to believe that the life was in the tree, and that she had only to eat of the tree, and this life would be hers. "When the woman saw," it is said, that it was "a tree to be desired to make one wise, she took of the fruit thereof." It is plain that she believed the tree able of itself to make her wise, and that it had been interdicted by God, either because he grudged her the good the tree had power to bestow upon her, or, what is more probable, that she had mistaken the command altogether. This, then, was the prime object of Satan's policy. He admitted, at least he did not deny, that God had promised her life; he admitted that that life was good, and that she should aim at enjoying it; and he admitted farther, that it was in connection with the tree that that life was to be attained. But the question was made to turn on the sort of connection; Whether did, or did not, the promised good reside in the tree itself? The command of God plainly intimated that it did not reside in the tree, but would be bestowed by himself, in the way of his ordinance, which took the form of a covenant, being observed. But the point which Satan laboured to establish was, that the good was in the tree, and that it was intended as the *efficacious means* of bestowing that good upon her. Such was the question the woman had to decide; and according to her decision would one of two inevitable issues ensue, — her obedience and life, or her disobedience and death. If she should reject the doctrine of *inherent efficacy*, so boldly and artfully propounded, she would of course look elsewhere for life, even to God, and would respect his command. Should she, blinded and led away by the subtlety of the serpent, embrace the doctrine of *inherent efficacy*, — should she come to believe that she had only to eat and to live, — she would of course look only to the tree, and would straightway partake of its fruits. Unhappily she adopted the latter belief, and we know the issue.

But here the whole policy of Satan stands revealed. Brought within the compass of this single transaction, we can study that policy to much more purpose than when displayed along so extended a line of operations as the Papacy presents. Here is the key to Satan's policy of six thousand years, and especially the key to the Papacy. This transaction exhibits unmistakeably all the worst features of that evil system. Here was the *opus operatum* of a sacrament the woman was taught that she had only to partake, and, in virtue of the act, would be as God, knowing good and evil. Here already were *works* substituted in the room of *faith*: instead of the passive obedience which the covenant demanded, in the *faith* that God would bestow the life he had promised, the woman was taught to do a certain work by which that life was to be attained. And here was the doctrine of human merit, — *salvation of man* substituted in the room of *salvation of God*; for the woman was led to look for life, not from God, but from the tree, in the way of using its fruits. All the master errors of the Papacy, — those errors which in the standard books of Rome take the form of canons or of pontifical bulls, and which in her temples take the form of gorgeous and idolatrous rites, — were promulgated for the first time in Eden, and by *this* preacher, not, indeed, in express terms, but by implication: the policy of Satan proceeded on a principle which embraced them all. Yet farther, we find Satan teaching Eve that she could not understand the command of God without note and comment, and offering himself as an infallible interpreter, and not more grossly perverting the *text* than Rome has done in aims of the innumerable instances since. The boastful claims of the Papist and the Puseyite to a high antiquity are not without some foundation after all. In one sense, Popery, and its modern Anglican form Puseyism, are mediaeval error; in another they are but a development of that false principle by which Eve was seduced, and mankind precipitated into condemnation and death.

We can clearly trace the policy of Satan in the early polytheisms; and we find that policy in its essential principles unchanged. The pagan idolatries were manifestly the substitution of the *counterfeit* for the *real*. Satan, their author, did not deny that there is a God, or that it is man's duty to worship him. He reserved these truths as a fixed point, on which to rest the lever by which he was to move the world. But in the room of God, one, invisible, and spiritual, he substituted those material objects which most reflect his glory, or most largely dispense his goodness; — the sun, as in Chaldea; eminent men, the founders of tribes or the inventors of the arts, as in

Greece; vile and creeping things, as in Egypt; and, as the course of this idolatry is ever downward, in some tribes we find that the very idea of God had well-nigh perished. Falsehood is its own greatest enemy: its tendency is to destroy itself. Polytheism corrupted the nations; it thus came to lose its power over the human mind; and the world had lapsed into scepticism, when Christianity, young, vigorous, and pure, came forth from her native mountains to renovate the earth, — to restore that faith which is the life of man, and that religion which is the strength of nations. This was the most powerful antagonist that had yet appeared in the field against the interests of Satan. It was the great original truth revived with new splendour, — man revolted from God, redeemed by the Son, and sanctified by the Spirit, — the truth which Satan had supplanted by his LIE of polytheism; and, powerful as true, it attested its power by planting its trophies and monuments above the abjured creeds and prostrate temples of paganism.

This antagonist Satan could confront with but his old policy. That policy took a new form, to adapt itself to new circumstances: its edge was finer, its complications greatly more intricate, and its scale of operation vastly larger; still it was the old policy, radically, essentially unchanged, beneath its new modifications and altered forms. Satan presented over again to the world the COUNTERFEIT; and he succeeded once more in persuading the world to accept the *counterfeit* and to banish the *real*. The great primal truth of God's unity and supreme and exclusive government was supplanted in the old world by the device of making men adore inferior deities, not as God, but as representatives and vicegerents of God. So in the modern world the leading Christian truth respecting Christ, and the oneness of his mediation, has been supplanted by the device of other mediators, and of another Christ, — Antichrist. Popery is the counterfeit of Christianity, — a most elaborate and skilfully contriven counterfeit, —a counterfeit in which the form is faithfully preserved, the spirit utterly extinguished, and the end completely inverted. This counterfeit Church has its high priest, — the Pope, — who blasphemes the royal priesthood of Christ, by assuming his office, when he pretends to be Lord of the conscience, Lord of the Church, and Lord of the world; and by assuming his names, when he calls himself "the Light of the World," "the King of Glory," "the Lion of the tribe of Judah," Christ's Vicar and God's Vicegerent. This counterfeit Church has, too, its sacrifice, — the mass, which blasphemes the sacrifice of Christ, by virtually teaching its inefficiency, and needing to be repeated, as is done when Christ's very body and blood are again offered in sacrifice by the hands of the priests of Rome, for the sins of the living and the dead. This Church has, moreover, its Bible, which is tradition, which blasphemes the Word of God, by virtually teaching its insufficiency. It has its mediators, — saints and angels, and especially the Virgin; and thus it blasphemes the one Mediator between God and man. In fine, it blasphemes the person and the office of the Spirit as the sanctifier, because it teaches that its sacraments can make holy; and it blasphemes God, by teaching that its priests can pardon sin, and can release from the obligations of divine law. Thus has Popery counterfeited, and, by counterfeiting, set aside, all that is vital and valuable in Christianity. It robs Christ of his kingly office, by exalting the Pope to his throne; it robs him of his priesthood in the sacrifice of the mass; it robs him of his power as Mediator, by substituting Mary; it robs him of his prophetical office, by substituting the teachings of an infallible Church; it robs God the Spirit of his peculiar work as the sanctifier, by attributing the power of conferring grace to its own ordinances; and it robs God the Father of his prerogatives, by assuming the power of justifying and pardoning men.

Thus the counterfeit Christianity of Rome is as extensive as the real Christianity of the New Testament: it substitutes other objects of worship, other doctrines, other sacraments; all of which, however, in the *letter*, have an exact correspondence with the true. The *forms* of Christianity have been faithfully copied; its *realities* have been completely set aside. Thus Satan has carried his object, not by erecting a system avowedly antagonistic, but by amusing and deluding men with the counterfeit. The policy adopted in Egypt of old to frustrate the mission of Moses, was that of bringing forward a class of magicians to counterfeit the miracles of the Jewish lawgiver. The same expedient has been adopted a second time. Satan has brought forward the magicians and necromancers of Rome, who have imitated the miracles of the gospel. And as Moses was withstood by Jannes and Jambres, so have the lying prophets of Rome withstood Christianity in its glorious mission of regenerating the world. Christianity has respect to time as well as to eternity; and in both departments of its mission has it been withstood by the Romish soothsayers, and that, too, exactly in the style of their Egyptian predecessors, who "did so with their enchantments." The temporal end of Christianity they have defeated, by persuading rulers that *they* were able to secure the good and order of society. Princes have listened to them, and refused to let the gospel have liberty; and thus society has been corrupted and destroyed. The eternal end of Christianity they have defeated, by persuading men that, without parting with a single sin, or acquiring a single gracious disposition, they might attain to heaven. They have thus retained men under the power of corruption, and sealed them over to eternal damnation.

But the Papacy may be viewed as of man. Primarily it is the emanation of satanic policy; secondarily, it is the fabrication of human ambition and wickedness. In order to discover its genius, viewed as the creation of man, it is necessary to keep in view the grand aim of the Papacy. Without this we cannot appreciate its marvellous adaptation of means to their end, and the relation of each part to the whole. There is not one of its arrangements, however minute, nor one of its doctrines, however unimportant it may seem, but has a direct reference to and a powerful bearing upon the object of the Papacy. In the vast and complicated machine there is not a useless cord or a superfluous wheel. The object of the Papacy is, in brief, to exalt a man, or rather a class of men, to the supreme, undivided, and absolute control of the world and its affairs. So vast a scheme of dominion the genius of Alexander had never dared to entertain. The ambition of the popes far outstripped that of the Caesars, and looked down with contempt upon their empire as insignificant and narrow. They aspired to be gods upon the earth. It was the majesty of the Eternal which they plotted to usurp. Pride can go no higher. Ambition finds nothing beyond for which it may pant. They reigned with equal power over the minds and over the bodies of men. They grasped the reins of secular as well as of ecclesiastical jurisdiction. They made their opinions the standard of morals, and their wills the standard of law, to the universe. They claimed not merely to be obeyed, but to be worshipped. They were not monarchs, but divinities. We do not affirm that this object was definitely proposed by the bishops of Rome from the outset. Nay, had they seen to what their early departures from the faith would lead, — that the principles which they adopted contained within them the germ of a despotism beneath which the religion and the liberties of the world would lie crushed for ages, — they would have stopt short in their career. The Omniscient eye alone can trace things to their issues. It was not till ages had passed away, and numerous usurpations had taken place, that the object of their policy was clearly seen by the pontiffs themselves, though the invisible prompter of that policy had doubtless proposed that end from the first. But by the time that object came to be clearly understood, all scruple was at an end. The pontiff panted to place himself upon the throne of the universe, and to prostrate beneath his feet all other dominion. The object surpassed in grandeur all to which man had ever before aspired, and the means brought into operation were vast beyond all former example. A policy unmatched in dissimulation and craft, — a sagacity distinguished alike by the largeness of its conceptions and the precision and accuracy of its conclusions, — a quiet irresistible energy, — a firm unalterable will, — a perseverance which no toil could exhaust, which no difficulty could discourage, which no check could turn from its purpose, which made all things give way to it, and which proved itself invincible, — a vast array of physical force when an antagonist appeared whom its other arts could not subdue, — lavishing its favours upon its friends with boundless prodigality, and visiting with vengeance equally unbounded its incorrigible enemies, — wielding these qualities, the Papacy saw its efforts crowned at last with a success which was as astonishing as it was unprecedented.

In the first place, Popery was exceedingly fortunate in the choice of a seat, when it selected Rome. The possession of such a spot was almost essential to it. It was itself a tower of strength. In no other spot of earth could its gigantic schemes of dominion have been formed, or, if formed, realized. Sitting in the seat which the masters of the world had so long occupied, the Papacy appeared the rightful heir of their power. Papal Rome reaped the fruit of the wars and the conquests, the toils and the blood, of imperial Rome. The one had laboured and gone to her grave; the other arose and entered into her labours. The pontiffs perfectly understood this, and were careful to turn the advantage it offered them to the utmost account. By heraldic and symbolic devices they were perpetually reminding the world that they were the successors of the Caesars; that the two Romes were linked by an indissoluble bond; and that to the latter had descended the heritage of glory and dominion acquired by the former. Herein we may admire that extraordinary sagacity which fixed on this spot, — the first, and certainly not the least striking, indication of the profound and unrivalled genius of Popery, — showing what that genius would become when fully developed and matured. The Seven Hills were the home of empire and the holy ground of superstition; and when the barbaric kings and nations approached the spot, they were fascinated and subdued by its mysterious and mighty influence, as the pontiffs had foreseen they would be. Thus the young Papacy had the penetration to discover that the sway of old Rome had by no means ended with her life, and, by serving itself heir to her name, continued to exercise her power long after she had gone to her grave. The genius that could turn to so great account the traditional glory of a departed empire was not likely to leave unimproved the existing resources of contemporary monarchies.

In the second place, the pontiffs claimed to be the successors of the apostles. This was a more masterly stroke of policy still. To the temporal dominion of the Caesars they added the spiritual authority of the apostles. It is here that the great strength of the Papacy lies. As the successor of Peter, the Pope was greater than as the successor of Caesar. The one gave him earth, but the other gave him heaven. The one made him a king; the other made him a king of kings. The one gave him the power of the sword, the other invested him with the still more sacred authority of the keys. The one surrounded him with all the adjuncts of temporal sovereignty, — guards, ambassadors, and ministers of State, — and set him over fleets and armies, imposts and revenues; the other made him the master of inexhaustible spiritual treasures, and enabled him to support his power by the sanctions and terrors of the invisible world. While he has celestial dignities as well as temporal honours wherewith to enrich his friends, he can wield the spiritual thunder as well as the artillery of earth, in contending with and discomfiting his foes. Such are the twin sources of pontifical authority. The Papacy stands with one foot on earth and the other in heaven. It has compelled the Caesars to give it temporal power, and the apostles to yield it spiritual authority. It is the ghost of Peter, with the shadowy diadem of the old Caesars.

Similar is the tendency and design of all the dogmas of the Papacy. These are but so many defences and outposts thrown up around the infallible chair of Peter: they are so many chains forged in the Vatican, and cunningly fashioned by Rome's artificers, for binding the intellect and the conscience of mankind. There is not one of the articles in her creed which is not fitted to exalt the priesthood and degrade the people. This is its main, almost its sole object. That creed, superstitious to the very core, exerts no wholesome influence upon the mind: it neither expands the intellect nor regulates the conscience. It does not set forth the grace of the Father, or the love of the Son, or the power of the Spirit. It has been framed with a far different object. It sets forth the grace of the pope, the power of the priest, and the efficacy of the sacrament. The pope, the priest, and the sacrament, are the triune with the mystery of which the creed of Popery is occupied. We have already pointed out the tendency of each of the separate articles as they passed in review before us, and it becomes unnecessary here to dwell upon them. Let it suffice to remark, that by the doctrine of *tradition* the priests are constituted the exclusive channels of divine revelation, and by the doctrine of *inherent efficacy* they become the only channels of divine influence. In the one case the people are entirely dependent upon them for all knowledge of the will of God; and in the other, they are not less dependent upon them for the enjoyment of divine blessings. It is easy to conceive how this tends to exalt this class of men. They have power *spiritually* to shut heaven, that it rain not upon the earth. By sprinkling a little water on the face of a child, the priest can remove all its guilt, and impart holiness to it. A whisper from the priest in the confessional can absolve from sin, or adjudge to eternal flames. By muttering a few words in Latin, he can create the flesh and blood, the soul and divinity, of Christ; and in saying mass, he can so regulate his intention as to direct its efficacy to any person he pleases, whether in this world or in the next. At his word the doors of purgatory are closed, and those of paradise fly open. He can raise to immortal bliss, or sink into eternal woe. These are tremendous powers; and the man who wields them, in the eyes of an ignorant people is not a mortal, but a god. "It is a most execrable thing," said Pope Paschal II., "that those hands which have received a power above that of angels, — which can by an act of their ministry create God himself, and offer him for the salvation of the world, — should ever be put into subjection of the hands of kings." The truths which the gospel makes known are intended to elevate the people; the dogmas of Romanism are intended to exalt only the priesthood, and to put the people under their feet. The miraculous power with which the Roman clergy are invested places them above kings; — they are raised to a level with the Deity himself.

Whatever order or government exists in society, Popery has had the art to seize and make subservient to her own aggrandizement. She infused herself into the governments of Europe. She possessed them, as it were, and made them really parts of herself. The various thrones of the west were but satrapies of the fisherman's chair. The princes that occupied them were always, in point of fact, and not unfrequently in point of conventional arrangement, the lieutenants and deputies of the Pope. They were taught that it was their glory to be so; that their crowns acquired new lustre by being laid at the feet of the successor of the apostles; and that their arms were ennobled and sanctified by being wielded in his service. The pontiff taught them that their life was bound up with his life; that without him they could not exist; and that in no way could they so effectually strengthen their own authority as by maintaining his. Thus did Popery poison at their source the springs of law and government, and bind the kings and kingdoms of Europe in one vast confederation against the interests of liberty and religion, and in support of that divinity who sat upon the Seven Hills. No doubt the members of that confederation sometimes quarrelled among themselves, and sometimes revolted against their sacerdotal master; but even when they hated the person of the Pope, they remained true to his system. They warred, it might be, against the pontiff, but they still were the yoke of the Papacy. They were revellers against Hildebrand or against Clement, but all the while they were obedient sons of the Church. In nothing does the genius of Popery appear more wonderful than in that it could bind to its chariot-wheel so many powerful and independent princes, and reconcile so many diverse and conflicting interests, and unite them all in support of itself.

If Popery has leant for aid upon civil government, and has known how to convert its functions into organs of its own, it has leant not less decidedly upon human nature, and has had the art to draw from it most substantial support. The nature of man it has profoundly studied, and thoroughly understands. There is not a faculty of his soul, nor a feeling of his heart, which is not known to it. There is not a phase of character nor a diversity of taste among the whole human race, of which it is not cognizant. Whatever talent it be which any of the sons of men possess, Popery will speedily discover it, and instantly find a fitting sphere for its exercise. Whether the faculty in question be a good or an evil one, matters wonderfully little, seeing Popery knows the secret of making both alike serviceable. It is a system adapted to man as he is. It runs parallel with the entire range of his hopes and his fears, his virtues and his passions. his eccentricities, his foibles, his tastes. There is no one therefore who will not find in Popery something that corresponds with his own predominant quality and taste. It is the most accomodating of all systems, and has therefore received an equal measure of attachment and support from men differing widely in their intellectual powers, their acquired tastes, and their moral dispositions. To the man of the world who delights in the glitter of show, and yields his submission only where he is dazzled by the splendour of rank, it presents a Church moulded on the pattern of earthly monarchies, — an imposing hierarchy, rising in successive ranks, throne above throne, from the barefooted friar up to Christ's vicar. To the man who is capable of being captivated with only an outward religion, here is a worship to his heart's content, — a gorgeous ritual, performed amidst the glories of architecture, of statuary, and of painting, amid the perfume of incense, the glare of lamps, and the swell of noble music. There is no revelation of God's holiness; there are no humbling views of the sinner's unworthiness and guilt communicated; everything is so contriven as powerfully to stir, not the conscience, which is left in its profound sleep, but the imagination; and to gratify, not the longings of the spiritual nature, which do not exist, but the cravings of the senses. In short, every ingredient that could intoxicate and madden, that could weaken reason and drown the man in delirium, has Rome mixed in her "witch's cauldron." The figure is almost apocalyptic, — the cup of sorcery.

To that large class of mankind who seek to reconcile their hopes of heaven with the indulgence of their passions, the religion of Popery is admirably adapted. The religion of Rome is not a *principle*, but a ritual; and the observance of that ritual will secure heaven, let the morals of the man be ever so corrupt. It is not necessary to part with any sin; no change of heart, no progress in holiness, is required; obedience to the Church is the one cardinal virtue. The want of this alone can damn a man. More lax and pliant than even Mahommedanism or Hinduism, there is not a ceremonial rite nor a moral duty in the system of Popery from which a few gold pieces may not purchase a dispensation. It is the most demoralizing of all idolatries. It spares the indolent man the trouble of inquiry, by presenting him with the infallibility. In fact, it makes his indolence a virtue, and thus, by sanctifying his vices, makes him more completely its slave. But farther, there is a lurking disposition in the heart of man to claim heaven as a debt due, rather than receive it as a free gift. This propensity Popery completely gratifies. Its grand characteristic, as a religious system, is *works*, in opposition to *faith*, — salvation by merit, in opposition to salvation by grace. And thus, while it traverses the grand idea of the gospel, it enlists on its side the pride of the human heart. This lays open to us one of the main sources of Popery's success. While the gospel is met by the whole force of unsanctified human nature, because it seeks to eradicate those principles which are naturally the most powerful in the heart of man, and to implant their opposites, Popery takes man as he is, and, without seeking to eradicate a single evil principle, finds him a sphere and sets him a-working. Passions already strong Popery nurtures into yet greater strength, and so creates a vast moving force within the man. If her fund of heavenly treasure be imaginary, not so her fund of earthly power. There exist within her pale elements of diverse character and tremendous force, and these Popery knows right well how to guide. The forces are completely under her control; and however noxious in themselves, and however destructive if left to act without restraint, she knows how to make them not only perfectly safe, but eminently serviceable. In few things is the genius of Popery more conspicuous than in this composition of forces, — this combination of elements the most various; so that from the utmost diversity of action there is educed at last the most perfect unity of result, and that result the aggrandizement of the Church. That Church provides convents for the ascetic and the mystic, carnivals for the gay, missions for the enthusiast, penances for the man suffering from remorse, sisterhoods of mercy for the benevolent, crusades for the chivalrous, secret missions for the man whose genius lies in intrigue, the Inquisition, with its racks and screws, for the man who combines detestation of heresy with the love of cruelty, indulgences for the man of wealth and pleasure, purgatory to awe the refractory and frighten the vulgar, and a subtle theology for the casuist and the dialectician. Within the pale of that Church there is work for all these labourers, and that too the very work in which each delights, while Rome reaps the fruit of all. "To him who would scourge himself into godliness," says Channing, speaking of the Church of Rome, "it offers a whip; for him who would starve himself into spirituality it provides the mendicant convents of St. Francis; for the anchorite it prepares the death-like silence of La Trappe; to the passionate young woman it presents the raptures of St. Theresa, and the marriage of St. Catherine with her Saviour; for the restless pilgrim, whose piety needs greater variety than the cell of the monk, it offers shrines, tombs, relics, and other holy places in Christian lands, and, above all, the holy sepulchre near Calvary. . . . When in Rome, the traveller sees by the side of the purple-lackeyed cardinal, the begging friar; when under the arches of St. Peter, he sees a coarsely-dressed monk holding forth to a ragged crowd; or when beneath a Franciscan church, adorned with the most precious works of art, he meets a charnel-house, where the bones of the dead brethren are built into walls, between which the living walk to read their mortality. He is amazed, if he give himself time for reflection, at the infinite variety of machinery which Catholicism has brought to bear on the human mind." "The unlettered enthusiast," says Macaulay, "whom the Anglican Church makes an enemy, and, whatever the polite and learned may think, a most dangerous enemy, the Catholic

Church makes a champion. She bids him nurse his beard, covers him with a gown and hood of coarse dark stuff, ties a rope round his waist, and sends him forth to teach in her name. He costs her nothing; he takes not a ducat away from the revenues of her beneficed clergy; he lives by the alms of those who respect his spiritual character and are grateful for his instructions; he preaches not exactly in the style of Massillon, but in a way which proves the passions of uneducated hearers; and all his influence is employed to strengthen the Church of which he is a minister. To that Church he becomes as strongly attached as any of the cardinals whose scarlet carriages and liveries crowd the entrance of the palace on the Quirinal. In this way the Church of Rome unites in herself all the strength of establishment and all the strength of dissent. With the utmost pomp of a dominant hierarchy above, she has all the energy of the voluntary system below."

But we have been able to unfold but a tithe of the wonderful and unrivalled genius of the Papacy. When one thinks of the amazing variety and endless diversity of qualities which here entered into combination, he feels as if the Papacy had summoned from their grave all the systems of policy and all the schemes of dominion which had ever existed, and, compelling them to lay bare the springs of their success and the elements of their strength, had selected the choicest qualities of each, and combined them into one system of unrivalled power. It united the subtle intellect of Greece with the iron strength of Rome. Qualities which never met before, Popery found out the means of reconciling and joining in harmonious action. The wildest enthusiasm and the soberest reason, the grossest sensuality and the most rigid asceticism, the most visionary genius and the coolest and most practical sagacity, the extreme of fanaticism and the extreme of moderation, Popery taught to dwell together in peace, and to work together in harmony. Nothing was so exalted as to be beyond its reach; nothing was so low as to be beneath its care. It accepted the labours of the peasant and the serf, and it taught the titled noble to stoop to its service. It arrayed itself in purple, and dwelt in the palace of kings; it put on rags, and companied with the outcast. Its marvellous flexibility made either character equally easy and equally natural. It entered with like avidity into the projects of princes, the intrigues of statesmen, the speculations of the learned, and the homely pursuits of the artizan. In this way the spell of its power was felt by all ranks of society and by all grades of intellect. Its spirit was operative at all times and in every place. To elude its eye or resist its arm was alike impossible. So terrible a system never before existed on the earth; and, once overthrown, it will, we trust, have no successor. Well may the Papacy be termed the perfection of human wisdom and the masterpiece of satanic policy.

Chapter II: Influence of Popery on the Individual Man.

The important question next presents itself, What is the INFLUENCE of this system? The system, we have shown, tried by the standard of Scripture and the test of reason, is thoroughly evil. Is the influence which it exerts also evil? This is a curious and a most important inquiry. It opens up a wide field, which, like some that have gone before it, we must hastily traverse, selecting only the more prominent of the proofs and evidences, and indicating rather than fully illustrating them. The subject resolves itself into three branches: — I. The influence of Romanism on the individual man. II. Its influence on Government. III. Its influence on society.

We shall confine ourselves to the first of these in the present chapter, — the influence of Romanism on the individual man. Religion is by far the most powerful agent that can act on man, and that for the following reasons. In the first place, its objective truths and its impelling motives infinitely transcend all others; and it is a law, not less in the moral than in the natural world, that the greatest *effect* must flow from the greatest *force*. In the second place, with religion is bound up man's own most important interests. Other departments of knowledge are speculative, or at best touch only the interests of time; but religion bears upon the entire of man's destiny. In the third place, it puts in motion the faculties of man in their natural order. As a moral being, man's moral sense is the moving faculty within him, and the intellectual powers are but its ministers and helps. Now, religion acts on the conscience, and the conscience calls into play the understanding, the affections, and the memory. In this way the mental powers act with the most ease and vigour, because this is their natural and healthful action. It is the action of life, not the action of spasmodic or galvanic effort. In the fourth place, religion acts *soonest* upon the mind. A child can feel its relations to God, and have its judgment and memory exercised about these relations, long before it is capable of a mental act in any other department of human knowledge. But for its religious exercises, which are always the earliest mental efforts of the child, years of intellectual dormancy would pass away, and when they came to an end, the child would bring to other subjects untrained and comparatively feeble powers. Besides, whatever makes the *first, coeteris paribus*, makes also the *deepest* impression upon the mind. In the fifth place, religion acts most *frequently* upon the mind. In early life especially, questions of duty must be of hourly occurrence. The decision of these questions involves the exercise of the reasoning powers. This is favourable to mental activity, and mental activity begets mental vigour. In the last place, religion acts upon the *greatest number*. Science, politics, and other subjects, have each their chosen disciples, but religion embraces all; for where is the rational being who cannot feel the force of its motives, and the extent to which his highest interests are involved in it? On all these grounds, we do not hesitate to affirm that religion, both as a motive power and as a moulding agent, wields over man, whether viewed individually or socially, an influence of such universal and resistless energy, that, compared with it, all other agencies are insignificant and powerless. Emphatically it is religion, — keeping out of view at present the unequal advantages of birth and of mental endowment, — it is religion that determines the social place and the terrestrial destiny of a man; it is religion that determines the social place and the terrestrial destiny of a nation. But we have already proved that Popery is opposed to Scripture, and contradicts reason. In the proportion in which it does so it is not religion; and in the proportion in which it is not religion, it does not possess and cannot exercise the influence we have described. It follows that the Papist is denied the benefit of an influence morally restorative and intellectually invigorating in an extraordinary degree, to all the extent to which Romanism comes short of religion. But we have already established that Popery is not merely a defective system of Christianity, — it is a system antagonistic to Christianity. It not only, therefore, does not possess the influence we have ascribed to Christianity, but it possesses an influence of a directly opposite character. It tends as much to degrade and pollute man's moral constitution as Christianity tends to elevate and purify it; and where the one quickens, expands, and strengthens the intellect, the other inflicts feebleness and torpor.

In proof of the vast intellectual quickening which Christianity always brings along with it, we may appeal to the state of the heathen world. The various nations of the earth occupy places on the intellectual scale ranged according to the proportion in which the elements of religion are retained among them. First come the more remote tribes, to whom the existence of a God is scarcely known, and whose mental powers scarce suffice to enable them to count ten successive numbers; next come the Hindoos of India, conspicuous alike for the grossness of their religious system and their utter intellectual and moral prostration; next in the intellectual scale come the various tribes of Western Asia, whose faith is Mahommedanism; then the popish nations of Southern and Western Europe; then the semi-popish nations of Northern Germany; and last of all, and very much in advance of all the others, are the Protestant nations of Britain and America. As is the religion of a people, the Bible being the standard according to which we judge of religion, so is the intellectual development and the social advancement of that people. This order obtains over all the earth. It cannot be regarded as a mere coincidence. To regard it as such would be not less unphilosophical than to regard as a mere coincidence the connection between stinted food and a dwarfed body, or that other connection which is found to exist in all ordinary cases between sufficient aliment and vigorous physical powers. A fact of such universal occurrence must necessarily have birth in some great and universal law. Neither climate, nor race, nor government, can solve the phenomenon. Solutions have often been attempted on one or other of these principles; but there are innumerable facts which defy solution on all of them, and which are soluble only with reference to the influence of religion. Not to mention other instances, we find in the very heart of the Mahommedan empire a small Christian society, — the Chaldeans of the Kurdish mountains. Their lovely and well-cultivated valleys, their clean, thriving villages, their pure morals, and cultivated manners and tastes, form a striking but most agreeable contrast to the barbarism, the sloth, the filth, and the vice, that on all sides surround them. They are under the same climate and government as their neighbours: in one thing only do they differ from them, and that is their religion. Thus, in all circumstances the influence of Christianity is the same. Here we find it, though existing in a very imperfect state, creating a very oasis of beauty in the midst of the waste wilderness of Mahommedan idolatry. And, to come nearer home, we have in Britain a striking fact standing in direct antagonism to the theory which resolves all these great national diversities into influence of race. We have the Celts of Ireland and the Celts of Scotland standing at the very antipodes of the moral and social scale. But we have not only the proof from analysis; the proof from direct experiment is equally conclusive. All our missionaries declare, that when Christianity is brought to bear upon the native mind of India, it brings a striking intellectual change along with it. Even where it stops short of conversion, it elevates the man from the mass of his countrymen: even where it does not bestow the heart of the Christian, it bestows the intellect of the European. There is a visible quickening and expansion of all the powers, intellectual and moral. The vast transformation which Christianity wrought on the islands of the Pacific is well known. She found these islands the abode of cannibalism, and she made them the home of the moral and industrial virtues. In short, what clime or tribe has Christianity visited where she did not bring in her train all the elements of terrestrial happiness?

If, as a wide induction of facts establishes, the religion of the Bible is by far the most powerful agent in quickening the intellect, and starting nations in a career of progress, and if, as we have already proved, Romanism is not the religion of the Bible, it follows that Romanism is devoid of this life-dispensing power. But further, if Romanism be a system the spirit of which is antagonistic to the religion of the Bible, as we have shown it to be, it follows that its influence on the mind of man is antagonistic also, — is as pernicious and destructive as that of religion is wholesome and beneficial. We might safely rest the matter, as regards the influence of Rome, on these general grounds; but we shall go a little into particulars, and show, first, from the *doctrines*, and, second, from the *practice*, of the Church of Rome, that the practical tendency and working of the system is ruinous in no ordinary degree.

We take first the doctrine of infallibility. Can anything be conceived more fitted to crush all intellectual vigour than such a doctrine? As an infallible Church, Rome presents her votaries with a system of dogmas, not a few of which are opposed to reason, and some of them even to the senses. These dogmas are not to be investigated; the person must not attempt to reconcile them to reason, or to the evidence of his senses; he must not attempt even to understand them; they are simply to be believed. If he demands grounds for this belief, he is told that he is committing mortal sin, and perilling his salvation. Here is all action of the mind interdicted, under the highest sanctions. The person is taught that he cannot commit a greater crime than to think; that he cannot more grievously offend against his Creator than by using the powers his Creator has endowed him with. Thus, while the first effect of Christianity is to quicken the intellect, the first effect of Romanism is to strike it with torpor. She inexorably demands of all her votaries that they denude themselves of their understandings and their senses, and prostrate them beneath the wheels of this Juggernaut of hers. While the Protestant is occupied in investigating the grounds of his creed, in tracing the relations of its various truths, and in following out their consequences, the mind of the Roman Catholic is all the while lying dormant. As the bandaged limb loses in time the power of motion, so faculties not used become at length incapable of use. A timid disposition, an inert habit, is produced, which is not confined to religion, but extends to every subject with which the person has to do. His reason is shut up in a cave, and infallibility rolls a great stone to the cave's mouth.

Not less injurious to the intellect is the doctrine of absolute and unreserved submission to ecclesiastical superiors. If the former afflicts with mental imbecility, this deals a fatal blow to mental independence. The Church issues her command, and the person has no alternative but instant, unquestioning, blind obedience. He acts not from the power of motive, but, like the beast of burden, is urged forward by the rod. Here are the two prime qualities of man destroyed. The one doctrine robs him of his strength, the other of his freedom: the one makes him an intellectual paralytic, the other a mental slave. To this double depth of weakness and servility does Popery degrade her victims.

The leading idea of Popery as a scheme of salvation is, that the sacraments impart grace and holiness, — the *opus operatum*. It is hard to say whether this inflicts greater injury upon the intellectual or the spiritual part of man. It injures vitally his spiritual part, because it teaches him not to look beyond the sacrament and the priest: it substitutes these in the room of the Saviour. The intellectual part it no less vitally injures: it cuts off that train of mental action, that intellectual process, to which the gospel so naturally and beautifully gives rise, by joining works with faith, the sinner's own efforts with the grace of the Spirit. Under the system of Popery, not a single quality or disposition need be cultivated; not the reason and judgment, for the Papist is forbidden to exercise these; not the power of sustained and patient effort, for all for which the Christian has to pray, and labour, and wait, is in the case of the Papist conferred in an instant, in virtue of the *opus operatum*: his power of self-scrutiny, his self-denial, and his self-control, all lie dormant. Here are the noblest and most useful of the moral and mental faculties, which Christianity carefully trains and invigorates, all blighted and destroyed by Popery. The very idea of progress is extinguished in the mind. The man is stereotyped in immobility. He is given over to the dominion of indolence, and shrinks from the very idea of forethought and reflection, and effort of every kind, as the most disagreeable of all painful things. These qualities the man carries with him into every department of life and labour; for he cannot be reflective, persevering and self-denied in one thing, and slothful, self-indulgent, and devoid of thought in another. Need we wonder at the vast disparity between Papists and Protestants generally? When called to compete with another man in the field of science or of industry, the Papist cannot, at the mere bidding of his will, call up those faculties so necessary to success, which the evil genius of his religion has so fatally cramped.

Faith is one of the master faculties of the soul. It is indispensable to strength of purpose, grandeur of aim, and that indomitable persevering effort which guides to success. But faith Popery extinguishes as systematically as Christianity cherishes it. She hides from view the grand objects of faith. For a Saviour in the heavens, who can be seen only by faith, she substitutes a saviour on the altar. For the blessings of the Spirit, to be obtained by faith, she substitutes grace in the sacrament. Heaven at last is to be obtained, not by faith on the divine promise, but by the mystic virtue of a sacrament operating as a charm. Thus Popery robs *faith* of all her functions. That noble power which descries glory from afar, and which bears the soul on unfaltering wing across the mighty void, to that distant land, teaching it in its passage the hardy virtue of endurance, and the ennobling faculty of hope and of trust in God, — lessons so profitable to the intellect as well as to the soul of man, has under the Papacy no room to act. In the room of faith, Popery, as is her wont, substitutes the counterfeit quality, — credulity; and a credulity so vast, that it receives without hesitation or question the most monstrous dogmas, however plainly opposed to Scripture and to reason.

In short, Popery teaches her votaries to devolve upon the priesthood the whole responsibility and the whole care of their salvation. The well-known case of the late Duke of Brunswick is no caricature, but is simply a plain and honest statement, — though not such, we admit, as a Jesuit would have given, — of the real state of matters in the Romish Church. "The Catholics to whom I spoke concerning my conversion," says the Duke, when assigning his reasons for embracing the Roman Catholic religion, "assured me that if I were to be damned for embracing the Catholic faith, they were ready to answer for me at the day of judgment, and to take my damnation upon themselves, — an assurance I could never extort from the ministers of any sect in case I should live and die in their religion." Thus the Church teaches her votaries that religion is entirely dissociated from morals; that it is to no purpose for one to put himself to the trouble of cultivating any one moral or spiritual quality — to no purpose to deny one's self any gratification, however sinful; that one may live in the flagrant violation of every one of the commandments of God, provided only he be obedient to the commandments of the Church; and the sum and substance of the Church's commandments is, that he practise a ritual associated with no act or feeling of the soul, and which produces in return no spiritual effect, and that whenever he fails in this somewhat monotonous and dreary task, he be ready with his money to pay for masses and indulgences. Thus the very first principles of morality are struck at. But the point we meant to bring mainly into view here is the habit of mind thus produced, which is that of sitting still, and leaving all which it belongs to one to do, to be done for him by others. This is fatal to the energy, not less than to the morality, of the man. It teaches him the needlessness of effort; it extinguishes the principle of self-reliance, and teaches the duty of divesting one's self of all care and forethought, — a habit of mind which, when acquired in the important matter of salvation, is sure to be carried into other and interior departments of life. It would form a curious subject of enquiry how far the feeling which leads Roman Catholics to lean so decidedly upon the priesthood for the life to come, is akin to that which leads them to lean so decidedly upon governments, and so little upon themselves, as respects the present life. The fiat of a priest, without any labour of theirs, can give them heaven, with all its happiness: why should not the fiat of a statesman, without any labour of theirs, be able to give them earth, with all its enjoyments? We have only to transfer their modes of thinking and their habits of action on the subject of religion, to matters of this world, and we have the woeful picture of sloth, and decay, and want of forethought, which Roman Catholic countries almost uniformly indicate. The internal powers of the individual Catholic lying undeveloped and running to waste, form but the type of his country lying neglected, with all its rich resources locked up in its bosom, because the poor popery-stricken man has neither skill nor energy to develop them. The one is more than the type of the other: they stand related as cause and effect.

Such are the characters whom Popery is fitted to create: such are the characters it does create. Every noble faculty it chills into torpor and death. The understanding of the man lies crushed beneath the dogmas of his Church: his independence is overborne by an infallible priesthood: his very senses are blunted; for Popery judges it unsafe to leave her miserable victims in possession even of these, and therefore she systematically outrages them in some of the more awful of her mysteries. And conscience, which, did the moral sense survive, might rise in its strength, and rending asunder these fetters of brass, set free the intellectual powers, Popery drugs, by her horrid opiates, into a death-slumber. A more pitiable and hopeless condition it is impossible to imagine. The man is divested of almost all that is distinctive of man. He becomes a mere machine in the hands of Popery. He trembles to assert his manhood. And these unreflective and slavish habits are inwrought into the very being of the man by daily iterations, and they attend him in every avocation of life, proving a certain source of failure and mortification.

Of the *practice* of Popery, as tending to degrade, we shall have a more legitimate opportunity of speaking when we come to exhibit the influence of Romanism upon society. And as regards the influence of the system upon the religious character of the man, we have so fully entered into this already, when discussing the several dogmas of Popery. that we do not here return to it.

Chapter III: Influence of Popery on Government.

To religion must we ever assign the foremost place among those beneficent agencies which the Creator has ordained to mould the character and determine the destinies of individuals and nations. She moves in her sphere on high, having no companion to share her place, and no rival to divide her influence. Nevertheless, there are secondary causes at work in moulding individual and national character, and amongst the most important of these we are to class government. Government, as regards its substance, though not its form, is an ordinance of God, intended, and eminently fitted, to conserve the order and promote the happiness of society. It is one of those things which must of necessity be a great blessing or a great curse. It will be the one or the other, according to its character; and its character will be mainly dependent upon the action of religion upon it. Wherever Christianity exists, she creates a standard of public morals, and purifies the whole tone of opinion and feeling. These soon come to influence the acts of the national administration, and to be embodied in the laws of the state; and as the stream can never rise higher than its source, so the morality of the law can never be higher than that to which Christianity has already elevated public sentiment and opinion. As is the Christianity of a country, so will be its laws and government. With a sound healthy Christianity, we will have wise laws, upright judges, independent and patriotic rulers, who will maintain the national honour, guard the public rights, and keep inviolate the homes and altars of a country. With the departure or corruption of religion will come the depression of public sentiment and morals; and the degeneracy rapidly extending to those who make and who execute the laws, there will soon be but too much reason to complain of the injustice of the one and the dishonesty of the other. The decay of religion has ever been signalized by the prostration of public principle, the betrayal of the national honour, the invasion of conscience, and the violation of the security and sanctity of the family. The decay of primitive Christianity and the rise of Popery were attended by all the evils we have now specified. The influence of the latter on law and government was of the most pernicious kind, and palpable as pernicious. As Popery waxed in strength, so did the corruption and oppression of government, till at last they grew to an intolerable height. The destruction which Popery works on individual character we have just had occasion to state; but in the department of government it has had more room to operate, and here it has left traces of its evil genius, if not more frightful, at least more palpable. This opens to us a new aspect of Popery.

Popery has corrupted government both in its *theory* and in its *practice*.

It has corrupted the theory of government. God has ordained twin powers in the moral firmament, — the civil and the ecclesiastical jurisdictions; and on the due maintenance of this duality depends the liberties of the world. As the organs of the individual are double, so those of society are double also. The same precaution which God has taken to preserve those bodily organs on which the existence of the individual so much depends, has he taken to preserve those essential to the wellbeing of society. If one is destroyed, the other remains. These two jurisdictions are distinct in their nature and in their objects. They occupy co-ordinate spheres, each being independent within its own province. This is a beautiful arrangement; it maintains an admirable harmony of forces; and so long as that balance remains undestroyed, the rights of society cannot be vitally or permanently injured. These two co-ordinate jurisdictions resemble two friendly and independent kingdoms, between whom a league offensive and defensive has been formed; so that whenever one is attacked and in danger of being overborne, the other hastens to its succour. The history of the world shows that civil liberty and ecclesiastical bondage cannot stand together, and that the converse of the proposition is true, — a people spiritually free cannot long remain politically enslaved. Thus has God provided a double safeguard for liberty. Driven from the one domain, she can retreat into the other. Expelled from the first ditch, she can make good her stand in the second. The outer rampart of civil independence may be demolished; she can maintain the battle, and, it may be, conquer, from the inner citadel. The present eventful period demonstrates not less clearly than preceding ones, that the two liberties are bound up together, and that they must fight and conquer, or sink and perish, together. But the modern Delilah found out wherein lay the great strength of the strong man. Popery confounded and incorporated the civil and the spiritual jurisdictions. This union, instead of bringing strength, as union generally does, brought weakness. It was a fatal blow aimed at the existence of both liberties. It put manacles upon the arm of both. Herein lay the great crime of Popery against the rights of society, and especially against the purity and efficiency of that order of government which God had ordained for the good of men. This act laid a foundation for the most monstrous usurpations and the most intolerable oppressions.

This error grew directly out of the fundamental principle of the Papacy. That principle is, that the Pope is the successor of the Prince of the Apostles, and the Vicar of Christ. In virtue of this assumed character, the pontiff claimed to wield on earth the whole of that jurisdiction which Christ possesses in heaven, — to stand at the head of the civil as well as of the spiritual estate, — and to be as really a king of kings as he was a bishop of bishops. From the moment this claim was advanced, all distinction between the two jurisdictions vanished, and a kind of government was set up in Europe which was neither secular nor spiritual, and which can be described only as a mongrel creation, in which the qualities of both were so mixed and jumbled, that while all the evil incident to both was carefully preserved, scarce an iota of the good was retained. This hybrid rule was of course styled government, but it had ceased to fulfil any one function of government, and it set itself systematically to oppose and defeat every end which a wise government strives to attain. This form of government was essentially, and to an enormous extent, irresponsible and arbitrary. For, *first*, it was a theocracy. God's vicegerent stood at the head of it. He was bound to render no reasons for what he did. He claimed to be an infallible ruler. He could plead divine authority for the most enormous of his usurpations and the most despotic of his acts. He had an infallible right to violate oaths, dethrone princes, and lay whole provinces waste. What would have been atrocious wickedness in another man, was in him the emanation of infallible wisdom and immaculate holiness. Against a power so irresponsible and tremendous it was in vain that conscience or reason opposed their force, or law its sanctions. These were met by an authority immeasurably superior to them all, at whose slightest touch their obligations and claims were annihilated. Reason and law it utterly ignored. 'The necessary co-relative of infallible authority is unquestioning obedience. It was the right of one to command, — the duty of all others to obey. He who presumed to scrutinize, or find fault, or resist, was taught that he was committing rebellion against God, and incurring certain and eternal damnation. A theocracy truly! It was the reign of the devil, baptized with the name of God.

But, in the second place, this scheme of government centralized all power in one man. This centralization is of the very nature of the Papacy. The vicegerent of God can have no equal; none can share his power; he must reign alone. It would be equally absurd to suppose that an infallible ruler could admit constitutional advisers, or take himself bound to follow their counsel. If the course they recommend is wrong, the infallible pontiff cannot follow it; and if it is right, infallibility surely does not need fallible prompters to tell him so: this, it is presumed, is the very course in which the pontiff would move if left to the guidance of his own supernatural instincts. The popes cannot admit, therefore, of a *consulta*, or popular assembly with judicial and legislative functions, such as those which in constitutional countries limit the prerogatives and divide the authority of the sovereign. In the hands of one man, then, all power under heaven came to be centred, — the legislative and the judicial, the temporal and the spiritual jurisdictions. The papal theory placed the fountain of law and authority on the Seven Hills, and there was not an edict passed nor an act done in wide Europe, but virtually the Pope was the doer of it. For ages as was the theory, so substantially was the fact. It would have been one of the greatest miracles the world ever saw if liberty had co-existed with this vast accumulation of power. Even in the hands of the wisest of men, fettered by constitutional checks, and bound to assign the reasons of his procedure, such overgrown power could scarce have failed to be abused; and if abused, the abuse could not be other than enormous; but in the hands of men who claimed to reign by divine delegation, and who on that ground sustained themselves as above the necessity of vindicating, or so much as explaining, their proceedings, and who claimed from men an implicit belief that even the most outrageous of their acts were founded on divine authority and embodied infallible wisdom, the abuse of this power far surpassed the measure of all former tyrannies. The despotism of an Alexander, a Nero, or a Napoleon, was liberty itself compared with the centralized despotism of the Papacy.

In the third place, the theory of the papal government necessarily and stringently excluded every particle of the democratic element. Its pretensions to infallibility and to a divine origin made it arrogate all power to itself, and utterly repudiate the claims of all others to participation or control. It abhorred the popular element, whether in the shape of constitutional chambers or constitutional advisers, or checks of any kind. The people were debarred from all share, direct or indirect, in the government. Their place was blind, unreasoning, implicit submission. Nor could the Papacy have admitted them to the smallest privilege of this sort without renouncing the fundamental principle on which it is built.

In the fourth place, though in one respect the most centralized of all tyrannies, the Papacy was in another the most diffused. The great primal Papacy occupied the Seven Hills, but it had power to multiply itself, — to reproduce its own image, — till Europe came to be studded and covered with minor Papacies. Each kingdom was a distinct Papacy on a small scale. This arrangement consummated the despotism of the papal rule, by making its sphere as wide as its rigour was intolerable. Had Rome not confounded the temporal and spiritual jurisdictions, matters would not have been so bad. Had the pontiffs confined their pretensions as divine rulers within the ecclesiastical domain, men might have enjoyed some measure of civil freedom, and that would have mitigated somewhat the iron yoke of ecclesiastical bondage; but all distinction between the provinces was obliterated; the pretensions of the Pope extended alike over both, not leaving an inch of ground on which liberty might plant her foot. Practically throughout Europe the two domains were confounded. If the Pope was the vicegerent of God, the kings were the vicegerents of the Pope, and, of course, the vicegerents of God at the distance of one remove. The same twofold character which the pontiff possessed, he permitted, for his own ends, every monarch under him to assume. They were kings by divine right, — accountable only to the Pope, as he to God. Thus did the Pope succeed in extending his sway far beyond the limits of the States of the Church. He reduced the whole of western Europe under the rule of the Papacy, by planting his system of government in each of its kingdoms, and by making its various kings dependents on the chair of Peter. There was not a single ruler, of whatever degree, from the monarch down to the petty subaltern, within the wide limits of the papal empire, who was not a limb of the Papacy, and who had not his place and his function assigned him in that vast and terrible organization which the popes set up for overawing and oppressing the world, and aggrandizing themselves. How religion was desecrated by this unhallowed connection between Church and State, — this monstrous blending of things civil and sacred, — we need not explain. Heaven was sought only to obtain earth; and religion was employed only to cover the basest practices, to palliate the most revolting crimes, and to vindicate the most enormous usurpations. The words of the poet are strikingly descriptive of a policy which, the more it pointed towards heaven, the more directly did it tend to hell.

"Quantum vertice ad auras
Aetherias, tantum radice in Tartara tendit."

But we dishonour religion by giving that holy name to what was so called within the Church of Rome. The piety of the times, as we have already shown, was essentially and undisguisedly paganism. Religion, appalled by these gigantic corruptions, which had only borrowed her name the more effectually to counterwork her purpose, had fled, to bury herself in the caves of the earth, or to find a shelter amid eternal snows and inaccessible cliffs. A vast theocracy wielded the destinies of Europe. A blind, irresponsible, and infallible despotism, issuing its decrees from behind a veil which mortal dared not lift, sat enthroned upon the rights and liberties, the conscience and the intellect, the souls and the bodies, of men. Such was the Papacy! — a monstrous compound of spiritual and temporal power, — of old idolatries and Christian forms, — of secret frauds and open force, — of roguery and simplicity, — of perfidies, hypocrisies and villanies of all sorts and degrees, — of priests and soldiers, — of knaves and fools, — of monks, friars, cardinals, kings, and popes, — of mountebanks of every kind, hypocrites of every class, and villains of every grade, — all banded together in one fearful conspiracy, to defy God and ruin man!

So deeply did Popery corrupt the theory of government. First of all, it confounded the two jurisdictions, and then set over them a head claiming to be divine and infallible, thus paving the way for encroachments to any extent on the conscience on the one hand, and on civil rights and liberties on the other. It enabled the sacerdotal autocrat to support his temporal usurpations by spiritual sanctions, and his spiritual domination by secular arms. And this form of government, moreover, necessarily implied the accumulation of all authority in the hands of one man, forming a centralized despotism such as had never before existed. It was also of the nature of this government that it absolutely excluded every iota of the constitutional or democratic element. Farther, being based on an element of a spiritual kind, it was not confined within political boundaries, but extended equally over all states, making Rome everywhere, and the world but one vast province, and its various governments but one irresponsible despotism.

These corruptions in the theory of government led necessarily and directly to grievous corruptions in its practice. In truth, the government of the Papacy, — the only government known for ages to Europe, — was but one enormous abuse. First, the Papacy, in self-defence, was compelled to retain its subjects in profound darkness. It knew that should light break in, its reign must terminate, seeing its pretensions were incapable of standing an hour's scrutiny. Obeying, therefore, the instincts of self-preservation, the Papacy was the great conservator of ignorance, — the uncompromising and truculent foe of knowledge. "Let there be light," was the first command issued by the Creator. "Let there be darkness," said Popery, when about to erect her dominion. The darkness fell fast enough, and deep enough. First, the great lights of revelation, kindled by God to keep piety and liberty alive on the earth, were extinguished. Next, classical learning was discouraged, and fell into disrepute. History, science, and every polite study, shared the same fate. They were denounced as wolves; and Rome, the mighty hunter, chased them from the earth. The arts perished. If painting, sculpture, and music survived, it was solely because Popery needed them for her own base purposes. But their cultivation, so far from tending to refine or elevate the general mind, powerfully contributed to enfeeble and pollute it. These arts were the handmaids of superstition, resembling beautiful captives bound to the chariot-wheel of some dark Ethiopic divinity. Thus the earth came a second time to be peopled by a race of barbarians. Italy herself became ignorant of letters. The ancient polytheisms possessed no such cramping effect on the genius of man. Greece and Rome established schools, patronized learning, and encouraged efforts to excell. Of all superstitions, that of Popery has been found the most injurious to the human intellect. She found the world civilized, and she sunk it into barbarism. She found the mind of man grown to manhood comparatively, and she reduced it into second childhood. She polluted and emasculated it by her foul rites, and the singularly absurd, ridiculous, and childish doctrines which formed the scholastic theology, the only intellectual food of the middle ages. She was the enemy of science, as well as of the Bible. Some of its earliest and most brilliant discoveries she placed under anathema, and she rewarded with a dungeon some of its most illustrious pioneers. Had the Papacy had her will, our knowledge of the world would have been not a whit more extensive than was that of the ancients. The Atlantic would have lain to this day unploughed by keel; and America would still have been hid in the mysterious regions of the unexplored west. The great law of gravitation, which first certified to man the order and grandeur of the universe, would still have been undiscovered; and the whole furniture of the heavens, fixed in their crystalline spheres, would have been performing a diurnal revolution round our little earth. We would have been trembling at eclipses, and helpless before the power of disease and pestilence. We would still have been engrossed in the pursuits of alchemy and judicial astrology, discussing quidlibets and quodlibets, and, for our spiritual food, listening to the mendacious legends of the saints. We would have been moved to compassion by the example of St. Francis, who divided his cloak with the mendicant, — stimulated to zeal by the story of Anthony, who sailed to St. Petersburg on a millstone to convert the Russians, — fortified against temptation by the courage of St. Dunstan, who led Satan about with a pair of red-hot pincers, when he tempted him in the likeness of a fair lady, — exhorted against the fear of danger by the story of St. Denis, who carried his head half a dozen miles after it was separated from his body, and schooled into devotion by St. Anthony of Padua's mule, which, after three days' fasting, left his provender to worship the host. Had the Papacy had her will, Milton would never have sung, Bacon and Locke would never have reasoned, the classic page of Erasmus and Buchanan would have remained unwritten, the steam-engine would still have been to be invented, and the age of mechanical marvels, which ennoble our cities, and give to man the dominion of the elements, would have been still to come. Our ships would have carried from our shores other products than those of our learning, our science, and our industry; and would have returned laden, not with those varied commodities with which distant countries abound, and of which ours is destitute, but with papal bulls, beads, crucifixes, indulgences, dispensations, and occasionally excommunications and interdicts. If our temporal wealth would have been less, our spiritual comforts would have been much greater. What rare and precious relics would have stocked our museums, sanctified our churches, enriched our homes, and protected our persons! We would have been able to boast of the legs, arms, toes, fingers, and skulls of great saints who flourished more than a thousand years ago, and eke the arms, fingers, and toes of saints who never flourished at all, but the virtue of whose relics is not a whit the less on that account. We would have possessed the pairings of their nails, the clippings of their beard, some locks of their hair, mayhap a tooth, or a rag of their raiment, or the thong with which they scourged themselves. We might have possessed one of the many hundred legs of Balaam's ass, a bit of the ark, or a nail from the true cross. In short, there would have been no end to the store of venerable lumber that might have enriched our island, but for our quarrel with Rome. True, we could not have had our science, to which nothing is impossible; nor our commerce, which encircles the globe. We could not have bored through mountains, or spanned mighty rivers and friths, or erected noble beacons amid the waves. We could not have bridged over the Atlantic, or brought India and China to our very doors, the products of whose climes stock our markets and lade our boards. Nothing, of all this would we have had; but we would have been more than compensated by the profitable trade we should have driven with Rome in the spiritual wares with which she has enriched all those nations who have trafficked with her.

For ages before the Reformation, the Church of Rome, with the wealth of western Europe at her command, did nothing for learning, beyond patronizing some of the fine arts mainly for her own ends. Since the sixteenth century, Rome has been obliged to alter her policy, not in reality, but in appearance. The Jesuits, finding that the human mind had escaped from its dungeon, ostentatiously took up a position in the van of the movement, that they might lead the nations back to their old prison. In those countries, such as Spain and Italy, into which the Reformation had not introduced letters, these zealous educators, the Jesuits, made no effort to disturb the primeval night. Ignorance is the mother of devotion, and they were unwilling to deprive the natives of so great a help to piety. But in other countries, such as Poland, where the Protestants had erected schools and colleges, the Jesuits dogged the steps of the Protestant teacher. They opened schools, and professed to teach, taking care, however, to convey the smallest amount of knowledge. They kept the youth studying the grammar of Alvar for ten or a dozen years, and learning almost nothing besides. The Augustan era of Polish literature and that of the Protestant ascendancy in Poland, were contemporaneous. When the Jesuits began to educate, literature began to decline; and the period of the Jesuit influence is the least intellectual and the least literary in the history of Poland. It has been the same in all other countries. The Roman Catholics kept Ireland as a preserve of ignorance for ages, and never thought of erecting school or college in it (Maynooth excepted), till the Protestants began to erect schools. And their teaching in the Irish schools is of such a kind as warrants us in saying, that the great outcry they have made is, not for liberty to educate, but for liberty not to educate. In St. Patrick's Roman Catholic school, Edinburgh, instances have been frequent of children four years at school, and yet unable to put two letters together, and of others who had been at school for ten years, and who could not read. The Jesuits build schools, and appoint schoolmasters, not to educate, but to lock up youth in prisons, miscalled schools, as a precaution against their being educated. But it is unnecessary to particularize. In all ages and in all countries the Papacy has leant upon ignorance. It has been one of the grand instruments by which it has ruled mankind. Its *acme* was the midnight of the world. Idolatry came in with a *promise of knowledge*, — "Ye shall be as gods, knowing good and evil;" but it perpetuated its reign through the *fact of ignorance*.

The Papacy employed to an unprecedented extent *espionage* in its system of government. Despotism is always base; and the Papacy, as the most despotic, has also been the basest of governments. Former tyrannies employed spies and laid snares, to discover their subjects' secrets or anticipate plots; but the Papacy had the merit of establishing a regular system, by which it took cognizance of thought, and made it as amenable to its tribunal as actions and words to other governments. This it accomplished by the machinery of the confessional. All were obliged to confess, These confessions were sent to Rome; so that there was not a thought or a purpose which was not known at head-quarters. This invested the Pope with omniscience. Not only did he know all that was *done* and *spoken*, but all that was *thought*, throughout his empire. From the Seven Hills he could see into every home and into every heart. Europe lay "naked and open" beneath his eye. What a tremendous power! Hitherto, under the most intolerable tyrannies, men's thoughts were free. Words the tyrant might punish; thoughts defied his power. But under the Papacy no man dared to think. He felt that the eye of Rome was looking into his bosom. She could drag him into the confessional, and compel him by the threat of eternal flames, to lay open his whole soul. From her eye nothing was hid. And to what purpose did she turn this knowledge of the secrets of men? To the purpose of strengthening her own dominion, and sinking her foundations so deep, that every attempt should be in vain to unsettle or raze them.

But again, the papal government effected the prostitution of the civil power to an enormous extent. The distinction between the functionaries of the Church and of the State was maintained, doubtless, during the middle ages. But civil government as distinct from spiritual government was scarcely known in these times. There was, in fact, during the dominancy of the Papacy but one government in Europe, as we have already shown, — a heterogeneous compound of temporal and spiritual authority, which took cognizance of all causes, and arrogated jurisdiction over all persons and all kingdoms. The Papacy was the uniting bond and the animating spirit of this system. But from this parent corruption, which we have already illustrated, there sprung innumerable lesser corruptions. One of these was the subjection and prostitution of the civil power to the ecclesiastical, and the perpetration of acts of tyranny in the State, in order to uphold a yet more odious tyranny in the Church. The Church of Rome felt that she could not reign by enlightening the conscience, and therefore she reigned by coercing it. Her union with the State enabled her to employ, as often as she would, the secular arm for the somewhat anomalous purpose of compelling obedience and enforcing belief. The policy of every government within the limits of the Roman Catholic Church was prompted by Rome, was papal in its essence, and insidiously managed for the interests of the Vatican. Not only were kings themselves the slaves of Rome, and not only did they feel that to rebel against her was to rebel against heaven; but they laboured to make their subjects her slaves also, feeling that a people bound in the fetters of the Church were thereby more amenable to regal authority. This supposed identification of their interests with that of Rome made them zealous supporters of her pretensions. They willingly give the force of law to her bulls; they lent the pageantry of state to her worship; well knowing that nothing awes the mind of the vulgar like state authority. The Pope and the King were the two divinities which the Europe of the dark ages adored. But further, not only did the vicious element of sacerdotalism infect the secular government, but that government was to a large degree administered by sacerdotal persons. Cardinals and priests were in innumerable instances the public ministers and secret advisers of monarchs. This was to some extent a matter of necessity, inasmuch as in that age the knowledge of letters and of business was confined almost entirely to ecclesiastics. But the practice was encouraged by Rome, who was able thus to penetrate the secrets and control the policy of governments. Thus all things, great and small, originated with the Papacy. The wars that convulsed Europe grew out of the intrigues of Rome. Princes were exalted to thrones, or hurled from them, according as it suited her interests. The wealth of the state was employed to debauch conscience, and the arm of its power to punish opinion.

If any of the governments recalcitrated, and refused to degrade themselves by doing the vile work of Rome, she speedily found means to reduce them to obedience. She knew the power of the superstition which she wielded; she knew that it placed in her hands the control of the masses, as well as of governments; and thus she could employ the people to overawe the throne, as well as the throne to oppress the people. She had but to issue her interdict, and the ties that bound subjects to their sovereign were dissolved, their oaths of allegiance annulled, and rebellion against their persons and government preached as a sacred duty; so that the unhappy prince had no alternative but to make his peace with Rome, or abdicate. At one time the Church of Rome has taught the doctrine of the divine right of kings, and at another she has propagated the opinion that the people are the source of sovereignty, as was done in France during the reign of Henry III., who joined the Protestants. So long as princes were submissive to the Romish see, their persons were sacred; the moment they revolted, their assassination was recommended as a holy service, and the crown of glory was held out to the murderer. Rome, to use her own phraseology, laid "the axe at the root of the evil tree," with orders "to cut it down." Herein lay the real supremacy of Rome, — not in her theoretic headship, which the kings of Europe acknowledged only at times, but in her actual headship, which was founded on the power of her all-pervading superstition. She filled Europe with darkness, and through that darkness became omnipotent. This made her the mistress of men's minds, and through that she became the mistress also of their bodies and their properties. When her voice sounded through the gloom, men heard it as if it had been the voice of God, trembled, and obeyed.

Another enormous abuse grew out of the sacerdotal government of Rome, namely, the maxim that princes are the constituted guardians of orthodoxy in their dominions, and are bound to employ their swords in the extirpation of heresy and heretics. This doctrine the Church of Rome wrote in blood in every country of Europe. A grievous perversion it was of the ends of civil government, and it led directly to persecution for conscience' sake. The Church of Rome has earned for herself unrivalled notoriety as a persecutor. Pagan Rome shed the blood of the saints, but papal Rome was drunk with the blood of the saints. We have already alluded to the numbers who, in the twelfth century, in central Europe, held the pure doctrines of the New Testament, and protested against the Church of Rome as the Antichrist of Scripture. These confessors abounded in the southern provinces of France, in the valley of the Rhine, in Lombardy, and in Bohemia. They occupied a belt of country of considerable breadth on both sides of the Alps, stretching from the mouths of the Po to those of the Garonne. They were as distinguished from their neighbours by the skill and industry with which they prosecuted arts and manufactures, as by their extraordinary acquaintance with the Scriptures, and the pure morality of their lives. The Reformation would have broken out in that century, or in the first half of the next, but for the violent and bloody measures of Rome. She saw the danger, she unsheathed the sword; nor did she return it to its scabbard till scarce a man remained to carry tidings of the catastrophe to posterity. The three centuries that preceded the Reformation were one continued massacre. The armed force of western Europe, led on by Rome, was employed to crush a peaceful and industrious, a virtuous and a loyal people, guiltless, but for the crime of refusing to bow the knee to the Dagon of the Seven Hills. Southern France became a perfect shambles. The Alps were swept with fire and sword. Bohemia and the Rhine were overwhelmed with armies, with dungeons, and with scaffolds. Three centuries of crimes, of wars, of bloodshed, at length completed their revolution, and Rome was able to announce that heresy was now exterminated, — drowned in blood. Crimes unparalleled! The French statesman would have said, folly unparalleled; and in sooth it was so. It was the flower of their subjects which these princes had destroyed. The towns they had converted into smoking ruins were the seats of trade and industry. The men whose blood dyed the soil and the rivers of their land were the stay of order. The vast armaments and the successive wars maintained by these zealous vassals of Rome inferred enormous expense. This double damage, — the direct cost and the indirect loss, — drowned in debt and permanently crippled all the states of Europe. Philip II. of Spain, "a beast of priestly burden," is said to have declared to his son, a little before his death, that he had spent in enterprises of this sort no less a sum than five hundred and ninety-four millions of ducats. The millions that France lavished in these crusades, and the hundreds of thousands of virtuous and industrious citizens whom she banished from her territory, can never be accurately told; but one thing is manifest, that in these proceedings she sowed the seeds of the frightful calamities she has since endured, and is now enduring. "Nearly fifty thousand families," says Voltaire, writing of the revocation of the Edict of Nantes, "within the space of three years, left the kingdom, and were afterwards followed by others, who introduced their arts, manufactures, and riches, among strangers. Almost all the north of Germany, — a country hitherto rude and void of industry, — received a new face, from the multitudes of refugees transplanted thither who peopled entire cities. Stuffs, lace, hats, stockings, formerly imported from France, were now made in these countries. A part of the suburbs of London was peopled entirely with French manufacturers in silk, others carried thither the art of making crystal in perfection, which was about this time lost in France. The gold which the refugees brought with them is still very frequently to be met with in Germany. Thus France lost about five hundred thousand inhabitants, a, prodigious quantity of specie, and, above all, the arts with which her enemies enriched themselves." From that period dates the decline of France and Spain, and of all the Catholic kingdoms of Europe. Ever since have they been running a downward career in wealth, in morality, in social order, in military genius, in manufacturing skill, and commercial enterprise. The men who committed these follies and crimes went to their graves, little dreaming what a legacy of dire revolutions they had bequeathed to their successors. These revolutions have come. The men who sowed their seeds sleep in their marble tombs, unconscious of the earthquake's throes and the tempest's thunderings, which are now overturning thrones which their perfidy had disgraced, and desolating lands which their violence had watered with tears and blood. But their sons, who have served themselves heirs of their fathers sins, by a continuance in their father's superstitions, must witness and endure these dire calamities. These persecutors dug the grave of the Church at the same time they dug their own, in the abyss of socialism. Truth is immortal, and she returned from her tomb; but for them, alas! there is no resurrection. When we think that this violence on the part of Rome delayed the Reformation for three full centuries, or rather, shall we say, has added six centuries of darkness and suffering to the history of Europe, we wonder why God permitted those triumphs to such a power. But it becomes us to bear in mind that, but for these six centuries, we never should have known the true character of Popery; or rather we never should have known the fearful malignancy and bloodthirstiness of that principle of idolatry set up by Satan in the world, which appeared so tolerant in early times, and whose true character has been fully developed only in these latter days. Nor, but for this violence, should we ever have known the mighty power of God in bringing truth from her grave, — restoring Christianity anew by the preaching of Luther and his co-reformers, after its confessors, almost to a man, had been cut off.

We must here notice, however briefly, the INQUISITION. Not content with being able to wield the swords of the Catholic princes, the Church of Rome erected a tribunal of her own, that she might the more summarily and effectually wreak her vengeance upon heretics. This is a thoroughly ecclesiastical court, and forms, therefore, a correct illustration of the true spirit and genius of the Papacy. It was erected by the Pope, sanctioned by councils, has been all along supported and governed by ecclesiastical authority, was wrought solely for ecclesiastical ends, and managed by priests and friars. In all the countries in which it was set up, — and it was introduced into most of the countries of Europe, — it caused unspeakable terror. Its victims were apprehended commonly at midnight. The familiars of the Holy Office surrounded the door of the house, whispered the name of the tribunal on whose errand they had come, and the inmates, transfixed by the dreadful words, delivered up their dearest relatives without pity or remorse. The person apprehended was consigned to a dungeon, generally below ground; he knew not his accuser; he was not told even of what crime he was suspected; he was often desired to divine the cause of his apprehension; and when he refused to criminate himself, the most horrible tortures were employed to extort confession. He was not confronted with the witnesses against him; their depositions even were not read over to him: he was allowed no advocate; his friends trembled to come nigh the place of his confinement, and put on mourning for him, as for one already dead. He knew not his sentence even, till, led forth to the *auto da fe*, he read it for the first time in the terrific symbols on his dress, or in the dreadful preparations of pile and faggot for his execution.

It is St. Dominic whom the world has to thank for this dreadful tribunal. St. Dominic, whom the Church of Rome canonizes as a great saint, was a Spaniard by birth, and by disposition a fierce, cruel, bloodthirsty bigot. His mother is said to have "dreamed before his birth that she was with child of a whelp, carrying in his mouth a lighted torch, who should put the world in an uproar, and set it on fire." This man it was who first suggested to Pope Innocent III. the erection of such a tribunal for the extirpation of heresy; and, having given abundant proofs that his own genius lay much this way, he was appointed inquisitor-general, though it was not till after his death that the Holy Office was regularly organized. In the beginning of the thirteenth century did Innocent give forth the bull which "decreed the existence of this tribunal, to finish what the anathemas of popes, the sermons of fanatics, and the brand of crusaders, had left undone. Wherever the poor Albigenses and Waldenses fled, the Inquisition followed them; and in a few years it was set up not only in Italy, Spain, and Piedmont, but in France and Germany, Poland and Bohemia, and in course of time it extended as far as Syria and India. The famous Inquisition at Goa is well known to every reader of Dr. Buchanan's "Christian Researches." Our own Mary is said to have contemplated the erection of the Inquisition in England, in order to aid her in her pious labours of purging the country of heresy by fire and sword. Spain, Portugal, and Italy were decimated by this tribunal. In an unhappy hour for her liberty and her commerce, Venice opened her gates to the familiars of the Holy Office. The *sbirri* and spies of the Inquisition swarmed on all sides. Stone walls were found to have ears and eyes. Secret denunciations poured in. Snares were sowed in the paths of citizens. Dark mistrust and suspicion banished the happiness of the hearth and the convivialities of the board; and the heaps of dead found in the canals, and seen on the public gibbets, told how well this secret tribunal did its work. If any commiserated the fate of the victim, that fate speedily became his own. If any doubted the justice of so cruel and summary a vengeance, he was sure to be himself ere long overtaken by it. Some deep pit became his prison, whose damp atmosphere froze his limbs, and whose mephitic vapours consumed his lungs; or a leaden furnace became his abode, where the powerful rays of a vertical sun, heightened by the nature of the prison, speedily brought on a burning fever or inflammation of the brain, and the wretched being, shut up in this terrible abode, ended his days as a raging madman, or sunk into heavy hopeless idiotcy. Such were the deaths reserved for the free and proud citizens of the Adriatic republic. Venice was unable to bear up under such a tyranny. Her ships disappeared from the ocean, and her merchants ceased to hold the first place on the *bourse* of the world.

But the country in which the Inquisition has reached its most flourishing estate is Spain. This tribunal was first introduced into Catalonia in 1232, and propagated over all Spain. It was re-established in greater pomp and terror in 1481 by Ferdinand and Isabella, chiefly for the spiritual good of the Jews, then numerous in Spain. The bull of Sixtus V. instituted a grand inquisitor-general and supreme council to preside over the working of the Holy Office; and under that bull commenced that system of juridical extermination which is said to have cost Spain upwards of five millions of her citizens, who either perished miserably in the dungeon, or expired amid the flames of the public *auto da fe*. The Jews were expelled, the Moors were reduced to submission, and the powers of the Holy Office were now put in requisition to purge the soil of Spain from the taint of Protestant pravity, both as regarded books and persons. In obedience to the behest of the Inquisition, Charles V. obtained from the University of Lorraine a list of heretical works. This list, printed in 1546, was the first *Index Expurgatorius* published in Spain, and the second in the world. In 1559, as Llorente informs us, was held the first *auto da fe* of Protestants at Valladolid. Men of learning were particularly obnoxious to suspicion. SANCHEZ, who enjoyed the reputation of being the first scholar of his age; LUIS DE LEON, an eloquent preacher and a distinguished Hebraist; MARIANA, the prince of Spanish historians, — were all summoned to its bar, and made to promise submission to its authority. But not only so; — princes of the royal blood, prelates of the highest rank, and men who had done good service to the cause of Rome, fell under its suspicion, and suffered in its dungeons. This tyranny endured till the period of the French invasion in 1808, when the Spanish Inquisition was abolished, to be restored on the accession of Ferdinand VII., who divided his time between the embroidering of petticoats and the worship of the Virgin.

It was under the reign of the Inquisition that the soul of Spain expired, and that a great power in arms and in arts, in literature and in commerce, fell from its high place into almost utter annihilation.

The author had once the fortune to be shown over a dismantled Inquisition, — one, too, famous in its day; — and as it illustrates this part of his subject, he may be permitted here to tell what fell under his own observation. In the summer of 1847 we found ourselves one fine day on the shores of the Leman. At our feet was the Rhone pouring its abundant but discoloured waters into the beautifully blue lake. The lake itself, moveless as a mirror, slept within its snow-white strand, and reflected on its placid bosom the goodly shadows of crag and mountain. Behind us, like two giants guarding the entrance to the lovely valley of the Rhone, rose the mighty Alps, the Dent de Midi and the Dent d'Oche, white with eternal snows. In front was the eastern bank of the lake, a magnificent bend, with a chord of a dozen miles, and offering to the eye, rocks, vineyards, villages, and mountains, forming a gorgeous picture of commingled loveliness and grandeur. The scene was one of perfect beauty, yet there was one dismal object in it. At about a mile's distance, almost surrounded by the waters of the lake, rose the Castle of Chillon. Its heavy architecture appeared still more dark and forbidding, from the gloomy recollections which it called up. It had been at once the palace and the Inquisition of the Dukes of Savoy, so celebrated in the persecuting annals of Rome; and here had many of the disciples of the early reformers endured imprisonment and torture.

We had an hour to spare, and resolved to pay a visit to the old Castle. We crossed the draw-bridge, and a small gratuity procured us entrance, and the services of a guide. We were first led down to Bonnivard's dungeon, "deep and old." There is here a sort of outer and inner dungeon; and in passing through the first, the light was so scant, that we had to grope our way over the uneven floor, which, like the landward wall, is formed of the living rock. Into this place had been crowded some hundreds of Jews; and we felt — for we could not be said to see — the little niche of rock on which they were seated one after one, and slaughtered for the good of the Church, which it was feared their heresy might infect. We passed on, and entered the more spacious dungeon of Bonnivard. It looked not unlike a chapel, with its groined roof and its central row of white pillars. The light was that of a deep twilight. We distinctly heard the ripple of the lake against the wall, which was on a level with the floor of the dungeon. At certain seasons of the year it is some feet above it. Two or three narrow slits, placed high in the wall, admitted the light, which had a greenish hue, from the reflection of the lake. This effect was rather heightened by the light breeze which kept flapping the broad leaf of some aquatic plant against the opening opposite the Martyr's Pillar. How sweet, we thought, must that ray have been to the Prior of St. Victor, and how often, during his imprisonment of six years, must his eyes have been turned towards it, as it streamed in from the waters and the mountains around his dungeon! We saw the iron ring still remaining in the pillar to which he was chained, and read on that pillar the names of Dryden and Byron, and others who had visited the place. The latter name recalled his own beautiful lines, descriptive of the place and its martyr: —

"Chillon! thy prison is a holy place,
And thy sad floor an altar; for 'twas trod
Until his very steps leave left a trace,
Worn, as if the cold pavement were a sod,
By Bonnivard! May none those marks efface!
For they appeal from tyranny to God."

This dungeon had its one captive, and the image of suffering it presented stood out definitely before us. The rooms above had their thousands, and were suggestive of crowds of victims, which passed before the mind without order or identity. Of their names few remain, though the instruments on which they were torn in pieces are still there. Emerging from the dayless gloom of the vault, we ascended to these rooms. We entered one spacious apartment, which evidently had been the "Hall of Torture;" for there, with the rust of some centuries upon it, stood the gaunt apparatus of the Inquisition. In the middle of the room was a massy beam reaching from floor to ceiling, with a strong pulley a-top. This was the *corda*, the queen of torments, as it has been called. The person who endured the *corda* had his hands tied behind his back; then a rope was attached to them, and a heavy iron weight was hung at his feet. When all was ready, the executioners suddenly hoisted him up to the ceiling by means of the rope, which passed through the pulley in the top of the beam: the arms were painfully wrenched backwards, and the weight of the body, increased by the weight attached to the feet, in most cases sufficed to tear the arms from the sockets. While thus suspended, the prisoner was sometimes whipped, or had a hot iron thrust into various parts of his body, his tormentors admonishing him all the while to speak the truth. If he refused to confess, he was suddenly let down, and received a severe jerk, which completed the dislocation. If he still refused to confess, he was remanded to his cell, had his joints set, and was brought out, as soon as able, to undergo the same torture over again. At each of the four corners of the room where this beam stood was a pulley fixed in the wall, showing that the apartment had also been fitted up for the torture of the *veglia*. The *veglia* resembled a smith's anvil, with a spike a-top, ending in an iron die. Through the pulleys at the four corners of the room ran four ropes. These were tied to the naked arms and legs of the sufferer, and twisted so as to cut to the bone. He was lifted up, and set down with his back bone exactly upon the die, which, as the whole weight of the person rested upon it, wrought by degrees into the bone. The torture, which was excruciating, was to last eleven hours, if the person did not sooner confess. These are but two of the *seven tortures* by which the Church of Rome proved, what certainly she could not prove by either Scripture or reason, that transubstantiation is true. The roof beneath which these enormities were committed was plastered over with the sign of the cross. In a small adjoining apartment we were shown a recess in the wall, with an *oubliette* or trap-door below it. In that recess, said the guide, stood an image of the Virgin. The prisoner accused of heresy was brought, and made to kneel upon the trap-door, and, in presence of the Virgin, to abjure his heresy. To prevent the possibility of apostacy, the moment he had made his confession the bolt was drawn, and the man lay a mangled corpse on the rock below. We had seen enough; and as we re-crossed the moat of the Castle of

Chillon, the light seemed sweeter than ever, and we never in all our lives felt so thankful for the Reformation, which had vested us in the privilege of reading our Bible without having our limbs torn and our body mangled.

That religion, whose birth-place is heaven, and whose mission is love, should be propagated over the earth by means of racks and stakes, is utterly repugnant to all that we know of her and of her author. No; it was not Christianity, but its counterfeit, which the Inquisition was erected to promulgate. These were not priests, but demons; this was not a "Holy Office," but a DEN OF MURDER. Of the enormous crimes and the horrible cruelties there enacted, much is known; but, alas! that much is but an insignificant portion of the whole. When we take into account the countries to which the Inquisition extended, the length of time it flourished, and the countless thousands of every rank, and age, and sex, who entered its gates, and never more saw the light of day or heard the voice of friend, — the virgin whose youth and beauty were her only crime, — the rich man whose possessions were needed to swell the revenues of the Church, — the heretic, for whom are reserved the strongest racks and the hottest fires of the Holy Office, — the imagination is overwhelmed by the number of the victims, and the awful aggregate of their sufferings. Yet, though but a tithe of these horrors is known, enough has been disclosed to cover the Church of Rome with eternal infamy, and to convict her before the world as but an assemblage of miscreants and villains, banded together in the name of religion, to rob and murder their fellows. And while we have the Papacy, we must have, in one shape or other, the Inquisition. Errors so monstrous as those of Rome cannot be maintained but by coercion. Those who talk of separating between Popery and her screws and racks would disjoin what the laws of superstition have made eternally one. So long as the one exists, both will continue, like substance and shadow, to darken the earth. When the papal government was temporarily suspended in 1849 by the Roman Republic, the Inquisition was found in active operation, and it was restored the moment the Pope returned to Rome. The various horrors of the place, — its iron rings, its subterranean cells, its skeletons built up in the wall, its trap-doors, its kiln for burning bodies, with parts of humanity remaining still unconsumed, — were all exposed at the time. These partial disclosures may convince us, perhaps, that it is better that the veil which conceals the full horrors of the Inquisition should remain unlifted till that day when the graves shall give up their dead.

In fine, as regards the influence of Popery on government, it were easy to demonstrate, that the Papacy delayed the advent of representative and constitutional government for thirteen centuries. Superstition is the mother of despotism; Christianity is the parent of liberty. There is no truth which the past history of the world more abundantly establishes than this. It was through Christianity that the democratic element first came into the world. That principle was altogether unknown in the ancient governments, which were either autocracies, or, in a few instances, oligarchies. The people, as such, were excluded from all share and influence in the government. Christianity was the first to teach the essential equality of all men, and the first to erect a system of government in which the people were admitted to those rights, and to that share of influence, which are not only their due, but which nearly concern the safety and stability of the state. The state began to model its government after the example of the Church, borrowing the idea which she had been the first to promulgate in theory and exhibit in practice; and ere this time of day the world would have been filled with free and constitutional states, had not the Church, abandoning her own idea, begun to copy, in her government and organization, the order of the state. The issue was the erection of the Papacy. The papal government is the very antipodes of constitutional government: it centres all power in one man: it does so on the ground of divine right; and is therefore essentially and eternally antagonistic to the constitutional element. Its long dominancy in Europe formed the grand barrier to the progress of the popular element in society, and the erection of constitutional government in the world. With the Reformation the popular element revived. "Geneva," says one who is no friend to Christianity, "in submitting to Calvinism, became a popular state." In the proportion in which the various states of Europe received the Reformation did they become free; and in the proportion in which they have retained the Reformation have they retained their liberty. The cause of the dissolution of the old empires was their slavery. Society was divided into two classes, — nobles and slaves. Wealth and luxury in process of time exhausted the aristocracy; and as they could receive no infusion of fresh blood from the other classes, the state was at an end. But Christianity, by teaching that all men are immortal, and that there reigns among them an essential equality, has abolished slavery, has effected a free circulation among the various classes of the state, like that which maintains the salubrity of the air and ocean, and has thus conferred upon kingdoms the gift of terrestrial immortality.

Chapter IV: Influence of Popery on the Morals and Religious Condition of Nations.

We come now to speak of the influence of Romanism on society. This part of our subject we have already illustrated to a large extent. All that we have said regarding the influence of Popery on individual man and on government bears directly on the question of its influence on nations. In the three foregoing chapters we have laid down and demonstrated the principles of the subject: in this, we shall attempt the proof from experience, or show the operation of these principles on society. If it be true that Popery tends to degrade man intellectually and morally, and if it be also true that it exerts a most malign influence on government, rendering it essentially despotic, and adverse in its spirit and actings to the constitution, the necessities, and the progress of society, then there must be a marked and palpable difference between popish nations and Protestant nations. We maintain, and now proceed to prove, that popish nations are vastly inferior to Protestant nations, — first, in general morality; and, second, in general prosperity and happiness.

I. There is a great and obvious difference between protestant states and popish states, in point of morality. Let it be remarked here, once for all, that we are not dealing with individual cases, but with broad and prominently marked national characteristics. There are individuals in Roman Catholic countries sincere, truthful, upright, honourable, just as there are individuals in Protestant countries lamentably devoid of every one of these virtues. We speak, of course, of the prevailing character of the mass. First, as regards truth: its obligations are felt in a much lower degree in popish than in Protestant countries. The importance of truth to society it is unnecessary to point out. It is the basis on which society rests; and its existence is taken for granted in all its proceedings, from the commonest business transaction up to the solemn acts of the judgment seat. The jesuitical morality of the Romish Church has deeply tainted the nations subject to her sway; and the maxim on which the Church has acted, that faith is not to be kept when it is to her advantage to break it, is of easy transference to her individual members. The power arrogated, and so often exercised, by the Pope, of annulling vows, promises, and oaths, has tended, too, to destroy all sense of truth, and all reverence for its claims. The Romish doctors have discovered two powerful instruments for banishing all sin from the world, or rather for transmuting all sin into virtue. These are *probabilism* and *intention*. According to the first, any course, however criminal in itself, becomes probably right should any doctor of the Church argue in its favour. It would be difficult to name the sin which some grave doctor has not defended, and which, accordingly, is not probably right. In this way contrary opinions may both be probable; and the inquirer, noways perplexed, chooses the one he likes best. A greater license to all kinds of sin than the doctrine of *intention* it is impossible to imagine. The famous Escobar teaches, that if men only direct aright their intention, that is, if they think not of the sin, but of the benefit flowing from it, there is nothing which they may not do with impunity. They may deal a mortal stab to their adversary, and yet do no murder, provided, in the moment of striking, they can so far control their mental emotions as to think, not of vengeance, but of the stain which they avert from their reputation. They may purloin the wealth or steal the property of others, and yet stand clear with the eighth commandment, if they can suppress the avaricious wish, and keep steadily before their mind the good they may be able to do with their increased means. They may lie, and yet be guilty of no falsehood, if they can only invent some imaginable good which they may accomplish by prevaricating. Such is the moral code of Rome's casuists. Its utter contrariety to the law given on Sinai, and written on stone, we need not point out. It confounds the essence of things; it annihilates all distinction between right and wrong; it exiles *truth* from the world. And yet this morality the Romish doctors have taught with applause. Need we wonder that the popish world has become a vast lazar-house, filled with all sorts of moral plagues, — its very stones and timber rotten with the leprosy? The corruption of public faith in papal Europe is notorious and admitted. Peculation and bribery are rife in all departments of government. Tricks, manoeuvers, and frauds are the main machinery by which it is carried on. This is notoriously the case as regards France, Spain, and Austria. The stereotyped and immemorial abuses of the pontifical court we leave altogether out of view. How rare is it to find in the service of any of these states, one who displays an honest adherence to the oath of office, or who forms his public acts on any higher principle than the good of family or of party, or who descends from power without the stain of the epidemic corruption upon him! The gross scandals which disgraced the close of the reign of Louis Philippe in France are yet fresh in the recollection of all. These disclosed a woeful lack of public principle on the part of the very highest servants of the crown. The prostration of truth in France is evident from the fact, that scarce any reliance is placed on the word of any man, from the highest functionary of state, down to the street porter. Take up the work of any traveller in the popish states of Europe, and you will find him complaining in every chapter that his utmost circumspection did not prevent his being imposed upon. Compared with the high principles on which British commerce is carried on, and the honourable character maintained generally by British merchants, how frequent in the papal states of Europe are bankruptcies, frauds in trade, and chicaneries of all kinds! How little feared is an oath in popish countries! How frequent is perjury! What a difference between the value of evidence in the courts of southern Europe, and its value in those of northern Germany, and especially in Britain! What else can be expected, where the great fountain of truth is sealed, and the eye is turned away from the great tribunal in the heavens, and the conscience of the man is made amenable to a judge on earth, who often, when an end is to be gained, absolves him from the obligation of speaking truth? In this respect all Roman Catholic countries are alike. The sanctity of oaths is almost universally disregarded. We may cite a few out of innumerable instances in proof. During the reign of the Republic in Rome, an agent of a Jesuit club waylaid and well-nigh murdered a Frenchman who was obnoxious to him. The case came to trial. The fact that the person who committed the outrage was abroad on that day was deponed to by twenty-six witnesses; nevertheless, those with whom he lived, including a countess, a bishop, an advocate, and a Jesuit, swore that their protégé had never been out of the house on the day in question. They were examined separately; and, though the Jesuit was skilful, they were all convicted of perjury. On the 1st of January 1850, an agent of the Irish Protestant mission was beaten in open day in the Cowgate of Edinburgh, in the presence of a mob of Irish Roman Catholics. The case came to trial; about a score of witnesses were examined, all of whom had been present in the mob, several of whom had shared its proceedings; but not one of them would identify the suspected perpetrators of the outrage. Some of the witnesses swore, in alternate sentences, that the agent of the society was beaten, and that they saw no one beating him. It is the same on a larger scale in Ireland. Assaults, murders, and crimes of all kinds are often perpetrated in that unhappy land, in the presence of numerous spectators;

yet, so lightly do they hold a false oath, that it is impossible in the majority of cases to procure a conviction. In the courts on this side the channel also, the vast difference between an Irish oath and a Scotch or English oath is well known. Thus justice is paralyzed in a Roman Catholic country. She sits powerless on her tribunal. The witness desecrates her most sacred forms, and the criminal defies her righteous awards.

It is also an admitted fact, that in Roman Catholic countries life is held much less sacred than in Protestant lands. The popish earth is defiled with blood, and the stain is deep in proportion as the Popery is intense. No one need be informed how dreadfully prevalent are assassinations and murders in Italy, in Spain, and in Ireland. In Paris, the Morgue furnishes awful evidence that suicides and assassinations are of nightly occurrence in the capital of France. The Countries south of the Alps and the Pyrenees, which are those most under the influence of the Church, are precisely those in which travelling is most dangerous. The towns swarm with assassins, and the roads are infested with banditti. Scarce a night passes without an assassination in the streets of Madrid. The slightest insult sends the man's hand to his poignard's hilt; or if he decline himself to shed blood, he knows that for a paltry sum he can hire a villain to undertake the deed. The facilities provided by the Church of Rome for enabling men to escape the future punishment of such crimes, is a main cause of their dreadful prevalence. So sensible was Napoleon of this, that he shut out the shriving priest from the condemned criminal. And we find Lord Brougham stating in his place in Parliament, that the same course was adopted by the Marquis of Wellesley in his colonial government, and that this judicious vigour was followed by a marked diminution in the commission of crimes. On the same occasion do we find the leading members of their Lordships' house tracing the noon-day murders and the midnight outrages, of so unhappy frequency in the sister island, to priestly influences, more especially to the confessional and altar-denunciations; and out of doors we find the *Times* journal, in less courtly phrase, branding the apostolic clergy of Rome as "surpliced ruffians."

The state of morality as regards the marriage vow is also much more lax in Roman Catholic countries. Infidelities are far from being unfrequent; concubinage is common. In a table recently compiled and widely published, of the "morality of great cities," the two cities that stood lowest on the list, as being the least moral in Europe, were the capitals of its two principal Roman Catholic countries, Vienna and Paris. In Paris, the illegitimate births were marked as being about one-half of the whole; and in Vienna the proportion was nearly the same. We speak not of the conventual establishments, which were the consecrated abodes of the twin vices of indolence and lewdness. Nor do we speak of the seduction and profligacy with which the law of clerical celibacy inundated private families. We speak of the state of general society as regards the great virtue of chastity, which is confessed far below that of Holland, of Britain, or of any Protestant country.

Analogous to this is the respect in which woman is held in Roman Catholic countries. Christianity alone gives woman her proper place. All idolatries agree in degrading her. Hinduism makes woman the slave of man; Mahommedanism makes her the toy of his pleasures. Modern Judaism teaches that they are "very inferior beings;" and several great rabbies have held, that for them there is no immortality. Romanism, true to its genius as a false religion, has degraded woman, by forbidding its priests to marry. "It cries up marriage for a sacrament, and yet at the same time bars its sacred clergy from it, because it will defile them." Thus all false religions, and Romanism among the rest, have struck at the highest interests of society through the sides of woman. Nothing could more powerfully tend to barbarize mankind. It deprives youth of its most persuasive instructor; it robs home of its chief attraction and its most endearing pleasure; and it deprives society of that strong though secret guard which consists in the delicacy, refinement, and purity of woman.

How rankly soever the passions shoot up beneath the shade of Popery, the domestic affections refuse to flourish in its neighbourhood. The confessional works sad havoc in families. We do not allude to the grosser pollutions and crimes to which it often leads, but to the fatal blight it inflicts upon the affections. Happy, guileless, unsuspecting youth becomes prematurely thoughtful; for persons of tender years are dragged into the confessional, — "the slaughterhouse of conscience," as it has with justice been termed, — and are there doomed to listen to what must pollute, revolt, and shock them. Like a biting frost upon the early bud, so are the questionings of the confessor upon the warm sympathies of youth: these sympathies become dwarfed and stunted for life. Dreadful images of crime are mixed up with the earliest associations and amusements of the person, which not unfrequently in after years ripen into deeds of guilt. How the hearth and the confessional can exist together it is impossible to conceive. How can there possibly be a full interchange of free, genuine, trustful sentiment and feeling between the different members of the family, when all feel that there, in the midst of them, sits one, though invisible, seeing and hearing all that is said and done? for all must be told over in the confessional. In the breast of the wife the husband knows that there is a secret place, which even he dare not enter, and to which none but the priest, with his curious and loathly questionings, has access. The same dark shadow comes between brother and sister, and the mutual and trustful confidence of their childhood years is blighted for ever. The father can mark, day by day, the dark stains of the confessional deepening on his daughter's soul, clouding the sunshine of her face, and restraining the free current of her talk. Infernal institution! invented in the pit, and set up on earth to root out all that is lovely and pure, and holy and free, among the human family. The confessional is slavery worse than death. How a people who have once tasted freedom could advocate the introduction of a tyranny so unspeakably odious and so perfectly unbearable, surpasses our comprehension. And yet there are not wanting at this moment some in England who seek to revive the practice of confession.

Another disagreeable feature of papal Europe, in which it contrasts most unfavourably with Protestant states, is the all but universal prevalence of the vice of gambling. Gambling-houses abound in all the great cities of the Continent. Most of the watering-places of southern Germany are nothing else than large gambling establishments. The Protestant part of the Continent, it is true, is not altogether free from this dreadful pollution; but such houses in protestant states are thinly planted, comparatively. In France and in southern Europe this vice has infected the whole of society, and obtrudes itself everywhere, — in private parties, in the common taverns, as well as in those houses specially set apart for it. The papal government, too, has its lottery, and attempts to compound with heaven by devoting the proceeds to the support of paupers. It is believed to yield seven millions of francs to the apostolic exchequer. The shops for selling lottery tickets are all open on Sabbath. Nothing could more fearfully demonstrate the power of avarice, first, over governments, who license these establishments for the sake of revenue; and, second, over the masses, who, impelled by an uncontrollable greed to possess the property of others, and altogether unscrupulous as to the mode of obtaining it, flock to the gambling-table, and there lose health, character, fortune, reason, and often life itself. How weak must be the power of principle where such courses are so generally indulged in! and how far must the heart of man have strayed from its rest, when happiness is sought amidst such maddening pursuits!

One other feature only is awanting to complete the dark picture of the popish world. It has no Sabbath. Who can calculate how much Christian lands owe to the Sabbath? It is equally impossible to tell how much popish lands lose by the want of it. The Sabbath descends upon the earth like a visitant from another sphere, laden with blessings, which grow not in this world. It is as if Eden had returned, with its innocence and its joy; or as if time, with its sorrows and its cares, had rolled past, and God's "unsuffering kingdom" had come. How many, worn out with toil, had withered and sunk into their graves ere their time, but for its rest! How many minds, never unbent, would have lost their spring, and ended in madness or idiotcy, but for the Sabbath! How many weak spirits would have yielded to temptations and been for ever lost, but for its salutary and oft-recurring counsels! How many had sunk, brokenhearted, under the afflictions of time, but for the prospects beyond earth which the Sabbath opened to them! It purifies the social affections, heightens the standard of public morality, elevating to a higher platform the general community. Even the man who never enters the sanctuary, — who habitually desecrates the Sabbath, — is the better for it. To him even it is a hebdomadal sermon about God and religion. The Sabbath is the bulwark of Christianity. Popery has perfectly comprehended its mission, and has been, in all countries, its uncompromising foe. Two hundred years ago, when Popery sought to reestablish itself in Scotland, it found that the Sabbath stood most in its way; and it began its assault upon the religion of Scotland by an attempt to abolish the Sabbaths of Scotland. The "Book of Sports" was intended to pave the way for the mass. On the Continent, Popery has steadily pursued the same end, — the abolition of the Sabbath, — first, by the institution of *fête* days, which are more numerous than the Sabbaths of Protestant countries; and, second, by teaching the people to pass the day in shows and amusements. Its policy has been crowned with complete success; and now, in popish lands the Sabbath is unknown, or exists only as a day of toil or of unhallowed pleasure.

The writer has had occasion to observe how the Sabbath is spent in several of the great cities of popish Europe, and may here be permitted to tell what fell under his own notice, as the matter bears directly on the moral and religious influence of Popery. In Cologne, — "the Rome of northern Germany," as it has been called, — work seemed generally forborne. There were, of course, far more idlers in the streets than on other days. A stream of foot-passengers and vehicles kept pouring into the town across the bridge of boats. Here and there in the crowd might be seen a female with prayer-book (the Romish of course) in hand, and a white-flowered napkin forming her head-gear, after the manner of the German maidens. Parties of young men paraded the streets. Some were regaling themselves with the long German tobacco-pipe; others were bearing on their heads baskets of fruit, which they carried to market; while others were laden with the produce of the dairy and the poultry-yard. The light blue of the Prussian uniform enlivened the more sober attire of the burghers, among whom, the writer is sorry to have to say, he observed some of his own countrymen, who were cheapening fruit in the market, while their servants followed, bearing bottles of Rhenish wine, — an excursion to the country being plainly meditated. We went to the cathedral, or Great Dom, that we might see what kind of instruction it is that Popery provides for her people on the Sabbath. This temple, the sublimest north of the Alps, and, were it finished, the noblest Gothic structure in the world, would contain within its vast limits the population of a city. At the great western gate we found a great crowd: some were thronging in, others were leaving the edifice; and the low murmur of the multitude mingled hoarsely with the grand music which came in overpowering bursts from the interior of the vast edifice. We passed on through its aisles, its nave, and its arches, and at last reached the choir. For beauty, and elegance, and grandeur, it appeared a splendid vision rather than a reality. It was a mighty temple in itself, railed off by richly-carved screens and tall graceful pillars, from the yet greater temple which enclosed it. Around the choir was gathered a motley assemblage of worshippers and gazers, of all ranks and of all countries. The gates of the choir were guarded by portly officials in scarlet dresses, bearing in their hands the symbols of office, — long staves surmounted by little chaplets of silver. Within the choir, at one end, was the high altar, on which were enormous lighted tapers, a crucifix, and an illuminated mass-book; while the archbishop, in the splendour of cope and scarlet tunic, was saying mass. Numerous priests in gorgeous vestments were assisting. Boys in scarlet dresses, with silver censers, were waving incense. In the other end of the choir, opposite the high altar, was a gallery filled with choristers, consisting of about four hundred of the *elite* of the youth of Cologne, who sung some of the finest pieces of the great masters. The music rolled on without pause: now it seemed to retreat into the remotest part of the edifice, and now it came forward in a noble burst, and rolled a magnificent volume of rich melody along the aisles and roof of the mighty Dom. it was a grand effort on the part of Popery; and nowhere, not even in Notre Dame at Paris, have we seen the Roman Catholic worship conducted with half the pomp. The organ pealed, the melody of the choir rose and fell in noble bursts, the tapers blazed, and the incense ascended in fragrant clouds. Beautiful little stalls, rich in paintings, ran round the cathedral, each with its altar, crucifix, and tapers, and its priest, in cope and stole, celebrating mass. There were renowned relics, in little marble chapels, before which were kept lamps which burned perpetually; and then, in the ever-beauteous choir, which, like the palace in the fairy tale, seemed to have arisen unaided by the hand of man, were numerous priests, tall of figure, in vestments of purple, and scarlet, and fine linen, and gold, who ranged themselves, now in rows, bearing burning tapers, and now mingled in curious maze, — their deep rich voices chanting the while the service of the mass. Before the high altar, in magnificent robes, stood the Archbishop of Cologne, bowing, crossing, kissing the crucifix, and occasionally clasping his hands in the attitude of one in rapt devotion. Not the least important element in this goodly show was the unrivalled grandeur of the temple in which it was enacted. As a mere spectacle, we never saw anything that made a tolerable approach to it. But it rose not beyond a mere artistic effort. There was not a single truth communicated. It was not in the nature of things that such a show (for the mass was chanted in a tongue which the people did not understand) should enlighten the conscience, or purify the heart, or elevate the character. Could any one be the better for such a Sabbath? Could any one be the better for the Sabbaths of a whole life spent in this way? The direct tendency of the service was to subjugate the mind in idolatrous reverence of the mass, and in degrading vassalage to the priesthood. Such was its manifest effect. Of the thousands which crowded the cathedral, two hundred or thereabouts might be engaged in counting their beads, or reciting prayers from their prayer-books. They were ranged in a line of three deep round the choir, — the holiest place in the building. But there was not a countenance on which the prevailing expression was not that of gloom and despondency. In fact, the genius of the Romish worship is towards gloom. All the objects to which the mind of the worshipper is turned are of a gloomy kind. Of this description are the images presented to their senses, which are almost all associated with death: Christ on the cross, pourtrayed often in the agonies of dying; figures of saints undergoing martyrdom, or half-exanimate from the effects of the prolonged fast, the iron collar, the hair shirt, or the lash. Over the gates of their cathedrals are not unfrequently sculpture-pieces representing the torments of the damned. The same scenes occur, with disagreeable though intentional frequency, inside their churches. There is a striking force of conception in these representations, which contrasts with the evident lack of power in their occasional attempts to depict the happiness of heaven. Thus the Church of Rome has made her appeal to the fears of her people. She attempts to awe and terrify, and thus keep them under her dominion. We have been at some pains to ascertain the actual effects produced on the mind by the Romish worship, as represented in the countenance. We do not recollect of having seen in one instance that kindling of delight, that expansive and radiant expression, which bespeaks intelligence and hope, which genuine devotion produces. We have seen earnestness, — earnestness amounting evidently to intense anxiety; but still the cloud was there. The prospect of purgatory, and of enduring there torments for an unknown period, which becomes nearer as life advances, must tell upon the general feeling. We do not think we ever saw an air of more dreary hopelessness upon human faces than on those of the old men and women of Belgium. In southern Europe this is not so perceptible. There, this feeling, or at least the expression of it, is counteracted in a good degree by the influence of climate and the livelier sensibilities of the people.

To return to Cologne and its Sabbath: the mummeries which began in the cathedral were terminated on the streets. The host was carried in solemn procession through the city, with drum and fife, and a goodly show of crucifixes, tapers, and flags. The crowds uncovered as it passed. During the forenoon business had been partially carried on. A third or so of the shops were open; and the vessels moored in the Rhine unladed them of their cargo. But in the afternoon and evening the whole city freely gave itself to pleasure and revelry. The children marshalled themselves in line, and, carrying branches and flambeaux, imitated the grand procession of the morning. All the taverns were open, and every street rang with the shouts of bacchanals, mingled with music, vocal and instrumental. The spacious gardens of the hotel, on the right bank of the river, adjoining the suburb of Deutz, were illuminated with numerous variegated lamps; gay parties danced or promenaded in them; while a band played airs at intervals, which came floating across the Rhine in the stillness of the evening. In this way was the day spent. There may be less superstition and less revelry; but with this exception, we believe the Sabbath of Cologne is a fair sample of the Sabbaths of Rhenish Prussia, and, indeed, of the greater part of Germany. Wherever Protestantism exists, and in the proportion in which it exists, do we find the Sabbath. The two most protestant cities of Switzerland are Basle and Geneva. The writer has passed Sabbaths in these cities, and he found a marked difference between the way in which the day was there kept, and its observance in Cologne; though still the best portions of Switzerland are far inferior to the worst portions of Protestant Britain. If we enter the south of France, we find ourselves again in the midst of the thick darkness, and we lose almost all trace of the Sabbath. We take Lyons as an example, — a city wholly given to the worship of Mary, and where might be set up, in the midst of her shrines and temples, an altar "To the UNKNOWN GOD." The writer would have found it impossible to have discovered from any outward sign that it was the Sabbath. No branch of labour or merchandise was suspended, in the forenoon at least: every shop was open. There was the same bustle on the quay of the Rhone, where steamers were arriving and departing. While the priests inside the cathedrals burned candles and incense, or chanted mass, or sung a requiem over the coffined dead, to mitigate, as their relatives fondly hoped, their purgatorial pains, the people over whom they bore sway were busy outside prosecuting their labours, and intent on making gain. Nay, the churches were approached through stalls of buyers and sellers, which covered the open space in front, and came close up to the gates of the cathedrals, so that the priest's chant blended with the hum of traffic outside. So few entered, and these for so short a time (for such went only to mutter a few prayers and retire), that they were never missed from the toiling and trafficking thousands of Lyons. The amusements of the evening were not unlike those of Cologne. A military band, consisting of at least an hundred performers, was stationed in the grand square, to regale the citizens, who were gathered around them in thousands, or sipped wine or coffee in the adjoining gardens.

The Sabbaths of Paris are, unhappily, too well known. But here we use a misnomer; — Paris has no Sabbath. The man who rises six successive days to toil, rises on the seventh also to toil. This shows us, by the way, what, in an economic point of view, would be the effect of the abolition of the Sabbath — it would be simply the substitution of a day of labour for a day of rest, — the addition of a seventh to the toil of man, not only without any additional remuneration, but with a very greatly diminished remuneration, owing to the over-production which it would create. In Paris all trades and professions are prosecuted on the Sabbath as on other days. The wheel of the mechanic and the tool of the artizan are as busily plied on that day as on any other. The mason builds, and the smith kindles his forge; the porter, the tailor, the shopkeeper, the merchant, — all are occupied as usual. In the forenoon a thin congregation assembles in the venerable aisles of Notre Dame, or in the more gorgeous temple of the Madeline. The worship consists of genufluxions, incensings, chantings, and other pagan mummeries, but has no reference to the verities of an eternal world. That *ouvrier* and that young woman, as they worship on bended knee an image or a Madonna, seem the very picture of devotion; but follow them in the evening to Franconi's circus, or to the dancing garden, and see how little they have profited by the morning's devotions. At that altar the Bible is never opened. Beneath that roof God's message of love is never proclaimed. In the city around, a million of men, with a few exceptions, are living in the grossness of superstition and vice, but no voice cries "Deliver from going down to the pit." The priests have taken away the key of knowledge; they enter not in themselves; and them that were entering in they hindered. At an early hour in the afternoon business is suspended, and pleasure takes its place. Then, indeed, does Paris rejoice. A gay stream of vehicles, equestrians, and pedestrians, pours along the Boulevards. Others hasten to the *Jardin des Plantes*, or to the *Champs d'Elysée*, where mountebank shows, and all kinds of games and amusements, are going on. Others assemble round the tea-tables in the gardens of the *Palais Royale*, or saunter in those of the Tuileries. All the theatres in the city are open, and are better attended on that evening than on any of the previous six. The saloons are brilliantly illuminated. Omnibuses and vehicles of all kinds thunder along the Rue St. Honoré and the Rue St. Antoine, filled with half-inebriated passengers, who shout or sing in their boisterous efforts to be merry. It is remarkable enough, that what certain parties in this country confidently and urgently recommend as an effectual preservative against drunkenness should in France be a main provocative of that vice. There is more wine and spirits drank in Paris on that day than on any three of the other days of the week.

We must not suppose that it is only in the cities of the Continent that the Sabbath has disappeared: matters are no better in the country. "It so happened," says a traveller, "that we reached Orleans, — a day's journey from Paris, — on a Saturday afternoon. My relatives forgot the fact that it was Saturday; and no external indication making Sunday palpable to the eye, I did not undeceive them, being anxious to return to Paris without delay. We started, then, the following morning, as usual, and travelled seventy or eighty miles through towns, villages, and hamlets, till we reached Paris, without my friends discovering that we had been travelling on Sunday." This speaks volumes, and requires no comment. To the south of the Alps matters are no better, and they could scarce be worse. The fact is too well known to require either illustration or proof. Such is the condition into which the Papacy has reduced western Europe: it has withdrawn men from the great fountain of morality — the Bible; it has thrown down the great bulwark of morality — the Sabbath; it has made the good of the Church the supreme law, and has thus confounded the essential distinction between virtue and vice; it his converted religion into a mere ritual, and government into a system of coercion; it has introduced corruption into public life, and fraud into private society; it has covered the Continent with concubinage, assassination, robbery, and gambling; it has eradicated from the minds of men all sense of obligation and duty. The Church now seeks in vain for faith, and the State for loyalty; and both have been brought to rest their continued existence upon the precarious tenure of military fidelity.

Chapter V: Influence of Popery on the Social and Political Condition of Nations.

Our second proposition is, that Popish nations are inferior to Protestant nations in respect of general prosperity and happiness.

The economic condition of a nation grows directly out of its moral and intellectual state. We have already shown how vastly inferior, in this respect, are popish nations to Protestant nations; but they are as inferior in point of wealth and general prosperity. The Reformation demonstrated that the doctrines of Popery were false; the three centuries which have since elapsed have demonstrated that their influence is evil. The former brought Popery to the test of the Bible; the other has brought it to the test of experience; and Popery has been cast on both grounds. It was convicted, in the first instance, of being the enemy of divine truth, and therefore, of man's eternal happiness; it has been convicted, in the second instance, of being opposed to political and economic truth, and therefore the foe of man's temporal welfare. The Reformation brought with it a great and visible quickening of mind; it released it from the fetters it had worn for ages, — awoke the intellect, — touched the sympathies and aspirations; and hence there was not a country into which it was introduced that did not start forward in a career of progress in all that relates to the greatness and happiness of man, — in letters, in science, and in arts, — in government, in industry, in manufactures, and in commerce. For the past three centuries Protestantism has been steadily elevating those countries into which the Reformation found entrance; Popery has been steadily sinking those in which Rome continued to bear sway. The difference between the two is now so great as to force itself upon the attention of the whole world. Could the two rival systems have had a fairer trial, — three centuries of time, and western Europe for an arena? and could anything be more striking or conclusive than the issue, — a progress steadily upward in the one case, — steadily downward in the other? The difference may be summed up in two words — ADVANCE and RETROGRESSION. The solemn verdict of history is this: — Popery is the barrier to progress, and the foe of man's temporal wellbeing.

Wherever we look, we find this evil system bearing the same evil fruits. Wherever we meet Popery, there we meet moral degradation, mental imbecility, indolence, unskilfulness, improvidence, rags, and beggary. No ameliorations of government, — no genius or peculiarities of race, — no fertility of soil, — no advantages of climate, — seem able to withstand the baleful influence of this destructive superstition: it is the same amid the exhaustless resources of the new world as amid the civilization and arts of the old: it is the same amid the grandeur of Switzerland and the historic glories of Italy, as among the bogs of Connaught and the wilds of the Hebrides. The first glance is sufficient to reveal the vast disparity between the two systems, as shown in the external condition of the nations that profess them. Let us compare Britain and America, — the two most powerful Protestant countries, — with France and Austria, — the two most powerful popish countries. What a difference as regards the present state and future prospects of these countries! Or, let us take Austria, the daughter of Charles V., and compare it with Prussia, the daughter of Luther; or let us take the United States, the offspring of Protestant Britain, and compare them with Mexico and Peru, the offspring of Catholic Spain. Why should not Austria be as flourishing as Prussia? Why should not Mexico be running the same career of improvement and growing wealth as the United States of America? Are not these countries on a level as regards their internal resources and their facilities for foreign trade? Austria is richer in these respects than Prussia; Mexico than the States. And yet their prosperity is in the inverse ratio of their advantages. Why is this? One solution only meets the case. In the one instance, Protestantism has elevated the moral character and strengthened the intellectual powers of the people, and hence the presence of all the elements of a nation's greatness, — skill, enterprize, sobriety, steadiness, and security; and there appears, therefore, no limit to their progress in the other, a demoralizing and barbarizing superstition still bears sway; the people are unskilful, disorderly, and improvident; their country has reached the limits of its prosperity, and is advancing backwards into ruin.

But it is not only when we take a large region into view that we are able to trace the peculiar effects of the two systems; a petty dukedom of Germany, or a Swiss canton, shows it equally well. The result is the same, however closely or minutely we examine. Let us take a rapid glance at the various popish countries of Europe, and see how they authenticate our theory, — that, be the genius of a people and the capabilities of their territory what they may, Popery will convert their country into a social and economic wreck. And here we may state, once for all, that as regards the countries north of the Alps, we shall state only what we have had personal opportunities of knowing, and which we challenge any competent witness to contradict or disprove.

We begin with Belgium, which, on the whole, is the most flourishing Roman Catholic country in Europe, but which, nevertheless, affords conclusive evidence of what we are now seeking to substantiate. Belgium enjoys a free government, a rich soil; is favourably situated for commerce with protestant states; and, above all, still retains the Protestant element, and, along with that, the arts and manufactures which the storms of former persecuting eras were the means of drifting to her shores. Those parts of Belgium where the French Protestants settled enjoy a high degree of prosperity, — a prosperity which is the result and the recompense of its former hospitality to the victims of persecution. But in the aboriginal parts, as in the south-west, where Popery settles thick and dense, we find the same indolence and wretchedness that prevail in Ireland. That district bears the same relation to the rest of Belgium which Ireland does to Britain. It is liable, like Ireland, to be visited with periodic famines, and at these seasons it endures like deplorable misery. The condition of these districts forms a frequent theme of discussion in the Belgian Chambers, as Ireland does in the British Legislature. As in Ireland, so in Flanders, agriculture and the arts are in a backward state, and the people are the prey of ignorance and improvidence. The land groans under a pauper occupancy; and the manufacture of thread, — the staple manufacture of the country — is prosecuted with the hand-wheel of their ancestors. Competition is hopeless with the rest of Belgium, which enjoys the advantage of improved machinery, and thus the Flemings have fallen behind in the race of national prosperity.

Let us contrast Belgium with the little Protestant state on the north of it, — Holland. Holland was originally a few scattered sand-banks at the mouth of the Rhine, when its inhabitants conceived the design of forcing a country amid shifting sands and roaring waves. Piece by piece did they rescue from the ocean an extensive territory; and, girdling it with a strong rampart, it became in time the theatre of mighty deeds, and the asylum of Protestant liberty, when the rest of Continental Europe fell under the power of tyrants. Every reader of history knows the long, unequal, but finally triumphant contest which they waged with the Emperor Charles, who sought to compel them to embrace the Romish faith. The glorious era of the nation dates from the time that the Hollanders threw off the yoke of Spain. From that period their social interests steadily advanced, their commercial genius expanded, the trade of India came into their hands, and they replenished their sea-girt home with the riches and the luxuries of the Orient. No nation teaches the lesson so strikingly as Holland, how little a people owe to the advantages of soil, and how much their greatness depends upon themselves. In all points Holland is the antipodes of Ireland. Without one good natural harbour upon their coasts, the Dutch built commodious havens amid the waves for their shipping. Their soil, which was originally the sand which the ocean had cast up, could yield nothing as a basis of trade. All had they to import; — timber to build their ships, — the raw material of their manufactures. Nevertheless, under these immense disadvantages did the Dutch become the first commercial people in the world. They owed all to their Protestantism, and to that element do they still owe their superiority among continental nations, in the virtues of industry, frugality, sobriety, sound morals, and love of freedom.

Let us ascend the Rhine, and mark the condition of the dukedoms and palatinates which lie upon the course of this celebrated stream. This was once the highway of Europe and at every step we meet the memorials of the commercial wealth and baronial power of which this region was anciently the seat. The banks of the river are studded with faded towns, once the busy seats of traffic, but now deserted and impoverished; while the crag is crowned with the baron's castle, now mouldering in the winds. We by no means ascribe to Popery the great reverse which the Rhenish towns have sustained, and which is plainly owing to those great scientific discoveries and political changes which have opened new channels to commerce, and withdrawn it from this its ancient route. But what we affirm is, that wherever there yet remains in this celebrated tract any commercial enterprize and prosperity, it is in connection with Protestantism. The commerce of Europe the valley of the Rhine can never again command; but its trade might be ten times what it is, were it not for the torpor of the people, induced by a superstitious faith; and to be satisfied of this, we have only to take into account that the Rhine connects the centre of Europe with the ocean, and that its course throughout is in a thickly-peopled region. Here, on the right bank of the Rhine, is the free Protestant state of Frankfort. It is some fifteen miles distant from the river; nevertheless it is the scene of extensive banking operations, of commercial activity, and of great agricultural prosperity. Its soil is rich and smiling like a garden, and offers an agreeable contrast to that of the semi-popish duchies and electorates lying around it. But in no part of Germany have the seeds of life which Luther sowed become wholly extinct; and therefore the whole of Germany contrasts favourably with the Bavarian and Austrian kingdoms on the south. As we advance towards the Adriatic the darkness deepens, and the ground refuses to yield its strength to the poor enslaved beings that live upon it.

No traveller ever yet penetrated the mountain-barriers of Switzerland who was not struck, not more with the grandeur of its snows and glaciers, than with the striking but mysterious contrast which canton offers to canton. A single step carries him from the garden into the wilderness, or from the wilderness into the garden. He passes, for instance, from the canton of Lausanne into that of the Valais. and he feels as if he had retrograded from the nineteenth back into the fifteenth century. Or he quits the kingdom of Sardinia, and enters the territory of Geneva, and the transition he can compare only to a passage from the barbarism of the dark ages to the civilization and enterprize of modern times. He leaves behind him a scene of indolence, dirt, and beggary; he emerges on a scene of cleanliness, thrift, and comfort. In the one case the very soil appears to be blighted; the faculties of man are dwarfed; the towns and villages have a deserted and ruinous look; and one sees only a few loiterers, who appear as if they felt motion an intolerable burden; the roads are ploughed by torrents; the bridges are broken down; the farm-houses are dilapidated; and the crops are devastated by inundations, against which the inhabitants have neither the energy nor the forethought to provide. In the other case the traveller finds a soil richly cultivated; elegant villas; neat cottages, with patches of garden ground attached, carefully dressed; towns which are hives of industry; while the countenances of the people beam with intelligence and activity. The traveller is at first confounded at what he sees. The cause to him is wholly incomprehensible. He sees the two cantons lying side by side, warmed by the same sun, their soils equally fertile, their people of the same race, and yet their bounding line has a garden on this side and a desert on that. The traveller discovers at last that the same order invariably obtains, — that the rich cantons are Protestant, and the poor cantons Popish; and he never fails to note down the fact as a curious coincidence, even when he may fail to perceive that he has now reached the solution of the mystery, and that the Popery and the demoralization before him stand related as cause and effect. "I met a carrier one day," says M. Roussell of Paris, speaking of his tour in Switzerland, "who enumerated all the clean cantons and all the dirty ones. The man was unaware that the one list contained all the Protestant cantons, and the other all the Popish cantons." Every one who knows anything of Geneva knows that it is crowded with thousands of laborious and skilful artizans. Here is a picture from the opposite quarter of Switzerland, — the canton of Argau, — where the Popery settles thick and deep: — "M. Zschokke, together with two Catholic gentlemen, was named inspecting visitor of the monasteries by the Argovian government. He found the population around the convent of Muri the idlest, poorest, most barbarous, and most ignorant in the whole canton; a long train of able-bodied beggars of both sexes to be seen at the doors of the monastery, dirty and in rags, receiving distributions of soup from the kitchen, but exhibiting the lowest average both of physical and moral wellbeing throughout the neighbouring villages."

It is but a few years since the author stood upon the frontier of Sardinia; but never can he forget the impression made upon his mind by that lovely but wasted country. Behind him was the far-extending chain of the Jura, with the clouds breaking away from its summits. In the vast hollow formed by the long and gradual descent of the land, from the Jura on the one side and the mountains of Savoy on the other, reposed in calm magnificence the lake of Geneva. Around its lovely waters ran noble banks, on which the vine was ripening; while here and there tall forest-trees were gathered into clumps, and white villas gleamed out upon the shore. In front were the high Alps, amid whose gleaming summits rose "Sovran Blanc" in unapproachable grandeur. In approaching the Sardinian frontier, the author traversed a level fertile country. Trees laden with fruit lined the road, and, stretching their noble arms across, screened him from the warm morning sun. On either side of the highway were rich meadow lands, on which cattle were grazing; while noble woods, and villas embowered amid fruit-trees, still farther diversified the prospect. At short intervals came a neat cottage, with its vine-trellised porch, with its garden gay with blossoms and fruit, and its group of happy children. The author crossed the torrent which divides the republic of Geneva from the kingdom of Sardinia; but ah, what a change! That moment the desolation, moral and physical, began. The fields looked as if a blight had blown across them; they were absolutely black. The houses had become hovels; nor had he gone a dozen yards till he met a troop of beggars. By the wayside stood a row of halt and blind, waiting for alms. Some of them were afflicted with the hideous goitre; others were smitten with the more dreadful malady of cretinism. They formed altogether the most disgusting and miserable-looking group he had ever seen. Their numbers seemed endless. Every other mile, in the day's ride of fifty miles, brought new groupes, as filthy, squalid, and diseased as those which had been passed. They uttered a piteous whine, or extended their withered arms, as if not to beg an alms so much as to protest against the tyranny, ecclesiastical and civil, that was grinding them into the dust. The grandeur of the scenery and the riches of the region, though neglected by man and devastated in part by the elements, could not be surpassed. There were magnificent vines, — trees laden with golden fruit, — patches of the richest grain; but the region seemed a kingdom of beggars, not driven out of their paradise, as Adam was, but doomed to dwell amid its beauty, and yet not taste its fruits. Cretinism, with which the popish cantons especially are overspread, is well known to be owing to filth, insufficient food, and mental stagnancy; and wherever one travels in the popish cantons of Helvetia, he is perpetually met by idiotcy, mendicancy, and every form of misery.

"ubique

Luctus, ubique squalor."

This was the land of the confessor as well as of the persecutor. Here, during many ages, burned the "Waldensian candlestick," shedding its heavenly light on a cluster of lovely valleys, when the rest of Europe lay shrouded in deepest night. This Church, the most venerable in Christendom, has enjoyed a revival in our day. Its Synod was holden in the present summer (1851); and the sound moral and physical condition of its people contrasts instructively with the ignorance and disease around them. It was stated that twenty-five per cent of the population was at school, and only one per cent in the hospital.

We turn northward into France. France, from its central position, extent and fertility of territory, and the genius of its people, was obviously meant by nature to be one of the first of European kingdoms. We find France taking the lead at the opening of modern European history, and, after a period of decadence, resuming her former place under Louis XIV. Since that time her progress has been steadily downward. No doubt she is nominally richer at this moment, both in population and in revenue, than she was under the *grande monarque*; but taking the actual value of money into account, and comparing the increase of France in the points specified, with that of Protestant countries, she is vastly poorer in these, as she is in all other points. This decline is directly traceable — indeed her greatest historians trace it — to her bigotry, by which, no sooner had her trade and commerce become flourishing, and no sooner had the principles of loyalty and virtue taken root among her people, than she made renewed and desperate attempts to extinguish both. Last summer M. Raudot published a work entitled "The Decline of France," of which an analysis appeared in the "*Opinion Publique*," to which we are indebted for the following facts. The first element of power is population. France had a population of thirty millions till 1816, which had risen to thirty-five millions in 1848. Russia had risen in the same period from sixty to seventy millions; England from nineteen and a half to twenty-nine millions; and Prussia from ten to sixteen millions. France during these years had added only a seventh to her population, while the other countries named had added about a third; that is, their rate of increase had been more than double that of France. Were a war to break out, the conditions of the struggle would be changed. France, an essentially agricultural country, has become unable to mount her cavalry with her own horses; and while the other countries have increased in this respect, France was obliged to purchase upwards of 37,000 in 1840. It is obviously unnecessary to compare the shipping of France with that of England. In 1788 the French tonnage was 500,000 tons, and that of England 1,200,000 tons. In 1848 the tonnage of France amounted only to 683,230 tons, and that of England to 3,400,809 tons. These figures speak volumes. The English shipping, which only measured somewhat more than double our tonnage in 1789, is five times greater at present. When a nation buys more than it sells, its wealth diminishes. In France, from 1837 to 1841, the excess of its imports over its exports was 71 millions, and from 1842 to 1846 it was 573 millions. M. Raudot, by calculations founded on the income tax, finds that the landed property of France, though its area is greatly larger and its productive power higher, yields a smaller revenue than that of England and Scotland. It is also to be taken into account, that the funded property in France is dreadfully overloaded with debt. M. Raudot finds also that there has been a diminution in the stature and the physical powers of Frenchmen. In 1789 the height for the infantry soldier in France was 5 feet 1 inch. The law of March 21, 1832, fixed the height at 4 feet 9 inches 10 lines. It was not without reason that the required height was reduced. From 1839 to 1845 there were on an average 37,326 recruits a-year fit for service, who stood less than 5 feet 1 inch French; and if the ancient height had been required, it would have been necessary to send away, as improper for service, one-half of the men called on to perform their turn of duty. In the seven classes called out from 1839 to 1845 there were 491,000 men exempted, and only 486,000 declared fit for service; whereas in the seventeen classes from 1831 to 1837 there had been only 459,000 exempted, and 504,000 declared fit for service; showing that in France the health as well as the stature of the people has declined. M. Raudot proves from the judicial statistics a similar downward course in morals. In 1827, the first year in which a return was made of suicides, the number was 1542 ; in 1847 the number was 3647. In 1826 the tribunals tried only 108,390 cases, and 159,740 prisoners; in 1847 the number of cases had risen to 184,922, and of prisoners to 239,291. This is a sad statement. M. Raudot investigates all the elements of a nation's power, population, army, navy, wealth, commerce, health, public force, morals; and his finding is the same in all, — DECADENCE.

But, would we see how great a wreck Popery is fitted to create, we must turn to Spain. Place a stranger on the summit of the gray rampart formed by the Pyrenees; bid him mark the rich valleys of Spain winding at his feet, and expanding, as they wind, into the fertile plains of Arragon and Navarre; bid him mark how on the north this rich and beauteous land is bounded by the magnificent mountain-wall on which he stands, while on the south it is mistress of the keys of the Mediterranean, still the highway of the world's commerce, and on the west receives the waves of the Atlantic; tell him that the country on which he is gazing, and which under the sway of the Moorish kings was the garden of Europe, possesses every variety of climate, vast beds of minerals, while its soil is covered with the cereals of the north, interspersed with the cotton and rice plants, the sugar-cane, the mulberry, and the vine. "This country," he will exclaim "nature clearly formed to be the seat of a great and powerful kingdom." And such Spain once was; and such it would have been to this day, but for its Popery. Ages of bigotry and of the reign of the Inquisition accomplished at last the utter demoralization of the people; and now Spain, despite her natural wealth and her historic renown, has sunk to the lowest depth of national infamy. Of political weight she is utterly bereft. How seldom is her wheat, or her wool, or her silk, met with in the market! Abroad her name has long ceased to be honoured; at home she presents a spectacle of universal corruption and decay, — an exchequer bankrupt, a soil half-tilled, harbours without ships, highways without passengers or traffic, and villages and towns, partially deserted and falling into ruin.

From Spain we pass into Italy. The nearer we come to the centre and seat of the Papacy, we find the darkness the deeper, and the desolation and ruin, moral and physical, the more gigantic and appalling. Than Italy the world holds not a prouder or fairer realm; but, alas! we may say with the traveller, when he first surveyed its beauty from the passes of the Alps, "the devil has again entered paradise." How much has the Papacy cost Italy! Her arts, her letters, her empire, her commerce, her domestic peace, the spirit and genius of her sons. Nay, not utterly extinct are the last, though sorely crushed and overborne; and now, after twelve centuries of oppression, giving promise to the world that they will yet revive, and flourish anew upon the ruins of the system which has so long enthralled them. Here is Lombardy, "storyful and golden." its sunny plains stretching away in their fertility, with corn and wine eternally springing up from them: yet the Lombards, the merchants and artificers of Milan excepted, are for the most part slaves and beggars. Where now is the commerce of Venice? On the quays on which her merchants trafficked with the world, mendicants whine for alms; and the sighing of four millions of slaves mingles with the wave of the imperial Adriatic.

Italy presents at every step the memorials of its past grandeur and the proofs of its present ruin. In the former we behold what the narrow measure of freedom anciently accorded to it enabled it to attain; in the latter, we see what the foul yoke of the Papacy has reduced it to. Its literature is all but extinct, under the double thral of the censorship and the national superstition. The Bible, that fountain of beauty and sublimity, as well as of morality, is an *unknown book* in Italy; and the popular literature of its people is mainly composed of tales, in prose and in verse, celebrating the exploits of robbers or the miracles of saints. The trade of its cities is at an end, and its towns swarm with idlers and beggars, who can find neither employment nor food. These are wholly uncared for by government. Its agriculture is in a like wretched condition. In some of Italy the farms are mere crofts, and the farm-houses hovels. In other parts, as in the plain around Rome, the farms are enormously large, let out to a corporation; and the reaping, which takes place in the fiercest heats of summer, is performed by mountaineers, whom hunger drives down every year to brave the terrors of the malaria, and the harvest costs on the average the lives of one half the reapers. Some tracts of this beauteous land are now altogether desert; and the salubrity of Italy has been so much affected thereby, that the average duration of human life is considerably shorter. The malaria was known to ancient Italy, but it is undoubted that it has immensely increased in modern times, and this is universally ascribed to the absence of cultivation and of human dwellings. "The Pontine marshes, now a pestilential desert, were once covered with Volscian towns; the mouth of the Tiber, whither convicts are sent to die, was anciently lined by Roman villas; and Paestum, whose hamlet is cursed with the deadliest of all the Italian fevers, was in other days a rich and populous city."

A perpetual round, extending from one end of the year to the other, of festivals and saints' days, interrupts the labours of the people, and renders the formation of steady habits an impossibility. The Roman Calendar exhibits a festival or fast on every day of the year. The most of these are voluntary holidays; but the obligatory ones amount to about seventy in the year, exclusive of Sabbaths. A great part of the land is the property of the Church. The number of sacerdotal persons is of most disproportionate amount, seriously affecting the trade and agriculture of the country, from which they are withdrawn, as they also are from the jurisdiction of the secular courts. "In the city of Rome," says Gavazzi, "with a population of 170,000 (of which nearly 6000 resident Jews, and a fluctuating mass of strangers, nearly of the same amount, formed part), there were, besides 1400 nuns, a clerical militia of 3069 ecclesiastics, being one for every fifty inhabitants, or one for every twenty-five male adults; while in the provinces there were towns where the proportion was still greater, being one to every twenty. The Church property formed a capital of 400,000,000 of francs, giving 20,000,000 per annum; while the whole revenue of the state was but eight or nine millions of dollars, — a sum disastrously absorbed in the payment of cardinal ostentation, in purveying to the pomps of a scandalous court, or in supplying brandy to Austrian brutality." In popish countries generally one-third of the year is spent in worshipping dead men and dead women; the people are withdrawn from their labours, and taught to consume their substance and their health in riot, and drunkenness. The clergy, exempt from war and other civic duties, have abundance of leisure to carry on intrigues and hatch plots. They oppress the poor, fleece the rich, and drive away trade. Vast quantities of gold and silver are locked up in the cathedrals, being employed to adorn images, which might otherwise circulate freely in trade; and in every parish there is an asylum or sanctuary, where robbers, murderers, and all sorts of criminals, are defended against the laws. To this, in no small degree, is owing the blood with which popish countries are defiled.

There is only one other country to which we shall advert. Its condition is so well known that we simply name it, — Ireland. Its natural riches, — its mineral wealth, — its amenity of climate, — its vast capabilities for commerce, — are all well known; and yet Ireland is a name of woe among the nations, and its wretchedness has clouded the glories of the British empire. There, IGNORANCE and POPERY, IDLENESS, and CRIME, grow side by side, and draw each other up to a marvellous height. In their shade raven all manner of unclean beasts. Rebellion roars from its cave, murder howls for blood, perjury mocks justice, and faction defies law; while hordes of its teeming population annually leave its shores in nakedness and hunger, to lurk in the fever-haunted dens of our great cities, or to be cast upon the frozen shores of Canada. "Take up the map of the world," says Dr. Ryan, Roman Catholic bishop of Limerick; "trace from pole to pole, and from hemisphere to hemisphere; and you will not meet so wretched a country as Ireland." But to what is this wretchedness owing? There is no man who acknowledges the least force in the principles we have demonstrated and the examples we have adduced, who can help seeing that the misery of Ireland is owing to its Popery. On the other side of St. George's Channel it is still the dark ages. There mind is as stagnant as before the breaking out of the Reformation. Nor has Ireland shared in the great industrial revolution of the sixteenth century, and vainly struggles to rival in wealth and comfort a country like England, which possesses the intelligence and wields the arts of the nineteenth. Her Popery has degraded and demoralized her; and out of her demoralization have sprung her sloth, her improvidence, her crime, and her misery. It is hard to say whether her vices or her priests now eat most into her bowels. Where the landlord cannot gather his rents, nor the tax-gatherer his dues, the priest collects his. Popery can glean in the rear even of famine and death: she has neither a heart to pity nor an eye to weep, but only an iron hand to gather up the crumbs on which the widow and the fatherless should feed. Compare Scotland with Ireland. How poor the one, despite her immense natural advantages; how rich the other, despite her no less immense natural disadvantages. We see Popery, in the one case, converting a garden into a wilderness, darkened by ignorance, swarming with mendicants, polluted with crime; while the wail of its misery rings ceaselessly throughout the civilized world. In the other, we see Protestantism converting a land of swamps and forests into a fruitful and flourishing realm, the home of the arts, and the dwelling of a people renowned throughout the world for their shrewdness, their industry, and their virtues.

Or we may take another contrast. At the one extremity of the European continent stands ITALY; at the other is SCOTLAND; — the centre of Roman Catholicism the one, the head of Protestantism the other. What was the relative position of these two countries at the beginning of our era? That a land of sages and heroes; this a country of painted barbarians. But eighteen centuries have accomplished a mighty revolution. Italy, despite the beauty of its climate, the exuberant fertility of its soil, the fine genius of its people, and the heritage of renown which the past had bequeathed to it, is a land of ruins. It has lost all; while Scotland has cleared its swamps, covered its wilds with the richest cultivation, erected cities than which the world contains none nobler, and filled the earth with the renown of its arts, its science, and its patriotism. Why is this? Popery is the religion of the one country, — Protestantism is the religion of the other. God never leaves himself without a witness. He may close his Word; He may withdraw his ministers; still we need no prophet from the dead. He continues to proclaim, by the great dispensations of his providence, the eternal distinction between truth and error. Here has He set up before the eyes of all nations, Italy and Scotland, — a witness for Protestantism the one, a monument against Popery the other. "Be wise, ye kings." Would we sink Britain to the degradation of Italy, let us endow in Britain the religion of Italy.

We have already demonstrated that Popery, looking solely at its character, and apart altogether from any experience of its working, is fitted to degrade man socially and individually. We have now shown, from nearly as extensive an induction of facts as it is possible to make, or as one can reasonably demand, that experience fully bears out the conclusion at which we had arrived on the ground of principle. Wherever we find Popery, there we find moral degradation, intellectual torpor, and physical discomfort and misery. Under every government, whether the free governments of England and Belgium, or the despotic regimeof Spain and Austria, — among every race, the Teutonic and the Celtic, — in both hemispheres, the states of the Old World and the provinces of the New, — the tendency of Romanism is the same. It is a principle that stereotypes nations. It depopulates kingdoms, annihilates industry, destroys commerce, corrupts government, arrests justice, undermines order, breeds revolutions, extinguishes morality, and nourishes a brood of monstrous vices, — murder, perjury, adultery, indolence and theft, massacres and wars. It enfeebles and destroys the race of man, and annihilates the very cement of society. Popery has been on its trial before the world these three centuries; and such are the effects which it has produced in every country under heaven where it has existed. It is truly "the abomination that maketh desolate." The man who will not hear what the Bible has to say of Popery, cannot refuse to hear what Popery has to say of itself.

To make the contrast complete, let us glance at the career of Protestant Britain during the past hundred years. In 1750, the throne of Britain was filled by the second George. Four years before, the hopes of the Stuarts had expired on the fatal moor of Culloden; France, under Louis XV. had scarcely passed her zenith; Francis I. and Maria Theresa ruled the destinies of Austria; Philip V. those of Spain; while Pope Benedict XIV. occupied the Vatican. England was but a second-rate power, not daring even to dream of the career of greatness which was just then opening to her. The British sceptre was swayed over not more than thirteen millions of subjects, including our North American colonies. We held at that time, no doubt, possessions both in the western and eastern hemispheres; but they were insignificant in extent, and precarious in point of tenure. The French were masters of Canada and Louisiana, and threatened to expel us from the American continent altogether. Our Indian empire was then limited to the British settlement in Bengal; and the French, who held the Deccan, threatened to deprive us even of that. Holland and Portugal rivalled us as commercial powers; France far eclipsed us in political importance; and Spain, mistress of the gold mines of Mexico and Peru, outstripped us in wealth. In all points we were inferior to the great powers on the Continent, save in one, our Protestantism. Since that period Britain has pursued a career unexampled in the history of nations. Canada has become ours. The Mogul empire has fallen under our sway. We have called hitherto unknown continents and islands from out the Pacific, and are peopling them with our race and our language, ruling them with our institutions and our laws, and enriching them with our commerce, our science, and our faith. Thus the chain of our power encircles the globe. We have become the mother of nations. During the same period we have made rapid progress in scientific discovery, and in the improvement of the arts, perfecting those already known, and summoning to our service new and extraordinary elements of power. Our commercial enterprise and monetary power have also experienced prodigious expansion. Thus, in the short space of a single century, from being but a second-rate state, whose language, laws, and influence scarcely extended beyond the shores of our island, overshadowed by the great continental kingdoms of Europe, we have risen, in point of population, extent of territory, and real power, to a pitch of greatness which is threefold that of imperial Rome. And, we must add likewise, that, though not blind to our shortcomings and sins as a nation, no candid and well-informed man will deny, that during the past century we have made great advances in the theory of liberty, and in the principles and practice of vital godliness; while abroad, we have been making, not so great efforts as we ought to have made, but greater than any nation ever before made, to diffuse the Bible and the gospel throughout the habitable globe. "Happy people the English!" was the exclamation of M. E. de Girardin, at a peace-meeting lately held in London. "Happy people the English! ever advancing in their onward course, while so many other nations progress only to retrograde." There never was seen on earth so sublime a spectacle as Britain at this moment presents.

To one element alone are we to trace the unexampled career and prodigious height of Britain, — her Protestantism. "Ascribe ye strength unto God; his excellency is over Israel; the God of Israel is He that giveth strength and power unto his people. Blessed be God!"

Book IV: Present Policy and Prospects of the Papacy

Chapter I: Sham Reform and Real Re-action.

Pius IX., on ascending the pontifical throne in 1846, found a crisis in papal affairs. Ages of misgovernment and superstition had borne their proper fruit, — universal decay and exhaustion. Nations were exhausted; the long thraldom they had endured had inflicted a fatal blight on their moral and industrial powers. Governments were exhausted; their numerous crusades and wars had sunk them into bankrupty. Churches were exhausted; superstition had worn out belief altogether, and plunged the masses into infidelity and atheism. Wickedness is short-lived, and in the end destroys itself. Thus, after twelve centuries of dominion and glory, it was seen that the Papacy was now verging to its fall, and that it was the author of its own overthrow. The Reformation had done much to weaken Popery: the progress of scientific discovery, and the working of a free press, — indirect consequences of the Reformation, — had contributed also to undermine this system. But, though it startles at first, Popery had done more than all these to work out its own ruin. Its superstition had passed into atheism, its tyranny into revolution, and the Papacy appeared doomed to a violent death at the hands of those evil principles which itself had engendered. His first glance at the Catholic world, after his elevation to the tiara, must have satisfied the Pope that the condition of western Europe was very different indeed from what it was in the fifteenth century, — different even from what it was in the middle of last century, — that the democratic element, which had burst out with such terror in the first French Revolution, and which had spent itself in the wars that followed, had been recruiting its forces during the period of quiescence since 1815, — that it now universally pervaded the west, — that it had summoned to its aid principles of unknown character, but of tremendous power, — and that there was not strength enough in either the secular or the sacerdotal system to withstand the coming shock, unless, indeed, both should come to be reinvigorated. Pius was aware especially, that in Italy a constitutional movement was in progress, and had been so in the latter years of his predecessor Gregory XVI. He knew that thoughtful Italians, both in and out of Italy, were painfully sensible of the demoralization of their country, — that they attributed that demoralization to the character and form of its government, — that they regarded the rule of a sacerdotal monarch as an anomaly, unsuited to the spirit and the wants of the age, and a barrier to progress, — that throughout all Italy, more especially in the States of the Church, where the evil was more felt, and even in Rome itself, the desire was universal among all classes for the disjunction of the temporal and spiritual sovereignties. All this was perfectly well known to Pius IX. on his elevation to the fisherman's chair; and it is necessary to keep this in view, as it explains the phase that Popery assumed, and the new tactics which it adopted, and likewise furnishes the key to its present state and prospects.

Popery, though outwardly strong, is inwardly and essentially weak. The reverse is the fact as regards Christianity: it is outwardly weak, but inwardly and essentially strong. Its power is within itself, and inseparable from its essence. It can lead those on whom it operates, whether an individual or a nation, to act contrary to their passions and interests. It originates and guides great movements, but is never dragged in their rear. Not so the Papacy. All its power is without itself. It governs men only in accordance with their passions: it watches the rising of great movements, links itself on to them, and appears to guide, while in point of fact it is constrained to follow. The crisis in which Pius IX. found the Papacy offered him the alternative of opposing the movement, or of siding with it, and so appearing to lead it. Either alternative was attended with immense risk; but on the principle we have stated, that Popery is powerless in opposition unless she can wield the sword, and that her great strength lies in casting herself upon the popular current, in whatever direction it may chance to be running, Pius chose the last, as the least perilous of the two courses open to him. No one can yet have forgotten the amazement which seized upon all men when they saw that power which for ages had been the head of European despotism, place itself at the head of the Italian movement, now sufficiently developed to be seen to be part of a grand European movement towards constitutional government. A new prodigy was beheld. That power which had warred with liberty during ten centuries, and ceased to assail it with its thunderbolts only when it was prostrate beneath its feet, — that power which had been the bulwark of despotic thrones, — which had provided a dungeon for science, and a stake for the patriot and the confessor, — whose motto was immobility, — had become the patron of progress, and assumed the lead in a grand movement towards free government! Those who were able to penetrate the policy of Rome saw clearly that the movement was distasteful and abhorrent to the

Papacy, — that it contained principles utterly destructive of the system, — and that it had placed itself at its head that it might strangle by craft what it was unable to crush by force.

Nevertheless, for some time the policy of the Pope was completely successful; and there even appeared some likelihood of its being finally triumphant. Flambeaux were burned before the gates of the Quirinal, and Rome resounded day and night with *vivas*. The journalists of Paris and London wrote elaborate and eloquent panegyrics on the reforming Pope. It had almost been voted by acclamation that Popery was changed; that the bloody deeds of past times were to be attributed to the barbarism of the age, and not at all to the spirit of the Papacy; and that the pontifical system was perfectly compatible with constitutional and liberal government, and the progress of the human race. This was what Pius IX. wished the world to believe; and had he but succeeded in making the world believe this, he would have carried his point; he would have added a lustre and authority to the chair of Peter unknown to it for ages. The revolted masses would have returned to the creed they had abjured, and come thronging back to the altars from which infidelity had driven them away. Recognising in Pius at once the pontiff and the reformer, — the high priest of religion and the foremost champion of liberty, — how willingly would the nations have surrendered the movement into his hands! and, once in his hands, he would have known well how to turn it to account, making it the harbinger of a new era of dominion and glory to the popedom, and of iron bondage to Europe. Such were the visions of the Vatican. The conspiracy was wide-spread. The bishops and priests throughout the Catholic world were taught how to play their part. The Church ostentatiously marched in the van, as if she had been the originator of the movement, and was nobly guiding it to its goal. Prayers were offered in the cathedrals and parish churches of France for Pius IX. and his reforms. The banners were taken into the chapels and blessed. Trees of liberty were set up amid papal benedictions; and in the public processions priests of all orders were seen to mingle. The blouse of the democrat and the frock of the bourgeoise were interspersed with the robe of the parish *curé*, the cowl of the Capuchin, and the rope of the Franciscan. There was at that time no small danger of the infidelity of the masses passing into superstition, and of Popery thus rooting itself afresh in the popular mind of Europe. But from a calamity so great it pleased Providence to deliver the world, by writing confusion upon the counsels of the Vatican. And when we speak of deliverance, we would not insinuate that all peril from the Papacy is at an end, but only that the insidious and dangerous device of Pius IX., maintained with great plausibility, and carried out with immense *eclat*, during well-nigh three years, has been completely exposed and defeated; and this we are disposed to regard as no light mercy. A crisis arose in the movement, which might have been foreseen, but for which no amount of papal ingenuity could possibly provide. Big promises and sham reforms, — all as yet which the reforming pontiff had given, — could no longer suffice. The masses were in earnest, and boons were now demanded, great, substantial and sweeping, such as would have laid the papal supremacy in the dust, — a free press, the secularization of the papal government, and the introduction of the representative and constitutional element in the form of chambers. It was to prevent such demands ever being made that Pius IX. had placed himself at the head of the movement. As astute an upholder of the infallibility and supremacy as any pope who ever flourished in the dark ages, Pius IX. resolved not to yield; and, after a short space spent in shuffling, be openly broke with the movement, and cast himself into the arms of the absolutist and reactionary powers. He commenced his reforming career with an amnesty which set loose from prison thieves, robbers, and even worse criminals; and he closed it with an amnesty which consigned to a dungeon, or drove into exile, the most virtuous and patriotic citizens of Rome. And thus the spell by which Pius had hoped to charm into peace the furies of the Revolution broke utterly in his hands. Driven from this high ground, the Papacy has renewed the struggle in a much less advantageous position. Having been obliged to drop the mask of reform, it advances against Christianity and liberty under its own form, and with its old weapons, — coercion and the sword. This so far is well. One plan, organized by the Jesuits, and worked by them, is at this moment in operation in all the countries of Europe; and when we trace its workings, so far as we have access to know them, we exhibit the *present state and tactics* of Popery. Popery, then, has gone back to its ancient and natural allies, from whom it had been parted for a brief space; and the two, having manifestly one interest, will probably remain united, till both sink into one common perdition. Matters have come to this pass, that nothing but the sword of the state can save the spiritual power, and nothing but the policy of the Church can wield the sword of the state. This both parties clearly perceive. Accordingly, the Jesuits, whom the revolutionary outbreak of 1848 had driven away, have been recalled, and a virtual compact entered into with them. Lend us your power, say the Jesuits, and we will give you our wisdom. We will save the vessel of the state, only we must sit at the helm. And at the helm they do sit. The Jesuits are at this moment the real rulers of Europe; and from the one end of it to the other they pursue the same object, and act upon the same tactics. Their scheme of reconquering Europe by the pretence of reform having come to nought, they have been compelled to fall back upon their ancient and approved method of rule, — open, undisguised force. Europe is at present under the government of the sabre. This is the Jesuit prescription for curing it of its madness. The first object of the Jesuits is to abrogate the liberties which the Revolution of 1848 inaugurated. They know that liberty and Protestantism are twin powers, — that the alliance between despotism and Popery is now of a thousand years standing, — and that the papal supremacy is incompatible with the order of things introduced by the Revolution, more especially with universal suffrage and a free press. The first requisites, therefore, to the restoration of their power is the suppression of the rights of 1848. They dare not by edict proclaim these rights null and void, but they provisionally abrogate them. The violence of the masses is the pretext alleged for placing the great cities and several whole kingdoms of the Continent under martial law. It isof course intended by the Jesuits that this provisional state shall become the permanent and normal condition of Europe. Thus they attempt insidiously to rivet their former chains upon the nations.

They are wise in their generation. A glance at the past history of Europe shows, that in every country in which Reformation advanced so far as to introduce constitutional government, Protestantism has kept its ground; whereas in those countries where the government was not reformed, whatever progress the reformed religion had made, the people have again fallen back into Popery. They know also enough of Europe at this hour to be aware that, were Poland, were Bohemia, were Italy, and, we may add, Spain, to acquire a constitutional government, these countries would not remain a single day under the papal yoke. It is their absolute *regime* alone that prevents the immediate erection of a Protestant national Church in Poland and Bohemia. A Christian Church would be formed at Rome, but for the sacerdotal government. No sooner did Piedmont become a constitutional kingdom in the spring of 1848, than the Waldensian Church obtained its religious freedom, and its members their constitutional rights; while the despotism of Russia to this day excludes the missionary from her

Asiatic provinces. These facts show that the Jesuits have good cause for plotting the overthrow of the liberties of 1848.

They have attacked these liberties one by one. First, the press groans in its former chains. In France, in Austria, in Naples, and, in short, all over Catholic Europe, the press is the object of prosecution, of fine, and not unfrequently of actual suspension. This rigour is not limited to newspapers, but extends to all useful books, and especially to the Bible. As an instance, we may mention that, in the spring of 1850, the priests prosecuted two printers of Florence for having, under the government of the republic, printed a translation of the New Testament in Italian, and that on the express ground of "their having published the gospel in the vulgar tongue, so that every one may be enabled to read it." Thus they show their dread of letters, and their hankering after the darkness of bygone times. The excuse put forward for these tyrannical proceedings is, that a free press is propagating communism. These persons forget that under the rigorous censorship of Germany nothing flourished so much as an atheistic pantheism. Occasion is taken on the same ground to molest colporteurs in their distribution of tracts and Bibles, especially in France, where this work is mostly carried on.

The Jesuits are making prodigious efforts in all the countries of Europe to get into their hands the education of the youth. In Ireland, the Synod of Thurles condemned the government colleges, and prohibited the Romanist youth from attending them, because their chairs were not filled solely with Romanists. This Synod, which enacted, in effect, that darkness is better than light, and that the light ought to be put under anathema all over Ireland, and all over the world if possible, was fittingly presided over by a man who believes that the Pope is infallible, and that the earth stands still. In France a bill was introduced into the Assembly by the Jesuit Minister M. Falloux, and passed, giving to the prefects the power of dismissing the departmental schoolmasters. So early as April 1850, not fewer than four thousand schoolmasters, suspected of a leaning to Protestantism or to communism, had been dismissed, on the complaint of the parish *curé*. These discussions on education brought to light the existence of a feeling in favour of a spiritual or mental tyranny in quarters where it was least suspected. We allude to MM. Thiers, De Tocqueville, and others. No sooner did the Jesuits regain their ascendancy at Naples than they commenced their war against education. By a decree of the 27th of October 1849, whoever is engaged in public or private instruction must appear before a council, to be interrogated on "the Catechism of the Christian doctrine," and can only exercise their office *by permission*; which simply means that the Jesuits are to dictate what is to be taught to the youth at Naples, whilst the civil law will punish any deviation from their orders. By a decree of the Minister of Instruction at Naples, issued in December 1849, all students are placed under a commission of ecclesiastics, and are obliged to enroll themselves in some lecherous congregation or society. All schools, public and private, are placed under the same arbitrary law. The schoolmasters are bound to take all their pupils above ten years of age to one of the congregations, and to make a monthly return of their attendance. Since that time, the atrocious catechism described by Mr. Gladstone, which teaches that kings are divine, that popes can dispense with oaths, and that all liberals are the children of the devil, and will be eternally damned, has been introduced into the schools, and is now conned by the children. In Austria and Germany they are not less busy attacking knowledge under pretence of diffusing it. Thus do the Jesuits strive to lead back the mind of Europe to its dungeon. The shackles which infidelity taught the fathers to throw off are to be riveted betimes upon the sons.

In the latter years of Napoleon's career, the condition of Roman Catholicism seemed desperate. It was then that a small but brilliant band of literary men undertook to restore its fortunes. Lamennais, de Maistre, Bonald, wrote argumentative and eloquent works, defending Romanism and attacking its adversaries. Their works made a great sensation, and gathered a party around them. They leant mainly upon the Roman Court, the restored Bourbons, and Metternich: they were absolutist in their politics, and their great success seduced them into measures of an extremely despotic character. Under Louis XVIII. bloody persecutions were recommenced in the south of France, and the Jesuits kept assassins in their pay. Marshals of France were obliged to walk in processions and carry a candle, under the penalty of forfeiting the favour of their sovereign. As a consequence, the Revolution of 1830 broke out, and fell upon the Jesuits like a thunderbolt. They saw their error, and resolved henceforward not to lean upon governments, but to operate directly upon the people, through the instrumentality of the press, the pulpit, and the confessional. The interval since 1830 has been occupied in this way by the priesthood. But it does not appear that their success has been great; for it is a fact too obvious to be denied, that infidelity, under its various forms of socialism, communism, and atheism, is more widely spread among the French people at this moment than it was in 1830. But every new disaster that befalls their system, instead of discouraging them, only stimulates to greater activity. And since 1848 their zeal has been prodigious: they are in course of filling the schools with teachers thoroughly devoted to the priests; new school-books have been compiled; and the main object kept in view in their compilation is the initiation of the youth into the absurdities of Popery. The following may be taken as a sample of these books: — Of the tracts of the "blessed Alphonse de Liguori," which the priests are in the habit of putting into the hands of their scholars and catechumens, there is one in great ardour of sanctity in the seminaries, convents of young females, and in all the institutions under the influence of the Romish clergy, entitled *Paraphrase de Salve Regina*. It was designed to recommend the worship of the Virgin; and amongst other methods to gain this end, it condescended to tell the following story: — "There lived at Venice [when, it is not said] a celebrated lawyer, who had enriched himself by fraud, and all sorts of illicit practices. His soul was in a most deplorable state, and the only thing that saved him from the doom he so richly merited was his reverence for the Virgin, to whom he every day repeated a certain prayer. This appeared from the following melo-dramatic occurrence. One day a Capuchin father, was dining with him. The lawyer, after having shown him all the curiosities of his house, told his reverend friend that he had one thing more wonderful still to show him, — 'an ape, the phoenix of its kind.' 'He serves me as a valet,' said the advocate, 'waits at table, washes the glasses, attends to the door, in fact does everything.' 'Ah!' said the Capuchin shaking his head, 'provided it is really an ape; let me see the animal.' The ape, after a long search, was found secreted under a bed, and would by no means move. 'Infernal beast!' cried the monk, come out; and I command thee, in the name of God, to say who thou art!' The ape replied that he was a demon, and that he waited for the first day that the advocate should omit to say his prayer the to the Virgin, to stifle him, and carry off his soul to hell, as the Lord had given him permission." Such is the instruction which Jesuitism furnishes to the youth of France. It would scarce be possible to show greater contempt for the human understanding.

"Signs and lying wonders" is one mark of the predicted apostacy. In all ages miracles have been wrought by the prophets of Rome in support of their pretensions. These are dangerous weapons in an age when knowledge is somewhat diffused. Nevertheless Rome has again in her straits had recource to them. Somewhere about the time that the Pope returned to

Rome, a famous image of the Virgin at Rimini was seen to wink. Intelligence was quickly spread of the miracle; crowds were assembled; the prodigy was repeated day by day, and day by day rich offerings continued to be heaped upon the shrine of the Madonna. It was now reported that another image at another Italian town had been seen to wink; and presently there was a whole shower of winking Madonnas. We ask, Is the Pope infallible? and we are answered by a wink. It is difficult seeing the logical connection between the wink and the infallibility. The faithful, of course, will take the wink as a proof that the Pope is infallible; but others may take it as meaning just the opposite. Did Rome understand her position, an attempt to establish her doctrines by miracles would be the last thing she would think of. The infallibility is the ground on which she rests all belief. When, therefore, she brings forward a miracle as a proof of any dogma, she in reality shifts her ground; she commits a grievous solecism in argument; and, instead of proving that she is infallible, proves that she is an impostor.

Paris, too, was the scene of some miracles. A Peter Perimond, a plain obese peasant from Grenoble, appeared in Paris in March 1850, and announced that he had seen the Saviour, and received from him a commission to heal the sick and convert the world. He lay during passion week, the *stigmata* impressed on his body, and the blood distilling drop by drop from his "sacred" wounds. When the sun went down the wounds ceased to bleed. He cured the diseased who visited him, by the touch. Peter Perimond was evidently a tool of the priests, by whom the whole affair was arranged with great adroitness. Some of the first anatomists of Paris examined the miracle-worker, and pronounced "the whole a juggle." A *Veronica* was seen to shed tears at Naples, doubtless over the misfortunes of the exiled Pontiff. A *Madonna* at Rome was observed to nod with special grace to certain of her devotees; but the priest was a bungler, and permitted the cords to be seen. Veritable portraits of Christ and the Virgin, said to have been discovered in some subterranean vault of the ancient palace of the Senate at Rome, where they had lain undiscovered for eighteen centuries, were hawked about in France. During winter, the friars in Naples and in some parts of Italy have been zealously warning their flocks from the pulpit against the three great evils, Revolution, Communism, and Protestantism. "I heard," says a Continental correspondent, writing from Naples last December, — "I heard a preacher, a few days since, from the pulpit of a church exclaim, 'Mind what you are about! You may ere long fall into the deplorable state of the English, and lose all hope of salvation.'" A deep veil rests above the confessional; but the activity of the priests of Rome in every other department at this moment leaves no doubt that that powerful engine is worked with energy and effect.

The Church of Rome has carefully noted every phase of society at this moment, and, with her usual flexibility and tact, she suits herself to all, and has a separate argument for each particular class. To governments trembling in the presence of the "fierce democratie" she represents herself as the only bulwark of order. She bids kings lean on her, and so save their thrones and sceptres, which otherwise will be swept away. She calls on those shocked by the impieties and blasphemies of socialism to ponder the consequences of forsaking the true faith; telling them that if they rebel against the reaching of the Church, they plunge into the abyss of atheism. To the propertied man, who trembles at the confiscation and pillage which a triumphant communism would bring with it, she exhibits herself as alike able to preserve his earthly and to augment his heavenly goods. In the panic that is abroad, she knows that men have not the calmness to inquire whether the Church does not need protection, rather than posess the ability to bestow it. The upper strata of society in France, too, are pervaded by a great anxiety to create power, — to discover new principles and sources of authority; and what so likely as the influence of the Church to tame and subjugate those passions which the Revolution has let loose? Up to the present hour, ever since the great outbreak of 1848, they have found out no principle of authority save downright force. The army and the police, pretty much blended into one, is their only instrument of government. They are not unnaturally anxious to supplement their vast array of physical force with a certain amount of moral power, by enlisting the priesthood on their side. They look to the Pope as a kind of moral Fouché, — a spiritual prefect of police for Europe. These statesmen, speaking generally, — for we must except MM. Montalembert and Falloux — care nothing for the Church as a Church. They never go to confession or to mass; but they need the Church for the maintenance of their own authority. Their religion is that of Pope's *Sir Balaam*, who, whilst he himself was seeking to make his fortune in corrupt politics, sent his wife and family to sermon. How far this perfidious alliance, prompted by fear and necessity, is likely to promote the ends of either statesmen or churchmen, we shall inquire when we come to glance at the favourable symptoms of Europe. Meanwhile we note it as one of the grand currents in the Catholic world, and one of the main causes which have led to an apparent return of many of the higher classes to Romanism. Thus everywhere we behold a movement towards civil and religious despotism. Rome is in the van of the march.

Chapter II: New Catholic League, and Threatened Crusade against Protestantism.

We greatly err if we regard the above in the light of unconnected efforts. They are parts of a colossal plan, hatched in the Vatican, for the purpose of restoring arbitrary government and papal domination all over Europe. The European DEMOCRACY is the modern Sphinx: the dynasties of the Continent must solve her riddle, or be torn in pieces. They must either rule that democracy or annihilate it. Should they resolve on the first, not only must they feign to be in love with what at heart they abhor, but they must be prepared to grant concessions unlimited in magnitude and endless in number. It is now too late to adopt such a policy; and none know better than the ruling powers themselves, that were it adopted, it would speedily issue in the complete suspension of their functions and the total annihilation of their authority. In the face of constitutions ignored, oaths and promises violated, and the profuse expenditure of blood, which darken the history of the past three years, the least approach towards conciliation would be sternly repulsed by the democratic party. The second alternative only remains,— coercion. The democracy, and, along with that, whatever is free, whether in religion or in government, must be crushed promptly and universally. The last spark must be trodden out, else the conflagration will blaze afresh. Now, in this war the infallible Church presents herself to the absolutist state as by far its oldest and staunchest ally. Her organization, which is the most flexible that exists; her influence, which operates in a domain from which that of the state is shut out,— for, till the intellect and the conscience are blindfolded by superstition, power cannot succeed in permanently enslaving men; are all now made available. Moreover, it is equally the interest of both to quell this revolt; and what so likely as that a community of interest should suggest unity of action? *A priori*, then, we might infer the existence of a grand conspiracy against the liberties of Europe, even did not the facts already stated, and those we now proceed to state, render the existence of such a conspiracy undoubted. We do not, of course, know the day or the hour when this criminal confederacy was formed,— such transactions belong to the darkness; but the public measures of the conspirators enable us to read the history of their most secret hours, and to unveil the character of their deepest plots.

A crusade has been undertaken simultaneously in all the countries of Europe against civil and religious liberty. This bespeaks concert. The agents who conduct that crusade are the same everywhere,— the priest and the *sbirro*. Does not this denote confederacy between the ecclesiastical and the civil authorities for their joint domination? The catechism and the bayonet,— the Jesuit and the *gendarme*,— the Church and the army,— are in combined and vigorous action all over Europe. Look at Rome. Under Pius IX. the era of the worst popes has been revived. The return from Gaeta formed the commencement of a policy as astute in its foreign relations, and more oppressive in its home administration, than even that of Hildebrand. Infallibility sits behind a hedge of bayonets; its assessors are described as "assassins, galley-slaves, and thieves;" and the subordinate agents of its government are undoubtedly spies and police. The patriot, the scholar, the constitutionalist, have all been swept off to prison, or sent into exile. Felons only are at large, who celebrate the saturnalia of license under the archfelon of the Vatican. The fisherman's net is of steel, as its victims know. The keys are no mere symbol now, seeing Peter's successor has become a jailor. Rome, full of dungeons and desolate hearths, and cinctured with fresh graves, sits cowering beneath the baleful shadow of pontifical despotism. The Word of God dare not enter those gates within which the vicar of God sits enthroned. An edition of Diodati's Bible, amounting to some thousands, which was commenced by the American mission under the Roman Republic, lies locked up in the vaults of the Quirinal. The incarcerated Bibles and the incarcerated Romans tell the same tale: they proclaim the unchanged and unchangeable hostility of Rome to religious and civil freedom.

At Naples the same object is pursued by precisely the same methods. Whatever coercion, mental and physical, can do to make a people swallow down the doctrine that kings are divine and popes infallible, is now being done at Naples. The government is conducted by priests, police, and soldiers; the capital is full of spies; the confessional is worked to discover opinion, and the police to extirpate it. There, too, as in Rome, light, and, above all, Protestant light, is the object of profoundest dread. The press is locked, the Bible is prohibited, and the Jesuit laborers in his special vocation as a propagator of ignorance, or of something worse. The few schools taught by British Protestants have all been closed, and the whole youth of the country are under Jesuit tuition.

On Naples the gaze of the civilized world has been fixed, by the astounding disclosures of a British statesman. Let us look narrowly at this model kingdom, and its model king, for such Papists account Ferdinand. Here we behold a specimen of what all kings would be were the jurisdiction and teaching of the Roman Church universal. The acts of Ferdinand, which have filled the world with horror, are but the dogmas of Liguori applied to the science of government.

The tragedy now in progress in Naples commenced in dissimulation and Jesuitism. In 1848 the king inaugurated constitutional government, by swearing, "in the awful name of the Most Holy and Almighty God, to whom alone it appertains to read the depths of the heart, and whom we loudly invoke as the judge of the simplicity of our intentions." Promises and oaths were speedily followed by perfidies and perjuries. The constitution, so solemnly inaugurated, and which included a limited monarchy and two houses, with a guarantee for personal liberty, and the legality of imposts only when imposed by parliament, has been abrogated in every particular. But this crime is small compared with the atrocious maxim which has been unblushingly put forward to justify it, that the king's right is divine, that his powers are unlimited, and that no oaths which restrict his prerogative can bind him. Right orthodox doctrine, according to Liguori. A "Philosophical Catechism" has been compiled by a priest, who acts, of course, under his superiors, and is now, in virtue of a government order, used in all the schools,— "a work, one of the most singular and detestable," says Mr. Gladstone, "I have ever seen." The doctrine of this catechism is, that all who hold liberal opinions will be eternally damned; that kings may violate as many oaths as they please in the cause of papal and monarchical absolutism; and that "the Head of the Church has authority from God to release consciences from oaths, when he judges that there is suitable cause for it."

In the history of the Papacy demoralizing doctrines have invariably been the prelude to dreadful tragedies: so has it been at Naples. A Jeffries *redivivus*, ferocious, cowardly, blood-thirsty, and as thoroughly the creature of the court as was the infamous minion of James VII., presides over the Neapolitan tribunals. The indiscriminate and insatiable tyranny of this man has swept off all who co-operated with the court in its brief but hollow attempt at constitutional rule; the patriot, the scholar, the gentleman,— all are in prison. From twenty to thirty thousand political prisoners, according to the estimate of Mr. Gladstone, are in the dungeons of Ferdinand. We wish that, like the novelist, we could take a single captive. This clanking of chains on every side, and this gathering of haggard faces, row upon row, till the woe-struck assemblage grows into thousands and tens of thousands, but distract and overwhelm us. These miserable crowds lie pent up in filthy prisons, heavily loaded with irons, and see the light of day only when it gilds the bars in the roof of their vault. Others have been disposed of in Ischia and the adjoining islands on the Neapolitan coast, where they rot in dungeons many feet below sea-level. One cannot point his foot on Neapolitan earth but it is above a dungeon. Where, in works of fiction, shall we find a tragedy like this? The genius of Shakspeare himself never painted a mightier woe.

But the question remains, Who is responsible for all this suffering? We reply by asking, Who taught Ferdinand to revoke the constitution? Who gave him a dispensation from an oath sworn "in the awful name of the Most Holy and Almighty God?" Who wrote the catechism which adjudges to eternal torments all who hold liberal opinions? And who, in fine, are the busy agents in this persecution? The priests of the Roman Church. That Church is responsible for all this suffering. The thirty thousand victims in Naples groan in chains, that such things as purgatory and transubstantiation, with all the revenues therefrom arising, may not be swept away, and the rule of infallibility exploded as a monstrosity. The Neapolitan *sbirro*, the French bombardier, and the Austrian Croat, are the triple alliance which props up the imposture of the Vatican; and whatever enormities they may choose to perpetrate, Rome must stand accountable for them at the bar of both human and divine justice.

Of the concordats with Spain and Germany we have already spoken. The object of these deeds is to bind these countries more firmly than ever to the Roman see. Claims are put forward, to which these governments would not have listened in ages termed less enlightened than our own; and, if granted, they will reduce the people to a pitch of vassalage unequalled by anything that obtained even in the dark ages. Of a kindred character is the concordat with Tuscany. This instrument establishes, for the first time since the existence of the Florentine state, the complete subjection of the State to the Church, in all matters which the latter may choose to call spiritual: it empowers the Pope to send any number of bulls into the country, and the bishops to enforce them, subject to no control: it erects an ecclesiastical censorship over books and opinions; and it declares that the property of the Church shall be disposed of, not according to the laws of the land, but according to canon law. Those sovereign rights which the Seignory handed down and the Medici defended, the secular power has conspired to surrender into the hands of the spiritual. Between the Croats of Vienna and the priests of the Vatican, liberty is extinguished throughout Italy. The Alps and the Pyrenees enclose a region where men walk about in chains. The Lucifer of this pandemonium is the Pope. If he can prevent it, never shall a single Bible cross the Alps, and eternal darkness must be the fate of Italy.

France is not so retrograde, only because party and the press have still some power there. Louis Napoleon has sold himself and his country to the Pope, that the Pope may make him President for life: he has gone to the Vatican, as Saul went to the Witch of Endor, that he may obtain by sorcery what he cannot command by talent. Thus it is that European Yezideeism goes on. The Pope worships the devil, that he may give him the world; and Louis Napoleon worships the Pope, that he may give him France. Hence a great apparent revival of Popery in that country. The Jesuits being masters of the President, have their own way, and are uncontrolled, save by the mountain and the socialist masses. Pretensions which have lain dormant in France for twenty years have been revived within the past twelve months. Congregations and confraternities are again springing up. Crosses and Calvaries are rising on every road. The Jesuits spend the night in hatching plots, and the day in running about to execute them: they get up, with equal adroitness, sermons and miracles; they enact the schoolmaster, and pull the strings at a Madonna show; they busy themselves in tracking and prosecuting the journalist and the *colporteur*; they haunt the clubs and the saloons, and introduce themselves into families, and into every sort of society. The Abbé Dauparloup and his associates could not be more bustling and important, though Charles X., in his character of a religious ascetic, had returned from the tomb. Everywhere Jesuitism is seizing on waxen youth, erecting new colleges, expelling liberal professors, dismissing the communal schoolmasters in thousands, and obliging those who fill their places to take the pupils to church and to all the services. The Jesuits are drawing their web over all the country, in the shape of friars of the Christian doctrine, and lay brothers. In most parts of Italy a confession-ticket is demanded as the passport to public office and private employment; and it is not improbable that it will soon be so in France.

Louis Napoleon, whom the Jesuits endure as the mere *locum tenens* of the Bourbon, leans upon the Church, and the Church upon Louis Napoleon; and a powerful army in the hands of the President has given unexpected but fictitious strength to Romanism in France.

In Austria, Prince Schwarzenberg has restored, in all their rigour, the twin-tyrannies of Jesuitism and absolutism. While all other religious bodies have had their privileges abridged, those of the Church of Rome have been fully restored. The *placetum regium* has been abolished, and the Pope now exercises in Austria uncontrolled power in the appointment of bishops. An association has been formed by the machinations of the Jesuits, called "The Young Catholic Association;" its recruits are drawn mainly from the youth in the schools. Every member, on entering, must swear fidelity to the Pope, and promise to concur in the establishment of missions throughout Austria, and in the realization of religious liberty,— a phrase which can mean only a right to extirpate Protestantism, seeing the Romanists already enjoy full liberty in Austria. During the summer of 1850, Jesuit intrigue had well-nigh precipitated Austria in sanguinary conflict upon Prussia. War was averted only by the concessions and humiliations of the King of Prussia at Olmutz. Protestant congregations in Hungary have been sadly harassed; and it was universally observed, that during the negotiations of 1850, the troops of Austria were quartered exclusively in Protestant districts, after the approved modes of punishing nonconformity set by Ferdinand II. at the beginning of the "thirty years' war," and by our own Charles II. during the "twenty-eight years' persecution." And now the house of Hapsburg has fully returned to its traditional maxims of rule, and has completed its reaction by its edict, in August of this year (1851), proclaiming the will of the Emperor the sole constitution of the country, and rendering the cabinet and the council of state accountable to the Emperor alone. Thus the last shred of constitutionalism has been swept away, and the naked fabric of pure unmitigated despotism has been set up in its room. Francis Joseph furnishes another example of the historical fact, that the vassals of the Church are uniformly the oppressors of their subjects.

That the Jesuit should nestle once more under the shadow of Schonbrunn, is not surprising; but it may well astonish us that Prussia should open its gates to these men. Yet the fact is as undoubted as it is melancholy. Frederick William, the professedly Protestant King of Prussia, has taken the viper to his bosom, and, with his kingdom, has joined the great anti-protestant league. This man's pedantry in speechmaking, and tinkering in the work of government,— his heroism in words and shortcomings in deeds,— his voice, which is the voice of a Protestant, and his hands, which are the hands of a Papist,— make him the James the Sixth of Germany. In a recent tour in his dominion, he received the popish bishops with smiles and genuflections, while he could find nothing but frowns and sharp reproofs for his protestant ministers. And why? Because they had permitted the Jesuits to outdo them in the courtly work of preaching the doctrine of "divine right" and "implicit obedience." Constitutional journals are silenced, and liberal professors are expelled. The Jesuits have undertaken to inculcate no precepts but those of order and loyalty, and therefore they are free of Prussia. They have descended the Rhine, bringing social dissensions and family discords in their train, and have now penetrated into all parts of the kingdom. There is no power in either the doctrines of Hegel and Fichte, or in the pietist party of Gerlach and Stahl, to resist the strides which despotic Austria is making towards political and ecclesiastical dominion in Prussia. Let Austria once get her barbarian but Catholic provinces into the German confederation, and the fate of Prussia as a Protestant power is sealed. The polypus arms of Roman Catholicism will be stretched over all northern Germany. Unhappy Frederick William! When he struck hands with Austria and the Jesuits, he little thought what woes he was entailing on his house and kingdom.

Nor is it without significance, as tending to prove that this re-action towards political and papal despotism in Germany is the result of concert and combination, that in the July of this summer (1851) the Grand Duke of Anhalt issued a proclamation "To my people." This document, which read as if some greater potentate had held the pen, told the world that "the German governments have pledged themselves to each other energetically to withstand the further development" of liberal principles. From the greatest to the pettiest despot, all have their faces turned towards Rome, as the grand central and model despotism. Every reforming and liberal influence is extinguished; every constitutional organ and party is crushed. The constitutionalist and the missionary are equally the objects of jealousy. The Jesuit and the jailor only can move freely about. Thus the arms of Continental Europe are once more at the service of a power which would stifle every aspiration towards liberty, and would entomb the world in the dense shadow of one colossal despotism.

The object of this league, avowed almost in so many words, is to undo the Reformation in both its political and spiritual effects. But success in this object is impossible, so long as Britain remains a free and Protestant country. This the papal powers very clearly perceive. Their policy, therefore, is either to convert Britain to Romanism and absolutism, or, if that is impossible, to put it down. To convert Britain is the design of the papal aggression, first, by the erection of the hierarchy; next, by introducing popish bishops into the House of Lords; next, by taking into their own hands the whole ecclesiastical and educational machinery of Ireland; next, by bringing over England to Romanism by means of tractarianism, aided by the multiplication of popish cathedrals, convents, and schools; and finally, by changing the coronation oath, marrying the heir-apparent to a popish princess, and, along with his conversion and accession to the throne, inaugurating their full domination in the country. But if we resist this aggression, we may prepare for one of a more physical kind. It is infallibility or the sword that Rome now offers to Britain. The exigencies of the times have forced this course upon the Papacy. Rome must advance. To stand still were, in her case, and in that of the absolutist powers, irretrievable ruin. They have an infidel democracy behind them; and, to conquer it, they must precipitate themselves upon Protestant Britain; for such despotisms as they are now attempting to set up cannot co-exist on the same globe with British constitutionalism and the Protestant faith. Self-preservation, then, dictates this course, and numerous and unequivocal indications point to it as resolved upon. When Cardinal Wiseman arrived in the country, all the papal powers sent him their congratulations. What was this but a defiance to Protestantism? Numerous hints have been dropped by Romanist preachers and organs, that if their rights are denied, the arms of the Catholic powers will enforce them. But the *Univers* has the merit of speaking frankly out. This is the leading Popish organ in Europe, and doubtless expresses the sentiments of its friends, when it preaches, as it now does, a new crusade against Protestantism. "A heretic examined and convicted by the Church," says *L'Univers*, used to be delivered over to the secular power, and punished with death. Nothing has ever appeared to us more natural or more necessary. More than one hundred thousand persons perished in consequence of the heresy of Wicliffe; still greater number by that of John Huss; it would not be possible to calculate the bloodshed caused by the heresy of Luther, and it is not yet over. After three centuries, we are at the eve of a re-commencement." Such is the dreadful tragedy which is plotted, and the plotters are not at the pains decently to veil their enormously diabolical purpose. One great St. Bartholomew in Britain, and the reign of absolutism will be established, and the triumphs of the Vatican complete. From Naples, with its twenty thousand chained captives, to Austrian-garrisoned Hamburg, there extends a chain of political forts, linking together the various countries in one powerful confederacy, which converges ominously on Britain. Pelion is piled upon Ossa, and Ossa upon Pelion. Of this towering mass, which threatens alike the pandemonium of democracy below and the heaven of constitutionalism and Protestantism above, the base is Russia and the apex is Rome.

The ghost of the middle ages,— for in this confederacy the political and religious dogmas of these ages live over again,— the ghost of the middle ages, we say, which the world believed had been laid for ever at rest, has returned suddenly from its tomb of three centuries, and now stalks grimly through the awe-struck and terrified nations of Europe, with the mitre of the Church upon its brow, and the iron truncheon of the State in its hand. Its foot is planted with deadly pressure upon the necks of its own subjects; and its mailed arm is raised, to strike down with one decisive blow that one country which is the home of freedom and of Protestantism.

Chapter III: General Propagandism.

The operations of the Roman Catholic Church extend far beyond the limits of her ancient domain,— the Roman world. Wherever British power or British enterprise have opened a path, there comes the missionary of Rome, to plant his spiritual and mental tyranny beneath the free flag of Britain. Let the reader glance over the table in the Appendix, exhibiting the stations of the Roman Church throughout the world, and he will see that she has fixed on points so numerous, and these so centrical, either already so or prospectively, that her aim, beyond all peradventure, is to become mistress of the globe. And the character of that Church affords an ample guarantee, that whatever organization, money, numbers of missionaries, and unflagging zeal can do, will be done to realize that aim. She has upwards of six thousand missionaries at this moment labouring in her service. They are spread over all lands, from the shores of Japan to the forests of the west. We need not speak of the countries of Europe,— the populous, and civilized, and wealthy regions of the globe. There we find her dignitaries in great splendour, and her orders in full force. But if we extend our view beyond, we find her agents planted thick along the line which divides the civilization of the world from its barbarism,— in the principalities of the Danube, where the barbarism of the east meets the refinement of the west,— in the plains of Mesopotamia and Syria, hanging on the skirts of Mahommedanism,— in India, where Hinduism comes in contact with British science and Christianity,— in China, where the stereotyped ideas and usages of the Celestial Empire are melting away before the encroachments of British commerce,— in Australia, in Oceanica, and over the New World, from Cape Horn to Canada. Her circle of operations encompasses the globe. Let us mark herein the policy of Rome. She takes care that the civilizing influences shall not outrun the Romanizing. It was much in this way that she founded her dominion at the first in Europe. She met the nations on their march from the north; and in their semi-barbarous state, without any instruction, she admitted them into the Church. In the same way is that Church now advancing to the semi-barbarous tribes of earth; and before they have been enlightened or Christianized in any degree, she procures their submission to her yoke. She communicates no Christian instruction; she exacts no confession of faith; they are still heathens in all save the name; but the nominal submission of the parents gives her access to the children, and these she trains in thorough subjection to her authority. It will not be the fault of Rome if there remains one individual in the most distant region of the earth who has not bowed the neck to her yoke. We see the Jesuits adopting all measures, and assuming every garb, to gain success in their work. Nor do they shrink from violence, when their object cannot otherwise be attained. In the latter years of Louis Philippe, the French ships of war were pressed into the service of the Propaganda. No one can yet have forgotten the massacre at Cochin-China in the spring of 1847, where the Jesuit missionaries, mounted upon the French ships of war, dealt out grape-shot to the inhabitants. Nor is the sad story of Tahiti forgotten, or ever will. The Jesuits found it a paradise physically and morally, with a Christianity blossoming there as pure and lovely perhaps as ever bloomed on earth. They dethroned its queen, and ravaged the isle with fire and sword, because the inhabitants refused to embrace an idolatry as foul as that from which they had been rescued. Popery is as much the wolf as ever. To see its real dispositions, we must not look at it in Europe; we must track it as it prowls along on the frontier of the heathen world. After centuries of massacre and persecution, its thirst for blood is still unslaked. Previous to the revolution of 1830, the funds of the French state were to a great degree at the command of the Jesuits; but since that event the French exchequer has been less accessible, and the missionary operations of the Romish Church have been supported mainly by the funds of the Propaganda, the head quarters of which are at Lyons, presided over by Archbishop Bonald. Latterly, by the help of the Propaganda, Pius has pushed his emissaries,— bishops, bishops in partibus, and vicars apostolic,— into parts of Hindustan, both within and without the Ganges, which have never heretofore been visited by such functionaries. Within the last eighteen months, parts of China, of Tibet, and of Chinese Tartary, have seen popish priests, with a breviary in one hand and a purse in the other, ready to preach, and to take tribute in behoof of Rome with both hands. The home supplies have much diminished of late, and foreign resources have been called into requisition. Belgium and Spain have been appealed to. The pauper Irish, both at home and in America, have given their alms; and Van Diemen's Land and Botany Bay have sent Pius many a crown, which his own subjects, who know him better and love him less, have heretically refused.

But not one of the schemes of the Jesuits, nor all of them put together, equals in magnitude and daring their present attempts on Britain. These have been concocted with a deeper policy, are being prosecuted with greater dissimulation and energy, and would, if realized, yield them a far greater return, than any other plan they have on hand. Britain is by much the paramount nation on the globe. In every region of the earth she is acquiring dominion and founding colonies. Her extension is the extension of Protestantism; at least it affords vast facilities for its extension. Since the beginning of the century, the Bible has been translated into one hundred and forty-three languages. Never before was the name of Christ proclaimed to so many nations. This has happened mainly through the instrumentality of Britain. It was impossible that the Pope or the Jesuits could be indifferent to this great fact, or fail to see to what it tended. Every consideration pointed to the conquest of Britain. Her political rank and vast moral and Christian influence made her their greatest barrier. It was plain that Rome must destroy Britain as a Protestant state, or be destroyed by her. Her conquest would give Rome the supremacy of the globe. The conversion of Britain to the Catholic faith is, and for some years past has been, the one grand object of the papal policy. Since the restoration of the Bourbons, at least since 1820, the Jesuits have been prosecuting this object with consummate craft, immense vigour, and very considerable success. They commenced operations in Ireland. Let us go back to the period preceding the passing of the Catholic Emancipation Act. The first step was to mission Dr Kenry, who had been brought up at the Jesuit College of Palermo, to Ireland, in the capacity of provincial head of the Jesuits. This man's task was to bring the educated laity, the men of influence in Ireland, under the Jesuit influence. For this purpose the College of Clongows was instituted. It was filled with Jesuit professors, and received the youth of the middle and upper classes. The next step was to reduce the priests of Ireland under the Jesuit influence. This could be done only by seizing upon the College of Maynooth, where the Irish priesthood was trained. The president of that institution became unable to fulfil his duties. He selected Dr. Kenry, the able head of all the Irish Jesuits, to supply his place. Although the thing had been pre-arranged (as doubtless it was) between General Roothan at Rome, Dr Kenry, and the president of Maynooth, it could not have happened better for the designs of the Jesuits. By and by

Jesuit professors began to be transferred from Clongows to Maynooth; a Jesuit confraternity was established among the students, termed the Sodality of the Sacred Heart; a Jesuit commentary on the Scriptures was introduced, which all the students were enjoined to study; and in this way was the college, and through it the whole Irish priesthood, brought under the Jesuit dominion. The people were under the dominion of the priesthood, the priesthood under that of Dr. Kenry, the head of all Irish Jesuits, and Dr. Kenry under that of General Roothan, the head of Jesuitism throughout the world. The political agitation that arose,— the result that crowned it, and which gave free admission to Roman Catholics and Jesuits into the British senate,— we need not describe. The principal scene of operations was now transferred by the Jesuits to England.

The Jesuits have a sort of intuitive sagacity in comprehending in what lies the strength of an enemy, and of course the point to attack. The Church of England, they saw, was the main barrier between them and political ascendancy. Provided they could Romanize it, the battle would be half won; and to carry this point all their efforts were put forth. But previous to beginning operations on the Anglican Establishment, there was a preliminary point to be gained,— the reduction of the old popish families to the Jesuit dominion. To effect this, the college at Stoneyhurst was erected. This institution is flourishing, and nearly all the first Catholic families in England are educated within its walls; and there they receive such a polish as is fitted to make them influential in English society. But the main battle was directed against the Church of England. They strove to quicken the dormant principles of a popish origin which had been suffered to remain in her ever since the Reformation; they availed themselves of her forms, some of which savour of superstition, to revive within her a love for Popery. Of course we have no direct proof that Jesuits took orders in that Church, and officiated as pastors, to expedite the movement; but few will be disposed to doubt the fact, who now consider the whole career of Messrs Wiseman, Pusey, Ward, Newman, and who consider the history and character of the "Tracts for the Times." Tract No. 90, where the doctrine of reserves is broached, bears strong marks of a Jesuit origin. Could we know all the secret instructions given to the leaders in the Puseyite movement,— the mental reservations prescribed to them, — we might well be astonished. "Go gently," we think we hear the great Roothan say to them. "Remember the motto of our dear son the *cidevant* Bishop of Autun, — 'Surtout, *pas trop de zèle.*' Bring into view, little by little, the authority of the Church. If you can succeed in rendering it equal to that of the Bible, you have done much. Change the table of the Lord into an altar; elevate that altar a few inches above the level of the floor; gradually turn round to it when you read the Liturgy; place lighted tapers upon it; teach the people the virtues of stained glass, and cause them to feel the majesty of Gothic basilisques. Introduce first the dogmas, beginning with that of baptismal regeneration; next the ceremonies and sacraments, as penance and the confessional; and, lastly, the images of the Virgin and the saints. Especially show the nobility the elegant position which Roman Catholicism reserves for them, and cause them to comprehend that the Church of Rome alone is in a position to resist democracy." Such is the course which has been followed. And behold the result! The last published list of Anglican ministers who had seceded to Rome, — certified as correct so far as regarded the individuals named, but incomplete as to numbers,— amounted to sixty-six; and the Anglican Establishment appears in not a little danger of being split in two, or broken in pieces, on the subject of baptismal regeneration. The extent and variety of machinery which Romanism has set up in England, as given below, is truly formidable and alarming.

Nor has the land of Knox been overlooked by the popish Propaganda. Scotland has been divided into three dioceses; and strong efforts are at present making to plant it with popish congregations, colleges, convents, and schools. Advantage has been taken of the relics of Popery in the Highlands, and the influx of Irish hordes in the Lowlands, to form centres whence to propagate popish influences. Fully one half of the funds that support these operations are sent from the Propaganda at Lyons. Many of the priests stationed in Scotland received their education in Jesuit colleges on the Continent, and are themselves most probably Jesuits. Their headquarters is in Brown Square, Edinburgh; and it were interesting to know the intrigues of which that house, with its perpetually darkened windows, is the centre. Popery is not making great progress among the lower classes of Scotland: the chief scene of its operations are the drawing-rooms of the New Town of Edinburgh; and there the unrivalled finesse and deeply-veiled craft of Popery have not gone without their reward. High-bred and thoroughly educated Jesuits are employed in this work. An evening is set, the party assembles, and those instructed beforehand so guide the conversation, that the popish dignitary who happens to be present is led, unwillingly as he would fain have it thought, to descant on the comparative merits of Protestantism and Roman Catholicism. Or, from some piece of statuary or painting that chances to be in the room, he contrives to drop a word in praise of the Virgin, and another in reprobation of that stern iconoclast John Knox. These sapping and mining operations are being prosecuted with great vigour: not a few perverts, chiefly ladies, have been made, who are employed, in their turn, in ensuring others. It is not long since the Protestant community was startled by the official announcement in the Catholic Directory, that seventy converts from Protestantism had been confirmed during the year 1848 in Edinburgh alone.

Of the agency devised for operating on the masses, we may point to the numerous nunneries and monasteries rising up in our cities, where provision is made for the instruction of Protestant children, for whose benefit these seminaries are mainly intended. We might point also to the popish ragged schools, and other institutions, in some of which provision has been made for the celebration of popish rites, as in the school in New Market Street, Edinburgh, which is marked by a gilt cross and where, as the Catholic Directory informs us, "*at the upper end is a neat altar, concealed, except when required, by a screen.*

Two societies have lately been formed in Scotland to aid in reducing the masses under the dominion of Romanism. The first we mention is called the "Holy Guild of St. Joseph," instituted in 1844: it unites the character of a "benefit club" with that of a "Christian sodality or pious confraternity, having reference only to the spiritual improvement of its members." Its real object is the advancement of Popery, veiled under the pretext of charity. Its ordinary members must be Catholics, and they bind themselves to the performance of certain religious duties. Its honorary members, which may be "*Christians of any denomination,*" are less strongly bound: they are admitted with a sole view to the benefit of the funds, being presumed to be more wealthy than the ordinary members. They are, however, required to participate in certain parts of the Romish worship, and are allowed, in return, to share in the benefits of the society, among which are the prayers of the brotherhood for them after their death.

There labours in the same work another society, termed "Brotherhood of St. Vincent of Paul." The native country of this fraternity is France. A branch of this society was established at Rome in 1836; another in London in 1844, and another in Edinburgh in 1845. Its ostensible object, like that of the former, is charity,— fuel and clothing to the poor; but "*these temporal succours are only the covering which conceals the spiritual good it does to souls.*" The Old Town of Edinburgh is divided into six districts, each under the care of two or more brothers. The hopes cherished by the Jesuits, from the operations of this and similar societies, may be gathered from the following passage:— "Wonderful things seem to be in store for our conferences in England," says the *Rapport Générale* for 1844; "and it will be a sweet and pious consolation for us to think, that in the movement which is drawing the people of Great Britain back again into the bosom of unity, our dear society will perhaps have assisted by its prayers and by its works in the religious regeneration of that mighty nation." There is scarce a Roman Catholic in Edinburgh whom these societies have not pressed into their service, and who do not ply the work of proselytism with the weapons of perverted texts and stale slanders.

There is not a colony under the British crown which is not the scene of popish stratagem and tactics. In Canada, a considerable portion of the lands have fallen into their hands. A glance over the American register, in Battersby's Registry for the whole World, shows how fast new cathedrals, convents, and schools are rising up in many parts of the United States. This body had in 1850, 4 archbishops, 30 bishops, 1073 churches, 1081 priests, and a population of one and a half million, according to the Roman Catholic Almanac. In British America they foment divisions, to obtain concessions and grants from government. Their grand maxim, both in Ireland and in Canada, is, agitate! agitate! and such will be their practice wherever and whenever they become sufficiently numerous. They have sisters of mercy, who offer their services to emigrants, and thus enlist them in the support of Popery the moment they arrive on the shores of the New World. Some of their priests have small salaries from the state, under pretext of doing certain official duties, as the Rev. M. Duguesney in Jamaica, who attests the Catholic soldiers in the camp barracks. In Gibraltar the Romanists have five hundred pounds annually from government. The chief increase of Papists in America is owing to hordes of Irish continually pouring into Canada and the States. Ireland, in fact, is a vast popish propaganda for both the western and southern hemispheres. The Romanists are vigorously working the press in America. In the United States they have one Quarterly Review, one Monthly Review, and twelve weekly newspapers, almost all of which are edited by priests.

To return to the old world. An attempt was made in March 1850, in Malta, by the popish governor, Mr. More O'Ferral, to make the Romish

Church in that important colony nominally what it is in fact, the dominant Church. According to one article of the Amended Code, the Roman Catholic Church in Malta was styled the "Dominant Church." According to other articles, it was enacted that, whoever should violate, *by word or gesture*, any article of the Roman Catholic Church, should be punished with imprisonment of from four to six months. A refusal to uncover when the host passed, or a word spoken against the Virgin and the saints, would have subjected the person to the penalties of the code. Here was a grievous encroachment on the principle of British toleration, and a jesuitical attempt to obtain legal recognition of the worship of the host and the dogma of transubstantiation. A few days after the appearance of this edict, mixed marriages were prohibited in Malta and its dependencies, unless on the solemn promise of the parties that the children of these marriages should be brought up in the Romish faith. This affords a fine sample of the intriguing and encroaching spirit of Jesuitism in all the British colonies. But on no field is Rome prosecuting her proselytising system so vigorously as in Australia and Oceanica.. She anticipates the future eminence of this young empire, which assuredly it will never reach if she succeed in imposing her yoke upon it. She will stereotype its condition, as she has done that of Lower Canada. Meanwhile she is sending to it shiploads of priests, sisters of mercy, and Irish Catholics. It has been felt for many years, that the emigration from this country is so conducted as to favour the spread of Popery in Australia. The vast proportion of those carried out thither at the public expense are Roman Catholics, particularly orphan girls from Irish workhouses. The object evidently is, to supply Roman Catholic wives for the English and Scotch Protestants of the humbler classes in Australia, and thereby to Romanize the Australian colonies through the artful and thoroughly jesuitical device of mixed marriages.

The rapid and portentous rise of the Romish Church in Australia is fraught with immense danger to both the colony and the mother country. This has happened mainly through the working of the Bounty Emigration Scheme. The waste lands of the colony are sold by auction, and the annual proceeds, now amounting to four hundred thousand pounds, are devoted to the importation of emigrants from the united kingdom. The scheme is farmed to speculators, who receive so much a head for their cargo of emigrants. Hordes of Irish paupers, Papist to a man, are collected in the south and west of Ireland, and, being shipped at Plymouth or Cork, are carried across the globe, and thrown upon Australia. In this way an Irish land-flood has been flowing steadily, during several years, upon this colony; and a new Ireland is rising in the Pacific. In 1822, two priests, one in New South Wales and the other in Van Dieman's Land, sufficed for the entire of Australia. But mark the strength of Romanism in the southern hemisphere now. Oceanica has been divided into eleven dioceses, which are under the management of one archbishop, ten bishops, and two hundred priests. These are supplemented by a numerous staff of sisters of charity, ecclesiastical students, and Christian brothers or schoolmasters, under a vow of celibacy and devotion to the Papacy. In all the towns there is a priest, and one, and sometimes several congregations; the membership ranging from four hundred to two thousand five hundred. At the head of the establishment is Dr. Polding, a native of England and created by the Pope in 1840, Archbishop and Count of the Papal States. Liberal grants are made from the colonial treasury to aid the erection of cathedrals and chapels. A model trust-deed is lodged in the Secretary's Office; the building is inspected by the government architect; and the sum required is ordered. As the mass-house is built in part, so the priest is salaried in part, by government. A list of seat-holders, with the amount of annual or quarterly rent paid by each, is transmitted to the governor, and an order is straightway issued for the payment of the stipend. Schools and schoolmasters are also aided from the treasury, and that in no stinted measure. In 1849 the sum voted was eighteen hundred pounds, and the sum placed on the estimates for the following year was upwards of twenty-six hundred. What makes this the more extraordinary and the more unjustifiable is, that there is a government system of education in operation in the colony. We thus see what a web Rome has spread over this fine portion of our colonial empire, and how much her boast is justified, that Australia is already all her own.

Australia, in point of geographical position, is the very citadel of the southern hemisphere: it is destined to give population and language, and, we fondly hope, freedom and religion, to all this region of the globe. But let Popery seize upon it, and she will convert what otherwise were a career of unbounded progress, into one of premature decay. Instead of growing into a great empire, Australia will sink down into the decrepitude of Ireland. And not only so; Rome will close the gates of the Pacific against the entrance of the gospel, and create here a dense mass of darkness and heathenism, which it may require ages to dispel. Nor will this be all; she will erect her batteries on this strong redoubt, and play with prodigious effect upon our missions in the east, and upon our Christianity at home.

Chapter IV: Prospects of the Papacy.

Societies, not less than individuals, reap as they have sowed; and in the convulsions and revolutions of our times, Rome is reaping the fruit of ages of superstition and despotism. The Papacy at this moment is fighting its third great battle. Its first was with the empire; in that it was victorious. Its second was with Christianity, in the persons of its Albigensian and Waldensian confessors; and in that, too, it was victorious. Its third great war is that which it is now waging with an ATHEISTIC COMMUNISM, which has risen contemporaneously, and with extraordinary intensity and power, in all the Catholic countries of Europe. Whence has come this new and destructive principle? It is the natural issue of the bondage in which the human mind has so long been retained, — of the violence done to reason and faith, — for superstition is the parent of atheism. The national mind in France long struggled to find vent through means of Christianity. This was denied it. It next sought liberty in scepticism, which speedily terminated in atheism. With French infidelity came French democracy. We have already said that the democratic element entered the world with Christianity, and revived again in the Reformation of John Calvin. There is this difference, however, that whereas the doctrine of Calvin would have given true liberty, — constitutional government, — to Europe, the doctrine of Voltaire gave it an anarchy which baptized itself in blood. Scepticism, engendered thus from superstition, has overspread Europe, and set free the masses from all divine control, and, by necessary consequence, from all earthly authority. The brood of revolutions which now torments Europe is the progeny of Rome. From her own loins has sprung the hydra that threatens to tear her in pieces. The sorceress of the Seven Hills, like the Hag of Pandemonium, is now

"With terrors and with clamours compass'd round

Of mine own brood, that on my bowels feed."

Herein lies the grand difficulty of governments, and especially of the popedom, — that the superstition which, while it was a principle of belief, enabled them to govern the masses as they would, is a principle of belief no longer. With superstition their power has departed. The element which endowed the Papacy, as the governing power of Europe, with a sort of omnipotence, is extinct. Both governments and the popedom have meanwhile replaced the spiritual element by the merely physical. Everywhere a paternal despotism has given way to a military tyranny. But how long can this last? When the habit of blind, unreasoning obedience has been destroyed, it cannot last long; so at least it appears to us. Were any great change to occur, of a nature fitted to bring about a mental enthralment throughout Europe, the Papacy might become as strong as before, and might govern Europe for centuries to come; but so long as it continues to lean upon the sword, and to be hated by the masses as at once an impostor and an oppressor, the chances are not great that it will regain its power. The alliance of the priesthood with an expiring and worn-out despotism will not tend to the strengthening of the popedom. The popular vengeance was directed full against the priesthood in the first French Revolution, because the priesthood had been thoroughly identified with the government. In 1830 the priests were again the objects of attack, because the elder Bourbons had made them political auxiliaries. In 1848 they escaped, because they had not meddled previously with politics. Their present identification with the governing powers all over the Continent is sure to render them again the objects of popular vengeance.

As a drought upon the waters, so has infidelity wasted and dried up the vitalities of Roman Catholicism. Socialism is the evil angel which God has sent forth to smite the host of his enemies. It is a moral simoom. The Reformation was a messenger of good tidings, — a preacher of repentance; but men repented not; and the messenger returned to Him who had sent him. Communism comes next: it rounds the doom of the papal world, and announces that the hour of judgment is come. Wherever infidelity is strong, Popery is weak. Pantheism is spread all over northern Germany, and it is difficult to say whether it has been more fatal to Protestantism or to Romanism. Along the Rhine, if one may believe the published reports, there are millions of atheists. Still rationalism has lost ground among the upper classes. The universities begin to be leavened with an evangelical and believing spirit, and some of the more influential of the clergy have experienced a religious revival. The "Inner Mission" of Germany is working vigorously, printing tracts and old devotional works, forming Bible Societies, and instituting Christian circulating libraries. These efforts, which extend into Saxony and Protestant Bavaria, and part of Westphalia, if not impeded by the reactionary tendencies of the government, must speedily work a change on Germany, which had retrograded far behind the shadow of the Reformation. Switzerland closely resembles Germany, as regards the spread of infidelity; only there the evil exists in a mitigated form. France is more than ever overspread by the disciples of Voltaire. The late revolution has produced a re-action among the upper classes in favour of the Church. The children of the Encyclopedists carry consecrated tapers, and kiss the hand of the priest, in the hope that he may lead the impassioned masses from the political arena into the silent halls of penitence. The device is seen through and contemned. The lower orders, instead of being conciliated, are becoming every day more hostile, and are likely to continue so, so long as the government and the priesthood pursue their reactionary and coercive course. In all the Catholic countries north of the Alps, we see the same indications of the decline of Catholicism which, according to Gibbon, signalized the decline of Paganism: the cathedrals are in great measure deserted, and the few who do frequent them are mostly women and elderly gentlemen. Enter Notre Dame in the forenoon of a Sabbath, and in an edifice that would accommodate from ten thousand to twenty thousand, you find a congregation of some three or four hundreds, and these mostly ladies and gentlemen who were born under the old *regime*. The modern Parisians go to the clubs or the Boulevards. In Lyons, the ecclesiastical capital of France, matters are in much the same state. In its numerous and magnificent cathedrals the priests sing mass in presence of a few hundreds, while the thousands of the city outside are intent on their labours or their amusements. As a mission-field there are few more inviting than France. We find Dr. Merle D'Aubigné bearing his testimony to this fact at a recent meeting of the Foreign Aid Society in London. "The Lord has breathed on this country," writes our evangelist in the east of France; "the way is open everywhere, and I do not know which way to turn." "It is impossible not to have meetings," says another; "for no sooner does one enter a house than all the neighbours come in also." You know that we have churches in Burgundy, full of spiritual life, who missionize, and are composed entirely of converted Romanists. Has Dr. Wiseman any churches in England entirely made up of converted Protestants? It has happened that entire parishes almost have declared that they would leave the Pope, and have invited a minister of Christ to come and dwell among them; and the municipalities have offered to defray all expenses of the service. Have you in England whole parishes which go over to Popery?" At the recent census in Paris, many thousands of Romanists registered themselves in the

Protestant column, while others signified their wish for some better religion than Popery.

South of the Alps infidelity has not taken such root. In Spain the Romish Church has shared deeply in the decline which has fallen on that unhappy country. A large portion of the ecclesiastical property has been appropriated by the State; and there are now in Spain bishops without revenues, and parishes without curés. We have occasion to know, that among the young priesthood of Spain, there are not a few earnest inquirers. They have begun to canvass the foundations of the Pope's authority; and some of them have openly declared to Protestant ministers from Britain that it will never be well with the Spanish Church till it has thrown off the authority of the Roman bishop; a step of reformation which would lead to other and greater reforms. A Protestant mission stationed at Gibraltar could at this moment act with effect both upon the south of Spain and the adjoining coast of Africa. The Spanish laity are ready to receive the gospel; the priests are contemned, but feared.

In the important kingdom of Piedmont a severe blow has lately been dealt the Romish Church. The parliament at Turin has abolished a variety of ecclesiastical privileges, and among others, the exemption of the clergy from the secular tribunals, the right of churches to afford sanctuary to criminals, and the abolition of penalties for the non-observance of holidays. The constitutional path on which the government has entered affords a guarantee for the permanence of these necessary changes. In the resurrection of churches at the expiry of the dark ages, Bohemia was the first to cast away her shroud: it is an auspicious omen that her grave is again opening. The Protestant church in Prague, under the Rev. Frederic Kossuth, now numbers eleven hundred members. Of these, seven hundred are converted Romanists, among whom are included three ecclesiastics. Thus that pure light which shone in the ministry of John Huss is risen again, and is shining on those who sat in darkness. We trust it will not be now as formerly, when first it was extinguished in blood, and next stifled by the fogs of error; but that this time its dawn will pass into day, soon to lighten the whole land of Huss. It is an equally remarkable sign of our times, that the true apostolic Roman Church, — the Waldensian, — has obtained political enfranchisement from her earthly sovereign, and spiritual revival from her heavenly King. After the death-like silence of ages, her voice is heard once more among her ancient valleys. The turtle-dove, chased so long by the fowler, sings again among the Alps. Oh that her song may truly be, — "Lo, the winter is past, the rain is over and gone!" Among the perishing kingdoms of Italy, it goes well with Piedmont at this hour, because she harbours the remnant of the early Christian Church. The Waldensians are preparing for missionary operations in Italy, for which, as an Italian-speaking people, they are peculiarly fitted. In the duchy of Tuscany an intense thirst has been awakened for the Word of God. A few weeks ago, Count Guicciardini assured the writer that there were now in that little state three hundred persons in the judgment of charity savingly converted; that hundreds more were reading the Scriptures, which, in instances not a few, were brought into the country in the knapsacks of Austrian soldiers; that the tracts of D'Aubigné, and M'Crie's "Italy," were being circulated in thousands of copies; and that, whatever might become of the population, it is, speaking generally, lost to Romanism. Lombardy, too, is the scene of a religious movement. There numerous Christian Churches exist, though in secret, with both an ecclesiastical and financial organization. These disciples are often tracked by the sleuth-hounds of the Inquisition. The oath of the confessional, which may not be violated to prevent a murder or a robber, is readily broken to denounce a Bible-reader. When Pio Nono was a professed liberal, the Austrian police permitted the circulation of the Scriptures in Lombardy; and the Croats stabled their horses in the churches, and anointed their shoes with the holy chrism; but now that the Pope is Austrian in politics, the Croat and the Jesuit go hand in hand in suppressing the Bible, and maintaining the cause of a Church which is founded upon the Inquisition, and to which Lucifer has promised that the power of truth shall never prevail against her.

Not Lombardy only, but all Italy, is awakening. An immense number of Bibles were circulated in that country during the Republic, by the presses of Florence, and the British and Foreign Bible Society; and the stringent measures of the Italian governments have not been able to arrest the movement then commenced. There exists in Italy a large Christian Association, which numbers among its members not a few priests. Its affairs are managed by a central committee, which issues its orders to inferior or diocesan committees. Churches have been formed in most of the principal towns, not excepting Rome itself. A large chest receives the offerings of the laity and the contributions of the priests, who, in relation to this association, are termed ministers. The money thus collected is devoted to the purchase of Bibles and the circulation of religious tracts and catechisms, and also to the support of poorer members. The Italians evince, above all things, a thirst for the Word of God; and often do they meet, in parties of half a dozen, in solitary places, and in the midst of morasses, to read the Bible and celebrate their worship, as did the Lollards of England and the Covenanters of Scotland. Beginnings such as these cannot but be blessed. It augurs well for the thoroughly apostolic character of the coming Italian Church, that not man, but the Bible, has been its teacher. And the analogies of all history deceive us if Providence do not order the political affairs of that country, so that these confessors may have an opportunity of declaring themselves before the world, before the Papacy's destruction. The true Roman Church will rise from her tomb to condemn the harlot. He that took Lot out of Sodom before its overthrow, — He who drew off the legions from Jerusalem, that the disciples might flee from the devoted city, — will yet, despite the consociated and sanguinary vigilance of the Croat, the Jesuit, and the Gaul, call these Christians out of Babylon, that they may not be partakers of her plagues.

We do not look that Italy shall become Protestant, at least to the extent of being nationally so. The stage of great iniquities must first be purified by great judgments. Nevertheless, a remnant will be saved. But we would be doing injustice to our own strong convictions did we not declare, that what we believe to be a-coming on the Papacy is not victory, but doom. The judgments of God are a great deep. The Papacy persecuted the confessors of old under the pretence that they were atheists and rebels. And now the Church that so long fought with the phantom is called to grapple with the substance. Rome stands face to face with an atheism which has for its mission the overthrow of all government and all religions. A destroying communism is making head, and will make head, there is reason to think, till universal and tremendous overthrow sweep away the Papacy, with all the power that has upheld it. This dark presentiment already oppresses the minds of its adherents. In terror of the "Red Spectre," they run to throw themselves into the arms of the northern colossus. This will not save them. The communism of the west will be found stronger than the despotism of the north. At the first revolution the people set up the guillotine; and now they are smarting for it. This time it is the kings who have set up the guillotine. One other revolution of the wheel, and the drama will close; "For the Lord shall rise up as in Mount Perazim; He shall be wroth, as in the Valley of Gibeon, that He may do his work, his strange work, and bring to pass his act, his strange act, . . a consumption, even determined upon the whole earth." For Britain we have no fear. The hostile attitude now taken up against her by the entire popish world does not dismay us. A year's peace with Rome will do us more damage than a hundred years' war. We believe that God has chosen Britain to stand erect as a monument of the truth of Protestantism, when the popish kingdoms shall lie crushed and overthrown.

But while we thus avow our convictions, it is well for all to bear in mind that the Papacy is still powerful, and has possession of many strong positions: it is backed by all the strength of governments; it has a perfect organization, — numerous agents, trained to prompt and unreasoning obedience; it has energy and zeal; it has union, which is sadly wanting in the opposite camp; it has the traditions of its former power, and the fruits of its past experience; it has men of varied and great accomplishments arrayed on its side; it has something positive to offer to the people, whereas socialism is a negation to a great degree; it is still strong, above all, in the evil principles of the heart of man, and the corruptions of society. Human nature is still unchanged. Men in the mass are still as fond as ever of a religion which will render the hope of heaven compatible with the indulgence of their passions. Moreover, though scepticism has set free the masses from the Papacy in the first place, it may in its ulterior effects contribute to their return. Its effect is to weaken the mind, and to prepare it for acquiescing in any absurdity; and should a recoil take place, which is possible in the case of men wearied of suffering and disappointed by the failure of their schemes, then, just as we have seen the mind of Europe pass from superstition to scepticism, so might we see it again pass from scepticism to superstition; and thus would the revolution return to the point from which it started. The very possibility of such an occurrence, fraught as it would be with tremendous consequences to both liberty and religion, is enough, surely, to rouse every Christian to ask what he can do to aid in overthrowing the Papacy. Now is the time to act, without the loss of a day. A few years hence the conflict will be decided, and the fate of Europe and of Protestantism sealed for centuries.

The work properly is twofold. There is first the overthrow of existing barriers; and second, the introduction of the truth. The destruction of those despotisms which have been all along the great props of the Papacy, — the *alter egos* of the Pope, — is the work of God. He will provide the agency for this part of the labour: it is not that kind of work which He usually assigns to his people. This, as it appears to us, is the end to be accomplished by present revolutions. Their mission is to batter down the strongholds of darkness, and to open a pathway, along which Christianity may advance to bless the nations.

But the second part is the work to which God specially calls his friends. But how? In what way are they to work? Now, here we have no ingenious or startling plan to propound, promising brilliant results, without much pains, and in short time. We believe that there is no royal road to the evangelization of the world. But though our plan is simple, we believe it to be practicable, and the only one that is practicable in present circumstances. Well, then, we must concentrate our efforts, and make the blow fall where it will do most execution. Rome is the head and heart of modern paganism, — the fountain of temporal and spiritual tyranny: let us strike at Rome. Could we displace Popery and plant Christianity in Rome, the loss would be unspeakable to the Papacy, — the gain would be immense to Protestantism. Let us estimate the loss on the one side, — the gain on the other. First, Rome is the see of Peter (in papal logic); and it is as the occupant of Peter's see that the Pope claims the primacy and the rank of Christ's Vicar; therefore, should he lose the see of Peter, he loses that on which he founds the whole of his claim. After that, he would not have a shadow of ground for the primacy. Not all the casuists or councils of Rome could by fair reasoning help him out of that difficulty. Of whatever see he was bishop, if not bishop of Rome, he is not Peter's successor, — is not Christ's Vicar, — is not Pope. But second, so extended an organization as the Papacy, in order to its efficient working, must necessarily have a centre, where are placed the headquarters of all its missions and agencies. That point is Rome. Should we possess ourselves of that point, we break up the organization of Rome at its centre, and cripple and derange it to its very circumference. But third, there is, as experience has proved, a certain mysterious connection between the possession of Rome and the fate of the Papacy. It has never thriven away from it. Rome gives prestige to the Romish system: it gives unity to it: it operates as a potent spell upon the Papist in the remotest quarters of the globe. Rome has ever been to the popes, in the old maxim, *urbs et orbis*. Now, it is of consequence even to destroy that influence, by breaking the tie between Romanism and Rome. This threefold loss would the Christianization of Rome inflict upon the Papacy. It would be a blow at the root of its system; it would incurably derange its organization, and would strip it of its prestige. The gain to Christianity would be proportionate. It would furnish it with a powerful centre of action, and place at the service of the gospel all the exterior helps which the possession of Rome and of Italy has given to Popery, — a land whose resources are almost inexhaustible, and a people who, to the power of forming the largest plans, and the ability to prosecute them with steadiness, would add the fervour and zeal of converts. The moment, we repeat, is singularly opportune: it is one of those rare occasions which occur at the interval of ages, to test the Church whether she has wisdom to seize upon it. Scepticism has set loose the masses from Rome, speaking generally; but scepticism is too much of a negation to retain its power over them for any length of time. Smitten by a destroying revolution, heartsick with the failure of their plans and hopes, they must and they will seek something more positive than infidelity. There are some such aspirations already springing up. German rationalism is on the point of being renounced. Even socialism turns its face towards Christianity. As we have seen the blind turn his sightless orbs to that quarter of the sky where the sun was, so socialism, amid the horrors of its night, seems faintly to descry the great effulgence of the gospel. We may be assured that the nations must soon have something higher and better than pantheism: they already begin to feel after the "Unknown;" and if they find not truth, they will embrace error; and how long they may continue under its power, who can tell? This, then, is a great crisis in the world's history. Let every Christian feel as if he were the only Christian in Britain, and as if the issue of the crisis depended upon himself. Let him give his prayers; let him give his labours; let him give his money. Ye Christians of Britain, the voice of Providence loudly summons you to the conflict. Arise, — arise instantly; arise as one man. You have everything on your side. You have the prayers of the martyrs, whose blood the Papacy has shed, on your side. You have the prayers of oppressed nations, who now accuse and curse the Papacy as their destroyer, on your side. Above all you have the promises of God, which dooms that system to perdition, on your side. "Up, for this is the day in which the Lord hath delivered" the Papacy "into thine hand."

But what are the means? If asked what is the first mean to regenerate Italy, we answer, the Bible; if asked what is the second, we answer, the Bible; if asked what is the third, we answer, the Bible. God is plainly announcing by his providence that He will overthrow the Papacy, regenerate Italy, and save the world, by his Word, to the exclusion of all else. No missionary could enter Italy at this moment; but the Bible will, can, and has entered Italy, and even Rome. There are two doors by which we can send the Bible into Italy at present. We can convey it by the

Simplon, the great highway from Switzerland into Italy. Covering this entrance, as it were, we have the Waldensian Church, ready and eager to assist us in this good work. Besides, the Austrian sway in Lombardy is milder than the Sacerdotal government in the States of the Church; and in Lombardy and the adjoining parts of Italy it is quite practicable at this moment to distribute Bibles by colporteurs. The other door is of course on the west. There are three free ports on that side of Italy, — Genoa, Leghorn, and Civita Vecchia. Let Bibles be conveyed thither. They cannot be refused admission, being free ports; and from these places it is quite practicable despite the Pope's myrmidons, to convey them all over Italy. This may be done by colporteurs; but they must be prudent men. They must not offer them on the streets; they must carry them by threes and sixes in their pocket, or secreted about their persons, and distribute them privately.

How encouraging the fact, that the Romans, and the Italians in general, are ready to receive the Bible, — are most earnestly desirous of having it! This fact has been well attested by a variety of evidence. The following beautifully simple and touching narrative contains all that we could wish on that head, and shows how much encouragement we have to embark in this work. It is the address, as reported in the public prints, of Dr. Achilli, at a Bible Society meeting in this country: — "You are aware that I am just come from Rome. My great work in Rome was about the Bible. I knew that the Bible alone is able to produce a religious revolution. When I speak of a revolution, I mean an entire change of man in his relations with God, with society, and with himself. This change in an individual is quiet; but in the masses it is agitated, because very often it is a rapid change of a whole system. This revolution I desire for the whole world, beginning at Rome. It was in the days of political liberty that the New Testament of Jesus Christ was published in Rome for the first time. At the same moment copies of the complete Bible were introduced, published by the English Bible Society. I and my friends showed this beloved book to the Romans, who were not slow in asking us for it. Our manner of presenting it was simple. We had the book in our pockets when we introduced topics of religion, and quoted on purpose texts of Scripture. We then took it out of our pockets, and read the quotations out of it. I found it better not to offer it, but to let them ask for it, and even as much as possible to let them be anxious to get it. When I gave it, I used always to exact a promise that they would often read it, — perhaps every day. I had the pleasure of seeing in many shops groupes of persons round the shop-keeper, the latter reading aloud the Bible which I had given him. The Bible was in the Constituent Assembly, in several public offices, and in several military quarters. Many soldiers defended their country on the walls of Rome with the Bible in their pockets. You will ask me, What effect has the Bible produced in Rome? I will tell you. I do not think anything can better answer your question than the encyclical letter of Pio Nono, in which he exclaims against the Bible, the missionaries of the Bible, the Bible Societies, &c.; because, he says, in this way Protestantism, — that is, pure Christianity, — has entered into Rome, and into many other parts of Italy. I might tell you that, after the Bibles were distributed, Roman churches were quite left by the people, very few going any longer to confession. They talked about religion in the houses, in the clubs, in the streets, and in the shops. It was not only the Pope-king, but it was the Pope-bishop, that they thought about. It is quite certain that the Pope is more afraid of this book than of the republican bayonets, because he knows that this is able to destroy his throne in the Vatican." To this minute and interesting account it is unnecessary to add a single word.

We are to march against Rome, then, with the sword of the Spirit, which is the Word of God. But how are Bibles to be provided? We redeemed the slaves in the West Indies with a sum of twenty millions: shall we grudge twenty millions of Bibles to redeem Italy from a worse slavery? Would it not be a noble act, — BRITAIN GIVES TO ITALY TWENTY MILLIONS OF BIBLES? Can it be that there is not enough of Christianity in Britain for this? Oh, in this age of great schemes, let us devise liberally for the evangelization of the world. Twenty millions of Bibles, which would cost about one and a half millions of pounds, would put a Bible into the hand of every man, woman, and child in Italy, from the Alps to Sicily. But this number is not required; one-fifth would suffice. Five millions of Bibles would give a copy of the sacred volume to every family in Italy. Let, then, every Christian family in Britain give but two copies of the Word of God for Italy, and the object is achieved. This would be an expense of but a few pence to each professing Christian. We want nothing but a plan and organization for an effort on an adequate scale. What we propose, then, is, that this plan, or some similar one that is definite and adequate, be put before the country. Let the Christian public be told the greatness of the crisis, the desire of the Italians for the Word of God, and how small an effort on the part of each can achieve all that is wanted; and let Italian committees be formed all over the country, — a small one in every town, or perhaps in every congregation. Were machinery set a-going, the sum needed would be easily and speedily realized. We ought to aim at a large and specific object, in which we will more easily succeed than in a smaller aim. Sixpence a-head from the professing Christians of Britain would furnish the requisite copies of the Word of God for an effective blow at the Papacy in Rome. Nothing is wanting but concentration and organization among British Protestants. Let no one stay back. "Curse ye Meroz," said the angel of the Lord, "because they came not forth to the help of the Lord, to the help of the Lord against the mighty." Let British Christians be told that it is a united effort they are to make for the overthrow of the Papacy, for which they have long been praying, and which the blood of the martyrs, still unavenged, the groans of enslaved nations, and the commands and promises of the living God, call upon them to essay. The cry is now loud; creation itself travails and is in pain for the hour. The very earth which Popery has cursed and blighted cries to Heaven against her! The cities she has depopulated, the kingdoms she has barbarized, supplicate the awards of doom on their destroyer! The cretin of Switzerland, as he titters his idiot whine, — the serf of the once rich Lombardy, and the beggar of the once proud Venice, as they ask an alms, — protest against a tyranny which has crushed them into wretchedness and idiotcy The murdered liberties of Hungary, — the clanking chains of the twenty thousand captives of Ferdinand, — the very streets of Vienna, and of Paris, and of Naples, and of Rome, so lately drenched with the blood of their children, cry for vengeance on the Papacy! Her own sins cry against her. The souls of the martyrs under the altar cry, "O Lord, how long!" Prophets and apostles, whom she has compelled to an unholy partnership in her idolatries, join in this cry! The cherubim and the seraphim, whom she invoked when she immolated her victims, cry from their thrones! Heaven and earth unite in one mighty cry to the throne of the Eternal! And shall British Christians sit still? Shall they only be unmoved? No. Let them arise; and if they strike in faith, the Papacy shall fall.

The Papacy once overthrown, what blessed prospects will begin to dawn upon our wretched and benighted world, wretched and benighted from lack of enterprise, union, and liberality among Christians! Let the Papacy be overthrown, and thou, Oh Christianity, the parent of liberty, the fountain of domestic purity and social order, whose office it is to guide alike to terrestrial renown and to immortal happiness, wilt go forth among the nations; and when they see the glory of thy form, they will love thee, and, in loving thee, they will love one another. At the sound of thy voice proclaiming peace, their angry passions will be hushed, and the tumult of the people will subside into profound and blessed repose. Touched by thy beneficent and omnipotent hand, their bleeding wounds shall be stanched, and their fetters for ever broken. Cheered by thee, they will forget all their woes; and their voices, attuned no longer to sorrow and sighing, will make the whole earth vocal with their songs of gladness.

Made in the USA
Las Vegas, NV
23 September 2022

55856526R00236